OPEN SECRETS

Open Secrets

*Literature, Education, and Authority from
J-J. Rousseau to J. M. Coetzee*

MICHAEL BELL

OXFORD
UNIVERSITY PRESS

Great Clarendon Street, Oxford OX2 6DP

Oxford University Press is a department of the University of Oxford.
It furthers the University's objective of excellence in research, scholarship,
and education by publishing worldwide in

Oxford New York

Auckland Cape Town Dar es Salaam Hong Kong Karachi
Kuala Lumpur Madrid Melbourne Mexico City Nairobi
New Delhi Shanghai Taipei Toronto

With offices in

Argentina Austria Brazil Chile Czech Republic France Greece
Guatemala Hungary Italy Japan Poland Portugal Singapore
South Korea Switzerland Thailand Turkey Ukraine Vietnam

Oxford is a registered trade mark of Oxford University Press
in the UK and in certain other countries

Published in the United States
by Oxford University Press Inc., New York

© Michael Bell 2007

The moral rights of the author have been asserted
Database right Oxford University Press (maker)

First published 2007

All rights reserved. No part of this publication may be reproduced,
stored in a retrieval system, or transmitted, in any form or by any means,
without the prior permission in writing of Oxford University Press,
or as expressly permitted by law, or under terms agreed with the appropriate
reprographics rights organization. Enquiries concerning reproduction
outside the scope of the above should be sent to the Rights Department,
Oxford University Press, at the address above

You must not circulate this book in any other binding or cover
and you must impose the same condition on any acquirer

British Library Cataloguing in Publication Data

Data available

Library of Congress Cataloging in Publication Data

Data available

Typeset by Laserwords Private Limited, Chennai, India
Printed in Great Britain
on acid-free paper by
Biddles Ltd., King's Lynn, Norfolk

ISBN 978–0–19–920809–8

3 5 7 9 10 8 6 4 2

Qui non intellegit res, non potest ex verbis sensum elicere.

Martin Luther

> Nichts ist drinnen, nichts ist draussen;
> Denn was innen, das ist aussen.
> So ergreifet ohne Säumnis
> Heilig öffentlich Geheimnis.

J. W. von Goethe

The art of life has a pudency, and will not be exposed.

Ralph Waldo Emerson

This mysterious wisdom proclaims what *no ear hath heard*. Have you then heard it, my hearer, and how? Was the preaching perhaps not mysterious, because the word of which we speak, once whispered in solitary places, is now proclaimed from the housetops. Is such proclamation mystery? If a person confides to another some secret word, and through this other person's carelessness or wickedness it leaks out and into the world, then the word is revealed, and it is bad if those two people try to imagine that they still have a secret. But this mysterious wisdom is certainly for him only who hath ears to hear, for only he hears it.

Søren Kierkegaard

The 'open secret' in the genuine and strict sense . . . occurs where the concealing of the mysterious is simply experienced and is lodged in an historically arisen reticence. The openness of the open mystery does not consist in solving the mystery, and thus destroying it, but in not touching the concealedness of the simple and essential and letting this concealedness alone in its appearance.

Martin Heidegger

'. . . I learned something out there I can't express.'

'The English language may not be able to communicate it,' the professor suggested.

'That is not it, sir. Now that I possess the secret, I could tell it in a hundred and even contradictory ways. I don't know how to tell you this, but the secret is beautiful, and science, *our* science, seems mere frivolity to me now.'

After a pause he added:

'And anyway, the secret is not as important as the paths that led me to it. Each person has to walk those paths himself.'

Jorge-Luis Borges

The face is of itself, and, if I may express it so, the mystery of all clarity, the secret of all openness.

Emmanuel Levinas

For Kay

Contents

Ackowledgements	viii
List of Abbreviations	ix
Introduction: the Pedagogical Circle and the 'Open Secret'	1

PART I

1. Imaginary Authority in Rousseau's *Emile*	17
2. The Comedy of Educational Errors: (A) Sterne's *Tristram Shandy* and (B) C. M. Wieland's *History of Agathon*	53
3. Goethe's Open Secrets: *Wilhelm Meister's Apprenticeship*	87
4. Pedagogy, Fiction, and the Art of Renunciation: *Wilhelm Meister's Journeymanship, or the Renunciants*	108
5. Nietzsche as Educator and the Implosion of *Bildung*	130

PART II

6. 'The Passion of Instruction': D. H. Lawrence and 'Wholeness' versus *Bildung*	165
7. The Importance of being Frank: Criticism, Collaboration, Pedagogy in F. R. Leavis	193
8. The Novelist, the Lecturer, and the Limits of Persuasion: J. M. Coetzee and Elizabeth Costello on the Lives of Animals and Men	217
Conclusion	235
Bibliography	243
Index	251

Ackowledgements

I wish to thank Michael Black, Michael John Kooy, Martin Swales, and Martin Warner for generously reading earlier versions of this book. Any errors or inadequacies are my own.

I also thank Ohio University Press for permission to adapt 'What is it like to be a Non-Racist? Costello and Coetzee on the Lives of Animals and Men', from Jane Poyner ed., *J. M. Coetzee and the Idea of the Public Intellectual* (Athens: Ohio University Press, 2006) pp. 172–92.

Abbreviations

Agathon	*Geschichte des Agathon*
ASZ	*Also sprach Zarathustra*
Cadell	*The History of Agathon*
DP	*Doubling the Point*
ELTU	*English Literature in our Time and the University*
Émile	*Émile, ou de l'éducation*
Emile	*Emile, or On Education*
Lives	*The Lives of Animals*
LP	*The Living Principle*
NSMS	*Nor Shall My Sword*
R	*The Rainbow*
RDP	*Reflections on the Death of a Porcupine and Other Essays*
SCAL	*Studies in Classic American Literature*
STH	*Study of Thomas Hardy and Other Essays*
TI	*Twilight of the Idols*
TS	*Tristram Shandy*
TSZ	*Thus Spoke Zarathustra*
UM	*Untimely Meditations*
WMA	*Wilhelm Meister's Aprencticeship*
WMJ	*Wilhelm Meister's Journeymanship*
WML	*Wilhelm Meisters Lehrjahre*
WMW	*Wilhelm Meisters Wanderjahre*
WMYT	*Wilhem Meister's Years of Travel*
WL	*Women In Love*

Introduction: the Pedagogical Circle and the 'Open Secret'

My theme is the limits of the teachable. Certain technical topics can perhaps be fully taught, but in the humanistic realm there is always an element that cannot be imparted by authority. Maybe this is only a small part, too small to notice, yet what if it is nonetheless the vital element on which everything else depends? And if there is such a black hole at the centre of the activity, how does this, or should this, affect the exercise of pedagogical authority? How far does authority surreptitiously substitute for understanding? The more powerful the teacher, the more urgent the question; which is why it was inescapably central for Socrates and Nietzsche. Conversely, what does it mean for the pupil to have understood in such realms? How is understanding imparted, and how do we know it has been imparted? If the pupil fully absorbs what has been taught, and reproduces it perfectly, can we, or the pupil, infer that it has been independently understood? Indeed, can these questions be given any truly useful force, let alone answers?

Since the topic is as elusive as it is important, it may be helpful to start with a homely example that all experienced teachers will recognise. I once concluded a course of 'introduction to poetry' in America by inviting the students to summarise the principles which had emerged from the classes. Having done so, they claimed that had these been given at the outset it would have made everything faster and easier. When assured that these principles had indeed been set out in the very first session, they stoutly, and with manifest sincerity, denied this but as they drifted from the room I was approached by the class note-taker. He was that familiar figure, the universal amanuensis to life, who if told to take no notes will solemnly inscribe the instruction. Bemusedly, he confirmed what I said, though his tone suggested that only the evidence of his notebook would have convinced him. Of course, the students were in a sense quite right. What was said on the first day had seemed comprehensible; neither the words nor the conceptions were unfamiliar or puzzling. But while the experience was lacking, the words had no real content and had been quite naturally and healthily discarded. At the same time, the instruction had not been futile; it was just the necessary first stage, a preliminary focus of attention, in a much longer process of assimilation. And more importantly, it may be that if they had retained the initial formulations as an act of dutiful memory, it would have blocked the later process of understanding.

Similarly, in Adalbert Stifter's *Der Nachsommer* (*Indian Summer*) of 1857, the young hero is suddenly overwhelmed by the beauty of a statue owned by his mentor and asks him:

'Why have you never told me . . . of the beauty of the statue on your marble staircase?'
 'Who has told you now?' he asked.
 'I have seen it myself,' I answered.
 'Well, now you will know it more truly, and believe it more firmly,' he replied, 'than if someone had declared it to you.'
 . . . . .
 'And why have you never spoken of it to me?' I asked.
 'Because I thought that after a while you would notice it for yourself and find it beautiful,' he answered.
 'If you had told me sooner I would have known it sooner,' I replied.
 'To tell someone that something is beautiful,' he said, 'does not mean putting them in possession of its beauty.'[1]

These two episodes, one historical and one fictional, enshrine a simple truth with extensive implications. It indicates, for example, a familiar fallacy with which almost all teachers have to struggle. For they usually have to deal not only with pupils and students, but with those who would seek to direct the process from above. In every generation there are those who wish to produce social and moral, as well as intellectual, effects through instruction. And belief in the efficacy of direct instruction tends to increase in proportion to its unlikelihood. A high rate of teenage pregnancies in Britain, for example, will always excite a cry for sexual 'education' in schools, sometimes quoting the better record in Scandinavia which is then attributed to such education in schools. It is likely, however, that the more mature sexual culture of Scandinavia is rather *reflected* in such education than *produced* by it. By contrast, seeking to instil by instruction values which, *ex hypothesi*, are lacking in the prevailing culture is as likely to produce damaging as beneficial effects, if only through the cynicism it engenders in the young and exposes in their elders. And it tends to be promoted where it is most felt to be needed, in other words in schools where children already suffer cultural deprivation. By contrast, a more ambitious general education might begin to meet the cultural blankness, narrow horizons, and low self-esteem which are the likely locus of

---

[1] Adalbert Stifter, *Der Nachsommer*, in *Gesammelte Werke*, ed. Konrad Steffen, vol. 7 (Basel and Stuttgart: Birkhauser, 1965) p. 75.

the problem. Of course, this is not an argument against having such lessons, which are often done well. It is merely against the perennially naïve faith in instructional short-cuts on the part of those who do not teach, and some of those who do.

The possibly illusory authority of the teaching relation may be imaged as a pedagogical counterpart to the hermeneutic circle over which philosophers have agonised. This posits a fore-understanding on which the process of interpretation depends, and by which it may therefore be governed. Pedagogical circularity is more disturbing in that it seeks to impart as independent understanding what is synthetically induced by the teaching, and the authoritative structure of pedagogy in relation to minds assumed to be less mature makes its circularity potentially the more vicious. The encircling of the pupil, as has been argued in the case of Rousseau's *Emile*, may be benign in intent yet imprisoning in effect. Such ambivalent circularities underlie, without necessarily disabling, or rendering illegitimate, all the pedagogical relations discussed in this study.

It is not simply disabling because, of course, the circle, however vicious in structure or intent, is never entirely closed. The pupil is a centre of otherness and open to many other influences. Hence the historical emphasis has been on the opposite anxiety: that the instruction will escape the authority of the instructor. When Robert Raikes and Hannah More sought in the late eighteenth-century Sunday School movement to teach the reading of the Bible, they had to assure the reactionary establishment of the day that they would not be increasing the readership of *The Rights of Man*.[2] Both parties in this case were seeking to indoctrinate but neither could ultimately control the uses of literacy. This last fact remains crucial and all educators might inscribe over their desks in a constructive, not cynical, spirit, the reflection that education does so much less damage than it might because students, especially the good ones, can always be relied upon to do something quite different with it. This positive truth is, of course, merely negative as far as the teacher is concerned: it does not absolve the responsibilities of the educator. Nonetheless, a reflective awareness of it may radically affect the spirit and conduct of the educative process.

Good teachers have the practical art of dealing with these complexities. The present study does not presume to advise at that level but traces an insufficiently noticed history of reflection on this theme by some of the most penetrating minds in European tradition. The familiar, yet infinitely mysterious, gap between instruction and understanding has found some of its most suggestive

---

[2] See Frank Booth, *Robert Raikes of Gloucester* (Redhill: National Christian Education Council, 1980) pp. 150–1.

formulations, for example, in Goethe whose recurrent phrase *offenes Geheimnis* (open secret) provides the *leitmotiv* of the present study. This is not a secret which everyone has discovered, but an utterance that few can understand. Indeed, although 'open secret' is the normal translation of this phrase, the German word *Geheimnis* has a range of meaning covering the English 'mystery' as well as 'secret'. A mystery is impenetrable to understanding, and in its Christian religious sense there is a sacral value in its being so. In its most ancient religious sense, such as the Eleusinian mysteries, it is not just sacral but the locus of dangerous energies fundamental to life. At the same time it is possible to penetrate a mystery, to become one of its adepts. It may then become a mystery in the mediaeval trade sense, as a craft to which one can be apprenticed. Or it may be a form of esoteric wisdom that must be kept from the profane. The adepts will then form a secret society to protect, as well as practise, the wisdom they have learned. Mystery may require the veil of secrecy, or of deliberate mystification.

Mystery is exploited by Goethe in all these senses, and the trope of the 'open secret' links the historical transformations of this topic. At the same time, Goethe's very prestige as an original thinker and great artist can make his authority in a measure troubling. Despite, or indeed because of, his profoundly exemplary value, his authority may be dangerous or delusive. In his educational fiction, Goethe focused such an 'anxiety of influence' in mentor figures who stand not just between the author and the character but between the author and the reader.[3] Mentor and author, in their parallel attempts to form the same human being, throw an analytic light on each other.

There are two principal aspects in which the responsibility of the mentor may be considered: the individual personality and motives or the structural conditions. My interest ultimately lies in the latter although it is inevitably revealed through, and affected by, the former. Teachers' personalities are the necessary medium of their function and it is always salutary to ask what motives impel the passion of instruction. The etymologies of 'convince' and 'persuade' suggest the hidden temptations of domination or seduction which flank the pedagogical relation, and it no doubt draws upon these motives. Even the motives of Socrates, the secular patron saint of humanistic education, have been questioned. It did not require Nietzsche to suspect the ugly and ageing philosopher of finding in dialectic a more compelling, and intimate, exercise of power over handsome youths than he, or perhaps anyone, could achieve by the more conventional means of wrestling. Some

---

[3] I reverse, of course, the meaning of Harold Bloom's title *The Anxiety of Influence: a Theory of Poetry* (New York: Oxford University Press, 1973).

such charge already lurks in the angry reactions of Socrates' own interlocutors such as Aidemantus in *The Republic*.[4] And their irritation may include the frustrated awareness that it was precisely Socrates' authentic pursuit of disinterested enquiry which made him so compelling, or seductive. Ultimately, the motives of a good teacher are irrelevant, although they may help to explain the limitations of a bad one, while the structural question of authority is inescapable.

The dual truth that all teaching is a relationship extended in time and that every significant relationship tends to be formative, suggests why some of the most fruitful treatment of this theme has been in the form of the novel. But as well as the realistic, formative process which novels may enact, there is a less evident significance in the sheer category of fiction. For even where the institutional authority of the teacher is a fact, its true and essential exercise may be closer to a creative fiction. For that reason, the present study revisits, among other things, the peculiarly self-conscious tradition of the *Bildungsroman*. The term is used, that is to say, in its specific German sense rather than its looser Anglophone meaning for any fiction in which a central character matures. The German sub-genre thematises within the fiction a self-conscious project of rounded humanistic education derived from such Enlightenment figures as J. G. Herder, Friedrich Schiller, and Wilhelm von Humbolt. In this tradition, a recurrent fictional self-consciousness, and even artificiality, a deliberately oblique relation to realism, points up a constant philosophical reflection on the process of formation and imparts to it, I wish to argue, a significant bracketing *as* fictional. The mentor figure has a special prominence as a focus of this self-consciousness and, therefore, in contrast to the more usual critical focus on the standpoint of the young hero or of the author, I focus on the mediating and problematic standpoint of the mentor. It will be helpful first, however, to rehearse aspects of the eighteenth-century context in which the modern phase of the story starts, and then to summarise the trajectory of the subsequent discussion.

---

[4] 'Here Aidemantus interposed and said: To these statements, Socrates, no one can offer a reply; but whenever you talk in this way, a strange feeling passes over the minds of your hearers. They fancy that they are led astray a little at each step in the argument, owing to their own want of skill in asking and answering questions; these littles accumulate, and at the end of the discussion they are found to have sustained a mighty overthrow and their first opinion appears to be turned upside down. And as unskilful players of draughts are at last barred by their more skilful adversaries and have no piece to move, so they too find themselves barred at last; for they have nothing to say in this new game of which words are the pieces; and yet they are sure the truth is not on your side.' *Republic*, 487b, *The Dialogues of Plato*, trans. B. Jowett, vol. 2, 4th edn. (Oxford: Clarendon Press, 1953) p. 346.

The mentor and the *Bildungsroman*

It will already be evident that this is not a philosophical, methodological study in the manner of Wilhelm Dilthey and H-G. Gadamer, nor an institutional study in the mode of Pierre Bourdieu, nor a practical handbook for teaching, although it would hope to complement all of these. It has a closer cousinship with Gary Peters's *Irony and Singularity: Aesthetic Education from Kant to Levinas* and Jacques Rancière's *The Ignorant Schoolmaster*.[5] But Peters's questioning of post-Kantian thought on the aesthetic and Rancières radical critique of instructional pedagogy both have rather different purposes and are mainly conducted at a level of general principle. What follows here is rather a study of the personal dynamics of the pedagogical relation from Enlightenment to modernity, as represented in a number of, mainly fictional, texts. The wording of the latter qualification needs to be stressed for the focus on fiction in this argument is not through the choice of texts to be discussed but through its significance as a category in the understanding of them. Accordingly, although the pedagogical theme in the early *Bildungsroman* had crucial antecedents in the period's great novels, such as *Tom Jones*, it also had philosophical antecedents and a significant cousinship with the philosophical tale, such as *Gulliver's Travels, Candide,* and *Rasselas*. These tales frequently concerned the relation of ideas to experience and, in doing so, expressed the period's often rather dichotomous understanding of these terms.

On the face of it, the philosophical tale might be thought to answer D. H. Lawrence's desideratum of philosophical fiction:

Plato's Dialogues, too, are queer little novels. It seems to me it was the greatest pity in the world, when philosophy and fiction got split. They used to be one, right from the days of myth. Then they went and parted like a nagging married couple, with Aristotle, and Thomas Aquinas and that beastly Kant. So the novel went sloppy, and philosophy went abstract-dry.[6]

But, of course, the philosophical tale exemplifies the very split of which Lawrence complains. A common thrust of the genre, as of the novel at large, was a Cervantean suspicion of the cultural and epistemological power of ideas as such, whether social, metaphysical, theological, or scientific. But these tales were typically satiric and polemical, rather than strictly philosophical, and their presentation of these categories tends to be reductively dualised.

---

[5] (Aldershot: Ashgate, 2005) and *Le maître ignorant: cinq leçons sur l'émancipation intellectuelle* (Paris: Fayard, 1987); *The Ignorant Schoolmaster: Five Lessons in Intellectual Emancipation*, trans. Kristin Ross (Stanford: Stanford University Press, 1991).

[6] *Study of Thomas Hardy and Other Essays*, ed. Bruce Steele (Cambridge: Cambridge University Press, 1985) p. 154.

Whereas Lawrence prized the novel form for its dialogic resistance to ideal control, its refusal of the author's thumb in the scale, these works were typically driven by an intellectually monologic conception even when their leading idea was precisely the suspicion of ideas. Hence, although these works addressed themselves explicitly to systems of ideas or views of life, it was the great realist novels of the period which frequently did the real philosophical work. The philosophical tale remains relevant, however, in giving a clue to what is happening in more implicit ways in such novels as *Tom Jones, Clarissa, Werther, Julie, Tristram Shandy*, and *Les liaisons dangereuses*.

By the same token, however, the brisk reductions of the philosophical tale may underlie and govern the apparent experiential complexity of what we may think of as the novel proper. We may say that, despite the felt weight of experience in the fiction of Swift, Johnson, and Voltaire, their direct appeal to the category of experience is characteristically abstract. Even when opposing ideas to experience, they offer only an idea of experience. This is, however, a relative judgement. On a hard-nosed view, it is ultimately true of all fiction, and indeed of all experience. As Augustine found with the notion of time, when the words 'idea' and 'experience' are subjected to direct analysis both begin to shimmer.[7] H-G. Gadamer remarks: 'However paradoxical it may seem, the concept of experience seems to me one of the most obscure we have.'[8] There is no experience without the concept, which can therefore neither be separated intellectually *from* experience nor equated *with* it. Hence, although the novel form increasingly dissolved the eighteenth century's often crude dichotomy of idea and experience, just as Kant deconstructed the dualism of world and consciousness, it could not resolve it theoretically and the question of an ideal authorial control has continued to dog the form throughout its history.

In this respect, one of Boswell's recollections casts a long shadow down the history of the novel. He records Johnson bringing the conflict of idea and experience to a typically dualised focus in a conversation on free will: 'All theory is against the freedom of the will; all experience for it.'[9] Johnson is wont to tread with pragmatic confidence over philosophical abysses but the topic of the will as caught between the notional categories of idea and experience has a central significance for the novel in general and the *Bildungsroman* in particular. A literary character cannot be literally free, yet must be dramatically so. Hence,

---

[7] Augustine, *Confessions*, trans. Henry Chadwick (Oxford: Oxford University Press, 1992) p. 230.
[8] H-G. Gadamer, *Truth and Method*, trans. revised by Joel Weinsheimer and Donald G. Marshall (London: Sheed and Ward, 1989) p. 346. See also Jerry Fodor, 'Is it a Bird? Problems with Old and New Approaches to the Theory of Concepts', *TLS* 17 Jan. (2003) 3–4.
[9] *Life of Johnson* (New York and London: Oxford University Press, 1960) p. 947.

the creation of characters with moral lives makes their free will a central issue *within* the narrative while the degree to which we are dramatically persuaded that the characters actually enjoy free will is inescapably a function *of* the narrative. A thin veil of convention, or a thickness of felt life, separates the two levels and fiction is in constant danger of falling into an abyssal problematic analogous to the theological, or philosophical, mystery of free will. Wherever the problem of the will presses in reality, the fiction is likely to reflect it formally, as in the late nineteenth-century naturalism classically discussed by Georg Lukács.[10] An element of Johnsonian pragmatism is required to keep the two planes distinct while an overt philosophical consciousness threatens to confound them. The teaching relationship, however, involves a version of the same doubleness and in the *Bildungsroman* the mentor figure thematises the parallel between the two planes.

In the latter part of the eighteenth century, the paradoxes of a 'fictional' free will were comically exploited in Diderot's *Jacques le fataliste et son maître* (1771, 1783) written in partial imitation of Sterne's *Tristam Shandy*. The novel's structural joke is that the master constantly loses his authority over the ebullient self-will of his avowedly fatalist man-servant, Jacques, who repeatedly evades the master's authority by appealing to the narrative destiny already inscribed 'above'; in other words in the real text of the novel. As if in a comic anticipation of Hegel's master/slave relation, Jacques controls the master in consciousness by virtue of his own formal unfreedom. Meanwhile, the master is not just personally, but ontologically, displaced into a limbo of impotence between the planes of the action and the text. Or maybe he can be seen as a surrogate reader as he enjoys the antics and tales of his hired servant. But whereas in Diderot's novel the somewhat hapless master stands in contrast to the witty control exercised by the real author, in the *Bildungsroman* the crisis of the authority figure suggests a closer parallel. Both novelists and teachers must exercise their formative authority with subtle indirection which may be why Dilthey speaks of teaching as akin to artistic creation.[11] In that regard, the aporia in Johnson's contrast of theory and experience is crucial. Free will must escape intellectual comprehension or it will lose its necessary incalculability. While good teachers and novelists tend to manifest this in their tactful handling of the will, rather than their theorising of it, the *Bildungsroman* typically seeks to raise the paradoxes of pedagogy to a higher level of self-consciousness without reducing them to ideas. But fictional self-consciousness always takes its meaning from the

---

[10] Georg Lukács, *Studies in European Realism* (New York: Grosset and Dunlap, 1964).

[11] This is a recurrent theme in Wilhelm Dilthey, *Pädagogik: Geschichte und Grundlinien des Systems*, in *Gesammelte Schriften IX* (Stuttgart and Göttingen: Vandenhoeck and Ruprecht, 1986).

model of fiction that is being assumed and it is important in relation to the pedagogical theme to appreciate some of the rival models that dominated the period.

Over the central decades of the eighteenth century, the novel enacted a remarkable shift from maximal illusionism to extreme formal self-consciousness. In Britain, this story might start with the illusionistic fictions of Defoe around 1720, some of which were taken as historical accounts. Richardson's serialised epistolary novels of the 1740s were a conscious exploitation of affective verisimilitude in which the emotions of reality and the indulgence of fiction were mutually intensifying.[12] Readers knew it was fiction but responded with emotional identification; a double effect achieved by the minimal framing of the story by the fictitious editor. In reaction to Richardson came the extreme formal self-consciousness of Fielding, to be followed in turn by the elaborate play with fiction in Sterne after 1760. It is as if the new genre were rapidly rehearsing, as in a *Vorspiel*, the more complex development through realism to self-consciousness which was to occur more slowly over the nineteenth and twentieth centuries. But of course the concentrated eighteenth-century trajectory does not have the same significance as the later evolution since the nineteenth century was to develop poetic, philosophical, and sociological modes of realism which would give in turn a quite different significance to twentieth-century reactions. In contrast, the eighteenth century, although it produced realist fictions of enduring power, was importantly governed by a literalistic, rather than realist, conception. Even Sterne's games with fictional representation, for example, assume a literalistic model as their template and butt. The literalism of eighteenth-century fiction is important to the present topic because of its close relation to a similar literalism in the assumed workings of human psychology and moral formation. In the literature of sentiment, as exemplified in Richardson, there was not so much a parallel as a continuity between the emotional impact of moral occasions, such as the spectacle of virtuous distress, and the response to an affective fiction. The structure of sentiment, therefore, had a decisive impact on models of moral formation.

The movement of sensibility, in attempting to base the moral life on feeling, put a premium on the sheer arousal of feeling whether in fiction or in life. What was at stake was the intuitive immediacy of the emotional response rather than internal discriminations of quality within the realm of feeling. And since strong sympathies were believed to be more readily, and appropriately, aroused in the face of real life occasions rather than merely fictional distresses,

---

[12] I develop the implications of the term 'affective verisimilitude' in *The Sentiment of Reality: Truth of Feeling in the European Novel* (London: Unwin, 1983).

a maximal impression of factual reality, as in the epistolary novel, was the favoured vehicle for the fiction of moral sensibility. As I have discussed elsewhere, sentimentalist fiction typically sought the immediacy of emotional literalism, a response to the object as if it were a real historical occurrence, and this reinforced the common assumption in the period that the moral effect of imaginative literature was a one-for-one, isomorphic moral impression.[13] For a literalistic view of moral exemplarity extended well beyond the disciples of sentiment and the mid-century as a whole had little theoretical space for aesthetic transposition. To be sure, sentimentalist and literalistic assumptions were questioned but it was some time before a fully developed alternative would emerge.[14] The eighteenth century was rather characterised, in its theory if not its practice, by a sharp conflict of opposing models without the mediating impact of later conceptions. In practice, the internal contradictions of moral sentimentalism led, in the great literature of the period, above all in the novel, to a richly dramatic self questioning. Lovelace, notoriously, did not respond to Clarissa's letters as a sentimentalist reader should. Between Johnson's abrupt alternatives lies the opacity and recalcitrance of the individual human material; the proper sphere of the novel. The mixture of psychological complexity and theoretical naivety in the fiction of sentiment provides the significant context for Rousseau's half-novelised treatise *Emile*, a foundational text for modern educational thinking, which, precisely because it is not a novel, sits revealingly at the heart of the literary/psychological complex of sentimentalism.

Resumé

In the first section of this study, the gap between idea and experience, or instruction and understanding, is focused primarily in Rousseau, Goethe, and Nietzsche between whom there is a detailed process of chiasmic reversal. Nietzsche inverts Rousseau with Goethe as the vital middle term. And in each case, even where the text is not fictional, the category of fiction is crucial. To emphasise this latter point, the literalism and assumed transparency of Rousseau's *Emile* (1762) are contrasted with Sterne's *Tristram Shandy* (1759–67) and Christoph Martin Wieland's *History of Agathon* (1766–7); the latter being commonly thought of as the first German *Bildungsroman*. Both these works focus on the problems of would-be educators grappling with the free will of their pupils. They are also highly self-conscious fictions in significant contrast to Rousseau's literalistic assumptions of psychological transparency. This is

---

[13] See *The Sentiment of Reality, op. cit.*
[14] I discuss this longer-term development in *Sentimentalism, Ethics and the Culture of Feeling* (London: Palgrave, 2000).

not to condescend to Rousseau, however, who conducted his thought experiment with such passion and rigour as to reveal its internal contradictions along with its exemplary ambition. His greatest inheritors benefited as much from his negative as his positive example, and Goethe's resistance to transparency, his love of mystification, may be seen in that light. His 'open secrets' are rather a sublation, than simple rejection, of Rousseau's transparency.

In contrast to *Emile*, Goethe's *Wilhelm Meister's Apprenticeship* (1796) adopts the viewpoint of the pupil rather than the mentor. But even as the mentor figure is apparently more marginal, his function is more significantly thematised and questioned. Mentorship, and the whole process of *Bildung* which it serves, are put under increasingly sceptical pressure. For if Goethe's novel is the acknowledged apogee of this tradition it also shows potential dangers. Indeed, the whole ideal of *Bildung* is perhaps unsustainable in the conditions of modernity and in the long-delayed sequel, *Wilhelm Meister's Journeymanship, or the Renunciants* (1829), both Goethe and his hero overtly reject the whole conception. Nietzsche was to question *Bildung* even more radically and yet even in doing so he retains much of the substance and structure of what he reverses. For just as Goethe's positive achievement includes a critique of the *Bildung* project, so Nietzsche's wholesale attack on it inevitably depends on possessing in some sense the viewpoint of a culturally formed individual, a truly *gebildete Mensch*, of which Goethe remained the supreme example. The significant critique of *Bildung* can only come from within and the resulting paradox of pedagogical authority was especially urgent in Nietzsche and reached its culmination in *Thus Spoke Zarathustra*. Nietzsche constitutes an ambiguous historical watershed, both cutting us off from the world of Goethe and providing a vital link with it. Likewise, his own legacy is highly ambiguous.

The second section of the study looks at the conscious dilemma of pedagogical authority in post-Nietzschean modernity. In so far as the *Bildungsroman* survives into modernity, as in Thomas Mann, it is largely by reflecting on the paradox of its own combined impossibility and necessity, a consciousness which was always at the heart of the genre. In literature, such aporetic self-reflection has dwindled to a postmodern cliché but it is nonetheless a significant emblem, and practical exemplar, of the internal paradox of humanistic education. To focus this theme I look at three writers who consciously thrust themselves, or find themselves thrust, against the limits of the teachable: D. H. Lawrence, F. R. Leavis, and J. M. Coetzee. The reason for their more literal predicament is not, of course, far to seek: in their time, the authority of cultural tradition as such, the notion of *Bildung* itself, was losing its presumed authority. Yet once again, even as their predicament is more literal, the category of fiction is crucial in their thought. And with mention of these three, whom some readers may think an eccentric choice, some further reflection on the overall choice of authors is appropriate.

In following a thematic complex principally through some eight writers I am not seeking to impose upon the world a hitherto undiscovered 'tradition'. Indeed, in contrast to the respectful emulation that might be denoted, for example, by the phrase 'epic tradition', the relations between these authors are more frequently unwitting or hostile. But there is nonetheless an *ad hoc* or *de facto* tradition in the way they engage a continuing predicament and modify it in the light of changing historical circumstances. Most of these authors have a pedagogical aspect and some have had a strongly pedagogical impact. But what especially characterises several of them, particularly in the modern period, is the radical controversy which defines their influence. All authors' readerships are limited by taste, experience, and circumstance, but these are writers for whom the boundary has been defined by active opposition of a quite personal kind, frequently bordering on hostility or contempt. This makes them very different from, say, Beckett or Kafka, in whom the problems of expression are incorporated into the dynamic of the work in a way that does not literally affront the serious reader. In presenting the chosen writers as worth discussing, I inevitably make a critical case for them but the underlying purpose is rather to illuminate the historically evolving predicament of which they are extreme and conscious instances. This latter point also explains why I offer an intensive reading of a few writers, and indeed texts, rather than the broad range that George Steiner, for example, has covered in his treatment of the pedagogical theme.[15] I expect that readers will readily think of many other authors and works that could come within the purview of this argument. Indeed, it would be disappointing if this were not the case. But as will become evident, the principal danger, as well as the theme, of the argument, is banalisation, and it is only in the intensive meditation on the given case that the topic has its proper force.

It will also strike some readers that the sequence of authors is not only male, but masculinist, for I am following a masculinist tradition in the *Bildungsroman*. I take it that the battle for recognition of women's experience, and women's writing, throughout the period is well and truly won. Even in that regard, however, the present argument makes a contribution in tracing the partly repressed, but still significant, impact of the female within this tradition. Some authors are more aware of this than others, and J. M. Coetzee's investment in the female *alter ego* of Elizabeth Costello is the culmination of a gradual recognition within this line of authors. It is, of course, a female principle which is in question here, rather than the empirical woman, and the development in

---

[15] George Steiner, *The Lessons of the Masters* (Cambridge Mass. and London: Harvard University Press, 2003).

question is not necessarily sympathetic to a political feminism. Nonetheless, it is a significant cultural index for a shifting appreciation of gendered values.

With all these considerations in mind, D. H. Lawrence is, I believe, the European author who provides for Nietzsche, as Nietzsche did with Goethe, the significant anti-type, which in his case makes him the truest development of his predecessor. Lawrence as European author has significant points of contrast with both Nietzsche and Goethe and carried their problematic of cultural transmission into the twentieth century. He found himself increasingly isolated from his home culture; a condition which became part of the thematised meaning of his work. In that respect, his diminished reputation in the Anglophone academy over the last decades of the twentieth century is a significant aspect of his story, and part of his link with the next writer to be discussed. In the mid-twentieth century, the influential literary critic, F. R. Leavis, identified increasingly with Lawrence and, more significantly, his understanding of literature and history reveals its full force and coherence when it is linked to Germanic thought for which he worked out, apparently unwittingly, his own equivalent. But his emphasis on criticism rather than philosophy obscured his possession of such a coherent understanding, and the authority, or communicability, of his own judgements became more and more problematic even to himself. This was not because he doubted them but because when they were not accepted their very transparency, as it seemed to him, could not be further enforced. Here the compelling analogy is with Rousseau, whose era in significant respects finds its close in Leavis. Finally, in his generic hybrid, *The Lives of Animals*, the novelist and academic, J. M. Coetzee, through his fictional novelist and lecturer, Elizabeth Costello, plays darkly contemporary variations on the limits of the teachable. Addressing an already different epoch from Leavis's, this work shows pedagogical reason confronting its abyssal other.

Yet the limits of the teachable are also, of course, the conditions of its possibility and the pupil's ultimate escape from the pedagogical circle is powered by the very concentration of forces that the circle enables. And just as the best pupil may be the one who most profoundly transforms what has been taught, the best teacher is the one for whom this is an active recognition. One might, therefore, expand Friedrich Schiller's argument for the educative value of the aesthetic to say that education should itself be conducted in the aesthetic spirit implicit in some of the great pedagogical fictions.[16] It is the more pertinent to do so as Schiller has become for many a negative icon representing a naive, and ideologically loaded, belief in the humanising

---

[16] Most notably in *On the Aesthetic Education of Man in a Series of Letters*, trans. Elizabeth M. Wilkinson and L. A. Willoughby (Oxford: Clarendon Press, 1967).

function of the aesthetic. Schiller's argument seems to me more subtle than it is often represented as being, and in ways that bear on the pedagogical theme. Pedagogical authority is best understood as an enabling fiction and humanistic teaching, especially in modernity, is ultimately a 'purposiveness without purpose' at the opposite extreme from the literalistic and coercive authority of, for example, Rousseau whose generosity of spirit and brilliance of insight nonetheless provide the appropriate starting point.

Part I

1

Imaginary Authority in Rousseau's *Emile*

Rousseau represents a decisive turn in European culture. *Emile* (1762) is a treatise setting out principles for bringing up a young man from birth to marriage. It rapidly established Rousseau as a world-historical thinker on education and it was also in his view the best introduction to his thought at large.[1] *Emile* seeks above all to form a personality able to exercise responsible freedom, and the note of liberation is struck by Rousseau's opening, and soon influential, attack on the customary swaddling of infants.[2] But freedom is not a straightforward matter and Rousseau's brilliant insights remain notoriously problematic when considered either as a practical regime or as universal principles. He therefore focuses, in a fruitful variety of ways, the continuing and intrinsic problems of pedagogical authority.

Rousseau, who gives in *Emile* a closely reasoned account of a successful, but essentially imaginary, education, was to be highly frustrated in his attempts to educate his contemporaries. His predicament was that, although the truths he had to tell were self-evident to him, he found himself to be radically at odds with the world at large, especially as represented by church, state, and educated high society. Much turns here on radical assumptions about essential human 'nature' and in this regard the figure of the pre-socialised child would be of crucial evidential significance if it were not itself the inevitable locus of myths. Rousseau is rightly associated with a belief in the natural goodness of the child in so far as he turned from a traditional emphasis on original sin: that we are, in the words of the catechism, 'prone to evil from our very childhood'. For Rousseau, corruption came from socialisation, and the mutual comparison it involved. But he is only too aware of the sub-text of the Eden story, that the first human pair were after all available to corruption, and the human, as Aristotle reminds us, is inconceivable outside

---

[1] *Oeuvre complètes*, Bibliothèque de la pléiade, ed. Bernard Gagnebin and Marcel Raymond (Paris: Gallimard, 1959–) vol. i, p. 933.
[2] *Émile, ou de l'education*, ed. Michel Launay (Paris: Garnier-Flammarion, 1966) pp. 44; *Emile, or On Education*, trans. Allan Bloom (London: Penguin, 1991) pp. 43–4. Subsequent references are to these editions although the translations are my own.

the social.³ Indeed, one might say that the serpent tempted Eve by means of social comparison at the mythical dawn of history and there is no historical moment without the corruption of the social. A radical ambivalence, therefore, underlies Rousseau's reflections on pedagogical governorship throughout. He partly assumes that it will be sufficient for the pupil to be raised, at least initially, within a *cordon sanitaire* protecting him from corrupting influence, but active development and guidance are also required, and especially so given the internal potentiality of corruption. And of course, as he thought within the broadly Lockean assumptions of the period concerning human psychology, he recognised the crucial impact of experience on the child's formation. The child should ideally grow up to be similar to himself and he veers between, on the one hand, the enormous pains required to bring up the pupil to this coincidence of personality and world view, and on the other hand, the belief that uncorrupted nature should produce this effect unaided. The tutor, or governor, has to intensify, refine, and aid the educative effect of nature. He is therefore in the uneasy position of wishing to exercise both the authority *of* nature and the authority, at least of a stage director, *over* it. To what extent does this structural position leave him open to the charge of unconscious cheating or self-deception?

Rousseau declared in his *Confessions*: 'Throughout the course of my life... my heart has been as transparent as crystal'⁴ and Jean Starobinski, in *Jean-Jacques Rousseau: Transparency and Obstruction*, locates the central problematic of *Emile* in Rousseau's belief in the essential transparency of human nature, especially his own. This belief obstructs Rousseau's vision of his own interventions, and therefore his capacity fully to question his own exercise of authority. Moreover, as Starobinski observes, awareness suppressed at one level in Rousseau's thought tends to return at another. So the highly controlled regime which he envisages for Emile is close to the one of which he imagines himself to be the object in his later paranoiac fantasies. ⁵ All that is well said, and yet *Emile*, as Starobinski himself shows, constantly eludes definitive judgement and I wish to argue that this is partly because of running ambiguities in its imaginative presentation and the nature of its claims. Its generic hybridity is a source of ultimately fruitful ambiguity.

Commentators commonly refer to *Emile* as a novel although one of the most important things about it is that it is not one. The misprision doubtless occurs

---

³ Aristotle's definition of man as 'a political animal' implies a social being and is often translated as 'social'. *The Politics*, trans. T. A. Sinclair, rev. Trevor J. Saunders (London: Penguin, 1992) p. 60.

⁴ *The Confessions*, trans. J. M. Cohen (London: Penguin, 1953) p. 415.

⁵ Jean Starobinski, *Jean-Jacques Rousseau: Transparency and Obstruction*, trans. Arthur Goldhammer (Chicago and London: University of Chicago Press, 1988) pp. 216–17.

because Rousseau's treatise draws strongly on fiction not just adventitiously but constitutively. The pupil figure, Emile, combines the significances of a philosophical hypothesis and a fictional character. These may legitimately overlap but they also answer to different protocols of truth claim. In this regard, the fictional cases of *Candide* and *Rasselas* illuminate the overdetermination of *Emile*. In these philosophical tales, the mentor simply focuses the satire. In *Rasselas*, the hero comes to recognise what his mentor has always known, and the mentor trusts the process of experience to bring him to this point. In *Candide*, Pangloss is a false mentor, whose idealised view of the world is belied by experience in a way that is immediately evident to the reader if not to the innocent hero. In both tales, however, there is a virtual coincidence between the final realisation of the hero and the world view of the fiction. Rousseau, by contrast, seeks to engage the real life problems for the mentor in closing this gap but the radical ambiguity lurking in his exposition is whether it is ultimately a more elaborated version of a similarly self-fulfilling, and essentially literary, structure. Does Rousseau offer, under the sign of imagination, a serious and workable conception of educational authority, or is his conception itself merely imaginary, a hopeful, and perhaps dangerous, illusion? To what extent is it a controlled philosophical hypothesis, or a naïve wish-fulfilment in which the author suffers the classic illusion of the pedagogue? The imaginary pupil allows for a peculiarly self-fulfilling version of the pedagogical circle working at the level of both literary 'character' and the philosophical exposition.

If Rousseau could not see the supposed elisions and contradictions of his thought as clearly as his critics, both then and now, this is partly because of internal rationales which had compelling grounds at the time, and which throw a continuing light on the problems of pedagogical authority. Indeed, it was in the nature of his insights to outrun theory so that they could be best explored in the fluid forms of later fiction. Hence, while endorsing the thrust of Starobinski's analysis, I wish to relate it to the following contexts and themes which will be developed in later chapters: the assumed psychology of moral sentimentalism; the resulting exercise of educational authority, the generic hybridity of treatise and novel; Rousseau's utopianism; and the text's awareness of itself as an historical intervention. I turn first to the authority accorded to Nature within the assumptions of moral sentimentalism.

Sentiment and Supplementarity

Rousseau was acutely aware of the internally damaging effects of false or artificial needs and desires. The founding intuition which launched his career as a *philosophe* was that as humankind expanded its possibilities through the civilised arts and sciences it lost or impoverished its natural feelings and capacities.[6] As he puts it in *Emile*: 'The more we distance ourselves from the state of nature, the more we lose our natural tastes; or rather habit creates a second nature which we substitute for the first, so that none of us any longer recognises it.' (*Émile*, 193; *Emile*, 151) And at more immediately practical levels: 'The many instruments invented to guide us in our experiments, and to supplement the judgement of our senses, make us neglect to exercise it.' (*Émile*, 227; *Emile*, 176) For Rousseau, since cultured desire is largely socio-genic rather than a simply natural need, it creates a realm of ontological illusion. The object of desire is strictly imaginary even when the literal object in question is both real and valuable. Moreover, since desirability no longer lies in the inherent properties of an object but arises from a subjective feeling projected on to it, the desire is doomed to remain unassuageable. This is the structure of romantic love as analysed by Rousseau's heroine, Julie, in the novel on which he was working just before the writing of *Emile*: '. . . such is the vanity of human things that, apart from the Being who exists in himself, nothing is beautiful except what does not exist.'[7] Despite his great contribution to European romanticism, therefore, he was in principle opposed to this form of romantic longing. Hence Rousseau's abiding distrust of supplementarity. To *want* more is practically equivalent to *having* less. Indeed, when in the *Confessions* he speaks of his habit of masturbation as a dangerous 'supplement', J. M. Cohen's widely used translation renders this as a 'means of cheating Nature'.[8]

Accordingly, a cardinal principle of moral education for him is teaching, or rather inculcating, a distaste for false supplements. In Book Five, addressing the question of female education, he imagines a young girl over-enamoured of beautiful dresses. Rousseau would encourage in her the idea that fine apparel is desirable in an inverse ratio to natural endowment:

When she comes to look on dress only as a supplement to personal beauty, and as an implicit avowal of needing it in order to please, she won't be at all proud of it. She will be humble; and if, when dressed up more than usual, she hears someone say 'How beautiful she is!' she will blush with shame. (*Émile*, 485; *Emile*, 372)

While his method is tough-mindedly puritanical, its effect could indeed be liberating and a source of strength. But, of course, even the little girl's least showy dress is still a supplement. There is no escape from the condition of supplementarity and the very process of education is a supplement to natural experience. Rousseau's governor, therefore, must seek as far as possible to

---

[6] *Discourse on the Sciences and the Arts* (1750)
[7] *Julie, ou La Nouvelle Héloïse* (Paris: Garnier, 1960) p. 682.
[8] *The Confessions*, op. cit. p. 108.

create the effect of unmediated experience. The pupil must always seem to exercise his own will and powers even as he is secretly controlled by the tutor in the constantly varying, unpredictable circumstances of every day: 'Let him not know what obedience is when he acts, nor what power is when he is acted upon. Let him feel his liberty equally in his own actions and in yours. Supplement the strength he lacks just so much as he requires in order to feel free but not imperious.' (*Émile*, 101; *Emile*, 85–6) Hence Rousseau requires the tutor always to disguise his exercise of authority from the pupil: he should seem merely to discover along with Emile the silent working of reality.

Moreover, as he explains his system to the tutor/governor, Rousseau assumes a comparable immediacy, a force of natural truth, in which his own expression is no more than the transparent medium through which the nature of things is articulated. As he assures us, he relies '. . . as little as possible on reasoning, and trusts only in observation'. (*Émile*, 331; *Emile*, 254) Indeed, he has immense persuasive power to which this comment is by no means irrelevant, and yet, of course, in making this claim he elides his verbal relation to the reader almost as the tutor is to hide his authority from the pupil; and with the same justification. In both cases any manipulation, or arrangement, of reality is not in principle deceptive because it is merely anticipating, focusing, and intensifying, the impact of reality itself. Just as a good way to hide is to remain, like the tutor, in full view but unnoticed, so Rousseau's effect of transparency lies in the evident sincerity of the good Jean-Jacques. He embodies personally the supposed coincidence of content and form, of internal experience and rational order, in his exposition-cum-argument.

Hence, although no argument or rhetorical style can be merely the presentation of experience, his language constantly insinuates a coincidence of reality and reason. An extended example helps to suggest the rhetorical impact of his voice:

There is no subjection so complete as that which preserves the appearance of liberty: in this way the will itself is made captive. The poor child who understands nothing, can do nothing, and knows nothing: is he not at your mercy? Do you not have complete power, as far as he is concerned, over every thing around him? Are you not master to influence him as you please? Are not his tasks, his games, his pleasures and his pains, all in your hands without him knowing? Doubtless he must only do what he wishes, but he must only wish to do what you want. He must take no step that you have not foreseen; he must not open his mouth without your knowing what he will say. . . .

By leaving him master of his own will, you avoid exciting him to caprice. Only ever doing what suits him, he will soon do only what he should. And even if he is in constant bodily motion according to his momentary sensory interests, you will see he is much more capable of developing the power of reason, and in a manner more appropriate for him, than in studies of pure speculation.

Thus, not seeing you seek to cross him, and having nothing to fear from you, he has nothing to hide, and will never deceive, never lie, to you. He will show you everything without fear, while you can study him with ease. You can arrange around him all the lessons you wish to impart, without his ever realising he is receiving one. (*Émile*, 150; *Emile*, 120)

Starobinski quotes this passage to exemplify the master's envisaged power over the child even when advising a method of apparently complete freedom, 'leaving him master of his own will'.[9] Rousseau predicts, with absolute confidence, the outcome of his educative regime: that the child will never deceive or lie. But the confidence has a source anterior even to the method which itself rests on the coincidence of nature and reason.

Rousseau is often thought to have championed nature against reason; and indeed he did oppose a narrow conception of reason. But J. G. Hamman, an influential figure behind the German Enlightenment, objected to him precisely as another French rationalist.[10] For Rousseau did something more problematic, and ultimately more fruitful. Beneath the rhetorical opposition of reason and nature, he pointed to a deeper identity between them, an identity inscribed in the very manner of the prose. The rhetorical questions in the opening paragraph of the above quotation, which seem to overwhelm the implied listener, are continuous with the confident assertions that follow. Both have the condensation of near aphorisms in which causal connections are tautly integral to the thought. Exploiting the summative tendency of the eighteenth-century balanced period, Rousseau constantly gathers implicit analytic arguments into asseverative statements of the 'order of nature'. The combination of impassioned advocacy and general maxims enacts the ideology, and assumed psychology, of contemporary moral sentimentalism: the belief that the objective requirements of the moral life may be based on the subjectivity of natural feeling.

The optimistic ideology of eighteenth-century sentimentalism can be seen in the mid-century use of the word 'sentiment' which typically combines the meanings of social or moral 'principle' and personal 'feeling'. Principle is thereby underwritten by the spontaneity of humane feeling while feeling has in itself an objective and general moral value. In the discourse of sentiment the traditional conflict between principle and feeling is ideally elided. At one level, this was an optimistic myth of the Enlightenment flying in the face of age-old experience and, not surprisingly, its internal strains can be seen in the rhetoric of sentiment. By the latter decades of the century, the movement of moral sentiment had on one hand become the full-blown, one-sided cult of

---

[9] Starobinski, *op. cit.* p. 217.
[10] Robert T. Clark, *Herder: His Life and Thought* (University of California Press, 1969) p. 46.

sensibility and, on the other, had given rise to an anti-sentimental reaction. Yet the story is complex, for the very instability of moral sentimentalism was the basis for the many transformations, such as a variety of romanticisms, through which feeling was to become an important, and positive, aspect of modern moral identity. To a significant extent, therefore, the period's conscious argument over sentiment and sensibility can be seen as the epi-phenomenal reflection of a profound, but less conscious, or articulable, change in the culture.

Most notably, great works of fiction in the period explored dramatically the tension between feeling and principle elided by sentimentalist ideology. Rousseau's own novel, *Julie, or the New Eloisa*, is a classic instance as the lovers' passion is both sublimated and intensified by their high-minded principles of virtuous renunciation. In *Emile*, there is a comparable tension between acknowledging the waywardness of the human material and trusting in its natural development. Over and again, the conceptual frame is not coterminous with the moral and psychological process although the frame is necessary for registering its significance. Where ideas are truly 'influential', it may be because they reflect, as much as cause, change and Rousseau's writing had precisely such an iconic and suggestive power for readers across Europe. In that respect, his conceptual tensions were as important as his affective power in making him so productive in the longer term. Accordingly, despite his professed transparency, his effect for us now is rather to bring home the opacity of the self. And likewise, even as he puts his case with dogmatic conviction, we may read him between the lines in something of the manner that we have learned to read the heurism behind Nietzsche's apparent dogmatism. Of course, he sought consistency and would have opposed for his own part Nietzsche's positive embracing of self-contradiction, yet he was a forerunner of the holism which underwrites the bracketed dogmatism of Nietzsche or D. H. Lawrence, to be discussed in later chapters. One can, therefore, probe the principled bases of Rousseau not just to deconstruct his thought but to understand his intuitive holism.

Having said that, however, there remains a significant *petitio principii* at the heart of the sentimental philosophy of the heart which was identified by Jacques Derrida specifically in the case of Rousseau as the logic of the 'supplement'.[11] Despite his radical suspicion of supplementarity, Rousseau is shown to be deeply ensnared in its logic. A supplement should be an extra source of support, but the very fact of drawing upon a supplement implies an insufficiency. If the supplement is necessary it is no longer a mere supplement.

---

[11] *Of Grammatology*, trans. Gayatri Chakravorty Spivak (Baltimore and London: Johns Hopkins University Press, 1976).

Over the course of the eighteenth century, this destabilising logic worked itself out in the relation of principle to feeling in the myth of moral sentiment.

The traditionally rational and theological grounding of the moral life was initially reinforced by the natural goodness of the human heart but increasingly the emotional supplement both focused and exacerbated an insecurity in the traditional belief. Early in the century, the widely influential writings of Anthony Ashley Cooper, the third Earl of Shaftesbury, managed to disguise the difficulty.[12] He kept the traditional order in place while suffusing it with an enthusiastic rhetoric of benevolence. In this way he was able to influence almost everyone, from politically conservative Anglicans to progressive French Deists.[13] His aristocratic confidence helped create a positive ethical example for the century—in Addison the 'bourgeois gentleman' of Molière ceased to be a comic oxymoron—and he gave respectability to the notion of 'enthusiasm', often regarded with suspicion as a manifestation of mass religious emotion in the lower orders. But the internal strains within Shaftesbury's assimilative rhetoric were to unravel over the course of the century with Kant as the strongest spokesman for the view that the 'categorical imperative' of the moral life was to be kept free from sentimentalist contamination.[14]

The relation between nature and culture in *Émile* is caught in this sentimentalist logic of the supplement. In one of his many cautions to the tutor to remain flexible, and to adjust Rousseau's principles to the individual nature and circumstances of the pupil, Rousseau speaks of the need to discover the pupil's individual character, or 'genius', so that the tutor may 'aid' (*seconder*) nature in an appropriate way. (*Émile*, 249; *Emile*, 192) Here the tutor's secondary, or supplementary, relation is made explicit. Elsewhere, however, the relation between nature and moral culture is more intrinsic and identical. We are not invited to notice the join: 'There is, then, in the depth of the soul an innate principle of justice and virtue by which, even despite our own maxims, we judge our own actions and those of others as good or evil, and it is to this principle that I give the name of conscience.' (*Émile*, 376; *Emile*, 289) The phrase 'innate principle'. bluntly states the founding idea of moral sentiment; asserts its primacy over conscious moral 'maxims', and lends a more secular inflection to the traditional religious term 'conscience'. A little later, the sentimental model is even more explicit as, echoing Shaftesbury, human sociability is attributed to 'innate sentiments'. (*Émile*, 378; *Emile*, 290)

---

[12] I discuss this in *Sentimentalism, Ethics and the Culture of Feeling* (London: Palgrave, 2000) pp. 16–18.
[13] On this see Dorothy B. Schlegel, *Shaftesbury and the French Deists* (Chapel Hill, NC: University of North Carolina, 1956).
[14] *Critique of Practical Reason* (1788).

When the unstable conjunction in these phrases was put under critical pressure, the whole claim began to unravel. In *Emile*, Nature, which Shaftesbury saw as supplementing the divine, is itself now to be supplemented by education. It always was in Shaftesbury, of course, but the logical relations became consciously problematic as the elements fell apart under the pressure of a changing social and intellectual world. A significant point of change has just been indicated. The tutor must adapt Rousseau's general principles not just to the given circumstances but to the individual character of the pupil. Much depends on how much weight and scope is given to individuality but once it is acknowledged at all it seriously compounds the underlying instability of sentiment. Shaftesbury's appeal to benevolent sentiment assumed a norm of highly socialised personality. Feeling, to be moral, must promote universalisable values and conduct. But as the century advanced, and the movement of sentiment gave way to the excesses of sensibility, feeling, and therefore moral authenticity, were increasingly associated with the irreducibility of the individual self in opposition to the social.

In Goethe's *The Sorrows of the Young Werther* (1774), for example, the young eponymous hero, as man of feeling, stands in explicit opposition to his friend Albert, the man of social principle. Werther feels in argument that, even beyond the particular issue, his individuality, his very being, is at stake in resisting Albert's appeals to universal, social principle.[15] In that novel, the unstable compound of the man of sentiment is literally blown apart in an act of self-destruction. Werther, as man of feeling, is Goethe's comment on Rousseau, or more strictly perhaps, on the impact of Rousseau. Goethe intended his work to be a critique of the man of feeling but, precisely because the Rousseauan spirit was now so widespread, readers almost universally responded to it in a spirit of romantic tragedy and sympathetic identification. They read it sentimentally rather than critically, or aesthetically. Moreover, Goethe elsewhere confessed himself deeply implicated in the character and wrote the story partly for the purpose, as Lawrence put it, of shedding his own sickness.[16] Of course, truly significant resistance to the man of feeling would only come from someone for whom sensibility was an internal experience and

---

[15] 'What Albert had just said in the presence of the official was highly objectionable to Werther: he believed he saw in it some animus against himself. And even although on further reflection it could not have escaped his keen mind that both men must be right, it was nonetheless for him as if he must deny his innermost self if he should admit it.' *Die Leiden des Jungen Werthers, Goethes Werke* (Hamburger Ausgabe) *Romane und Novellen I*, ed. Erich Trunz (Munich: Beck, 1982) p. 97, my trans.

[16] *Conversations with Eckermann*, trans. David Luke and Robert Pick (London: Oswald Wolff, 1966) p. 126. D. H. Lawrence to A. W. McLeod, 27 Oct. 1913. *The Letters of D. H. Lawrence*, vol. 2, ed. George J. Zytaruk and James Boulton (Cambridge: Cambridge University Press, 1981) p. 90.

at least partly a positive one. In this respect, Goethe's ambivalence precisely reflects on Rousseau in whom the elements that were later to come apart were still in an unstable compound.

In general, Rousseau follows the ideology of sentiment in assuming that human feelings are predominantly generic and universal. He states explicitly that 'our individuality is the least part of ourselves'. (*Émile*, 97; *Emile*, 83) And he readily accommodates the individuality of the child into the logic of his system. Nonetheless, Rousseau is for good reason the mythic representative of a new valorisation of the individual in modernity even if the subsequent tradition has often vulgarised his conception. His commitment to a notion of self not reducible to social terms was an underlying cause of his break with Diderot, and his own career would increasingly feel the embattled diremption analysed in *Werther*.[17] The impulse to write the *Confessions* had the same ambiguity. He declares the public interest of his intimate self-revelations on the basis of his uniqueness, that there is no one like him, and yet there would be little point, or even comprehensibility, if he were not implicitly claiming to be in some way representative, and indeed exemplary.[18] A comparable tension runs through *Emile* as a universally valid demonstration by means of an individual case.

All educational theory or practice must accommodate the individual, but Rousseau envisaged his method purely in his imagination, and in a period when what we can now recognise as the formation of modern individuality was occurring within a highly universalistic discourse. The modern tradition of *Bildung* was formed within this matrix and Rousseau's effective elision of the child's individuality is suggestive for its subsequent development. If the novel in general was increasingly to valorise the individual, the sub-genre of the *Bildungsroman* is a running reflection on the problems this poses for an educational process.

The strongest manifestation of Rousseau's universalism is his constant, confident prediction of outcomes. From the outset, the tutor must anticipate not just the child's overt actions and words but his inmost feelings: '. . . observe him, watch him without pause and without his noticing, anticipate all his feelings and prevent those he must not have . . . ' (*Émile*, 244; *Emile*,189) After such a regime, and even after the two year's travelling that completes Emile's

---

[17] Rousseau took personal offence at a remark in Diderot's 'Conversation on *The Natural Son*' to the effect that the solitary man is evil. Diderot's play presents its Rousseauan central character sympathetically and we could say that the title phrase, in which the word 'natural' combines the meanings of 'goodness' and 'illegitimacy', suggests Rousseau's cultural predicament. *The Confessions, op. cit.* p. 423

[18] 'I am made unlike anyone I ever met. I will even venture to say that I am like no one in the whole world.' *The Confessions, op. cit.* p. 17.

education, Rousseau stakes all on the minute predictability of the outcome: 'Either I have been mistaken in my method, or he must reply to me more or less as follows...' (*Émile*, 618; *Emile*, 471) The circularity of the argument according to which his method is justified by the results he himself predicts is so self-fulfilling as to arouse scepticism even in readers broadly persuaded of his case. Yet the universalist confidence is double-edged in so far as it also subtends the radical principle of delay. 'Look on delays as advantages: it is a great point to advance towards the end without loss. Let childhood mature in the child. Whatever lesson becomes necessary, make sure you do not give it today if you can without danger put it off till tomorrow.' (*Émile*, 113; *Emile*, 94) Rousseau wishes experience to be the teacher and, in his guise as merely an older friend, the governor is to avoid as far as possible both didactic instruction and direct orders. Experience can be trusted because of the universal reason to which it leads. But non-interventional delay would also enable individuality to develop and reveal itself. The same method, therefore, allows scope for an opposite principle to the universalist and it was this aspect which was to be crucial to the *Bildungsroman* in whom the mentor figure, not usually charged with the formal responsibility of educating, carries the principle of non-interference to a further degree. Indeed, the all-important principle of delay is already in Rousseau fraught with implications which it is fruitful to unravel a little further.

Delay and the Authority of Nature

Rousseau's guiding principle is distrust of instruction by authority. He trusts natural process so much that where necessary he will seek to simulate it, or supplement it, rather than frankly substitute for it. And where he has to intervene in the natural course of things he will seek to disguise his intervention. Hence, through all the changing methods adopted for each new stage of development from child to young man, the underlying, constantly emphasised, principle is deliberate delay, not precipitating the pupil into premature, and most likely false, consciousness. The readiness is all. This principle was to become central to the *Bildungsroman* and within his daily, twenty-four hour commitment to the education of Emile, the governor must exercise a pedagogical renunciation which is a distant forerunner of Goethe's inflection of this theme.

Time and again, explanations are withheld by the governor because their apparent efficacy may be illusory, and may block true understanding. During instruction on astronomy, for example, Emile interrupts by asking what it is good for, a question he has been encouraged to ask of every activity and all branches of knowledge. The tutor immediately breaks off the lesson and arranges for them both to get lost a few days later in the countryside where they eventually find their way only through observing the skies. As he says, the boy will now know the value of astronomy as well as having had a practical lesson in it. Emile will never in his life forget what he learned on this occasion, whereas the formal lesson that was interrupted a few days before would have been forgotten the next morning. (*Émile*, 235; *Emile*, 182–3)

As an opposite turn on the same theme, when Emile is old enough to have a strong will of his own and the capacity to exercise it, it may be better in situations of potentially foolish behaviour to give him the appropriate advice before he acts while fully recognising that he is likely to ignore it. In this case, the essential emptiness of purely verbal instruction is equally recognised in not withholding it. It is an example of the open secret put to use, and its pedagogical efficacy depends on not insisting further at the time, and above all on not saying afterwards: 'I told you so.' (*Émile*, 322; *Emile*, 247) The governing principle is still self-restraint on the part of the tutor, and provided the tutor does not set up a resistance to the pupil's acknowledgement, the subsequent experience will imbue the earlier advice with the meaning it then lacked.

The principle of delay bears upon one of the continuing predicaments of child-rearing: to what extent is it appropriate to reason with a child on matters of moral behaviour? In Rousseau's view, this is worse than useless, it is positively damaging. The reasoning is beyond what the small child can appreciate and it is actually the adult's superior force and will which carry the day; a fact which is much more felt, even if not consciously articulated, by the child. It is better, therefore, that the child simply accept both the force and the moral practice as facts of life without being incited to precocious questioning. 'In seeking to persuade your pupils of the duty of obedience, you join to this supposed persuasion force and threats, or, even worse, flattery and promises. And so, lured by interest or constrained by force, they pretend to be convinced by reason.' (*Émile*, 108; *Emile*, 90) Accordingly, when Emile reaches the age to be positively taught, Rousseau recommends selecting only those matters useful to him and within his range:

From this small number, remove those truths which require, for their comprehension, a fully formed understanding; which presuppose the knowledge and relationships of an adult, beyond the child's reach; matters which, though true in themselves, would lead an inexperienced mind to think falsely on other topics. (*Émile*, 213; *Emile*, 166)

Indeed, on all subjects, the enemy is not so much ignorance, or even error, as the illusion of understanding. The child is, therefore, to experience the necessity of nature, the order of things, rather than the justifications of reason.

Reason excites, if not rebellion, then the independent exercise of an immature capacity for rational judgement, as the experience of natural necessity does not. Moreover reason requires human language, even when it is seeking merely to express the logic of events, whereas Nature teaches by experience without linguistic articulation. The child who fails to absorb the experience of others when articulated as reason is made more subject to the delusion of understanding. 'Remember, remember always, that ignorance has never done any harm, and only error is fatal. We go wrong not by what we do not know, but by what we believe we know.' (*Émile*, 213; *Emile*, 167)

The absence of true understanding may continue undetected by either teacher or pupil since the same form of words may well remain the best expression of the 'idea'. And conversely, we might add, if true understanding is achieved, it may be equally undetectable at the level of linguistic expression, and remain in that sense a private awareness like the achievement of Pierre Menard in J-L. Borges' fable.[19] The eponymous hero of 'Pierre Menard, Author of the *Quixote*' attempts to imagine a possible early twentieth-century meaning, sentence by sentence, for the complete text of Cervantes' *Don Quixote*. To imagine the seventeenth-century text as it might be conceived in his own day would be a stupendous achievement but, if successful, it would remain entirely within Menard's own mind and concealed within the words of the original. Outwardly, he would only have reproduced Cervantes' text. Similarly, when the matter remembered from purely formal instruction is properly understood there may be no verbal sign of the difference. Borges' fable, of course, concerns not writing, but reading, and expresses the impossibility of a reception that does not already modify the text. The fable affirms that there is always a measure of escape from the pedagogical circle, but Rousseau does not value that possibility which reasoning might open up. He wishes the moral impress of Nature to be immediate, isomorphic, and authoritative.

Premature reasoning is, therefore, one of the points on which Rousseau differs from Locke whose *Reflections on Education* are otherwise an admired model, and who provides the intellectual sub-structure for Rousseau's child-centred, developmental conception.

> To reason with the child was Locke's great maxim. It is the one most in vogue today, although its success seems to me hardly to justify it; and for my part I see nothing more foolish than these children who have been reasoned with so much. Of all the faculties of man, reason, which is only, so to say, a composite of all the others, is the one that develops last and with the most difficulty. And that is what they want to use to develop the first ones! The crowning achievement of a good education is to make a reasonable man; and yet they want to raise a child by means of reason! (*Émile* 106–7; *Emile*, 89)

---

[19] *Labyrinths*, trans. James Irby and Donald A. Yates (London: Penguin, 1970) pp. 62–71.

In this passage the reified powers of the old faculty psychology inherited from the middle ages, and which still persisted as ghostly verbal presences within Lockean sensationalist discourse, are visibly breaking up. Rather than a single faculty which comes to the child at the 'age of reason', and can then be developed, Rousseau sees a complex overall development of which rationality is the outcome. The capacity to reason, and still more to reason appropriately, arises as an indeterminate precipitate of the rational and the empirical, what we can only call the effect of experience. Likewise, the boundaries of the other traditional faculties, memory and understanding, begin to blur within the larger developmental process. As Rousseau questions the functioning of these faculties, the gap between a formal comprehension of language and a true understanding of the object is so much the more significant: 'All their knowledge is in sensation, nothing has reached the understanding. Their memory is hardly more complete than their other faculties, since they almost always have to learn again as adults the things for which they learned the words as children.' (*Émile*, 133; *Emile*, 108) Only experience can bridge this gap.

For Rousseau, then, 'the first stage of education must be entirely negative', and the continuing watch word is never to do 'today what you can, without danger, put off (*différer*) till tomorrow.' (*Émile*, 113; *Emile*, 94). For modern readers, Rousseau's use of the verb '*différer*' here locates his educational psychology more sharply in relation to his suspicion of instruction in language. Jacques Derrida's encompassing argument about 'deferral' as an inextricable aspect of linguistic meaning took Rousseau as one of its primary instances.[20] If Saussurian synchronic 'difference' is the basis of positive meaning in the linguistic sign, then Derrida complicates it with the temporal process of articulation in which the consummation of meaning is constantly deferred. According to Derrida, we generally fail to notice this because of the 'metaphysics of presence', the implicit presence of the speaker which, even in written texts, lends apparent substance and purpose to utterance. But whereas 'deferral' for Derrida is an inescapable condition of the production of meaning, for Rousseau it is a vital condition of understanding. Rather than reflecting a hidden hollowness *within* language, Rousseau's deferral acknowledges a process of interaction with the world *through* language.

The characteristically twentieth-century insistence that the human world is linguistically constituted may be taken in stronger or weaker senses. The danger of the stronger interpretation is that language itself is fetishised. When we get language, as D. H. Lawrence might have said, 'in the head', it is seen as coterminous with world, as if what leaves no trace in language does not exist. In fact, Derrida's deconstructive practice acknowledges a

---

[20] *Of Grammatology*, op.cit.

certain 'remainder', but his mode of critique, at least as it has been widely received, tends to elide the factor of experience, or see it only as illusory. Yet if experience as such cannot be put directly into language that does not mean it is non-existent, inconsequential or incommunicable. As Walter Ong observes of Derrida's argument: 'it hardly follows that because A is not B, it is nothing.'[21] In Rousseau, then, the urgent problem of language lies not at the level of intra-linguistic meaning, but in the relation to experience, whether in acquiring or communicating it, and the importance of the delaying principle is that it allows something other than the governor, what we can only call 'experience', to intervene, and thereby circumvent the premature closure of illusory understanding. The space opened by delay is far from empty although it may be difficult to articulate and the admonitory notion of a 'metaphysics of presence' is likely only to exacerbate the elision of experience.

Yet Rousseau, too, has a tendency to elide experience in so far as he wishes Emile to feel the direct impress of Nature. From the viewpoint of a later and more scientifically-minded culture, the physical world of Nature is less self-evident than it may have seemed to Rousseau. If in its muteness it does not actively deceive, it nonetheless requires immense labours of interpretation. Of course, what a later scientist means by the physical world is different from what Rousseau means by Nature but, as his botanising suggests, the distinction is not yet so active for Rousseau. He sought systematically to record rather than penetrate behind the appearances of Nature. Hence he warns at the outset of the educative process that, although the governor is to commit twenty-four hours of every day to the pupil from birth, he will have only limited control since he must share his formative influence with both society and Nature. His skill will lie in minimising the influence of the former and maximising that of the latter. In effect, the punning hint in 'defer' must be taken from English rather than French, so that the pedagogical deferral in Rousseau's delaying principle links not to Saussurian 'difference' but to moral respect or acknowledgement. It is a way of 'deferring' to Nature as the ultimate authority: '... at birth the infant is already a disciple, not of the governor, but of nature. The governor merely studies under this first master and prevents its efforts from being checked' (Émile, 68; Emile, 61) and later: 'Let nature act for a long time before thrusting yourself forward to act in its (or her) place...' (Émile, 131–2; Emile, 107) Indeed, Rousseau's personification of Nature illuminates his conception of educational authority. The noun is feminine in French and, taken in isolation, his remarks may often suggest the motherly, nurturing

---

[21] Walter Ong, *Orality and Literacy: the Technologising of the Word* (London and New York: Methuen, 1982) p. 167.

aspect of Wordsworthian Nature, and this would not be entirely wrong. But his emphasis is different. For him, Nature is rather a figure of impersonal, male authority whose reticence expresses the non-negotiability of the reality principle. It is rather the tutor who approximates the maternal role. He should be as close in age as possible to the pupil, whom he never punishes, and indeed he always places himself on the child's side, while nature 'punishes' remorselessly. Even though the tutor is responsible for arranging almost all of the experiences by which the child is 'punished', the punishment must seem to come simply from the logic of events, or what Rousseau repeatedly calls 'the order of things'. When recounting, for example, the method of reforming a wealthy spoilt child by arranging for him to get into humiliating difficulties, Rousseau affirms that 'the lesson always came to him from the thing itself.' (*Émile*, 156; *Emile*, 124)

The studied indirection and the mixture of gender in Rousseau's way of exercising the authority of Nature is significant in the light of his commitment to separate spheres for men and women. His conservatism in this regard may initially be surprising in view of his general progressiveness yet it reflects the dualisms and elisions in his thought. The cover of the 1966 Garnier edition of *Émile* quotes Michelet's approving comment that it is 'a very male book'. This is undoubtedly true but some decades later it seems less obviously a compliment and in this respect Rousseau anticipates an important aspect of the *Bildungsroman* as an unembarrassedly male genre.[22] If Book V, concerned with Emile's meeting with, and eventual marriage to, Sophie has less intellectual and dramatic power than the former ones, this is partly because of an abrupt reversal by which, having steadfastly opposed the uncorrupted nature of Emile to the prevailing social formation, he now takes the social construction of the female as straightforward evidence of her true nature. And above all, the woman's biology destines her to motherhood. Of course, all this is not to be read anachronistically. The book is about rearing a child from birth and is part of what we can now see as the invention of modern childhood, and to that extent motherhood too. Rousseau's encouragement of breast-feeding was immediately influential along with the general significance accorded to the earliest stage of childhood. Even modern working mothers would not usually reject the central thrust of Rousseau's legacy and his separation of spheres was more plausible, and economically necessary, in his day although it was rejected by such sympathetic women readers as Mary

---

[22] Much has now been written on the female side of this history as for example in Susan Fraiman, *Unbecoming Women: British Women Writers and the Novel of Development* (New York: Columbia University Press, 1993) and Gayle Green, *Changing the Story: Feminist Fiction and the Tradition* (Bloomington and Indianapolis: Indiana University Press, 1991).

Wollstonecraft, or Madame de Staël who would quietly adapt him to her aristocratic requirements.[23]

Rousseau tends both to idealise woman and to identify with her. Moreover, Rousseau's woman is herself a rather contradictory being: a figure of both strength and weakness. On the one hand, her supposedly innate capacity for wholeness of being, and her resulting capacity to live in closer harmony with the natural, made her the guardian of moral culture. In this respect she represents the ideal to which men have to be educated. Mme de Warens, Rousseau's adoptive 'Maman' in the *Confessions*, strikingly exemplifies this natural wholeness. Her purity of heart is impregnable not just to the bad principles of her confessor but even to the likely consequences of her own behaviour.[24] Yet the woman as weaker vessel and repository of familial honour also requires the most carefully guided upbringing and continuing male authority. In *Julie*, the heroine fulfils both ideals. Her father, and her husband, Wolmar, are the authoritative mentors for the young lovers but, once her conscience has been pricked and the affair is broken off, it is she who performs this function most directly for her former lover, Saint Preux.

The qualities and methods Rousseau attributes to the woman are, *mutatis mutandis*, strikingly close to those he has been recommending for the governor throughout the preceding books. Both exert a more powerful authority by appearing not to do so:

I expect many readers, remembering that I accord to woman a natural talent for governing men, will accuse me of contradiction. But they will be mistaken. There is great difference between arrogating the right to command, and governing the one who commands. The woman's power is one of sweetness, tact and willingness to please. Her orders are caresses, and her threats are tears. She must rule in the house as a minister in the state, by getting others to command what she wishes to have done. It is quite consistent that the best managed households are those in which the woman has the most authority: but when she fails to recognise the voice of the master, and seeks to usurp his rights and commands, the only result is disorder, poverty, scandal and dishonour. (*Émile*, 535; *Emile*, 408)

Rousseau has reason perhaps to feel some suspicion of Sophie's influence and the iron fist of control beneath the velvet glove of simulated friendship is more nakedly felt in the following, late comment on her than it has been with Emile. Despite her own excellent upbringing, Sophie, as a generic female, requires firm handling. 'Women are adroit and know how to disguise themselves: the

---

[23] See Germaine de Staël, *Lettres sur les ouvrages et le caractère de J-J Rousseau* (1788) and Mary Wollstonecraft, *A Vindication of the Rights of Woman* (1792).
[24] *The Confessions*, op. cit. pp. 190–1.

more she murmurs in secret against my tyranny, the more careful she is to flatter me. She feels that her fate is in my hands.' (*Émile*, 589; *Emile*, 449) If Sophie's intrinsic duplicity as a woman did not make her transparent *a priori* to Rousseau, his own skill as a manipulative governor might help him to detect her. It takes one to know one.

Sophie, however, is no match for Rousseau's imagined authority and a further reason for this is hinted at in the last passage quoted for it is hardly reading against the grain to recognise a deeper sense in which her fate is indeed in his hands. Although Rousseau refuses at the outset the awesome labour and responsibility of being governor himself, and writes only to advise a younger man, for purposes of exposition he imagines a hypothetical pupil of his own. This is harmless in so far as Rousseau imagines himself as governor but it is more ambiguously freighted in so far as the governor's authority and foresight are those of the author himself. This is where the generic, as well as gender, ambiguity of the text becomes significant.

The point may be clarified by comparison with an earlier text. As part of his epochal impact, Rousseau transposes on to a naturalistic plane what was expressed allegorically in the major educational fiction of the preceding epoch. Archbishop Fénelon's *Télémaque* (1699) was written as an idealistic model of princely education for the young sons of Louis XIV. It was admired throughout continental Europe and *Emile* is a conscious attempt to replace it for a new era in which the king is no longer the representative human type. Sophie has read and admired *Télémaque*: Emile has not read it but embodies the hero's virtues. *Télémaque* recounts the moral education of the son of Odysseus in the Homeric world as perceived through the lens of contemporary French classicism. Rousseau modifies this in a number of ways although with unconscious continuities. Telemachus is guided at crucial points by his father's old associate, Mentor, who is actually the goddess Minerva in disguise. This is echoed in the gender ambiguity of Rousseau's mentor figure: overtly male, secretly female. Just as Fénelon's Mentor in *Télémaque* is actually a female divinity, so a secret substitution of gender subtends the exercise of authority in *Emile* as the indirection of womanly power rather supplants than supplements male authority. No less importantly, however, the womanly indirection masks another kind of secret working in the imagination of authority.

In Fénelon's classical fiction the Gods intervene with a significant, though not complete, foreknowledge. The hidden divinity suggests the characteristic doubleness of the mentor in subsequent tradition, but in Rousseau's case the running together of governor and author means he is at once a secret divinity in the world of Emile and an acknowledged one in that of *Emile*. This matters because, just as the overt function of the governor is underwritten by his secret arranging of Emile's experiences, so the efficacy of these educative charades is underwritten in turn by the author. As always, Rousseau does not see this as a problem. He is quite transparent about it as part of the asserted confidence of his method. But in what is now a highly naturalistic treatise, as opposed to an allegorical fiction, it means that his authority is more imaginary than he imagines. Indeed, the image of divinity is unwittingly relevant towards the end of the text when Rousseau has Emile declare: 'It is you, Oh my master, who have made me free in teaching me to yield to necessity.' (*Émile*, 618; *Emile*, 472) Emile's grateful appreciation of his education into freedom may for us echo the theological mystery of free will since Rousseau as the governor-cum-author has indeed 'made' him what he is to a greater extent than Emile can know. Rousseau is not deliberately playing on these theological echoes since he wishes to emphasise the psychological independence of the pupil. Yet the unconscious echo is appropriate in so far as, like the Savoyard vicar, who expounds Rousseau's natural religion in Book IV, he largely elides the distinction and speaks as governor in his own name; he wishes a natural order to take over the function of the theological. By the same token, however, Rousseau himself, as author of *Emile*, cannot know how far the pupil has indeed been 'made' by the method. And the sense in which he has been entirely made, or made up, excites a scepticism upon which the text itself can put no authoritative limit. The figure of the mentor, in so far as it mediates between the planes of character and author, may act as a reflective device raising to consciousness the parallel predicaments of author and mentor. But in *Emile* the governor-cum-author unconsciously represents Rousseau's unembarrassed deployment of an over-determining power, and the problem is felt by the thoughtful reader precisely to the extent that it is not noticed by the author.

The questions raised here have long-term implications for the novel of education. In contrast to the *Bildungsroman* in the Goethean tradition, the eighteenth-century to modern novel more generally has been acknowledged to be a strongly female form, even when written by men. Leon Edel, for example, comparing Henry and William James, contrasts the male spirit of the philosopher in William to the female spirit of the novelist in Henry.[25] Rousseau enjoys a version of this gender combination in himself. If the philosopher and novelist in Rousseau answer in a significant measure to a comparable gendering, they are both present in *Emile* but not as a single combined mode of authority. Having recently written in *Julie* a work which was to become a

---

[25] The contrast between William and Henry is a major theme of Edel's biography and is frequently linked to the influence on Henry of his mother as, for example, Leon Edel, *Henry James*, vol. 2 (London: Penguin, 1977) pp. 252–3.

classic of European fiction, and which had been an immediate popular success in its day, Rousseau was aware of the fictional potential of *Emile*. Indeed, he signals this overtly by introducing the last of its five books as the fifth 'act'. (*Émile*, 465; *Emile*, 357) But rather than fully develop this potential, or write the work squarely as a novel, Rousseau seems to elide the generic difference of novel and treatise, which is a different matter. The consequences of this are worth examining more closely as they reflect on the subsequent history of educational fiction.

Treatise and/or Novel

The generic hybridity of *Emile* is particularly significant because of Rousseau's ambivalence towards fiction. He is highly suspicious of it as a product of the imagination, and hence another dangerous supplement. On the face of it, one could say that the initial idea of 'a treatise on education' (*Émile* 32; *Emile*, 34) is developed by its own internal logic till it assimilates something of the psychological complexity and dramatic thickness associated with later European novels. In fact, as Peter Jimack showed long ago, Rousseau's earlier drafts are in the relatively impersonal mode of a treatise and only later did he imagine himself as the governor educating a boy himself.[26] He speaks, for example, of his 'imaginary pupil' (*Émile*, 54; *Emile*, 50) and invites the reader 'to picture (his) Emile' (*Émile*, 314; *Emile*, 241). Yet the fictional potentiality is restrained not just by the residual structure of the treatise, but by a philosophical and didactic will that is resistant to fiction in principle. At the same time, although Rousseau will not let the novelistic dimension escape, or take over, from the treatise, he seems not consciously to pose the question in this way. Somehow he both wants, and does not want, it to be a fiction.

This is because, although he is highly self-conscious about the truth claims of the work, he does not conceive of these in terms of fictionality. On the contrary, what most characterises his awareness of the fictional potentiality of the text is his apparent indifference to it as a category. It is evident from his *oeuvre* at large that his notion of fiction lacked the positive and self-conscious ontological transposition we would now regard as its defining characteristic. As Schiller was to point out, despite his artistic talents and sensibility, Rousseau lacked a positive conception of the aesthetic. Or more precisely, when he did see the ontological transposition it was most typically under a negative sign, the sign of illusion.[27] Rousseau's *Letter to d'Alembert* (1758) arguing against the

---

[26] *La Genèse et la Rédaction de l'Émile de Jean-Jacques Rousseau. Étude sur l'histoire de l'ouvrage jusqu'à sa parution. Studies on Voltaire and the Eighteenth Century*, vol. xiii (Geneva, 1960).

[27] *On the Naïve and Sentimental in Literature*, trans. Helen Watanabe O'Kelly (Manchester: Carcanet Press, 1981) pp. 49–50.

latter's proposal for a Genevan national theatre is the most famous expression of his suspicion of the fictive. Beneath the various social evils he associates with theatre, lies a more radical objection, a metaphysical horror at the very nature of acting as a deliberate self-division and promotion of illusion. Compared to Rousseau, the Johnson of the *Preface to Shakespeare*, for all his hostility to fancy, is an aesthete. Just as revealingly, Rousseau's account of the writing of *Julie* in the *Confessions* acknowledges its partial origin in his frustrated feeling for Mme d'Houdetot, the acknowledged lover of his friend Saint-Lambert.[28] The real life situation was one of near voyeuristic sublimation and little more ontological transposition was required to turn it formally into fiction. His ambivalence towards his achievement encompasses both shame at its origin in emotional fantasy and pride in its compelling power over aristocratic women readers; the latter triumph, of course, being no ontological negation of the former condition. And although he goes on to make a moral case for the novel this is based precisely on its literalistic moral exemplarity, not on an aesthetic appreciation of it as a crafted fiction.

In *Emile*, Rousseau wishes to press a more urgent and hard-headed truth claim. He introduces the named figure of Emile precisely as a reality check against the assumption of efficacious authority to which a systematic treatise would inevitably be susceptible. (*Émile*, 54; *Emile*, 50) Rousseau's literalistic view of fiction is reflected in his invoking the imaginary pupil in this way as having the presumptive value of a real test case. As he seeks to offer not the 'merely' imaginary but an unrecognised truth, his claims would be undermined by the illusionistic power of the fictional imagination, and indeed he points this up by his occasional references to the work's fictional possibilities. At a late stage, for example, he comments that if he has succeeded only in writing a novel, or romance (the semantic closeness of the two words in French is obviously relevant here), it is a novel true to human nature, and it is rather the depraved reader who will see it as (merely) a novel. (*Émile*, 545; *Emile*, 416) Despite Rousseau's frequent association with pre-romantic *Schwärmerei*, the imaginatively focused emotion he sought to arouse in *Emile*, in contrast to conventional treatises on education, was a respect for the reality principle. Hence, as with the educative charades created for Emile, fiction is permitted only when it has the value of reality. But that, of course, given the affective verisimilitude of the age of sentiment, leaves a back door wide open to the fictional.

If fiction for Rousseau is justified only by its doing duty for reality, it is not surprising that the fictional propensity of the text often creeps up on the reader, and it seems on Rousseau too, by a constant slippage. The

---

[28] *The Confessions*, op. cit. pp. 410–15.

sudden leap from the hypothetical child to the named Emile indicates the ontological elision that occurs throughout. Emile's future wife, Sophie, for example, comes into being through the gradual personification of an ideal construction. These fictional effects remain local and *ad hoc* additions. They are ontologically unmarked and the fictional characters are intermingled with equally exemplary discussion of supposedly real instances of children, good and bad, from Rousseau's acquaintance. (*Émile*, 136, 152, 179; *Emile*, 110, 121, 141) As in *Julie*, Rousseau certainly imagines a situation, but he imagines it *as if* it were real, and the successive 'Prefaces' to that novel are a classic instance of sentimentalist equivocation on the reality status of the action designed to enhance its emotional, and hence moral, impact as a reality.

Rousseau's restraining of novelistic potentiality within a literalistic conception of fiction, was common in the period and reflected the moral and responsive psychology assumed in the movement of sentiment. Sentimentalist fiction was doubly literalist. It assumed that moral power was exerted on the reader through emotional identification; a one-for-one arousal of sympathetic feeling, likely to be most powerfully effected where the object has the maximum illusion of reality. Typically, the reader is invited to identify emotionally with virtue in distress. And by the same token, therefore, the moral or didactic impact of the work is isomorphic with the moral nature of the characters. The reader is assumed to identify sympathetically with the model whether good or bad and hence the widespread concern that immoral characters not be attractive, or go unpunished. Rousseau's remarks on fiction in *Emile* reflect this literalistic moral conception. His discussion of La Fontaine's *Fables* (*Émile*, 139–45, 323–4; *Emile*, 112, 248–9), a strange mixture, as we might now feel, of psychological acuity and literalistic obtuseness, is an extended example, though it is relevant to note his consistent hostility to their explicitly didactic conclusions. In keeping with his overall educational conception, he wishes them to work experientially, not propositionally, on the child. Hence, when Rousseau put educational advice into *Julie* and employed novelistic methods in *Emile*, the formal categories admitted for him no truly ontological transposition.[29] All the material is there with the same value of felt reality.

The one work of fiction he recommends for Emile as a boy is *Robinson Crusoe* (1719) which antedates the fiction of sentiment and yet appears to invite a literalistic response to its studied verisimilitude. Rousseau strips away the elements which might give Crusoe's narrative the thematic depth of fiction.

---

[29] The essential project of *Emile* can be seen in a single letter of *Julie* (pt. 5, letter 8) *op. cit.* pp. 598–600.

Emile would concentrate simply on Crusoe's experience on the island in a spirit of identification. (*Émile*, 238–9; *Emile*, 184–5) The book would be a practical guide to self-sufficiency, just as the art of drawing is practised elsewhere not to awaken artistic sensibility but for an accurate perception of objects. (*Émile*, 183; *Emile*, 143–4) Yet precisely within this literalism, Rousseau reads it for a philosophical and thematic meaning. Crusoe's sojourn on the island demonstrates the limited nature of real human needs when uncorrupted by social influence; and also the truth that no man is an island, that all men have a need for social collaboration. (*Émile* 240, 250–1; *Emile*, 185–6, 192–3) In fact, *Robinson Crusoe* is especially open to Rousseau's moral and philosophical use since, within his literalistic response, the experience of Crusoe is not embedded in a prior set of thematic meanings created by its internal literary structure. It simply presents itself as a body of raw material available for his own moral interpretation; an interpretation, moreover, which appears to him as no more than the transparently immediate impact of the events narrated. Defoe's real*ism* stands, in Rousseau's mind, for the reality principle he prizes in nature.

But if for Rousseau a different kind of imaginary from the fictional is at stake in *Emile* it is also evident, even from the above remarks, that fiction is a vital and constitutive element within it. It is fiction through and through. Even as Rousseau resists the ontological category of fiction, he creates an essentially imaginary being, and the imagined pedagogical process itself depends on a multitude of internal fictions by which the pupil is to be surrounded. The imagined governor himself, of course, is the pivotal locus of all the resultant ambiguity. He is the principal fiction in playing the role of innocent friend and he is the means of at once exposing to the reader and guarding from Emile the fictional status of the boy's experiences. So for example, to initiate Emile into the notion of property, he is encouraged by the governor to plant seedlings on a patch of ground actually cultivated by the gardener, Robert. (*Émile*, 119–21; *Emile*, 98–9) The labour of caring for the seedlings creates in Emile a positive sense of the meaning of property but one day Robert discovers them and digs them up as transgressing his prior right. In order to give Emile this rough lesson all the adults have to play a carefully prepared charade while, just as importantly, using the elements of the real world. Robert really is the gardener.

If Rousseau's use of fiction is open-handed at the level of content and repressive at the level of the category, this doubleness can be uneasily felt in many such episodes. Acting out the painful and manipulative fiction of the seedlings might strike some observers as more morally suspect for the participants in the pretence than the overt art of acting is to the actor.

Rousseau, after all, objects to acting as an exercise in duplicity in which the evil lies in the condition itself even more than in its effects on others. It is the deliberate splitting of the self, the psychological self-laceration, which arouses his moral horror. Emile, by contrast, is to be an integral being, one for whom even the polite duplicity of ordinary social relations will be alien. But what a Samuel Beckett character would later call the 'quantum of wantum' remains constant, and duplicity is displaced rather than eradicated. In the tutor's organised charade, the attempt to honour and produce an ideal integrity in one being requires a systematic duplicity in the rest of the social group. It is significant in this connection that Rousseau's attack on acting in the *Letter to d'Alembert* is contrasted with early memories of a Genevan *fête champêtre*: an authentic performance of the social self in which all the elements of theatre, music, dance, and spectacle, are performed collectively by the community.[30] *Julie* contains a similar episode.[31] So too, the charade over the seedlings might claim to be the moral obverse of theatre. From the adults' point of view it might even be regarded as a dramatic ritual of initiation into the social community. Indeed, seen in that light, the reading of fiction could be regarded as a form of social initiation and Goethe's novels will develop the possibility of sliding internally from realism to ritual, but if *Emile* were to become an overt fiction, it would envelop the whole experience in what Rousseau would see as the suspect mode of the imaginary. It is one thing for Nature to educate the boy, even if it is given some supplementary assistance along the way, but frank acknowledgement of the fictionality of the method would turn it from a natural development into an artificial product of social purpose with all the problems of justification that would entail. He wants the text to have the demonstrative force of reality that Emile encounters, albeit deceptively, in the seedlings episode.

Yet for all Rousseau's repression of it, there is a true instinct and an emblematic significance in the way fiction in *Emile* strains at the leash — strains both to perform its practical function and to be acknowledged as a category. Just as the period's great fiction of sensibility had a dramatic power and complexity beyond its moral literalism, so *Emile* unconsciously acknowledges the constitutive function of fiction in pedagogical formation. The outcome is that Rousseau offers Emile as the universally representative case whom he can treat with the sovereign power of a novelist over a character. And as he does so he constantly draws on the powers of fiction. So for example, although Emile is to read little fiction, when another privileged youth is to learn of the uncertainties of human life, he must have more than cold

---

[30] *Lettre à d'Alembert* (Paris: Gallimard, 1995) pp. 31–43.
[31] *Julie, op. cit.* pp. 588–98.

instruction. His imagination is therefore terrified with such literary staples as captive labour in Algerian galleys. (*Émile*, 291; *Emile*, 224) Once again, the function of fiction, even of a popular sensationalist kind, gets in by the back door even as the official entry is closed. Likewise, Rousseau is sceptical of historical study as having little relation to the pupil's own life, but the historians he admires are those who have the novelistic capacity to illuminate character by the use of telling psychological detail. By a characteristic circularity in sentimentalist theory, the methods of fiction support the category of history by whose virtue the use of the fictional is then justified. (*Émile*, 313; *Emile*, 241)

An obverse indication of the peculiar status of fiction in *Emile* is that the work is comparatively weaker where it comes closest to being frankly fictional. Its truly powerful fiction is the unconscious, philosophical one at the heart of the project, and centred in the early books, while in the fifth book fiction is allowed to become more openly dominant. The culmination of the treatise is Rousseau's analysis of emotional illusion and Emile's sentimental education encompasses the critique of romantic love which subtends the whole tradition of the French novel, including Rousseau's own *Julie*. (*Émile*, 94–5, 431; *Emile*, 81, 329) But Emile is still innocent of this recognition and the material therefore calls most notably at this point for novelistic treatment. But here we feel the imaginative limitation of the governor-cum-author's controlling viewpoint. As the love between Emile and Sophie develops, Rousseau hovers in his characteristic posture of confidant and go-between, vicariously excited by their mutual attraction even as he sees its necessarily illusory character as romance, but justifying his and the reader's emotional participation by the innocence of the principals. This extends into an invitation to participate in all the roles within an internal theatre of the imagination: 'O who that has a heart cannot create for himself the delicious tableau of the different situations of father, mother, daughter, governor, pupil . . .' (*Émile*, 557; *Emile*, 424–5) The simultaneous participation in the lives of all the characters, although presented here in the contemporary form of the sentimentalist tableau, is a classic ambition of the novel. But whereas in *Julie* Rousseau's tendency to vicarious emotion took on a genuinely dramatic life, in *Emile* the omniscience of the author merges with the control of the governor so that Emile and Sophie can only be lay figures with no dramatic independence. The resistance to novelistic transposition is at its most striking where it is nearest to being overt and permitted.

Conversely, Rousseau was to continue the lovers' story by examining, in a fully novelistic form, the collapse of their married relationship. The intended novel, *The Solitaries*, remained unfinished but it is highly suggestive that he should consider such an outcome and turn to fiction to explore the possible reworking of Emile's education. In *Emile*, he had repressed such doubts along with its fictional potential and it was likewise the fictional which perhaps held the key to deeper explorations. Many eighteenth-century novels used fictive characters to enact demonstrative experiments in human nature. When virtue is tested, for example, in Richardson or Laclos, the inhumanity of the process is devolved on to characters such as Lovelace or Valmont. Despite their drawing on the power of sentimentalist verisimilitude, the fictional status of these works permits their destructive investigations of human possibility. *Emile* is another such demonstrative experiment but Rousseau's literalism is at one with his dogmatism in not allowing novelistic freedom to his imagined characters.

But Rousseau's dogmatic literalism serves a useful function in bringing to the surface the inherent tensions of all educative authority and showing their significant parallel with the structures of fictional control. A novel typically adopts an innocent narrative present despite the reader's knowledge that its future is already written. Rousseau's treatise, by contrast, foregrounds the predictive control which the governor shares in some measure with the author. At the same time, there is a generous insistence that the child should live fully and genuinely for the present rather than for some future goal, and that this will prepare him best for the future. (*Émile*, 91–2, 273; *Emile*, 79, 221) And the governor is to participate in this present even while remaining in command of the process. (*Émile*, 117; *Emile*, 97) As in a good novel, the teleology is to be felt only as an immanent aspect of the moving present.

Rousseau rightly insists on the importance for the educator of this double awareness of time. It is a commonplace that teaching is performative in the sense of holding an audience, but the teacher also performs less obviously to the pupil by inhabiting a double timescale like that of the novel. In teaching, the rival necessities of encouragement and correction have to find an essentially fictional balance which has to be convincingly, and one might say sincerely, enacted at each present moment. In the early stages particularly, this intuitive calculation is crucial. The teacher must be partly, yet genuinely, where the pupil is at any given time. Rousseau's manipulative charades are in effect allegories of the teacher's sincere acting. In a novel, the pupil as hero might well have exactly the experience that is arranged for Emile and, since it would be a natural event in the world of the fiction, the question of teacherly duplicity would not arise. But the generic uncertainty of Rousseau's text exposes, for good or ill, the author's position and focuses the underlying structure of the educative relation as a participative fiction. The text's only partial consciousness in this regard suggests a further general dimension which Rousseau seems likewise both to exploit and yet not fully acknowledge. For as well as being a literalistic treatise half suppressing its own fictionality, it is also a work of utopian imagination whose very literalism is constantly, if ambiguously, raised to an allegorical power.

Emile as Utopian Allegory

I have suggested that Rousseau's ontological premises with regard to fiction faced him with an apparently stark choice between the literal and the illusory, and with a consequent need to avoid the contaminating middle ground of fiction. At the same time, his avoidance of the merely imaginary in that sense did not exclude, and indeed, in his mind it served to protect, a more philosophical order of truth claim. He wished to establish general and ideal principles of education which the governor is to adjust appropriately to circumstances. But just as the fictional is kept under restraint without quite being acknowledged as a category so another important mode, or motive, also strains to be acknowledged in the text: the utopian. A utopian impulse, although not usually a formal qualification, is an essential requirement for good teaching. Despite its frequently adopting the protective camouflage of cynicism, utopianism is the motive power of education. For similar reasons, perhaps, it often expresses itself in fiction, but it is not the same as fiction. In Rousseau's case, where fiction itself is ambivalently suppressed, the utopian motive is left with a similarly pervasive and ambiguous presence in the text. In his Preface, after all, he called it, as well as a treatise, the 'dreams of a visionary on education'. (*Émile*, p. 32; *Emile*, p. 34)

The ambiguously utopian element is evidenced in the history, especially the early history, of his reception. Despite Rousseau's advice that his recommendations were to be taken at a level of general principle and adjusted to the individual character and circumstamces, this did not answer the uncertainty of many readers about his specific examples. In the early, controversial decades of his reception, a constant motif for both critics and disciples was the frequent impracticality of his method although individuals often differed in their cherry-picking from it. One writer, La Fare, without mentioning Rousseau by name, evidently had him in mind in claiming that his own *Le Gouverneur, ou Essai sur l'éducation* (1768) was no merely 'imaginary system'. Pierre-Samuel Dupont, while acknowledging the 'magnificent poem of the philosophe from Geneva', thought its commitment to a completely private education was impractical.[32] The title of Richard and Maria Edgeworth's *Essays on Practical Education* (1811), a work which repeatedly challenges Rousseau in details but from within his acknowledged influence, indicates the principal

---

[32] I owe this information to Jean Bloch, *Rousseauism and Education in Eighteenth-Century France* (Oxford: Voltaire Foundation, 1995) pp. 42–5, 47.

locus of their critique and their deliberate avoidance of system.³³ Yet as these critiques themselves demonstrate, the work seemed to be offered as, and was widely assumed to be, a practical handbook. Once again, as with the question of fiction, Rousseau's literalism promotes this uncertainty by not recognising the category, but it also throws the question into relief. If we feel sceptical when Rousseau recommends a particular practice in an apparently pragmatic and literal spirit, this reflects not so much the manic obsessiveness and naivety of the writer, as a poetic, allegorical, utopian power implicitly at work in the text.

Some instances are both marginal and persuasive. He advises, for example, that a baby who is still learning to 'read' the world and interpret apparently two-dimensional visual impressions as spatial disposition should be carried around as much as possible in order to acquire the necessary experience. At a later stage, when the child wishes to handle a particular object, he should be taken to it rather than it be given to him. (*Émile*, 76; *Emile*, 66) This practical detail contains a symbolic wealth. The apparent kindness in fetching the object for the child reinforces its natural, but ultimately illusory, tendency to feel itself the centre of the world. Taking the child to the world, introducing it to reality, has an allegorical significance surely in excess of its likely impact in practice. Yet in so far as the action expresses a general and considered disposition in the parental adult, it is not only touching as a piece of performed poetry, it represents a more elusive background influence which is the true, and not unlikely, source of formative efficacy. The parental adult who does this will express a general disposition to the world that the child will be likely to imbibe.

Similarly, he advises distracting a persistently crying child with a fresh object. Nurses are adept at this, he acknowledges, but for Rousseau it is vital that the distraction not be perceived as such; that the child should discover the new interest as if by itself. (*Émile*, 80; *Emile*, 69) As always, the child is to experience the world rather than a human intermediary. This is a brilliant *aperçu*, yet one may feel sympathy for the nurse obliged to carry out the series of instant charades this technique would be likely to require. Moreover, as with the literalism elsewhere in the text, he assumes an unambiguous impress of experience on the child's mind. For there is a possible counter-argument for the value of the relationship fostered by the nurse's manifest good intention towards the child in providing the distraction. Indeed, there is a larger theme here about the young child's need to experience sociability: a need which is in fundamental tension with the principle of the *cordon sanitaire* and indeed

---

³³ Originally written by Maria as *Practical Education* (1798), the third edition was co-published with her father.

with the general suspicion of the social in Rousseau's thought. For although the capacity for personal and social relationship is theoretically the ultimate goal of Emile's education, this is precisely the dimension in which Rousseau's individualism is compounded by his own personality traits to create a major blind spot.

There is an unpredictable gap between parental practice and the child's impression; and language, as the pre-eminently social medium, is a peculiarly ambivalent area for him. For example, Rousseau goes on to advise that the nurse should not excessively talk to the child since it cannot yet understand anything except the tone of voice. (*Émile*, 81; *Emile*, 70) A more modern view might be that the continuous relationship, and precisely the intentional tone of communication in the voice, are the vital stimulus by which the child acquires linguistic attention. Relationship precedes language and at that stage conceptual meaning positively does not matter. Yet if the nurse's instinctive and traditional practice now seems wiser, and more efficacious, than Rousseau's theory at this point, this recognition comes from a refinement of appreciation within his legacy. It is in Rousseau's spirit that we now give greater weight to the earlier, pre-conceptual entry into the domain of language. But more importantly for present purposes, one can begin to feel a significant tension between practice and principle which either reveals an underlying naivety or suggests a principled intention aiming over the head of his own literalistic practicality.

Indeed, Rousseau's practical advice sometimes represents larger principles in ways that seem to overwhelm the pragmatic value. He would prefer, for example, that Emile should make all requests in the imperative mood rather than in false forms of politeness. (*Émile*, 102; *Emile*, 86) His reasoning is that since even the socially privileged child is in a position of relative weakness with respect to others, even servants, it will feel the need consciously to adopt the *tones*, and therefore feel the emotional disposition, of request and appreciation. By contrast, the conventional forms of politeness in the world of such a child are actually, and unthinkingly, imperious. Once again, there is a brilliant psychological recognition here, and one that encapsulates Rousseau's essential critique of culture focused in commonplace linguistic behaviour. Yet one must surely question the practical outcome of allowing a child, albeit only for a while, to run so much against the grain of the language. But then again, precisely as the thought becomes more impractical, it is harder to determine its true point. For if Rousseau is naive here, it is difficult to locate precisely where the naivety lies. The very quaintness of the advice makes it more like a literary trope, the innocent naivety of the child providing a vehicle for the darkly knowing, sombrely humorous, naivety of Rousseau himself. It has something of the sardonic charge of Swift's Houyhnynms who have no word in their language for a lie, and have to speak of 'the thing that was not'.³⁴

A more extreme example of this ambivalent shimmer of the allegorical and the practical is Rousseau's proposal that when the child sees someone in a state of anger it should be explained to him as a sickness. (*Émile*, 117; *Emile*, 97) He imagines the child gently sympathising with a woman in angry conflict. An advantage of this trick is that when the child himself succumbs to anger he is treated as if he were ill and confined to bed till he recovers. Again, this feels less like a practical regime of psychological engineering than a flight of Swiftian imagination on Rousseau's part, himself angered at all-too-human failures of rationality. But where Swift characteristically entraps the reader in the highly controlled, encircling ironies of his fictive personae and narrative voices, Rousseau's extravagance trips us up in the middle of an otherwise sober and literalistic treatise. Or that at least is the effect. In truth, it is likely that Rousseau's potential as a satiric poet is half emergent and only half aware of being such.

Part of Rousseau's elusiveness in this regard is that his earnestness does not exclude humour, which is constantly exercised in the turns and condensations of his argument. So for example, his play on the term 'raise' (*élever*) when, anticipating the social decorum that will resist his proposal, he nonetheless follows Locke in training the socially privileged Emile for an artisan's trade: 'I wish to give him a rank he can never lose, and which will honour him at all times: I wish to raise him to the rank of man.' (*Émile*, 254; *Emile*, 196) More elusively again, Rousseau's humour is directed not just to the reader but into the educative process in so far as the governor's fictive charades have the aspect of practical jokes played on the pupil. In one instance, Rousseau speaks of chastening the spoilt young son of a wealthy family by arranging for him to be humiliated when he ventures outside by himself. (*Émile*, 152–6; *Emile*, 121–4) If this material were transposed into frankly fictional form, it would be recognisable as part of a venerable literary and theatrical tradition including picaresque fiction, Cervantes, several Shakespeare plays, and Calderón's *Life is a Dream*. All provide examples of moral illusion dispelled by brutal trickery for the traditional form of practical joke, or *burla*, was an ambivalent mixture of malice and morality. In such works, the educative purpose was usually aimed primarily at the audience and typically depended on rather two-dimensional characterisation, whereas Rousseau wishes to promote the process of moral understanding within the character as a fully rounded individual. *Emile* is a transitional text in which early modern

---

³⁴ *Gulliver's Travels*, (pt. 4, ch. 4) ed. Peter Dixon and John Chalker (London: Penguin, 1985) p. 286.

robustness can still be seen within the sentimental turn of modern culture. Goethe's educational fiction was a decisive moment in the internalising of the picaresque but he also kept its ghost alive, and partly by winking at the reader over the young hero's head. If Rousseau does not quite do this at the level of a formal self-consciousness, it is partly because he is already doing it so overtly and literally in his educative charades. His transparency is the opposite of such fictional self-consciousness, yet also at some level a half-witting version of it.

Conversely, if the running deception of Emile is a benign form of *burla*, Rousseau uses the natural gaiety of the child to turn the serious business of learning into a continual game. Emile is to be habituated to physical rigours such as early rising and cold washing for, Rousseau claims, there is nothing for which children cannot be given a taste, even a positive passion, if approached in the right way. 'In all games where they are convinced it is only a game, they endure without complaint, and even with laughter, what they would not otherwise suffer without floods of tears.' (*Émile*, 164; *Emile*, 130–1) When games are in earnest and life itself is a game, the categories are elided to produce a confident psychological outlook. Just as Emile's education for freedom is through the recognition of natural necessity, so necessity itself acquires the characteristics of the rules of a game: restraints designed to concentrate the powers and skills of the players. Play is another form of participative theatre, and is as close as Rousseau allows himself to come to the positive ontological transposition of the aesthetic. Play actions are framed within a self-delighting purposiveness without purpose which, precisely on that condition, may serve a larger formative end. But where Kant and Schiller were to develop the notion of play towards an ontological conception of the aesthetic, Rousseau's practical use of this liminal category characteristically avoids breaching his pragmatic and literalistic frame.

In sum, then, Rousseau's literalism throws into relief questions of interpretation which might have been more diffused, and invisible, if handled in a fully fictional mode. The text is packed with supposedly practical advice the efficacy of which is often best understood allegorically, the nuggets of advice being taken more as poetic *images* of the principles at stake than as practical *techniques* for enacting them. In this respect, Rousseau anticipates the distinctive doubleness of the *Bildungsroman* which, while it adopts the mode of psychologically realist fiction, maintains an open-handed sense of artifice pointing to an allegorical and philosophical interest beyond the immediate action. But whereas the *Bildungsroman* seeks to hold these planes in a significantly distinct relation, Rousseau's literalistic treatise constantly strains to conflate them. This is largely because of Rousseau's challenging desire literally to change the world at least, in the first instance, in the form of a single child. This raises a question concerning education in relation to history. What historical sense is actually exercised in *Emile*?

Emile and History

History is a further category of truth claim which is at once half-acknowledged and half-repressed, yet is powerfully active, in *Emile*. It is worth pausing on this because of its continuing importance for the pedagogical theme in later writers. *Emile* was intended as an historical intervention in explicit conjunction with *The Social Contract* (1762) which is quoted extensively and verbatim in the latter part. The co-presence of *The Social Contract* reinforces the ambiguity of the utopian and the practical in *Emile*, and raises the question of the logical and psychological priority of the two works. To what extent does the educational process of *Emile* produce, or instead depend upon, the larger social order? And does it matter? Is this a vicious circle, as philosophical opponents will object, or a virtuously self-fulfilling one as political sympathisers may hope? This 'bootstraps' question is one of several notorious circularities in Rousseau's thought and arises partly from his tendency to base his arguments on absolute starting points, real or hypothetical. In so far as starting points are historical, his historical claims are important yet, as with his attitude to fiction, he has a limited and suspicious view of history so that the right hand does not quite see what the left hand does.

Rousseau is notoriously slippery on the historical status of the 'social contract' as the founding act of the legitimate state. It has to be understood as a regulative idea, or philosophical fiction, rather than an historical claim.[35] Yet his rhetoric sometimes accords it the apparent value of an historical truth. As with the equivocation on fiction, he wants it to have the force of reality, in the sense of what has actually occurred, and he also wants it to have the unmediated impact of an intrinsic truth not dependent on historical contingency or interpretation. In other words it is essentially a myth, not in the sense of a mere falsehood, but as a foundational and enabling narrative enshrining a general truth. But he does not quite think of it that way. Whereas such a positive understanding of myth grew to consciousness within the historical sense of the European Enlightenment, Rousseau's work achieves its effect within the thought world of a rationalistic universalism. The German Enlightenment in particular was to develop, notably in J. G. Herder, a profound sense of the formation of culture, and of national cultures, as

---

[35] Ernst Cassirer, for example, suggests that the 'state of nature' is a regulative idea rather than an historical truth and the 'social contract' was an 'as if' *image* of law-making. What Rousseau defined as experience, Kant translated into idea. *Rousseau, Kant, Goethe* (New York: Harper, 1963) pp. 24, 35.

products of a collective historical process. In turn, this would affect the sense of the development of the individual within, and as a microcosm of, that process. In comparison, *Emile* seems to predate such a consciousness; yet it reflects its epoch in some ways the more tellingly for its innocence of historical relativity. Although Rousseau is keenly alive to his own historical moment, and predicts the end of the French monarchy, this insight derives less from a sense of historical process than from his philosophical universalism, his search for intrinsic principles and starting points. (*Émile* 252; *Emile*, 194) His rhetorical and analytic power comes from his belief that you really can start from first principles. This parallels his belief that, by means of his *cordon sanitaire*, such a fresh beginning can be made in the life of the individual.

Not surprisingly, therefore, the historicity of *Emile* is to be felt rather between, than in, the lines and Rousseau invokes earlier writers as one discussing with his contemporaries rather than recognising their historical distance. He admires the toughness of Roman and Spartan education, and praises Plato's *Republic* as a work on education. (*Émile*, 40; *Emile*, 40) His admiration for the latter is especially universalist for Plato's conception of education is radically collectivist. It is not just that the individual serves the purposes of the state: the model of the individual psyche is that of the political macrocosm. The same principles of order and disorder are at work in both, and there is little discursive scope for the separate category of the individual. And, by the same token, there is little discursive room for it to become problematic. Although Rousseau, by contrast, sought to create an ideal social order through the free and responsible individual, the discourse available to him, and the methods he envisaged, are actually close to Plato's although applied on an individual scale and through the devious means of the governor. But if the governor's charades are a disseminated equivalent of Plato's 'great lie' or 'myth', their difference is crucial. Plato's lie is maintained to keep a whole social order in place whereas Rousseau's deceptions will be outgrown by the pupil's achievement of free responsibility. For of course, the spirit of modern individuality asserts itself powerfully from within *Emile* and this is the sense in which its historicity can be felt between the lines.

The underlying emotional investment in the value of the individual can be seen in Rousseau's implicit identification with both Socrates and Christ. He is Socratic in his refusal to 'understand' his contemporaries, and in his emphasis on the minimal wisdom of avoiding the common illusions. But his attack on sophistry is not just through dialectical argument but by an appeal to the obdurate reality of the world and to the authenticity of his own being. This latter belief, that he had a direct, internal access to universal and ultimate truth, identifies him with Christ who, unlike Socrates, died deserted by most of his friends. (*Émile*, 403; *Emile*, 308) Likewise, whereas Socrates accepted his legal execution, administered in a relatively peaceful form, in a spirit of lucid rationality, Christ's brutal and unjust crucifixion was as a martyr to a transcendent principle. This fate was echoed in Rousseau's felt need, Werther-like, to affirm his principle of selfhood against the world.

The prescient pressure towards modern individuality and interiority is especially apparent in Rousseau's relation to his major philosophical model, John Locke. Rousseau assumes in many respects the Lockean sensationalist model of the mind but, along with the movement of sentiment, he reacts against the mechanistic limitations from which this model was increasingly perceived to suffer. In an empirically based conception of the mind, the inculcation of correct habits would be crucial to moral and intellectual formation, and Rousseau enacts this in his pedagogical method, but in so far as the affective element is to be seen as foundational, the sufficiency of the empirical is thrown into question. Rousseau saw that social and moral formation can indeed be achieved through Lockean association and habit but precisely without the appropriate motivation or feeling. So, for example, the wealthy child who is encouraged to give to the poor learns not to perform genuine charity at real cost to himself but a socially approved practice from which he is most likely to gain. (*Émile*, 127; *Emile*, 103–4) Likewise, Rousseau criticises Locke's method of allowing a child to learn reading through the use of dice. Once again, he focuses not on the mechanism but the motivation. (*Émile*, 145; *Emile*, 117) When the child really wants to read, the mechanism will be inconsequential. For Rousseau, there is all the difference in the world between a *tabula rasa* to be impressed and innate generosity to be developed. Furthermore, on the 'Pierre Menard' principle noted earlier, overt social behaviour and verbal formulae may conceal the inner difference. Likewise, although Locke's system was in its day kindly and child-centred, the one fault he would punish severely was 'obstinacy'.[36] Rousseau, like the Edgeworths, takes issue with this and in subsequent tradition what Locke would call 'stubbornness' is increasingly valorised, or at least subjected to more problematic discrimination.[37] Just as Rousseau pointed out the difficulty of distinguishing in a child real stupidity from the apparent stupidity of the exceptionally intelligent (*Émile*, 131; *Emile*, 106), so 'obstinacy' too can be variously judged. Once again, this is an index of the shift towards acknowledging individual and innate difference. At the same time, while Rousseau in these respects points towards the future,

---

[36] John Locke, *Some Thoughts Concerning Education*, ed. John W. and Jean S. Yolton (Oxford: Clarendon Press, 1989) p. 139.

[37] Richard and Maria Edgeworth, *Essays on Practical Education* (1811) p. 239.

his whole method of imaginary authority in the writing of *Emile* was a systematic elision of the pupil's will which Locke at least frankly acknowledged.

In sum, *Emile* is a utopian fiction challenging its contemporary world all the more for its compelling literalism while its categorial elisions and unexamined assumptions, as on the question of gender, left a rich field for future reflection. Rousseau may have had his own doubts about the efficacy of his project, doubts which he was to explore in *Les solitaires*, the overtly fictional, but unfinished, sequel to *Emile*. Some such scepticism was to be richly developed in Goethe's educational fictions but it is worth pausing first on two works nearly contemporary with *Emile* which are unconscious ripostes to Rousseau's highly rationalised educational optimism: Laurence Sterne's *Tristam Shandy* and Christoph Martin Wieland's *History of Agathon*.

2

The Comedy of Educational Errors

(A) *TRISTRAM SHANDY*: 'I OUT-DO ROUSSEAU A BAR LENGTH'

Laurence Sterne's *The Life and Opinions of Tristram Shandy* (1759–67) was begun before Rousseau's *Emile* and in no way undertakes consciously to answer it. Yet his one parenthetical comment on Rousseau, 'I out-do Rousseau a bar length', is very apt to the present theme in so far as the book constitutes an implicit comic riposte to over-confident pedagogical authority and is couched in what Sterne leads us to see as an essentially musical mode circumventing the conceptual power of language on which simpler versions of pedagogical authority tend to depend.[1]

Notoriously, *Tristram Shandy* defies summary and teases the understanding. The narrator, Tristram Shandy, a frank *alter ego* of the author, gives a new meaning to Samuel Richardson's phrase for epistolary narrative: 'writing to the moment'.[2] He reminisces in the 1760s about the life of his family circle in Shandy Hall as far back as the Malborough campaigns in the first decade of the eighteenth century and beyond. Hence, although the title suggests he will present himself as his own subject-matter, and he indeed does so very vividly in his capacity as narrator, at the level of narrative content he exists principally in his account of the family by which he has been formed. Moreover, he privileges the momentary act of writing in which, with comic pretence of incompetence, he enacts a masterly control through continual digression, flashback, and self-commentary. In this way, although many of the events have taken place long before his conscious experience, he is less their chronicler than their orchestrator, and even creator. There is in other words a curious double viewpoint whereby he may be *known* as the outcome and yet *felt* as the progenitor of the family life described. That in turn is consequential

---

[1] *The Life and Opinions of Tristram Shandy, Gentleman*, ed. James A. Work (New York: Odyssey Press, 1940) p. 620.
[2] See Richardson to Lady Bradshaigh, 25 Feb. 1754. *Selected Letters of Samuel Richardson*, ed. John Carroll (Oxford: Oxford University Press, 1964) p. 296.

in so far as his father, Walter Shandy, had high ambitions for forming him. The whole narrative enacts a tussle over pedagogical control.

Given the richness and diversity of *Tristram Shandy* it is understandable, but still remarkable, that in all the voluminous commentary it has attracted, relatively little attention has been paid directly to the pedagogical theme *per se*. For Walter Shandy's abortive attempt to educate his son by a preconceived system is the principal motivating force of the book's digressive energy. It is the initial pressure against which Tristram's narrative largely defines itself. Like Tristram, Walter is also a writer trying to bring to order the complexity not just of a human being but of his own thoughts:

> The first thing which entered my father's head, after affairs were a little settled in the family, and *Susannah* had got possession of my mother's green sattin nightgown, ⸺ was to sit down coolly, after the example of *Xenophon*, and write a Tristra-*paedia*, or system of education for me; collecting first for that purpose his own scattered thoughts, counsels, and notions; and binding them together, so as to form an INSTITUTE for the government of my childhood and adolescence. (*TS*, 372)

All this, of course, goes wildly astray and Walter's passion for instruction, along with his desire to control, provides not just the narrative premise, but the comic and moral foil, for the other characters. As in all double acts, Tristram's lovable Uncle Toby depends above all on Walter to establish his positive ethos, while Toby's other comic partner, Corporal Trim, is also one who 'lov'd to advise, ⸺ or rather to hear himself talk'. (*TS*, 95)

Walter himself meanwhile is the enduring archetype of the failed pedagogue. In anachronistic contemporaneity with the Enlightenment encyclopaedists on the other side of the Channel, Walter's portmanteau neologism, Tristra-*paedia*, which appears in mixed font at its first mention, immediately suggests a forced and unhappy connection of individual and system, while the whole project has arisen in intended compensation for disasters already suffered from Tristram's earliest moments. Moreover, it quickly becomes evident that, like *Tristram Shandy* itself, it will take longer in the writing than the living.

> In about three years, or something more, my father had got advanced almost into the middle of his work. ⸺ like all other writers, he met with disappointments. ⸺ He imagined he should be able to bring whatever he had to say, into so small a compass, that when it was finished and bound, it might be rolled up in my mother's hussive.
> (*TS*, 373)

The writings of father and son are paralleled and at one point Tristram explicitly takes over his father's project by writing up the intended chapter upon sash-windows: 'in order to render the *Tristrapaedia* complete, ⸺ I wrote the chapter myself.' (*TS*, 384) Tristram's own narrative becomes a parodic, or inverse, *Tristrapaedia*: a seemingly endless compendium of pedagogical mishaps in which the only consistent principle to emerge is the law of unintended consequences. With an interrupted conception, a botched christening, and an obstetric accident to the usually impressive family nose, Walter's formative project miscarries from the outset while providing the positive content for Tristram's.

Emile was to be very grateful, and no doubt rightly so, for the education he had received from Rousseau's governor, but for this we only had the word of Rousseau himself *as* governor, and offered in anticipation of his success. In *Tristram Shandy*, it is the pupil himself who describes in retrospect the process of his upbringing. In that respect it anticipates two later classics: the *Autobiography* (1873) of John Stuart Mill and Edmund Gosse's *Father and Son* (1907). In all three cases the father exercises a highly directive authority from which the son needs to escape. Indeed, the model of father as pedagogue throws into relief the oedipal necessity for the pupil to break out of the influence. Tristram is luckier, in that regard, than Mill or Gosse in that his father's educational ambitions and methods are so ineffective. They have a much harder time escaping but in doing so they also express more overtly what is only implicit in *Tristram Shandy*. Escape from formative influence is always relative, and both Mill and Gosse are fully mature only when they are no longer in a state of reaction against their upbringing. Their memoirs are most touching for their appreciation of the paternal love which motivated the educational regimes under which they suffered. Indeed, they are mature when they can acknowledge the father in themselves. Tristram handles it very differently but his relation to his father is similarly one of assimilation rather than rejection. Tristram has his father's traits, as well as those of Uncle Toby and Parson Yorick, but they are turned in a different direction so that he is rather the sublation of his father's qualities. Or as the present author's mother would say: he is just like his father, except you can reason with him. In that respect, *Tristram Shandy* in its pyrotechnic narrative control and its delight in pedantry, for example, is less a parody than the genial realisation of the *Tristrapaedia* as the unwitting outcome of Walter's spirit. In this case, unlike that of *Emile*, fiction takes over the treatise from the inside.

Tristram's relation to his father is echoed with philosophical resonance in Sterne's relation to a major philosophical mentor of the period, John Locke. In a book where intended communication so often breaks down and understanding is constantly achieved by whimsical byways, Locke's *Essay Concerning Human Understanding* is a continual point of reference although, as Tristram says, 'many have read it who understand it not'. (*TS*, 85) Locke's model of the psyche was in important respects a secular and liberating one in which every individual started with a *tabula rasa*. His thought was of crucial importance to the European Enlightenment, which sought a comparably clean sheet in history, and Sterne, like Rousseau, moved within Locke's orbit. For Locke, sensory impressions were the basis of ideas for which words were the fixed symbols. The 'association of ideas' was one of the mechanisms by which the human mind organises, or fails to organise, the mental precipitate of sensory experience and Locke was especially concerned that verbal meaning be kept accurate and uncontaminated. Rousseau disagreed in detail with Locke's views but his conception of character formation drew its cogency from the underlying Lockean conception, the insistence on the formative value of personal experience. Sterne is likewise respectful of Locke, and accepts his model of the mind, but as a sceptic, humorist, and sentimentalist he submits it to a comic testing more radical than Rousseau's disagreements. For to a new generation, the Lockean conception was to prove too mechanistic. In particular, feeling, creativity, and humour were three areas that were hard to accommodate positively within Locke's model and they would all prove vital for later romantic challenges to eighteenth-century associationism. All three properties are combined in the figure of the English eccentric, such as Tristram himself, through whom the principle of individuality is hyperbolically celebrated. Having visited continental Europe in 1741 as governor to another young man, Tristram has noted in contrast the great variation in character 'in this unsettled island, where nature, in her gifts and dispositions . . . is most whimsical and capricious'. (*TS*, 25) But Sterne is still at an early stage of this epochal reaction to Locke and is not yet equipped with a conscious and coherent alternative. He does not so much satirise Locke directly, therefore, as satirise man, but he sees the absurdities of man in such a Lockean manner that it slides into a *de facto* satire of the Lockean conception, especially in Walter.

Walter Shandy, with his love of abstruse scholarship and theological minutiae, is in the first instance part of the Rabelaisian academic satire with which the book seems to have originated. In devising an ideal system of education for Tristram, or Trismegistus as he intended to have him christened, he draws constantly on the classical world for his authorities. But as a contemporary figure, Walter is Lockean both in his views and in his character. Like Locke, he cannot abide a pun, in which meaning and communication are sidetracked by false association, whereas sexual *double entendre* is one of the staple means of Tristram's narrative. More importantly, his own personality has the mechanistic absurdity of the Lockean conception made flesh. The opening episode of the weekly marital coitus interrupted by the associated idea of winding the clock confounds Walter with a Lockean mechanism as his own mechanical behaviour is reflected back on him by Mrs Shandy's digressive question: '*have you not forgot to wind up the clock?*' (*TS*, 5) Once again, Tristram's disastrous conception, the intended starting point for the *Tristrapaedia*, provides instead the opening of *Tristram Shandy* itself in which digression sparked by unexpected association remains the narrative staple.

In contrast to Walter, Tristram's more direct and positive mentor is his Uncle Toby who, as a man of feeling, albeit in a very different mode from Werther, typically exercises emotional rather than intellectual understanding. At his first introduction, following the botched conception of Tristram, we are told that 'my Uncle, Mr. *Toby Shandy*, who had often been informed of the affair, ──── understood him very well.' (*TS*, 7) As the book goes on, we see how the emphasis here falls less on 'understanding' than on 'understanding *him*'. He does not just understand Walter's theory but sympathises emotionally with the fact of his obsession. Similarly, Toby makes little or no attempt to instruct Tristram but has made an evident impression on him morally and emotionally. This is Rousseauan enough, and the episode in which Toby releases rather than kills a fly is the iconic image that lingers for Tristram as well as for the sentimental reader. As Tristram says: 'I often think that I owe one half of my philanthropy to that one accidental impression.' (*TS*, 114) Moreover, the first-person retrospective mode of the whole narrative means there is no need here or elsewhere to belabour the impact of the episode on Tristram since all the characters only enter the story through his memory and associations. They exist for him, and for the reader, only in so far as they have been his formative influences, are part of him.

If Toby's highly internalised influence is more powerful for being less direct, and less directed, this makes him another example of the feminised man of feeling. That is not because of the shadow lying over his manhood resulting from his war wound to the groin. The wound is rather an aspect of his maleness in so far as it is part of the running male-anxiety joke about the size and functioning of the penis, and the Widow Wadman clearly does not see him otherwise as feminised. It is his excessive modesty and sexual naivety which associate him more intrinsically, albeit quaintly, with the female. As Tristram explains to an imagined female reader, Toby had 'an extream and unparallellel'd modesty of nature... and it arose to such height in him, as almost to equal, if such a thing could be, even the modesty of a woman.' (*TS*, 66) As in *Emile*, therefore, an unacknowledged 'female' influence acts from within an overtly male authority while the feminised man of feeling, as is often the case, displaces the real woman. Mrs Shandy appears to have little influence on her son and in the Shandy family at large, apart from Aunt Dinah, 'the females had no character at all'. (*TS*, 65) But whereas in *Emile* the 'female' influence comes from the official governor mediating ambiguously between the pupil and the stern authority of Nature, in *Tristram Shandy* the official authority is invested in the male pedagogical will of Walter. Walter exposes the personal exercise of authority that was both hidden from Emile and repressed in *Emile*.

Toby, as one who communicates by emotional sympathies rather than by the clarity of Lockean words and ideas, is the primary foil to Walter. And rather than Tristram, it is Toby, along with Mrs Shandy, who excites Walter's most acute pedagogical frustrations. Walter typically seeks an isomorphic conveyance of ideas, not their internal digestion by another being:

his aim in all the pains he was at in these philosophical lectures, ⸺ was to enable my Uncle *Toby* not to *discuss*, ⸺ but *comprehend* ⸺ to hold the grains and scruples of learning, not to *weigh* them. ⸺ My Uncle *Toby*, as you will read in the next chapter, did neither the one nor the other. (TS, 238)

Despite his different motives and means, Walter's isomorphic model of understanding is reminiscent of Rousseau's governor. Yet while Toby's imperviousness to such instruction constantly strains their relationship, it never breaks it, for he recognises that Walter's passion for instruction is just that: an urge that needs to be satisfied for its own sake. He recognises it because the need to express individual being through the impress of a personal activity is a human universal which he experiences even more strongly in his own life. His frustration when attempting to explain the precise circumstances of his war wound leads to the elaborate model military campaigns he conducts with Corporal Trim on the converted bowling-green. Toby becomes the archetypal instance of hobby-horsical obsession and creates the vortex of association by which any innocent word, such as 'breeches', used by others may be drawn into his military obsession. His hobby horse, however, is more genial than Walter's and precisely to the degree in which it detaches itself from its initial motive of explanation to become an end in itself.

Toby's military hobby horse is a Lockean disaster: it goes well beyond the occasional pun to become a running source of confusion. It challenges Locke, however, not just by sowing confusion, for that would merely prove Locke right. It challenges him through the positive value of enjoyment and communication it embodies. The military games grew from Toby's need for self-expression and are literally life-saving in aiding his recovery from the wound. Through the games he expresses his emotional solidarity with the life of the regiment from which his wound has now excluded him, and they also give a slightly different twist to his innocence: just as he is feminised without being female so he is childlike without being a child. An ostensibly childish game played with great concentration and seriousness by an adult with no ulterior purpose except as a self-delighting expression of deeply held personal values provides all the elements of 'play' from which Schiller was to develop his idea of the aesthetic as essential to humane education. And indeed, the moment of conceiving the military games is one of several in which characters break into a spontaneous duet aria when their emotional enthusiasm finds a shared, or contrasting, theme:

> My uncle *Toby* blushed as red as scarlet as *Trim* went on; ⎯⎯ but it was not a blush of guilt, ⎯⎯ of modesty, ⎯⎯ or of anger; ⎯⎯ it was a blush of joy; ⎯⎯ he was fired with Corporal *Trim*'s project and description. ⎯⎯ *Trim*! said my uncle *Toby*, thou hast said enough. ⎯⎯ we might begin the campaign, continued *Trim* on the very day his Majesty and the Allies take the field and demolish them town by town as fast as⎯⎯ *Trim*, quoth my uncle *Toby*, say no more. ⎯⎯ Your Honour, continued *Trim*, might sit in your arm-chair (pointing to it) this fine weather, giving me your orders, and I would⎯⎯ Say no more, *Trim*, quoth my uncle *Toby*. ⎯⎯ Besides, your Honour would get not only pleasure and good pastime, ⎯⎯ but good air, and good exercise, and good health, ⎯⎯ and your Honour's wound would be well in a month. Thou hast said enough, *Trim*, ⎯⎯ quoth my uncle *Toby* (putting his hand into his breeches pocket)⎯⎯ I like thy project mightily; ⎯⎯ And if your Honour pleases, I'll, this moment, go and buy a pioneer's spade to take down with us, and I'll bespeak a shovel and a pick-ax, and couple of⎯⎯ Say no more, Trim, quoth my uncle *Toby*, leaping up upon one leg, quite overcome with rapture, ⎯⎯ and thrusting a guinea into Trim's hand, ⎯⎯ *Trim*, said my uncle *Toby* say no more; ⎯⎯ but go down, *Trim*, this moment, my lad, and bring up my supper this instant.   (*TS*, 97–8)

The interjected phrases have an iconic and gestural value rather than being used for their notional meaning. Toby's 'Say no more' is rather a sympathetic accompaniment than an attempt to arrest Trim's progress. Or rather one might say that the language pauses and repeats, as in an operatic aria, to feel an emotional moment suspended in time. And yet the language is in character as Trim loves to advise and hear himself speak. So too, the real life brutality and horror of war is not unrecognised by the two wounded soldiers even as the games they are envisaging will, like art, allow the genuine virtues of the military life to be celebrated harmlessly. This is a language of emotional communication, and the shared expression of something individually felt. The operatic analogy suggests how the game comes as close as could be to aesthetic transposition. It is still a big step, of course, from Uncle Toby's games to Schiller's notion of the aesthetic, but one can see why Sterne, whose own narrative is figured as a similarly self-delighting hobby horse, was to fascinate later German writers reflecting philosophically on the nature of the literary. The immediate point, however, is the substantial counter-value he already posed to the Lockean conception as it appeared by the latter half of the eighteenth century.

Indeed, one would not wish to make Tristram/Sterne into a Schiller *avant la lettre* precisely because this would rob him of his peculiar quality as expressed in his own hobby-horsical narrative. His genial obliquity is that he does not oppose Locke with an alternative philosophy or system any more than Toby engages in argument with Walter. In fact, Toby gives a significant clue to Sterne's own technique in his practice of whistling *Lilliburlero* instead of engaging in argument. For the musical image runs throughout the book and as far as education is concerned it enables Tristram/Sterne to offer a constantly surprising series of variations on the theme rather than a coherently organised view. Its peculiar virtue is to reflect the infinite unpredictability of pedagogy in practice. So, for example, when Corporal Trim recites the ten commandments as a military-style drill, Walter is scornful of it as merely external and mechanical memory such as Rousseau would also have suspected. He is sure the corporal has no 'determinate idea annexed to any one word he has repeated'. (*TS*, 393) But the episode throws up the ambiguity of what it means to learn 'by heart' for, when Toby asks Trim what is meant by 'honouring thy father and thy mother', Trim tells of how he supported his parents in their old age. He does indeed have the heart of the matter at heart though precisely how that relates to his drilled recitation of the decalogue is still open to question. Walter is doubtless right that its *instructional* value is nil. It is like the military duet with Toby, more of a celebratory ritual than a consciously articulated meaning.

A similar stumbling on to the unexpected occurs when Walter prepares to explain to Toby how we derive our notion of time. He is brought to a halt by Toby's impeccably correct Lockean answer: '____ 'Tis owing, entirely, quoth my Uncle *Toby*, to the succession of our ideas.' (*TS*, 189) It is the Menard principle again, and all teachers will recognise this moment when a pupil who surely cannot truly understand pre-empts a complex exposition with a verbally correct answer. Such episodes throughout the book do not lead, individually or collectively, to any overall pedagogical principle other than the continued frustration of Walter's pedagogical will.

Yet Walter's topic of time is, of course, one of the significant vortices of association governing Tristram's own narrative. Time is not only thematically central, it is inscribed in the narrative method. The work is positively structured on a delaying principle: 'my work is digressive, and it is progressive too, ____ and at the same time.' (*TS* 73) But the principle of delay here is far from that of Rousseau's experiential pedagogy, it is more akin to the narrative structure of a joke in which the punchline must be deferred till the end. Rousseau's experiential delay is obviously important to the novel form generally in so far as it is traditionally concerned with the acquisition of experience. The novel characteristically privileges the process of temporality in its narrative form and Goethe in *Wilhelm Meister's Apprenticship* was to identify the 'delaying' character as one of the necessary conditions of the novel.[3] Yet although time was vital in *Emile* for the same reason as the stated principle of delay, the book

---

[3] *Wilhelm Meisters Lehrjahre*, bk. 5, ch. 7. *Goethes Werke*, ed. Erich Trunz (Munich: Beck, 1948–69) vol. vii, pp. 307–8; *Wilhelm Meister's Apprenticeship*, trans. H. M. Waidson, 3 vols. (London: Calder, 1977) vol. ii, 94.

itself did not make significant dramatic use of temporality. It had no obligation to do so in so far as it was a treatise and not a novel, but even in so far as it became a *de facto* fiction its proleptic confidence in its own method allowed it at all points to collapse the present into the future. Tristram's narrative collapses time in the opposite direction: many different moments of the past, even times before Tristram's birth, are collapsed into a narrative present which takes on thereby a multi-layered imaginative depth. We see little, dramatically speaking, of an immature Tristram: where we do so technically it is only through the mature voice of Tristram the narrator. We hardly experience Tristram, therefore, as victim of his father's pedagogical obsession but only as he triumphs over it.

There are a number of reasons for Tristram's concentration on the present as a fictive space filled with reminiscences of the past. As the narrative goes on, and Tristram/Sterne is increasingly sick, his narrative escape from gravity becomes more directly an attempt to escape the grave. He finds, if not infinite, then indefinite, refuge in a present animated by the past. Sterne is an eighteenth-century Proust in his resistance to mortality through a self-conscious fictional present that denies time.[4] Hence figures from the past are treated as if co-existing with his present. There is, for example, a curious blurring of temporality in this passage:

From the first moment I sat down to write my life for the amusement of the world, and my opinions for its instruction, has a cloud insensibly been gathering over my father. ──── A tide of little evils and distresses has been setting in against him. ──── Not one thing, as he observed himself, had gone right: and now is the storm thicken'd, and going to break, and pour down full upon his head.   (*TS*, 215)

Once again, as Tristram writes his life and opinions his comedy does not just supplant but sublate his father's endeavours. The verbal tenses run together, by a temporal zeugma, the time of the father's misfortunes within the narrative and that of the narrative itself. So too, when Tristram recollects being with his father on the grand tour, this is not felt as a return to the past but as a transposition of the past into the eternal present of the narrative act.

For I am at this moment walking across the market-place of *Auxerre* with my father and my uncle *Toby*, in our way back to dinner──── and I am this moment also entering *Lyons* with my post-chaise broke into a thousand pieces──── and I am moreover this moment in a handsome pavillion built by *Pringello*, upon the banks of the *Garonne*, which Mons. *Sligniac* has lent me, and where I now sit rhapsodizing all these affairs.
(*TS*, 516)

---

[4] I develop the comparison with Proust in 'Sterne and the Twentieth Century', *Laurence Sterne in Modernism and Postmodernism*, ed. David Pierce and Peter de Voogd (Amsterdam and Atlanta Ga., Rodopi, 1966) pp. 39–54 (43–8).

The narrative elision of time means that Tristram is never experienced as being truly, which is to say imaginatively, *in statu pupillari* in relation to Walter. On the contrary Walter is rather Tristram's creature: creatively and morally, the father is child of the man. Indeed, Walter is, in an important sense, Tristram's fiction.

Since the whole work is conventionally taken as a classic of fictional self-consciousness, the point at stake here may need clarification. First, it must be remembered that Sterne's play with fiction is still in many ways a comic transposition of contemporary literalism. After all, however obliquely and humorously, he is still a sentimentalist and he rather exploits literalism than exposes it. Also his more purely formal humour is itself a jokey literalism of authorial presence, as when Tristram/Sterne, for example, emphasises the gravity of a point by removing his cap and laying it 'upon the table close to (his) inkhorn'. (*TS*, 236) More importantly, however, within the world of Tristram's narration, Walter is not the pure fiction he is to the reader, and it is within that world that he is importantly recreated as a character in Tristram's imagination. To say that, as readers, we cannot tell how far any of the comic eccentrics we encounter are true to their originals or are created for, and by, Tristram's enjoyment of them, is not to make a literalistic point about the historical original of, say, Dr Slop or Phutatorius. It is an internal literary point about Tristram's fictionalising of his family. The narrative enacts his emotional relation to them in his affectionate-satiric creation of them as near caricatures. At one level, therefore, Tristram's detailed descriptions are evidence of the family's influence on him, but by virtue of the double viewpoint mentioned at the outset of this chapter, they equally indicate his present imaginative independence of that influence. Tristram's fictional hobby horse trumps his father's pedagogical ass:

I must here observe to you, the difference betwixt
    My father's ass
    And my hobby-horse...   (*TS*, 584)

Far from being governed by his father, Tristram is governed by his own 'pen'. (*TS*, 416) In Rousseau, it was the absence of fiction as a category which figured the unreflecting pedagogical will power of the imagined governor. By contrast, Tristram's fiction nested within Sterne's is a means of transforming the possibilities of the pedagogical relation from the inside. His fiction expresses the internal overcoming of the pedagogical and other influences which are nonetheless the condition of his present existence.

Significant consequences for later educational fiction emerge subtextually from all this. Tristram/Sterne's fiction creates a world within a world: indeed, the relativity of 'world' is thematised within the narrative.⁵ Most striking in this regard is the shift in proportions between the public world of history and the private world of Shandy Hall, and indeed of the individual mind. As Tristram puts it, the book 'is a history-book, Sir, . . . of what passes in a man's own mind'. (*TS*, 85) The private world fills the imaginative space of the book within which the public world is miniaturised. Likewise, the shifting semantics of the word 'hobby' suggest the same epochal process as it is figured so tangibly in the narrative subtext. The 'hobby-horse' is in one meaning the old cant term for a prostitute, a woman whose most intimate functions are made over to public use. But if, as with all Shandy males, the sexual act seems blocked or diverted, and in Tristram's case sublimated into a narrative replete with innuendo, so a certain more or less happy inefficacy underwrites the emergent modern meaning of the word 'hobby' as a harmlessly absorbing pastime.

Xenophon's *Cyropaedia* concerns the character and education of a prince; and indeed, it is still a touching and telling example for any authority exercised in the form of pedagogical leadership. But the *Tristrapaedia*, in contrast to the encyclopaedia, is concerned with a private individual and, more importantly, its writing is conducted as an obsessive hobby. Hannah Arendt speaks of the modern hobby as a regrettable symptom of the decline of the public sphere. She endorses Marx's analysis, but not his evaluation, 'when he foresaw that "socialized men" would spend their freedom from laboring in those strictly private and essentially worldless activities that we now call "hobbies" '.⁶ Arendt likewise sees the common modern translation of Aristotle's *zoon politikon* as 'social', rather than 'political', animal as reflecting the same shift.⁷ For Aristotle, man is not just social, like hive or herd animals, but participates actively in the command of a collective destiny. But just as politics has become a specialised activity, so lurking in the overt comedy of Walter's failed pedagogical ambitions is the increasing modern relegation of humanistic cultivation to the status of a hobby. Sterne's fiction does not present this as an analytic recognition but registers it as a suffusively imagined truth and with the ambivalence that characterises most historical change when not seen from the angle of a particular *parti-pris*. Moreover, Cyrus, however personally benign, lived in a world of right by force of military conquest and it might be argued that the Marlborough campaigns were still closer to this

⁵ As for example: 'The midwife had acquired, in her way, no small degree of reputation in the world;—by which word *world*, need I in this place inform your worship, that I would be understood to mean no more of it, than a small circle described upon the circle of the great world, of four *English* miles diameter, or thereabouts, of which the cottage where the good old woman lived, is supposed to be the centre.' (*TS, op. cit.* p. 11).

⁶ Hannah Arendt, *The Human Condition* (Chicago and London: University of Chicago Press, 1958) pp. 117–18.

⁷ Ibid. pp. 22–8.

ethic than to either a Christian or a secular concept of a just war. And yet the era of sentiment represented a significant shift at the level of sensibility if not of state policy. In *Tristram Shandy* the military theme is focused on the sentimental Toby and, even as another war with France was in progress during the first years of its composition, and one which laid important foundations for British imperial success, the novel expresses a long-term, ambivalent shift in sensibility.[8] Toby's way of meeting argument by whistling *Lilliburlero* infuses nationalistic sentiment with humanitarianism. Against that background, the failure of the argumentative Walter to measure up to his classical model acquires a note of satire against the moral anachronism of his ambitions.

Overall, then, the novel places at its centre a pedagogical enterprise which fails at the level of willed purpose while providing the occasion for an extraordinary exfoliation of personality replete with epochal resonances. In so far as Walter's project is merely the irritant, the grain of sand, that produces the pearl, it is not surprising that the pedagogical premise as such has received relatively little commentary. But precisely in this lies an important lesson to be found in other pedagogical fictions too: neither the pedagogical benefit to the character, nor the educative value of the book, are to be identified with the success of the educational project enacted within it. At the same time, however, if the pedagogical value for the character, or for the reader, lies beyond the will of the pedagogue, neither can it be separated from the workings of that will. Pedagogical success is somehow inextricable from failure and it is the varied workings of this double principle which will be seen in subsequent texts.

---

[8] The Seven Years War (1756–63) established crucial British command in India, Canada, and at sea.

(B) *THE HISTORY OF AGATHON*

Christoph Martin Wieland (1733–1813) was a highly pedagogical author who had a crucial impact on German literary culture just before the generation of Goethe. He produced the first complete translation of Shakespeare's plays, wrote in a variety of genres, and made the German language the medium of a graceful and witty prose.[1] The extraordinary efflorescence of German literature and philosophy in the late eighteenth century was from an apparently unlikely starting point as much cultural expression before this time had been felt to be merely secondary to French and English example. Wieland's role in this change left him ironically vulnerable to two contrary misappreciations: he managed in rapid succession to be before his time and apparently *démodé*. He also experienced, on several occasions, the difficulties of conducting public office in unfavourable cultural climates and Thomas Mann was to have recourse to him when working on *Joseph and his Brothers*, his own novel using an ancient setting for reflecting on a modern political context.[2] It is not surprising, therefore, that, despite his own pedagogical commitment shown in his love of Xenophon's *Cyropaedia*, on which he based an uncompleted verse epic, a number of his works are devoted to ironising the pedagogical process.

Wieland was also among the first German authors to absorb Sterne in a philosophical spirit; the height of this Sternean influence coming with his *Dialogues of Diogenes of Sinope* in 1770.[3] Where the historical Diogenes expressed his extreme consciousness of pedagogical inefficacy by withdrawing from society to live in a barrel, Wieland assimilates this stance to that of the Sternean eccentric. However, in his acknowledged masterpiece his two-part novel *Geschichte des Agathon*, published in its original version in 1766–7, the dominant English exemplar is Henry Fielding, for this work sought to perform for German fiction what Fielding had done for the English novel: to make it into a work of conscious art, highlighting the process of moral assessment, in contrast to the literalistic illusionism and moralism of the novel

---

[1] For a useful general account of Wieland in English see John A. McCarthy, *Christopher Martin Wieland* (Boston: Twayne, 1979).

[2] He returned to his home town of Biberach as Councillor 1760–9; sought to reform the University of Erfurt during his tenure of a professorship 1769–72; and initially suffered from court intrigue when appointed as tutor to Karl August of Saxe-Weimar 1772–5.

[3] For a thorough account of the Sternean influence see Peter Michelsen, *Laurence Sterne und des deutschen Roman des achtzehnten Jahrhunderts* (Göttingen: Vandenhoeck und Ruprecht, 1962) pp. 177–224. On *Socrates Mainomenos, oder die Dialogen des Diogenes von Sinope*, see esp. pp. 205–11.

of sentiment.⁴ Sure enough, the contemporary critical climate, in so far as it still reflected the didactic outlook of Johann Christoph Gottsched, objected to the lack of clear moral direction in Wieland's novel. But it was highly praised by the greatest German critic of the day, G. E. Lessing, and then by Friedrich von Blanckenburg in his important *Essay on the Novel* (1774).⁵

For present purposes, however, *Agathon*, as well as being a work of intellectual substance and considerable charm with permanent, as well as period, interest, provides a *de facto* riposte to Rousseau's pedagogical optimism, and indeed a substantial part of its narrative is based on Plato's Seventh Letter telling the story of his abortive education of Dionys, the young king, or Tyrant, of Syracuse. In so far as the authenticity of the Platonic letter is uncertain, its equivocal basis as history or fiction underscores its mythic significance as the most prestigious archetype of failed humanistic education, and it is in this capacity that Wieland embeds it within his own narrative which may be seen as a dramatised critique of pedagogical reason. He also incorporates elements from Plutarch's life of Dion which enhance the public and political aspects of the theme.

The novel maintains a double historical consciousness: the ancient Greek world of the action and the Enlightenment world of its narration. The doubleness is multiply significant, and not least in promoting the pervasive self-consciousness of the narrative which is established at the outset by a preface in which the novel is presented as the translation of an ancient Greek manuscript. In the age of sentiment such devices as the found manuscript were often used to enhance verisimilitude and the anonymous translator of the 1773 English edition, which is still the only widely available translation, responded with gross literalism. He judges that the illusion of an ancient Greek original is not well sustained, and that the author would have been better advised not to draw attention to it.⁶ But before the age of sentimental literalism, the hoary device of the found, and translated, manuscript was most typically put to metafictional use, as in the classic instance of *Don Quixote*, another work much admired, and imitated, by Wieland.⁷ The opening sentence of Wieland's Preface establishes an irony as palpable as that of Cervantes' Prologue: 'The editor of the present history sees so little likelihood of convincing the public that it has really been taken from an ancient Greek manuscript that he thinks it

---

⁴ I use the original version. *Geshichte des Agathon*, ed. Fritz Martini (Stuttgart: Reclam, 1979). Expansions in the later editions of 1773 and 1794 seem largely to make his intentions more explicit.
⁵ See Lessing's *Hamburgische Dramaturgie* no. 69. Gotthold Ephraim Lessing, *Hamburgische Dramaturgie*, ed. Klaus L. Berghahn (Stutgart: Reclam, 1981, 1999) p. 356.
⁶ *The History of Agathon*, 4 vols. (London: Cadell, 1773) vol. i, p. xiv.
⁷ He wrote a Quixotic novel *Don Sylvio de Rosalva* (1764).

best to say nothing at all on the subject and leave the reader to make of it what he will.'[8] The double historical consciousness created by this device reflects the Enlightenment universalism of this early *Bildungsroman* for as Wieland lovingly recreates the ancient Greek world, and invokes the early Greek novel, it is always with a view to its bearing on the present world of the reader. Universal questions which took their classic form in ancient Greek thought have modern inflections so that his hero is a compound of ancient and modern as Platonic goodness is overlaid with Rousseauan sensibility while his major opponent, the Sophist Hippias, speaks for a modern materialism.

The work has several thematic interests perhaps arising from a multiplicity of impulses behind its creation. One impulse, for example, seems to have been a comparative study of political orders, as in Montesquieu, and of historical cultures, as in Herder. At the same time, the novel had a strong autobiographical basis in the experience of disappointed love, as is reflected in the inwardness of the hero's sentimental development. The work is, therefore, open to different readings according to whether the hero's journeying is seen as the necessary narrative thread on which to string a series of philosophical experiences, or whether they are the context for an inward process of his education. The latter reading, sanctioned by a long-standing critical tradition, internalises a lengthy philosophical tale into the first major example of the *Bildungsroman*. Without displacing these, I suggest a further reading which lends them a different rationale. Rather than concentrating on what the hero learns, the book exposes the failures of teaching and persuasion. The hero's name, Agathon (Greek: 'the good'), is as allegorical as Candide, and it indicates not just the moving centre of an internal development but the challenging material upon which a process of pedagogical formation is experimentally exercised. If the hero's internal development is seen as the object, rather than the subject, of the work this also explains more cogently why some episodes are accorded a detailed dramatic unfolding while others are given in narrative summary. The narrative emphasis falls on the episodes of pedagogical struggle which, in contrast to *Emile*, explore the limits of persuasion against the recalcitrance of the human material involved. So for example, a long discourse of Hippias in Book Three and the lengthy episode of the Platonic letter, which have both been criticised as over-extended digressions, become thematically more germane and richer in their irony.[9]

---

[8] *Geschichte des Agathon, op. cit.* p. 5; *History of Agathon, op. cit.* vol. i, p. xvii. All subsequent English references are to this edition although the translations are my own.

[9] Although these criticisms are well discussed, and discounted, by Wolfram Buddecke, my reading lends the apparent digressions a further point. See *C. M. Wielands Entwicklungsbegriff und die Geschichte des Agathon* (Göttingen: Vandenhoeck and Ruprecht, 1966) pp. 176–8.

Since Platonic antiquity and the European Enlightenment were both moments of high investment in the power and sufficiency of human reason, they were also periods which excited acute insight into, and concern for, its limits. In that respect, the novel's broad-ranging cultural comparativism provides more than a varied narrative setting; it rather suggests how individual characters may be unamenable to moral judgement or comparison if their life experiences are incommensurable. The work has in that respect a philosophical and moral openness at its heart which stands in striking contrast to its overt artistic control. Whereas Rousseau exercised a tightly imagined control over his pupil within a loosely fictional envelope, this work exercises an overt fictional and formal control within which the human material remains in some measure unaccountable. Self-conscious artistic control does not necessarily betoken closure of evaluative judgements. On the contrary, as Schiller was later to argue more systematically, a strong sense of the aesthetic may be the vital protective from over-determination in the sphere of practical judgement. Hence, if Fielding showed the capacity of the novel to become a significant art form, and thereby to offer a coherent view of man and society, the German author invoked a comparable artistic order, and irony, to explore the limits of coherence. In this respect, Wieland's humorous handling of pedagogical uncertainty within a consciously aesthetic fiction is at the opposite extreme from Rousseau's predictive literalism. He explores through conscious fiction problems which Rousseau had elided.

Starting *in medias res*, the classic formula of epic narrative, the story exploits flash backs and foreshortenings to focus the novel's thematic interests as distinct from the chronological progress of the action. Told chronologically, Agathon is brought up in an Athenian temple where he is initially ignorant of his respectable parentage. He thus enjoys in some measure the moral and social *cordon sanitaire* that Rousseau worked so hard to create for Emile. As his name implies, he has a natural goodness which hardly requires the supplement of virtue, and he might well have progressed in due course to the priesthood. His idealistic nature draws him to the Platonic academy where his innate outlook is given philosophical endorsement. His striking good looks, however, compounded with his moral goodness, are a source of disaster. He has to leave the temple owing to the jealousy of an older priestess, Pythia, whose passion for him he cannot pretend to return. A further reason for his difficulty and her jealousy is his loyalty to another young foundling of the temple, Psyche, with whom he has fallen in love. His subsequent adventures take him to four major cities, Athens, Smyrna, Syracuse, and Tarentum, which cover not only much of the physical space of the ancient Greek world but a variety of cultural possibilities. He experiences in turn: a political career in the philosophical and artistic sophistication of republican Athens; a prolonged encounter with a Sophist, and a love affair, in the Asiatic sensuality of Smyrna; a pedagogical experiment in the militaristic monarchy of Syracuse; and retirement to a private life of self-cultivation in the mercantile practicality of Tarentum. His gradual, enforced move from the public to the private sphere casts a long proleptic shadow down the history of the *Bildungsroman*.

In Athens, when his parentage is revealed, he enters public life and has a period of highly successful direction of war and peace till he is brought down by jealous intrigues occasioned by his success. Arriving in Smyrna as a slave, he enters the household of the famous and successful sophist, Hippias, whose name at least, like Agathon's, has an original in the Platonic *Dialogues*. Hippias gives Agathon the name Callias (Greek: beautiful) and seeks to win him over to his own philosophical viewpoint. Having failed to persuade him either by intellectual argument or worldly temptations, he seeks to seduce him with the beautiful, older courtesan, Danae, and is disconcerted when they fall genuinely in love. When Hippias subsequently poisons Agathon's love for Danae he goes to Syracuse where he is once again drawn into public affairs but in effect repeats the disaster of his period in Athens. He pursues an initially successful conduct of home and foreign affairs but is once again brought down by the intrigues of rivals. On this occasion, however, the situation is compounded by his attempting to act as mentor to Dionys, the young ruler of Syracuse, in whom Plato has already failed to instil the virtue and wisdom of a philosopher king. He finally settles in Tarentum where, after his father's death, he lives within the excellent moral example, both public and private, of his father's friend Archytas, discovers that Psyche is his sister, and is reunited in respect and friendship with Danae although without the symbolic closure of marriage.

As this summary indicates, the narrative focuses on several major occasions of humanistic pedagogy or mentoring. And there are more parenthetical instances too. While he is still in the temple, for example, a hypocritical priest seeks to seduce him by a charade which might recall those of Rousseau's governor. (*Agathon*, 221–8; Cadell, ii, 143–56) Central to the narrative, however, are Hippias' sustained attempt to convert him from Platonism, and his attempt in turn to impart a Platonic formation to Dionys. In both cases the intended pupil proves frustratingly recalcitrant.

Wieland's narrator has a technical omniscience which gives a strong effect of transparency reminiscent of Fielding, if not of Rousseau. Yet the significant impact of his constant conversation with the reader over the head, as it were, of the characters does not lie in the literal guidance he gives concerning the complexity or uncertainty of the questions he raises. These are often merely rhetorical and ironic. He rather highlights in principle the difficulty of understanding and judgement. In this way, if he does not quite create the 'three-dimensional' opacity of later novelistic characterisation, he does something comparable which can be understood by comparison with the Platonic *Dialogues* invoked in the narrative. When Lawrence spoke of these as 'queer little novels' he was thinking of argument conducted in fiction, not as the authorial puppetry into which it may descend, but as a passionate focus of personal being. As a novelist who privileged argument as a major narrative action, he saw that it is the very purity of philosophical interest in the *Dialogues* which gives them their novelistic concentration. Hence, although the figures in the *Dialogues* are known through little more than their participation in philosophical exchange, they are individually characterised, and usually have a strong living stake in the beliefs they express. If 'thought', as Lawrence put it, 'is man in his wholeness wholly attending' then the *Dialogues* constantly enact such wholeness, or expose its absence.[10] Hence, notwithstanding the traditional view of Socrates as a proponent of reason, a view put strongly by Nietzsche and Heidegger, his pursuit of objective, or rational, truth was also through a truth to self, a personal wholeness. When Socrates finds a chink in an opponent's argument, it is usually a chink in the self. In that respect, Nietzsche's notion of the Socratic dialectic as wrestling by other means might be taken less as a damaging comment on Socrates' motives and more as an image of personal urgency. Similarly in *Agathon*, philosophical arguments are not disinterested explorations of truth but manifestations of the will to power, in which reason itself constantly comes up against its other, and the character's whole way of being is at stake.

In this respect, the philosophical exchanges in *Agathon* bring to the surface what lurks between the lines of the *Dialogues*. For although Socrates repeatedly recognises the limits of his own, and others', understanding, and draws crucially on poetic or mythopoeic means, he always seeks to assimilate these to the ultimate standard of reason. He treats the personal factors which are recalcitrant to reason as occlusions to be overcome. In contrast, Wieland, in keeping with the cultural relativism already noted in the work, actively explores the limits of reason with respect to fundamental life questions and to personal disposition. He anticipates Nietzsche's reflections on the *uses* of 'reason', both in Socrates and in the Enlightenment itself. Hence, despite its urbanity, the novel carries a significant charge of fundamental life questions invested in argument not as the impersonal pursuit of truth but as acts of persuasion deeply significant to the would-be teacher or mentor. Why, after all, the obsessive need to instruct for which Walter Shandy is the parodic extreme? Where they fail to persuade, the mentor figures are repeatedly drawn in beyond

[10] 'Thought', *The Complete Poems of D. H. Lawrence*, ed. Vivian de Sola Pinto and Warren Roberts (New York: Viking, 1964) p. 673.

their original intentions, which is why the dramatic and philosophical interest lies so much in the viewpoint of the mentor.

The first extended pedagogical episode is Hippias' attempt to convert Agathon to his philosophy. If this is a moral test for the hero, it is equally a pedagogical test for the Sophist. Hippias' project echoes that of other eighteenth-century fictional characters from Richardson's Lovelace to Laclos's Valmont and the Marquis de Sade who seek to prove their own view of human nature demonstratively on other characters. The philosophical demonstration is usually entangled with other motives such as seduction, revenge or falling in love. Hippias, too, has such personal motives but his philosophical purpose in forming a young person is as intrinsic as Rousseau's. Approaching the end of his successful career as a sophist, he seeks a successor who will be a living vindication of his philosophy. Despite his personal insincerity, which is transparent even to Agathon, his methods are true to his beliefs, and the distinction from the benevolent educator, such as Rousseau, begins to blur in so far as both are obliged to follow a similar educational logic.

Hippias first attempts to win Agathon over by argument. At this point he knows little of his pupil's character and is indeed indifferent to his true identity, or even his name. By calling him Callias he privileges his beauty and elides his goodness although Agathon embodies their commonly assumed connection in Greek culture, a connection most famously affirmed in Plato. Hippias separates the beautiful from the good, or makes it his only good. His initial reason for purchasing Agathon in the slave market was for his voice as well as his looks. He wants someone to read to him with a musical voice and a high level of dramatic skill. Hippias is an artistic connoisseur and surrounds himself with beautiful objects, including his servants. His household bespeaks the highest development of all sensual pleasures with artistic objects included on the same terms. They are imaginative reflections of the sensory. He is a *gebildete Mensch*, a cultivated man, as an image of false *Bildung*.

Wieland embodies in fiction recognitions that were to be given discursive articulation by Kant and Schiller. Kant was to say that appreciation of natural beauty is a sign of the morally good, for which beauty itself is a symbol.[11] And yet he also expressed scepticism about the morally educative power of art as such and drew, as one confident of a notorious truth, on the empirical example of artistic connoisseurs as peculiarly vain and selfish. 'Connoisseurs of taste not only often, but generally, are given up to idle, capricious and mischievous passions, and . . . they could perhaps make less claim than others to any superiority of attachment to moral principles.'[12] Hippias' separation

---

[11] *Critique of Judgement*, trans. J. H. Bernard (New York: Hafner, 1972) pp. 143, 198.
[12] Ibid. p. 141.

of the good and the beautiful is a self-conscious and systematic example of Kant's observation, just as his personal character also answers to Kantian moral terms. For although Hippias initially uses Agathon not unkindly, he makes him a means rather than an end in himself. Hippias, in a subsequent exposition of his sophistical practice, defines it precisely as persuading others to become of their own free will the instruments of one's own pleasure. (*Agathon*, 96; Cadell, i, 155) He is an aesthete for whom the aesthetic stands in active opposition to the ethical and he challenges the morally educative value often attributed to art.

In his way, however, Hippias is sincere in his world view and he naturally expects a young man with Agathon's personal advantages, and in a household where no social hypocrisy is required, to give immediate assent both intellectually and practically. He therefore seeks him out in the garden, where Agathon frequently takes refuge, and draws him into a conversation which is set out in dialogue form throughout the following chapter. The characters, the garden setting, and the apparent casualness of a personal encounter, all reflect the familiar method of the Platonic dialogue. Yet as Agathon's Platonic world view resists Hippias' hedonistic materialism, it is not through a successful use of Socratic dialectic but by an internal self-evidence comparable to that of Rousseau's Savoyard vicar. The transparency of his ideal affords the hero, at least in his own eyes, a direct and truthful vision of the world: ' "I see the sun, so it exists; I feel myself, so I exist; I feel, I see this highest spirit, so he exists too." ' (*Agathon*, 61; Cadell, i, 88) Hippias sees this as merely youthful illusion and *Schwärmerei* which he seeks to dispel. In effect, it is Rousseauan sensibility rather than Platonic idealism which he detects as the problem in Agathon.

Meanwhile, from Hippias' point of view, his own philosophy is equally self-evident and his materialism is no less an appeal to the authority of nature. Therefore, since he is persuaded of Agathon's intelligence, he decides that 'Agathon would be better convinced by a frank exposition than through the rhetorical arts which he took care to use, with good effect, on weaker souls.' (*Agathon*, 73; Cadell, i, 109–10) Accordingly, he sets up another meeting and expounds his views over several chapters, and with a cogency that disturbed some of the early reviewers. Socrates usually sought to prevent his sophist opponents from getting into their rhetorical stride, and Hippias' extended exposition shows the tactical wisdom of this. Yet Agathon is still not overcome. Just as his mode of 'reply' in the initial encounter had been to commune with himself (*Agathon*, 65–8; Cadell, i, 97–103), so his response now is ironically attributed by the narrator to his 'unteachability' (*Agathon*, 108; Cadell, i, 180); although the irony does not specify to what extent this is real or strategic. He thanks Hippias politely for his fine speech, acknowledges the logical force of its conclusions and the practical benefits they promise, but declines the happiness, or the kind of happiness, which is offered. All he can, or will, oppose to it is his own experience and feeling, a Rousseauan or Wertherian appeal to his irreducible individuality. There is already a hint here of the way Thomas Mann's 'simple' hero, Hans Castorp, in *The Magic Mountain*, listens to the extended discourses of the intellectuals, Naphta and Settembrini, but responds essentially to their personal dispositions as their arguments float over his head. It is not so much their reasoning which is at fault, as that reason itself encounters its other.

The Savoyard vicar disclaimed any capacity to prove his beliefs, and talks to a young man who is already prepared to absorb what he has to say. His world view cannot be imposed by reason; it can only be offered as personal example to be freely accepted or not although Rousseau is confident that it combines reason and reality, with reality as the senior partner. By contrast, Hippias, who also believes his case to be both rationally compelling and empirically self-evident, is disconcerted, and then angered, to find that, after forty years of successful dissemination of his views, he has not only failed to convince this obstinate young man but has misplaced his trust in Agathon's response. His philosophical frustration, that is to say, is compounded by the consciousness of a pedagogical error. From his point of view, if Agathon has not agreed, this can mean only that he has not understood, which in turn must mean, given his evident intelligence, that he was not ready to understand. But by prematurely assuming his pupil's readiness Hippias has exhausted in vain his pedagogical armoury. And by showing his hand so frankly he has most likely inured Agathon from any future agreement since Agathon now 'understands' Hippias' position from the standpoint of his own prior views rather than being led to see it in its own terms.

Hippias demonstrates an intrinsic danger in the pedagogical circle. The conviction of rightness or self-evidence creates its own peculiar blind spot: it cannot readily distinguish pedagogical failure from radical disagreement. Whereas the self-fulfilling circularity of Rousseau's imaginary authority allowed him to elide the problems of possible dissent, Wieland sees the self-fulfilling comedy of errors that lurks in the pedagogical circle. In failing, where his own beliefs are concerned, to appreciate the gap between his compelling argument and another's experiential conviction, Hippias falls victim to his own rhetoric. Ironically, if he had a more genuine sense of the other, a truly 'sophistical' awareness might have been deployed in a creative recognition of his pupil's difference from himself. For if the skills of the sophist can serve a variety of convictions, they might also sensitise one who possesses them to possible differences of conviction within the pedagogical relation.

Despite his personal deceptiveness, however, Hippias is pedagogically sincere in so far as he believes in his own philosophy. By the same token, he realises that if this 'strange young man' was truly 'what he appeared to be' then he constituted a 'living disproof' (*Agathon*, 117; Cadell, i, 200) of his system. And if this were so Hippias would find it a greater 'insult to his principles' than the 'acutest critique' (*Agathon*, 120; Cadell, i, 205) made in formal argument. He therefore determines to overcome Agathon's resistance by whatever means and, although it is professional and personal pique which now impels him to do so, it still constitutes a genuine pedagogical project since only an authentic conversion would meet the case. The accent on 'living' disproof, however, following on the fiasco of his attempts so far, suggests that an even more radical change of method is now required. He turns from direct rational argument, which Rousseau eschewed even for the mature pupil, and adopts something closer to Rousseau's blend of indirection and immediacy. The pupil is to learn, like Emile, from direct, 'living' experience without being aware that he is having a specially arranged lesson. Otherwise expressed, he is now to be educated as a character in a novel rather than by the methods of philosophy.

Hippias puts Agathon off guard by renouncing the fruitless attempt to make him change his views (*Agathon*, 114; Cadell, i, 194) but he secretly begins to construct a charade involving Danae, a beautiful courtesan from Smyrna. He introduces Agathon to her circle so that he comes to know her as if by chance. She is to seduce him and, by initiating him into the life of the senses, she will dispel his Platonic illusions and provide experiential 'proof' of Hippias' sensual materialism. Unfortunately for Hippias, and in contrast to Rousseau's self-fulfilling charades, the educative plot gets out of control and succeeds only too well but in the wrong way. Agathon's initial resistance intrigues Danae and throws his natural goodness into relief. In the ancient world, and especially in the sensual culture of Smyrna, her profession is not so morally disreputable as its equivalents might be in later Northern European cultures. Furthermore, her own history has been of misfortune in love rather than a free choice of her current way of life. Indeed, her former relationships were with Alcibiades and with the younger Cyrus, also praised by Xenophon. (*Agathon*, 128; Cadell, i, 222) Agathon meanwhile has no prospect of being reunited with Psyche and the outcome is that they fall genuinely and mutually in love. Hence Agathon does indeed acquire an appreciation of the sensual realm but, to Hippias' chagrin, this is not at the expense of his idealism. The sensual and passionate attraction is part of a genuinely loving relationship.

The psychological process of their growing attraction is a mixture of ancient terms and modern meanings. More subtly than Hippias, Danae seduces Agathon not through ideas but through his emotional idealism, an idealism which is both Platonic, as in an apparent allusion to the description of physical love in the *Phaedrus*, (*Agathon*, 156; Cadell, ii, 22) and Rousseauan in an explicit comparison with Saint-Preux. (*Agathon*, 181; Cadell, ii, 68)

The key episode occurs in her house during a dance performance of the legend of Apollo and Daphne. If love is the significant other of reason in the realm of personal feeling, so is myth in the life of a rationalist culture; and no less so for its being consigned to a primitive phase of cultural evolution. Agathon is initially critical of the young woman performing Daphne as, while she is in flight, she seems half to entice Apollo. Another spectator explains that the talent of the dancer is precisely not to present Daphne as a prude but as a young girl half desiring the encounter. Danae replaces the young dancer, who has a close resemblance to Psyche, and suffuses the role with her own sensuality, thereby enacting the assimilation of the ideal and the erotic which Agathon is about to experience. While the dance episode provides a highly sophisticated aesthetic and psychological means of enticement for Agathon, it also invokes a myth of metamorphosis. In fact, the novel's opening *in media res* found Agathon alone in wild countryside in dangerous proximity to Thracian bacchantes. The historical world of *Agathon* is on the cusp of a radical cultural shift which Ezra Pound defined in relation to Ovid by saying that 'he walked with the people of myth'.[13] In other words, Ovid no longer inhabited the world of myth himself but he, and his audience, were still close to its power even as he turned it into literature. So here, the dance has an artistic sophistication comparable to Ovid's literary treatment of myth while arousing something of the mythic force of metamorphosis for the couple who fall in love. A change (*Veränderung*) comes over both Danae and Agathon which is increasingly referred to as a metamorphosis (*Verwandlung*). Hippias, as connoisseur in both spheres, appreciates both the aesthetic sophistication of the dance and the progress of the seduction without realising the deeper emotional transformation that is occurring before his eyes.

When he becomes aware of the situation his campaign against Agathon is pursued with even more cunning obliquity. He invites the couple to his house as part of a large company in which the formerly rather anti-social, Rousseauan outsider, Agathon, now begins to shine through his wit and conviviality. But when Hippias congratulates him on being now so clearly 'one of us' (*Agathon*, 199; Cadell, ii, 101), the compliment shocks Agathon who retains his disapproving view of Hippias and of the whole atmosphere of his house. His virtue reasserts itself, he dreams of Psyche, and Danae senses something is wrong. Encouraged by her to disburden himself, he takes the risk of telling her his life story and revealing his true identity. In true epic style, the early part of his story is now told at such length as to last virtually till the end of Part I. His telling of his early life as an intimate and trusting act gives the relationship a new emotional depth as Danae then takes an even

---

[13] Ezra Pound, *The Spirit of Romance* (London: Peter Owen, 1952) p. 16.

greater risk, from the point of view of the relationship, by also recounting her own past, albeit in a summary and discreetly veiled form. She is the only other character for whom we are given a personal history and who experiences change. She is also referred to as one of the *Schöne Seele* ('beautiful souls', *Agathon*, 593; Cadell, iv, 225) a phrase which was to have significant history in subsequent German thought. Their mutual narration is a psychological metamorphosis which, in deepening the relationship for the reader, drives a wedge of emotional otherness into the middle of Hippias' rationally and materially conceived educational project. The long narrative flashback, only revealed through a risky act of love, brings to life the inner world of the other. What Hippias has sought to manipulate as a means, becomes truly felt as an end in itself.

Part I of the novel ends in uncertainty as Agathon's loving conception of Danae is now a necessary, but perhaps fragile, condition for his idealistic world view. Part II opens with the final stage of Hippias' attempt to poison his idealistic love. Danae is a loyal friend and, after so much exclusive time with Agathon, she visits her friends in Smyrna although with the further motive that her absence may revive Agathon's love. During her absence, Hippias insinuates to Agathon Danae's previous promiscuity as a fact of public knowledge. Agathon initially resists this view of her but it severely damages, not so much his love, as the idealism on which it is too much based. Subtly, Hippias does not overtly criticise Danae but rather argues a positive case for erotic variety. He enthusiastically enumerates a variety of female types to be enjoyed in a manner reminiscent of Leporello listing Don Giovanni's conquests. (*Agathon*, 336; Cadell, iii, 21) His pretence lures Agathon into an unguarded counter-argument: a declaration of his love for Danae so passionate and complete that '. . . it would require either the malice of a Hippias, or the friendly hard-heartedness of a Mentor, to be capable of wrenching him from so happy an illusion. (*Agathon*, 337; Cadell, iii, 23) This parallel is suggestive: while opposing the *motives*, it identifies the *functions*, of Hippias and 'a Mentor'. It is precisely Hippias' malice which aligns him here with the benign function of the mentor.

The narrative develops both levels of this irony. On the one hand, it is questionable whether Agathon's view of Danae is simply an illusion and the judgement is ambiguously placed between Hippias' perception and narrative endorsement. After all, despite her partial veiling of her past to Agathon, her love for him is genuine and that indeed is her motive for wishing not to lose credit in his eyes. And as the narrator remarks a little later, the two versions of her past given by Hippias and by herself differ in their emphases rather than their substance. Her own account of her 'weaknesses' and 'misdeeds' presents them not just in a 'milder', but actually in a 'truer light' than the world's perception (*Agathon*, 338; Cadell, iii, 25). Yet in so far as Agathon's love is over-idealised, Hippias, whatever his motives, performs the function of the mentor authentically. He does so subjectively in that he genuinely believes in his own conception, and objectively in that Agathon undergoes the relevant experience through his agency. The difference in motive points up the functional identity.

Agathon's response at the end of the conversation affirms this. Despite being in a significant measure deceived by Hippias as to the fact, he is not so as to his character. He recognises the malicious intent, and feels overwhelming contempt for him. Indeed, the last straw for his resistance is precisely Hippias' claim to have been offered, and to have received, Danae's favours. '"Ye Gods! A suitor to Hippias. What could be more ignoble!"' (*Agathon*, 341; Cadell, iii, 30) Yet as he says: 'Hippias, under the smiling mask of friendship you have pierced me with a poisoned dagger—yet I thank you—your malice has performed a more important service for me than your friendship could have done.' (*Agathon*, 341; Cadell, iii, 14) That Hippias should perform an educative function irrespective of his motives is reflected in his becoming at this point an overt device of the plot; as if momentarily raised to the level of the loquacious narrator who constantly discusses the rationale of the action with the reader. For although Hippias never possesses the omniscient foresight of the author, or that accorded to Rousseau's governor, his self-confidence constantly aspires to it and, earlier in the same conversation, once he has said enough to do the damage, we are told: 'It is easy to foresee what course the events of this scene would have to take, and after all that has been said about the Sophist's purposes it can be left to the reader's own imagination.' (*Agathon*, 337–8; Cadell, iii, 37) Hippias is allowed both to anticipate and drive the action here. Indeed, the narrator later remarks that, if Agathon had not been made to withdraw from his passion for Danae, there would have been no second part to 'his history'. (*Agathon*, 345) But Hippias' anticipation of the outcome in this episode is momentary and ironic. His intentions are constantly at variance with the events and he is not the first, nor the last, educator of whom this is true. Where wise educators incorporate this uncertainty into their function, Hippias is incapable of doing so and he thereby enacts the pedagogical temptations which are raised to a further power in the next major episode.

The disillusioned Agathon, hovering uncertainly between awaiting Danae's return and using her absence to break with her, hears of a ship just about to leave for Syracuse. He embarks, and is drawn into a second public career which includes acting as mentor to the young ruler, Dionys. Having been the object of a malicious, and highly manipulative, regime of mentoring, Agathon now finds himself, with his quite different disposition, in the position of mentor.

He experiences the inner logic, and unpredictable dynamics, of the educative relationship from the other side. Such thoughts are far from his mind in advance, however, and the situation only arises because he is caught in the rivalry between Dionys' competing mentors.

The journey to Syracuse encompasses several chapters in which Agathon reflects on the meaning of his experience in Smyrna. He now deprecates his tendency to idealistic enthusiasm and even appreciates the relative realism of Hippias. In this respect, Hippias represents a note of classical, pagan sanity as opposed to the christianised emotional idealism associated with Rousseau. For example, Alcibiades is censured by the Athenians not for his sensual flings but for allowing them to interfere with public affairs. (*Agathon*, 378–9; Cadell, iii, 99–101) Such a perception of classical sanity looks forward to Goethe even as Wieland's general presentation of an eternal human pettiness equally evident in ancient Greek life would temper Winckelmann's exalted conception of the classical ideal. The narrator closes his reflections on the classical world through a Sternean exchange with an imaginary moralistic reader, Theogiton, who claims to have seen through Agathon from the outset. (*Agathon*, 383–4; Cadell, iii, 110) The narrator regrets that this reader lacks the requisite organ to understand the book which is about to explode even more thoroughly the aspirations of mentors. For Agathon arrives in Syracuse, in a seemingly matured frame of mind, but still with high moral ambition, just after the famous Platonic experiment in mentoring.

Dionys, the young king, or Tyrant, of Syracuse had succeeded to the throne on the death of his brutal father who had taken no care of his education. It is suggested that Dionys had better potential if he had had the right education. (*Agathon*, 390; Cadell, iii, 124–5) From a mentor's point of view, however, his character offers the opposite difficulty to what Hippias encountered in Agathon. It is not just that he is less virtuous than Agathon, but that his character is excessively malleable. Where Agathon was difficult to change, or even impress, Dionys changes so readily, and even enthusiastically, that no change can last. In this respect he is too much like his fellow citizens. The Syracusans are seen as like the Athenians, among whom Agathon suffered his previous failure in public life, except that the same faults of private self-interest and collective fickleness are so extreme as to render them effectively incapable of governing themselves at all. Hence everything depends on their having a king able to rule with wisdom and authority. Dionys, however, is not just an unlikely candidate for this responsibility; his instability makes him a veritable microcosm of the city itself. Just as the court and the people take the stamp of the ruler, so they are an effective psychomachia expressing his inner state. As in Plato's *Republic*, where the same principle of order applies within the individual and the state, so a comparable continuity pertains between the moral lability of Dionys and that of the citizens.

At this critical moment, Dionys' brother-in-law, Dion, an erstwhile pupil of Plato, is asked to act as mentor to the young king. Dion has been living in virtual seclusion since his high conception of virtue makes it difficult for him to function in the world at all. He is universally admired but effectively useless. (*Agathon*, 394; Cadell, iii, 131) Yet as the only person with the requisite qualities, he agrees to take on the task although initially he has no impact on his young relation whose life is given over to pleasures. There is a surprising turn, however, after a three-month festivity held in honour of the king's namesake, Dionysus, in which Dionys enacts the part of the god. The sensory pleasures, heightened by art, are so complete that the king feels he has exhausted the possibilities of the sensory realm while finding himself both exhausted and unsatisfied. He therefore turns to Dion, who does not sufficiently detect the merely reactive nature of the young man's sudden turn to virtue and philosophy, and, in his enthusiasm at the change, persuades the initially sceptical Plato to come to Syracuse as mentor to the king. Dion's high-mindedness leads him to misread his pupil just as Hippias' materialism did with Agathon. Once again, personal conviction proves a pedagogical stumbling block.

When the king takes to philosophy, the courtiers adopt it as a fashion. Their philosophical beards, mantles, and conversations are a parody of the Platonic academy, although Plato accepts this as the first stage of withdrawal from previous mental habits and as a 'kind of preliminary exercise' in the taste for knowledge and self-improvement. (*Agathon*, 408; Cadell, iii, 157) There is some plausible pedagogical wisdom in this, and in the way he concentrates on the king himself. In the spirit of Rousseau's governor, he seeks not to instruct, but to provide him with good habits and example so that 'without allowing it to be too clearly recognised' these 'would bring him by unnoticed degrees to have these thoughts for himself'. (*Agathon*, 409; Cadell, iii, 159) But the very malleability of Dionys, his lack of inner resistance to the educative process, renders it empty and Plato should after all have read the merely fashionable behaviour of the court as a reflection of the king's own mind. For all his high intelligence, Plato is open to the illusions of the educator and does not see that his pupil is now merely 'drunk on Platonic ideas' and a new kind of admiration, as he formerly was on Dionysian sensuality (*Agathon*, 410; Cadell, iii, 161). A shallower observer might have seen more clearly and when Plato allows himself a 'premature rejoicing at his success' (*Agathon*, 411; Cadell, iii, 162) it is because the conditions of the Platonic academy have not prepared him for 'the great stage of life' (*Agathon*, 412; Cadell, iii, 163). As Rousseau might have predicted, Dionys is actually made worse by this education. The 'discourses of the wise Athenians' swell his 'natural vanity' into an illusion of being an intellectual patron, an artistic connoisseur, and one of the finest spirits of his time. (*Agathon*, 436; Cadell, iii, 208) This is, of course, a mythical Plato of other-worldly idealism rather than the tough thinker of the *Dialogues*, and he meets his match in the over-eagerness of the only too 'ideal' pupil. But the underlying point is less a comment on Plato than on the limits of pedagogical reason.

At this juncture some rival mentors enter the scene. Philistus and Timocrates are two shrewd courtiers anxious to get the king back to his normal state, and under their influence. They insinuate to him that Dion and Plato are working to undermine his power which in a sense, by making him unworldly, they are. The two courtiers are not, of course, presented *as* educational mentors. They are seeking to break up the educative process. But that is why their parallel activity is significant in requiring the same methods. Are they to be seen as simple opposites to Plato, or are they the dark shadow of educational influence? Like effective mentors, they exercise the principle of delay, allowing Dionys to come to the desired conclusion himself (*Agathon*, 416; Cadell, iii, 172). The eventual consequence is the banishing of Dion and the end of the Platonic experiment in educating a philosopher king. It is only after this extended flashback on the archetypal instance of failed humanistic education that Agathon arrives in Syracuse.

His initial intention was to withdraw to private life in Tarentum with his father's old associate, Archytas, but, like Plato, he is seduced into the role of mentor. He meets an Athenian, Aristippus, who tells him the story of the failed venture in Platonic education. Aristippus recognises the likely futility of intervention such as Plato's but he is a conscious spectator at the theatre of life and, in telling Agathon this story, he entices him, in an almost experimental spirit, to take on the mentorship of Dionys. Agathon is intrigued by the idea, which Aristippus allows him to think of as his own, and he is especially attracted to the thought of succeeding where Plato has failed.

With discreet stage management from Aristippus, Agathon becomes the new enthusiasm of Dionys who appoints him, while he is still a near stranger, to plenipotentiary direction of state affairs. One of his steps towards this is a speaking competition in which, expecting to be a judge, he is suddenly asked to speak himself on the theme of the best form of government. It is a political trap in so far as he is not in favour of monarchy, which would damage him in Dionys' eyes; yet he cannot support it without displeasing the populace. In the event he satisfies all parties by making a case for monarchy as wise paternal governorship avoiding democratic anarchy and aristocratic oppression. In a monarchy it is necessary for only one man to be good and wise, and he can be educated for this. As the narrator insists (*Agathon*, 469; Cadell, iii, 270–1), there is no need to doubt Agathon's sincerity, but the speech is clearly designed for its context and prepares the way for his own ambition. A shadow of the all-purpose rhetorical expertise of the Sophists hangs over his achievement, and he is admired for his skill as much as for the substance. From the outset, then, he has to employ the same methods as his enemies, and by slow degrees he is enmeshed in court intrigue even as his motives remain unimpeachable.

Although the education of a powerful and self-willed ruler presents different problems of governance from Rousseau's private citizen, it throws into relief the generic tensions of tutelage. Dionys is any pupil writ large and with the stakes raised. The mentorship starts well as Agathon lays down conditions reminiscent of Rousseau's: as well as the right to withdraw whenever he loses the confidence of Dionys, he is not to receive monetary reward, and is to be a friend rather than a figure of authority to his pupil. Given their ages, his position is rather like Goethe's with the young Duke, Karl August of Saxe-Weimar, for whom Wieland himself was tutor up to the age of eighteen. Agathon's successful management of internal and external affairs of state is partly owing to his lack of personal ambition so that he achieves peace with other Sicilian city-states, for example, by ceasing to foment unrest and by inspiring personal trust. In this regard, Xenophon's Cyrus would be a significant model. At the same time, his rise is sustained not just by his intrinsic success but by vindicating Dionys' choice of him; a choice motivated by the good that Agathon may do *for* him rather than *to* him. For Agathon will provide an acceptable face for his monarchy. (*Agathon*, 466; Cadell, iii, 264) Meanwhile, Agathon has learned from his own experiences, and is properly modest in his ambitions. Eschewing any 'plan based on Platonic ideas' (*Agathon*, 476; Cadell, iv, 9), and knowing he can never make a model ruler out of Dionys, he nonetheless hopes to 'mitigate the worst effects of his vices' and turn his 'good moods', even his 'weaknesses', to use. (*Agathon*, 477; Cadell, iv, 11) One of his hopeful methods in this respect is to refine the king's sensual tastes with artistic appreciation (*Agathon*, 478; Cadell, iv, 12–13) but Dionys, as in the three-month Dionysian feast, tends to use even the aesthetic, or potentially aesthetic, realms in a sensual spirit. Just as Plato read overoptimistically his pupil's enthusiasm, so Agathon's error is to misread Dionys' apparent virtues as more substantial than they are. His labile character, and lack of settled purpose even for ill, give his very vices the occasional 'colour of virtue' (*Agathon*, 477; Cadell, iv, 12) on which Agathon hopes to build.

The opportunity for other courtiers to bring him down occurs when a beautiful woman falls in love unrequitedly with Agathon and also catches the attention of Dionys. Agathon is caught in the middle and, seeking to handle the affair with tactful confidentiality, incurs the resentment and distrust of all the parties. His own goodness blinds him to the likely behaviour of others while, objectively speaking, he is drawn into employing the same manipulative hypocrisy. He becomes vulnerable to the charge of conspiracy and, however unfair, this points to the element of conspiracy which always lurks within the educational project and was overt in Rousseau. He cannot be absolutely frank with his pupil. And despite the difference in motive, he finds himself, like Hippias, drawn in, somewhat corruptingly, beyond his initial pedagogic commitment. A further insidious temptation of the pedagogical circle is that, just as it is hard to assess success, so it is hard to judge when it has completely failed. It is inevitably a long-term project with many setbacks to be expected along the way. At what point should it be abandoned, and failure acknowledged? Agathon was to withdraw when he lost the trust of Dionys, but his 'self-love was now wounded in its most sensitive part'. (*Agathon*, 520; Cadell, iv, 91) He comes to think of Dion with more respect and, making contact with him in his banishment, is drawn into a real political conspiracy. He has to leave Syracuse having failed again, in a kind of second Athens, to maintain a public role and having been seduced into an educational project which, for all its good motives, places him in ironic parallel to both Hippias and the conspiring courtiers.

Aristippus, who effectively set up the pedagogical experiment, also frames its conclusion. He points out that the project was always doomed to failure since no court would be worthy of Agathon. Assuming a quasi-authorial perspective, he continues: 'I could pretty much have told you all this beforehand, when I helped you persuade yourself to go in with Dionys, but it was better that you should be convinced through your own experience.' (*Agathon*, 516; Cadell, iv, 83) In so far as he has acted as mentor, and with near authorial prescience, to Agathon, Aristippus has adopted the method of complete non-intervention and his remark states the typical function of the mentor in the *Bildungsroman*. With a rather tactless frankness, accentuating the pedagogical comedy of the episode, he spells out the necessity of not imparting the relevant truth before the experience. At the same time, he helps to focus the significance of the experience for the reader, and helps Agathon to see it *as* experience. Having done so, however, and with the experiment completed, he now advises Agathon directly, and with lucid reasoning, to abandon the project. But his reversal of method is only apparent since his advice provides an equally classic example of the open secret: '... Agathon would have done well to follow such good counsel. But how could one who performs the main part in a play exercise the relaxed judgement of a simple spectator.' (*Agathon*, 517; Cadell, iv, 85) Even at this stage, Agathon is unable to follow the advice. He overrides it just as he overrode his initial misgiving when Dionys was immediately willing to place him, still a virtual stranger, at the head of state affairs. Agathon remains impenetrable to both instruction and experience and this conversation, turning on the paradox of the open secret, enshrines the central problematic of the *Bildungsroman* of how experience is transposed into understanding.

After leaving Syracuse, Agathon effectively retires from public life and devotes himself to personal improvement by cultural pursuits such as travel and reading. The two extended pedagogical experiments discussed so far constitute most of the book's action and also raise further themes and topoi which are significant for subsequent tradition.

To Agathon, who unites in his own person the good and the beautiful, artistic beauty is intuitively connected to the good. His early life in the temple surrounded him with statues and other art-works which he believes have had an ennobling effect. When he meets his father, the psychological inheritance is symbolised partly in the discovery of his father's art collection, and his own ability to appreciate it. The son's discovery of the father's art collection only when he is mature enough to appreciate it is a narrative trope of later *Bildungsromane* such as the statue episode in Adalbert Stifter's *Nachsommer*. It implies that art itself cannot have its proper impact prematurely. And indeed, art as such has patently not ennobled other characters, such as Hippias and Dionys, who lack the proper disposition; or, as the narrator says of his religious interlocutor, who lack the necessary 'organ'. In this respect, Aristippus uses a suggestive image when advising Agathon to leave Syracuse. He points out the radical impossibility of success with Dionys for whom Agathon is of no more significance than 'his apes and parrots'. (*Agathon*, 516; Cadell, iv, 84) His citing animals known for their empty imitation of the human may suggest what artistic representation means to Dionys. In fact, the image of Aristippus himself as a 'spectator' is part of a running image of theatre in the Syracuse episode in which it has the Rousseauan implications of social falsity. Even the exchange quoted just above, in which Agathon is unable to exercise the 'relaxed judgement of a spectator', implies an underlying dualism of art and moral understanding.

Although mistaken, however, it was not unreasonable for Agathon, on the basis of his own experience, to suppose that Dionys' sensualism might be sublimated by art. His optimistic error casts a long shadow down European history, right down to the performances of classical music in concentration camps. Friedrich Schiller, in his *Letters on the Aesthetic Education of Man* accommodated this recognition as he combined the sentimentalist belief in the moral efficacy of art through emotion with Kant's notion of art as play. He showed sensibility to be the unconscious of the aesthetic and the aesthetic to be the unconscious of truly moral sensibility. On this view, art may make the good wiser and more self-reflective, but it cannot transform the evil, the selfish, and the frivolous. Unfortunately, indeed, these latter are rather likely to debase the aesthetic, as happened in Hippias and in some measure with late nineteenth-century aestheticism. The radical ambivalence of artistic culture is reflected in Wieland's narrative through the extended semantic field of the word *Bildung*. Along with its positive ambition it incorporates the verb *einbilden* suggesting conceit and illusion. As a work of high classical culture, *Agathon* reflects radically on the limitations of its own ideals.

But as Schiller was to argue, if art has no power to educate or ennoble where the human material is lacking, this fact does not cancel the value of the aesthetic, although it remains a crucial condition to bear in mind. Nor does such a conclusion imply elitism in the vulgar sense of exclusion or condescension but simply a condition of the experience. Two observers may look at an artwork and only one of them see it *as* an artwork at all, let alone respond to its proper power. At the same time, a great work of art will be ennobling for the right spirit. This ambivalence applies to *Agathon* itself which, in its self-conscious artistry, points to the special, self-selective terms on which the reader enters its world. With its pervasive register of transparent irony, it draws a hieratic, yet diaphanous, veil around itself.

The ambivalence of art as an 'open secret' had significant implications for the future, both literary and political. Agathon fails twice in public life and retires to a pursuit of personal cultivation in his newly rediscovered home. This feels to him, and perhaps to the reader too, like a *pis aller* although Archytas, who has himself pursued a successful public career, affirms its oblique value to the public realm. (*Agathon*, 580–1; Cadell, iv, 201–2) Archytas focuses in himself a final utopian dimension of the work, and it also transpires that Agathon has produced for Archytas the memoir on which the third person narrative is based. If the whole story is to that extent their joint production, this fact underwrites its mixed implication. On one hand, the pedagogical pessimism of the story has been reinforced by its double historical focus: in essential respects, humanity has made little moral progress since the ancient world. Furthermore, as Peter Michelsen has noted, Wieland saw a happy private life as the highest human goal but precisely because it produced the best *citizens*, while the happiness of the individual depends upon the collective.[14] Yet the pessimism of his vision in principle is belied in *Agathon* by the humour of the narration while the final section suggests a necessary utopianism underlying the treatment throughout. Where Rousseau's utopianism was pervasive but only half acknowledged within the practical advice of his treatise, Wieland's fiction enables him to define its motivating value without obscuring his pessimistic analysis. Most significant in this respect, perhaps, is the reader's having learned throughout not to identify the meaning of the book with

---

[14] Michelsen, *op cit.* pp. 217–18.

its action. Or rather, the most important pedagogical action of the book is its education of the reader, and in this respect it was, eventually, successful. As modern critics, such as Martin Swales, have especially emphasised, the self-consciousness of the *Bildungsroman* generally is designed to achieve this focus on the reader's education often in contrast to the character's failures.[15] None does this more strikingly perhaps than this first great example of the genre.

Nonetheless, the relation of humanistic *Bildung* to the public sphere is a continuing theme notably taken up in the wake of the French Revolution by Schiller's *Letters on the Aesthetic Education of Man*. The leading models of education in the classical world, including Plato's *Republic*, assumed it was for the purpose of participating in public life. Just as Hannah Arendt noted the declining force of Aristotle's definition of man as a 'political animal', so the purely negative use of the term 'sophist' reflects not just the triumph of the Socratic critique, but the lost context of public speaking in which it sought its justification. It was always a high, if not impossible, ideal, as can be seen in the sardonic utopianism of Plato's image of the philosopher king.[16] Even the life of Cyrus, the great historical examplar, is somewhat idealised by Xenophon and acquires a utopian tinge at the end as his descendants and disciples fail, after his death, to maintain his moral regime. As *Agathon* carries the sceptical aspect of the classical archetypes into Enlightenment modernity, the logic of the 'open secret' already bears not just on the education of the individual but on the relation of high culture to the public sphere. As it is used in *Agathon*, the word *offentlich* covers the English meanings of both 'open' and 'public' while variations on the terms public (*offentlich*) and home (*Heim*) are incorporated into the resonances of the 'open' and the 'secret'. Just as the individual aphorism may be only apparently comprehensible without the experience of which it speaks, so the collective understanding of the past in great art may remain incommunicable even when made available to a general public.

Accordingly, as Agathon effectively withdraws from public life, the logic of the 'open secret' is attributed to the very language of the published text. He makes his way from Syracuse reflecting with rueful incredulity on how he could have 'allowed himself to be persuaded to become the mentor of Dionys' (*Agathon*, 531; Cadell, iv, 111), at which point the same futility is attributed to the narrative itself. The fictional editor remarks, in true Cervantean style, that this chapter of the Greek story has many fine reflections arising from Agathon's experience in Syracuse but unfortunately the manuscript is so badly

---

[15] Martin Swales, *The German Bildungsroman from Wieland to Hesse* (Princeton: Princeton University Press, 1978).
[16] Mainly discussed in *Republic*, bks. 2–3, (484a–541b) *op. cit.* pp. 343–407.

damaged by damp and rats that it 'would be easier to read the leaves of the Cumaean Sibyl'. (*Agathon*, 532; Cadelll, iv, 112–13) These fine general reflections have arisen from Agathon's digestion of his experience, but we may infer, metaphorically, that the general maxims and reflections to which his experience gives rise are unfortunately of no use for passing it on. They may as well be eaten by rats. Although they are pregnant with experience, they are as obscure, in their apparent openness, as the utterances of the oracle whose predictions, usually sought on matters of grave public policy, were commonly understood only in the retrospect of bitter experience. The dubious impact of moral maxims and wise aphorisms was to be explored by Goethe increasingly throughout his fictional *oeuvre*. The physical dissolution of these manuscript pages prefigures a cardinal moment when Goethe's Wilhelm Meister completes his 'apprenticeship' and is given an anti-climactic sheet of maxims. For him, although the paper does not dissolve, its contents do. Wieland's urbane and cultured comedy inaugurates the tradition of the *Bildungsroman*, not least by placing its own educative capacity *en abyme*.

3

Goethe's Open Secrets: *Wilhelm Meister's Apprenticeship*

Nichts ist drinnen, nichts ist draussen;
Denn was innen, das ist aussen.
So ergreifet ohne Säumnis
Heilig *öffentlich Geheimnis*.[1]

In post-Victorian Anglophone culture, Goethe himself has been something of an open secret. Educated readers know of him, and most have encountered one or two of his works, but an inner appreciation of his stature is rare. Moreover, in my experience, rather than the presumptive respect accorded to other insufficiently read foreign classics, such as Dante, Goethe attracts a confident intuition that his reputation is inflated the judgement being usually volunteered as a point of critical penetration rather than sheepishly admitted as a default judgement. His name invokes an image of worthily portentous, Germanic reification of culture and T. S. Eliot, in a late lecture on 'Goethe as Sage', reflected on the difficulty of getting beyond this view, or of communicating this to others if you do so.[2] Eliot's word 'sage' focuses the problem. The ascription of wisdom is as elusive as it is ambitious and one has somehow to appreciate what Goethe's admirer, André Gide, meant by his 'banalité supérieure' for part of Goethe's special interest was to have experienced this question as an epochal phenomenon, and to have thematised it in a variety of ways, throughout his *oeuvre*.[3]

---

[1] Nothing is inner, nothing is outer, | For what is inner, is outer. | Therefore grasp without delay | The sacred, open secret. From 'Epirrhema', *Goethes Werke* (Hamburgischer Ausgabe), vol. i, ed. Erich Trunz (Munich: Beck, rev. ed 1981) p. 358.
[2] *On Poetry and Poets* (New York: Farrar, Strauss, and Giroux, 1966) pp. 240–64. For substantial views on Goethe's anglophone reception see Nicholas Boyle, ed. *Goethe and the English-speaking World* (Rochester NY: Camden House, 2001).
[3] I borrow this apt phrase of Gide's from R. H. Stephenson, *Goethe's Wisdom Literature: a Study in Aesthetic Transformation* (Bern: Lang, 1983) p. 258.

Although wisdom itself is not banal, its expression is peculiarly susceptible of being, or seeming, so. If it is not usually thought so in Homer, Dante, or Shakespeare, that may suggest that there is something historical as well as personal at stake. As so often in Goethe, and that is part of his elusiveness, the personal proves to be inseparable from the consciously epochal. In contrast to these earlier authors, Goethe is peculiarly concerned with the problematics of wisdom as such, and how the meaning of experience can be communicated. If the supposed late twentieth-century incredulity with respect to 'grand narratives' is itself perhaps too grand a narrative, it has certainly become a common point of wisdom to suspect claims to wisdom.[4] If few later writers attract the category *Weisheitsliteratur*, the reason is not that wisdom is no longer sought or needed, but rather an embarrassment about the claims of the term. George Eliot was perhaps the last major English writer in whom expressions of generalised moral wisdom are still prominent and powerful, although less so in the incipiently Jamesian *Daniel Deronda* (1876) than in *Middlemarch* (1871–2). The aphoristic in Nietzsche or Proust has a different kind of internal relativity and in so far as later nineteenth- and twentieth-century literature provides positive modern instances it is at best, and most typically, through the rejection of 'wise sawes'. Goethe is on the cusp of this shift, and he constantly makes the banality of general reflection palpable. Most peculiarly, he does so as much in the mode of acceptance as in the mode of critical irony.

His poetry can express such a positive acceptance with an effect at once monumentally impersonal and personally earnest as in the four lines quoted above. The first two lines, denying the separation of inner and outer, state a general principle that might have a philosophical, artistic or scientific bearing: 'Nothing is internal, nothing is external; for what is inner, is outer.' It has long been understood that Goethe developed an intuitive equivalent of the Kantian epistemological recognition while remaining apparently indifferent to the philosophical discourse and mode of thinking in which it was couched. These lines exemplify this. Their generality is contained within a tight repetition of terms and structure, so that the meaning emerges from the very compression of the simplistic formulae even as it remains genuinely simple. At the same time, the everyday idiom suggests a recognition emerging on the spot from some immediate concern of the speaker while the move from negative to positive form in the first two lines anticipates the active injunction of the third line to 'grasp' this truth: 'So grasp, without delay, (the) sacred open secret.'

While much of Goethe's poetry expresses positive generalities of this kind, his fiction problematises such expression with increasing overtness and

---

[4] This is the central claim of J-P. Lyotard, *La Condition Postmoderne* (Paris: Minuit, 1979).

centrality. This can be missed *as* a thematic focus, however, partly because it is so assimilated to what is more readily thought of as the dramatic action, and partly because of the disarming lucidity of his prose. In a sense, the 'open secret' theme starts right there, in the narrative language. The narrative voice of *Wilhelm Meister's Apprenticeship*, for example, frequently refers to the 'strangeness' of characters and events yet, as Schelling remarked, the high art of Goethe's style, like Cervantes', is to maintain an apparently unruffled serenity and clarity in recording the course of an action replete with oddity and abruptness.[5] It is as if one needs to be told of the strangeness because the narrative voice hardly acknowledges it, even while the strangeness of the content constantly sets the narrative tone into relief. This creates a recurrent uncertainty, as if something might have been said, or hinted at, that one has not quite caught. In this way, the narrative prose maintains a genuine openness of surface while constantly turning objects and events into personal symbols. Precisely because Goethe's fiction is so full of overt mystification, it is too easy to overlook the mysteries that may lie in the apparent lucidity of the prose.

This has a bearing too on the peculiar openness of the novel's irony. As in *Agathon* the narrative viewpoint eschews Rousseau's foresight and progresses along with the young hero's understanding. At the same time, in sharp contrast to the naive readerly identification to which the first person narrative of *Werther* had proved susceptible, the narration of *WMA* is overtly distanced. But its precise degree and locus of irony is more elusive than first appears. Indeed, one might usefully think of it less as an ironic narrative than as a single fabric which presents a different understanding as the pattern is viewed from either side. At the apparently culminating moment when Wilhelm receives his Certificate of Apprenticeship the reader is invited to review the whole preceding story in precisely such a way. The one viewpoint does not ironically trump the other so much as create a mutual illumination that modifies our understanding of both.

Wilhelm is the son of a merchant family who has an enthusiasm for theatre dating from his childhood play with a puppet theatre. In reaction to his apparent betrayal for a wealthier lover by the actress, Marianne, with whom he is in love, and to whom he has recounted his boyhood obsession, he

---

[5] 'Hence, the novel seeking to achieve the objectivity of the epic as regards form, yet with more restricted subject matter, has no other choice than prose, which is the highest indifference. Yet this implies prose in its highest perfection, where it is accompanied by a quiet rhythm and ordered periodic structure, one which, to be sure, does not command the ear like rhythmic meter, but which on the other hand displays no trace of coercion and thus requires the more careful cultivation.' Friedrich Wilhelm Joseph von Schelling, *The Philosophy of Art*, trans. Douglas W. Stott (Minneapolis: University of Minnesota Press, 1989) p. 231.

undertakes a distant business trip for his father. He quickly falls in, however, with a travelling troupe of actors who are the source of many adventures, artistic, emotional, moral, and social. He imposes a measure of order on the unruly group and directs a production of *Hamlet* in which he performs with some success the title role. When the actors stay for a while in an aristocratic household he causes a major psychological, and spiritual, shock for the count who accidentally sees Wilhelm dressed in the count's own clothes and interprets it as an admonitory vision. The novel's rapid action with constant changes of location allows him to meet many people some of whom become important to him. The troupe picks up a mysterious, melancholic harpist; a small boy, Felix; and a pre-pubescent girl, Mignon, who attaches herself strongly to Wilhelm. She is rescued by him from a troupe of travelling acrobats but continues to evince some secret suffering. After the group is attacked by robbers on the road, Wilhelm is treated by a beautiful woman, dressed in male hunting attire, and with whom he falls in love despite not seeing her again and knowing her only through his image of her as the 'Amazon'. Among the characters met casually are several who seem to take a special interest in him, give him brief words of advice, but do not stay to reveal themselves. These include an apparently clerical older man, later known as the Abbé, whom he meets on a couple of occasions, and who appears mysteriously at the last minute, and at that point anonymously, to enact the worryingly vacant role of the ghost in *Hamlet*. At a late stage in his adventures, Wilhelm is given to read an autobiographical manuscript memoir by a local canoness recounting her youthful spiritual experience as a 'Beautiful Soul'. This interpolated narrative comprises the whole of Book Six of the novel, after which the two remaining books take on a different quality from the preceding ones.

As it happens, the aristocratic family are connected with the 'Amazon', whose real name is Natalie; with the 'Beautiful Soul' who was her aunt; and with a group, including the mysterious Abbé, who have been taking a guiding interest in Wilhelm's educative experiences. They are a self-styled 'Society of the Tower' pursuing humanistic goals of altruism, personal development, and mutual guidance, in a manner strongly reminiscent of freemasonry. While still unaware of all these connections, Wilhelm goes to the estate of Natalie's brother, Lothario, whom he has not met, to remonstrate with him over the death of Lothario's former lover, Aurelie, whom he seems to have heartlessly abandoned. Here, however, the multiple layers of these relationships, and therefore of the preceding narrative, are gradually revealed to him, including the fact that Felix is actually his son by Marianne who had died faithful to him and whom he had abandoned without hearing her story. He finds himself in a less and less strong position to remonstrate with Lothario. The apparent climax of his development occurs at the end of Book Seven as he is allowed to enter the Tower, receives ceremonially his 'Certificate of Apprenticeship', and sees in the surrounding library cases, among many others, the 'scroll' of his own life story.

The pedagogical theme of the Wilhelm Meister novels provides an abundance of testing occasions for the theme of communicating experience, or the wisdom of experience, and, no less importantly, for raising this question to the level of a conscious and general problematic. With their mutual habit of thinking in the larger tradition of the genre, Schiller spoke approvingly of Goethe's revealing the epic 'machinery' (or divine intervention) of the novel when the figures who have been watching over Wilhelm's development are made known. Whereas the stage device of the *deus ex machina* is often used to resolve a human situation, in Goethe's novel the revelation opens further complexities within the educative machinery itself. For the 'strangeness' of Wilhelm's encounters is not just authorial but arises partly from the manipulations of other characters even if this distinction is constantly blurred within a larger providentiality. On the one hand, his secret mentors, like Rousseau, want him to learn authentically from experience while, on the other hand, the authorial artifice of the narrative is itself thematised as part of an obscurely purposive process whose aims and methods, powers and purview, remain uncertain and problematic. Much happens 'providentially' to Wilhelm as chance experience is made into meaning within the benign optimism of Goethe's narrative world. Any mentor who shares Goethe's outlook may also, therefore, assume a certain providentiality, or benignly creative fatedness, in the formative relation.

Schiller's analogy with the divine 'machinery' of the epic is very pregnant, therefore, with respect to the kind of power and knowledge ascribed to, or assumed by, some of the mentor figures, even as the expression reaffirms the pupil as the central and dynamic interest which this mere 'machinery' is there to serve. When we meet the Abbé properly, we are interested not just in the machinery, but in the ghost in the machine. And as his character is revealed, it transpires that, while he has a peculiar insight into the potentiality of the individuals in whom he takes a guiding interest, he tends to behave as if enjoying the kind of omniscience we would more readily associate with gods or authors and has a 'penchant to play the part of fate'.[6] Indeed, this perspectival turn at the end of Book Seven could be understood more radically as a shift in the narrative interest towards the processes and responsibilities

---

[6] *Wilhelm Meisters Lehrjahre, Goethes Werke, op. cit.* vol. vii, p. 554; *Wilhelm Meister's Apprenticeship*, trans. H. M. Waidson (London: Calder, 1977), vol. iii, p. 114. All subsequent references are to these editions.

of guidance and, arising from that, an interest in the process of the narrative itself. For when Wilhelm's education is taken as the major theme, the eighth and last book of the novel may appear anti-climactic but not if the process of his guidance is taken as the central focus. If the 'Certificate', which he sees and reads along with the reader, represents the conclusion of Wilhelm's apprenticeship, the scroll on which his story has been written by his secret mentors is an internal parallel to the book itself. It is not, of course, the text of *WMA* but an internal possibility of it reminding us of the different version, the mentor's perception on the other side of the fabric, which is inseparable from the version we are reading.

In that respect my initial formulation, that Goethe reverses Rousseau in seeing the educative experience from the viewpoint of the pupil rather than the mentor, requires some modification. As in *Agathon*, the pupil may be seen as the object, or occasion, of the pedagogical process as well as its subject. For while the inner life of the pupil is indeed being privileged in the narrative, the problem of guidance is itself being tested *through* the experience of the pupil. He is unwittingly testing it. In *WMA*, Wilhelm begins his educative adventures under his own initiative but gradually becomes aware that he is being watched, someone is seeking to give him guidance, and his experiences are deliberately obfuscated if not arranged. It is as if Emile were gradually to suspect that he was the object of the preceptor's educational charades. Of course, Wilhelm is never so entirely enclosed in manipulative fictions as Emile: indeed the interplay between the genuine chances of life and the providential working out of a personal destiny is an important aspect of the educational process with which guidance must not interfere. But the fact of his being the object of such attention at all is crucial as, over the course of the novel, he becomes increasingly puzzled, suspicious, and finally aware. 'Finally aware', at least, at the level of the facts, for the apparent culmination of Wilhelm's educative process only exposes more deeply the problems of both finality and awareness.

The narrative turn as the machinery of mentorship is exposed bears on the authorial irony towards Wilhelm. That the narrative is ironic has always been recognised, but in quite what way, and to what effect, has remained a matter of debate. A traditional reading of the novel, which still largely pertains outside of a specialist Germanist scholarship, emphasises how Wilhelm, despite his errors, has reached a significant point of maturity. He has outgrown his infatuation with the theatre, found his life partner, and assumed the responsibilities of fatherhood. But in recent decades, this generally positive reading, by which the *Bildung* process is ultimately vindicated, has been subjected to more radical questioning. It is not just that Wilhelm is no Goethe, but that the whole project of *Bildung*, and especially the role of artistic experience in this process, is thrown into question.[7] The full impact of this comes with the sequel novel, *Wilhelm Meister's Journeymanship*, which is very different, less accessible, and was written so much later that for the majority of readers it has never had its full impact within the Wilhelm story. But the later books of *WMA* already indicate the radical turn which the later novel was to consolidate and develop.

It should be said at this point that the question of irony within the book is compounded by a curious circular irony within this reception history. Goethe himself is generally acknowledged as the classic and triumphant instance of the conscious process of self-formation known as *Bildung*. It is therefore reasonable to think of him as endorsing it in general, whatever the limitations of his hero. But it is his whole *oeuvre* which properly embodies that process as far as his own case is concerned, a fact that is especially focused in his autobiography significantly entitled *Poetry (or Fiction) and Truth out of my Life*. The elusiveness of the categories in this title arises from Goethe's conscious tendency, as Nicholas Boyle emphasises in his biography, to create out of the events *in* his life, symbols *of* it.[8] In the fictional story of Wilhelm, however, by contrast with his own autobiography, he analyses someone who is not truly an artist and for whom the experience of art therefore has a different meaning. Wilhelm is long caught in the illusion of the dilettante, one who mistakes artistic interest and sensibility for creative capacity. It is made clear to Wilhelm by Jarno, the most bluntly spoken of his Tower mentors (and a figure partly based on Goethe's early mentor, J. G. Herder) that his relative success in playing the part of Hamlet did not come from his capacity as an actor but precisely the reverse: from the overlap between his own personality and his perception of the role. He achieved significant performance only fleetingly and by chance through emotional identification, not through artistic command. (*WML*, 550–1; *WMA*, iii, 111)

Dilettantism opens up a larger question beyond the personal maturity of the hero or the irony of the narrative. It represents a fundamental divide between Goethe and his hero. At the same time, it was precisely because Goethe was a genuine artist that he was so sensitive to the question. Up to the age of forty he still hovered between the careers of sculptor and poet, and the recognition that the former was not his calling was by high internal criteria. In this respect Goethe raises the problematic of Rousseau to a new power. In Rousseau, the question of uniqueness versus universality unconsciously

---

[7] For a resumé in English of modern scholarship on this topic see *Reflection and Action: Essays on the Bildungsroman*, ed. James Hardin (Columbia SC: University of South Carolina Press, 1991). There is also a good summary relevant to the present theme in Michael Minden, *The German Bildungsroman: Incest and Inheritance* (Cambridge: Cambridge University Press, 1997) pp. 48–59.

[8] *Goethe: The Poet and the Age*, vol. i (Oxford: Clarendon Press, 1991) p. 109.

dogged the supposedly rational and natural transparency of his educational method, as of his thought at large. In Goethe, what is at stake is the uniqueness not just of individual personality, but of creative genius. By a circular but effective logic, therefore, Goethe's genius most significantly separates him *from* Wilhelm while simultaneously providing the body of attested cultural significance which is continually read *into* him. Meanwhile, all the positive, impulsive, trusting, and life-affirming aspects of Wilhelm's character lend a colour of conviction to taking him as a vehicle for Goethe's own experience.

At the same time, just as some of the novel's internal would-be pedagogues seem to usurp the authorial function, so the elusiveness, and therefore the potential misreading, of Goethe's authorial relation to Wilhelm are illuminated by the pedagogical model. Authorial irony is a familiar, and generally prized, category. It is commonly taken as the sign of true control over the material. But the 'Flaubertian' model of the author as an indifferent deity, as expounded by Joyce's Stephen Dedalus in *A Portrait of the Artist as a Young Man*, and which often springs most directly to mind in this connection, is not the only possibility.[9] Apart from such tonal irony at the character's expense, there is a more long-term structural irony of outcome and growth which assesses the character's experience or attitude only in retrospect, and perhaps acknowledges in doing so that the earlier moment was necessary to the achievement of the later viewpoint. This is the kind of irony that typifies such otherwise different authors as Thomas Mann and D. H. Lawrence. Of all major novelists, Lawrence has perhaps most suffered the same reception problem as Goethe in the over-identification of central characters with the author. Moreover, an author's relation to the character, which inevitably governs the reader's, is a powerful symbol of human relation at large, including the pedagogical relation and not the less so for being thought a merely literary choice or technique.

Profoundly pedagogical authors are least likely to exercise irony against their characters. All teachers keep a certain detachment from their pupils but overt irony is not the best form of this; especially not old-fashioned schoolmasterly sarcasm which is more likely to serve the pedagogical self-image. The reality principle is always likely to impose itself eventually on pupils, many of whom will have a more immediate and overwhelming need of sustained self-confidence, the naivety required to keep embracing experience. Hence, whereas 'Flaubertian' irony tends to fix a view of the character, the pedagogical relation is always open to the dynamic of development even if that

---

[9] 'The artist, like the God of creation, remains within or behind or beyond or above his handiwork, invisible, refined out of existence, indifferent, paring his fingernails.' *A Portrait of the Artist as a Young Man*, ed. Chester G. Anderson and Richard Ellman (New York: Viking, 1965) p. 215.

never materialises. Character is understood *in* the moment but not identified *with* the moment. In this way, Wilhelm often speaks as one who has gained definitive insight into his experience, and he still does so towards the end of the novel, without being an object of overt irony. The very generalised ironic detachment that the narrative establishes towards its hero allows for a fluid and momentarily uncertain judgement of him at any given time. The same withholding of local judgement has troubled, or misled, readers of Lawrence in the twentieth century as it did some of Goethe's Victorian readers discussed by George Eliot.[10] It feels like simple endorsement of the character and for unwary readers both authors have seemed immoral in their suspension of judgement in situations that seem to call out for it. But the formation of judgement with respect to individuals is in itself a primary question pervading Goethe's fiction. It is inextricable from the dynamic of guidance and could hardly *be* thematised if an overt authorial judgement were constantly in place. In this way, we come to feel from the inside how such overt judgement is itself susceptible to banalisation.

Moral judgement was a central issue in *Werther*. In a series of arguments, Werther, the man of feeling, opposed the general moral maxims of his friend Albert, the man of social principle. Werther affirmed the irreducibility of personal feeling against the generality of principle. He complained angrily that his passionate convictions were met with platitudes. An argument over suicide, conducted in the company of a magistrate, extended Albert's sense of general principle to the level of a legal universality, while at the same time, in anticipating the manner of Werther's own death, it thematised the meaning of the novel itself. Importantly, Werther did not merely appeal to feeling here, he invested it in the emotional concreteness of story. In telling, against Albert's disapproval of her action, the story of a young girl who had committed suicide in a state of despair, Werther suggested that we cannot judge her unless we understand her emotional state. But to understand her in his terms would be to enter so fully into her condition that judgement would be impossible since one would then be emotionally identified with her. On this argument, to be detached enough to make the judgement is to be humanly disqualified from making it. But while Werther invoked this story in the sentimentalist mode of literalistic emotional identification, the novel suggested the error of this in the culminating episode of Werther's reading of Ossian with Lotte which was the emotional trigger for his suicide. The episode demonstrated how not to read fiction, including *Werther*. Yet Goethe himself was to some extent caught in the same sentimentalist double bind. While setting out the intrinsic logic of

---

[10] See George Eliot, 'The Morality of Wilhelm Meister', in *Selected Critical Writings*, ed. Rosemary Ashton (Oxford and New York: Oxford University Press, 1992) pp. 129–32.

Werther's condition, he refrained from direct authorial judgement and was obliged, as in Werther's own logic, to make the emotional condition of his hero fully compelling to the reader. To that extent, his sentimentalist readers were responding to something in the text and, as the figure of Werther was transposed into later romantic heroes, as in Senancour's *Obermann* (1804), he did in a sense escape Goethe's artistic containment.

The problematic of judgement and understanding, invested in the competing modalities of general principle and individual story in *Werther*, is carried over into the Wilhelm Meister novels. But whereas the arguments in *Werther* represented a static and polar stand-off between the competing mid-century meanings of 'sentiment' as feeling and principle, in the later novels the pedagogical theme transposes this apparently irresolvable contrast into a dynamic, and more open-ended, process. Both terms become more problematic. On the one hand, maxims, aphorisms, and generalities are subjected to testing of their experiential claims while story, on the other hand, becomes a constantly thematised vehicle of understanding and/or judgement. Most notably, as Wilhelm encounters the histories of several other characters, these are frequently written down as a way, not just of recording the events, but of transposing their experience into a meaning made fully objective and available to third-party discussion. Rather than the simple, emotional identification assumed by Werther, the reading of these stories is a complex act of understanding and judgement requiring a written and objectified text.

The most striking case in *WMA* is the long memoir of the 'Beautiful Soul', unless we think in this way of the 'scroll' of Wilhelm's own life as an image of the book itself. For, no less than in *Werther*, the interpolated narratives provide hints for reading the novel itself. Just as the 'Confessions of the Beautiful Soul' reveal against the writer's own grain something questionable in her spiritual intensity, so the reader of the novel has actively to interpret, rather than passively receive, any given judgement; however apparently authorial or authoritative. In that respect, these 'Confessions' stand in sharp contrast to the Savoyard Vicar's 'Profession of Faith' which otherwise occupies a similar structural position in Emile's education. Whereas the Vicar provides a body of notionally oral reflection with which the reader, and by now Emile too, can be assumed ready to identify, the written narrative of the 'Beautiful Soul' provides the active generic challenge of a first-person female narrative athwart the highly male main story of Wilhelm.[11] It becomes an object of debate for her readers within the text and, whereas the Ossian episode in

---

[11] I have discussed the impact of the 'Confessions of a Beautiful Soul' more fully in 'Narration as Action: Bekenntnisse eine Schönen Seele and Angela Carter's *Nights at the Circus*', *German Life and Letters* 45/1 (Jan. 1992) pp. 16–32.

Werther taught how not to read, this provides a positive lesson in literary criticism.

Focusing the irony of the book at large helps in understanding a subtle but palpable shift in the quality of the narrative in Books Seven and Eight following the 'Confessions'. The episode, for example, in which Wilhelm receives his Certificate and initiation into the Society of the Tower is a strange blend of genuine solemnity and gimcrack theatricality, reflecting the mixture of seriousness and hollowness at the core. The pasteboard aspect throws into relief what is genuine, or symbolic, in the ritual, while the narrative itself is transposed into a ritual mode much as Mulligan's parody of the daily Mass at the opening of *Ulysses* suggests the bid for artistic eternity in Joyce's book of the day. Goethe is a great lover of mystification, such as secret caskets, rooms or societies, and here he blends Masonic overtones with the conventions of the 'secret society' novel which was popular at the time.[12] But typically when you get there the cupboard is usually bare, and that applies equally in the realms of knowledge and wisdom. And so the Certificate, which Wilhelm starts to read, consists of general maxims about learning, and especially the development of artistic ability which can only partly be learned. The maxims are pithy and pertinent, yet their very generality bespeaks an implicit recognition of their own hollowness for anyone not already in possession of the relevant experience. And indeed their principal theme is to warn of the relative fruitlessness of words even while implicitly acknowledging, and enacting, their inescapability:

Only a part of art can be taught, the artist needs it complete. Whoever half-knows art is always in error and talks a lot; whoever possesses it fully likes only to act and talks rarely or at most late. The former have no secrets and no strength, their teaching is tasty like bread that has been baked, and is satiating for *one* day... (*WML*, 496; *WMA*, iii, 66)

Good advice of this generalised kind has been given to Wilhelm over the course of the novel, as from the then unknown Abbé, and it has often been couched in a language that this episode leads us to see more clearly as one of well-meaning platitude. The aphorism speaks from and to experience, but it cannot substitute for it, and Wilhelm has repeatedly failed to appreciate the advice he has been given. By the same token, however, the perspectival turn of the narrative in thematising this question also shifts the focus: it is not so much a personal failing of Wilhelm, or of his mentors, as a structural feature of language in relation to experience. This may seem a distinction without

---

[12] See Rosemary Haas, *Die Turmgesellschaft* in *Wilhelm Meisters Lehrjahre: zur Geschichte des Geheimbandromans und der Romantheorie im 18 Jahrhundert* (Bern and Frankfurt, 1975).

a difference, simply the consequence of looking at the same fabric from the other side, but major pedagogical insight often starts with the perspectival turn of ceasing to blame the pupil.

If the reader, like Wilhelm, is a little puzzled as to how seriously to take this strangely theatrical scene, with its odd note of intellectual anticlimax, it is carried off dramatically by the Abbé's simultaneous revelation that Felix is Wilhelm's son. This discovery is both an immediate distraction from, and a longer-term deepening of, the ambivalence of the episode with respect to Wilhelm's maturity. Like many of us, Wilhelm does not so much mature as find the responsibilities of maturity suddenly thrust upon him. If the one often has to do duty for the other, so that what passes for maturity may be merely a longer experience in handling one's immaturity, there is a literary equivalent here in the way the initiation scene has been read loosely as a symbolic expression of Wilhelm's maturity despite the fact that Felix proves to be the focus of new errors. It is, for example, with a view to finding a mother for Felix that he talks himself into proposing marriage to a worthy, but not quite suitable, young woman called Therese, still unaware that Natalie, the 'Amazon', is nearby and a member of the family. When he finally meets her, he does not know that all the other characters are aware of his love for her, and their resulting charade while awaiting his resolution of the situation maintains the same structure as the long process that preceded his initiation. The Tower group continues to exercise Rousseau's principle of delay so that the development will occur genuinely from within. At the same time, especially through Friedrich, the impetuous younger brother of the family, Wilhelm's secret is made an item of public comedy still without his recognition. As Schiller puts it, Friedrich roughly shakes the ripened fruit from the tree.[13] The group go to the very edge of direct revelation as if pushing Wilhelm to see the point. The open and comic extremity of this, now that the reader is in possession of the secret from all sides, reflects back on the behaviour of the mentors throughout.

While they continue resolutely to exercise the principle of delay, we can now see that their restraint has also been a matter of anxiety and frustration to themselves. Wilfried Bauer has traced the increasing urgency of the four major interventions through which Wilhelm was warned of his emotional and theatrical entanglements, although these moments of directness only reaffirmed the principle of the open secret in that he was unable to profit from them.[14] The strangeness of these gnomic interventions, which seems like

---

[13] Schiller to Goethe, June 1796. *Goethe: Gedenkausgabe*, vol. 20, ed. Ernst Beutler (Zurich and Stuttgart: Artemis, 1950–64) p. 181.
[14] Wilfried Bauer, in *Goethe's Narrative Fictions: The Irvine Goethe Symposium*, ed. William J. Lillyman (Berlin and New York: de Gruyter, 1983) p. 89.

mystification as read from Wilhelm's side of the narrative fabric, is revealed as arising from the mentors' internal conflict between restraint and instruction. Unlike Rousseau's confident governor, they fear for the unguided outcome and cannot leave the process to take its course. If as Rousseau says, you should never do today what you can without danger put off till tomorrow, such a policy is an active risking of harm at the responsibility of the mentor. In the light of Wilhelm's experience, the Abbé's willingness to take this risk, his resolutely positive view of error, that 'an error can only be cured by erring' (*WML*, 550; *WMA*, iii, 111), may suggest that it is more than a possible *route* to understanding, but somehow *intrinsic* to it. Error on this model is not merely a derogation and distraction from the truth, its possibility has to be implicit in the act of understanding which otherwise remains insecure as long as it does not encompass the understanding of error. In that sense, recovery from prior error may be the only guarantee of understanding.

When the situation is revealed to him, Wilhelm is not just slow in taking up the group's invitation to join them, he is suspicious and resistant. There is an internal logic to this, of course, as revealing a conspiracy against someone is not necessarily the best way of inspiring their confidence, and Wilhelm reacts as Emile might do if he were to discover the charades being played around him. In retrospect, therefore, it makes sense that a premonitory step towards his assimilation into the Society of the Tower was his being reluctantly drawn into such a conspiratorial charade himself. Seeking out Lothario to remonstrate with him over his abandonment of Aurelie, he arrived just as Lothario suffered a serious wound. The extravagant bedside anxieties of another young woman called Lydia, who is in love with Lothario, place his recovery at risk and Wilhelm reluctantly agrees to remove her for a while by taking her on a false errand around the neighbourhood. He initially resists this 'strange and questionable mission', despite its good motive, on the principle that deception is bad in itself and 'would take us too far, if we were once to start deceiving for the sake of what is good and useful'. (*WML*, 439; *WMA*, iii, 21) Jarno replies with a general observation that casts an incidental light on Rousseau: 'it's impossible to educate children except in this way', a proposition from which Wilhelm does not dissent. Yet neither does he accede to the main point, although he is willing to put his principles temporarily aside for the sake of Lothario, and then even more so when he believes that the mission may bring him to the Amazon. By degrees, he becomes more sympathetic to Lothario, general principles are necessarily flexible, and when the occasion finally arises for Wilhelm to be able to tax Lothario with his treatment of Aurelie, he finds himself taking a more lenient view of his new friend's behaviour: ' "Let it be," Wilhelm replied, "we can't always avoid what is blameworthy, nor that our opinions and actions are deflected in a strange way from their natural and true course...'" (*WML*, 468; *WMA*, iii, 44) Moral generalisations in Goethe can be used, benignly or not, as a way of avoiding moral responsibility.

By the same token, even as Wilhelm is being assimilated to the group, his suspicion is intensified. His distrust impedes his response to their benign intentions, and throws a questionable light on them for the reader too. If the initiation episode is as much a beginning as an ending for Wilhelm, the conduct of his would-be mentoring is likewise revealed to be even more uncertain than its mystificatory façade might initially suggest. The group of mentors is internally divided and made up of manifestly imperfect personalities. There are in fact two layers of mentoring in that the Abbé has overseen the upbringing of younger members of the group including Lothario, Jarno, and Natalie. The two younger men, although impressive and serious characters, indicate the limitations of his achievement in that regard, while Natalie is endowed with a natural wholeness of personality which, as Schiller argued, makes her, rather than her aunt, the true instance of the Beautiful Soul.[15] The difference in female upbringing partly reflects the gender distinction that was even more marked in Rousseau, while Natalie was a conscious image for Schiller of the innate wholeness which he called her 'aesthetic' character, her natural merging of inclination and duty. In a general essay on this theme, he defined such intuitive and unstrained wholeness as 'grace', and likewise attributed it especially to the female.[16] To that extent we may infer that Natalie required relatively little mentoring and perhaps for that reason she sets little store by fruitful error which would be a more dangerous principle anyway for young females of the period. When she takes charge of a number of young girls, and differs from the Abbé in being more overtly directive in her education of them, he accepts this divergence from his own principles as right for her.

Jarno meanwhile chafes under the restraints of the Abbé's style of mentoring and it is he, with his need to speak out, who later confirms the reader's possible suspicions about the gimcrack mystification of the initiation scene. Having had the group's manipulations opened to him, Wilhelm is only the more suspicious of their powers and purposes, and complains to Jarno:

'... it would be remarkable if those secret powers of the Tower that are always so busy were not to work on us now and fulfil with and on us some strange purpose or other. From what I know of these holy men, it always seems to be their praiseworthy intention to separate what has been joined together and to join together what has been separated. What sort of fabric can arise from this may indeed remain an enigma to our unholy eyes.' (*WML*, 547; *WMA*, iii, 108)

---

[15] Schiller to Goethe, 17 Aug. 1995. *Gedenkausgabe*, vol. 20, *op. cit.* p. 190.
[16] *On Grace and Dignity* (1793).

Jarno speaks deprecatingly of the ceremonial as 'the relics of a youthful venture' in which the element of mystery attracts a young person of some 'depth of character'. (*WML*, 548; *WMA*, iii, 109) It has to be understood, therefore, despite its 'first quasi-mystical impressions... almost allegorically'. (*WML*, 549; *WMA*, iii, 110) But such obliqueness is contrary to Jarno's blunt character. As he confesses: 'I myself have been the least use to the Society and to people; I am a bad teacher, I find it unbearable to look on when someone is making clumsy efforts...' (*WML*, 549; *WMA*, iii, 110). He has frequently argued this point against the Abbé's principles of maximal delay and fruitful error.

Jarno's explanations do not inspire the confidence that the mature Emile had in his governor. Moreover, in giving this explanation to the angry and suspicious Wilhelm, he irritates him further by reading yet more wise aphorisms from his certificate while acknowledging that 'they will seem empty and obscure to someone who recalls no experience in their context'. (*WML*, 548; *WMA*, iii, 109) And indeed, Wilhelm has just described them as 'magnificent, secret words of wisdom, most of which we don't understand'. The scene redoubles with a more intense urgency the critique of aphoristic wisdom already implicit in the initiation episode, which was itself a retrospective recognition of this principle in relation to the whole preceding narrative. Wilhelm's arrival at his presumptive goal has started a radical unravelling of the narrative process by which he got there; a turn reminiscent of Wittgenstein's principle that when you understand his conclusion you will appreciate the 'nonsensical' nature of the argument and see it as like a ladder that may be kicked away after it has enabled you to climb.[17] The implications of this analogy for the narrative itself, however, are even more radical than may at first be evident.

The investigation of educational direction and authority in the last book is significantly deconstructive both of itself, and of the preceding process for which Wilhelm has provided the focus and test case. But it goes even further in questioning the very fictional mode in which his educative experience has so far been conceived. As Schelling put it: 'The background reveals itself towards the end and displays an infinite perspective on all the wisdom of life behind a kind of illusory game, for the secret society is actually nothing other than precisely this, and it dissolves itself at just the moment it becomes visible.'[18] A substantial portion of the final book is devoted to providing a rational and material explanation of the two mysterious figures, the Harpist and Mignon,

---

[17] *Tractatus Logico-Philosophicus*, trans. D. F. Pears and B. F. McGuiness (London: Routledge and Kegan Paul, 1963) p. 151.
[18] *The Philosophy of Art*, op. cit. p. 235.

whose poetic aura is one of the generally acknowledged triumphs of the novel. Schiller admired the manner in which the story of these figures is resolved: it draws the dreadful pathos of their fate from the theoretical monstrosity of 'stupid superstition'.[19] In a sense, however, Goethe was thereby dissolving his own poetic creations and it was only with the appearance of *WMJ* that the radical nature, and logic, of his narrative turn in this respect became fully evident. He was moving towards a different conception of fiction reflecting a shift in his pedagogical theme. As the later work concentrates more squarely on the temptations and problems of the mentor rather than the pupil, and questions the whole notion of *Bildung*, so it develops a new mode of fiction.

This will be taken up in discussing the sequel novel, but something of the significance of the shift is already evident in *WMA*. The melancholic harpist, now known by his highly suggestive given name of Augustin, is discovered to be the father of Mignon by his sister, Sperata, to whom he was secretly betrothed in ignorance of their true relationship. The betrothal is secret because he fears his father's disapproval. With typical Goethean naturalism, the narrative does not condemn the incestuous relationship as such and Augustin, who was otherwise entering a monastery, rather suffers a religiously induced depression of guilt anxiety. Indeed, the internal understanding and treatment of the characters in the whole affair sits between the rival authorities of religious belief and medical science, the former of which comes out of it especially badly. The original error arises from Augustin's father who, having fathered Sperata at a late stage in life, fears social embarrassment and has had her brought up as the daughter of another family. When the lovers' situation is revealed, although not to Sperata, authority passes to a priest, an ecclesiastical father, who practises a piously protective deception leading her to believe that the sin lies in Augustin's being destined to the religious life, and that he is therefore to be kept separate from her. The priest acts in good faith according to his convictions but with some self-satisfaction in exercising a productive authority, in changing the course of events to conform with his beliefs. His religion and status give him unquestioning belief in his own authority, but the outcome is Sperata's madness and death followed by Augustin's self-exile and lifelong psychological malady. Once again, this story is not directly narrated but is deliberately written down first so as to become a text for the other characters too. Writing moderates the intensity of emotional involvement for the character, Augustin's brother, who would otherwise narrate it personally, and provides an internal rationale for assimilating it to the manner of the whole Goethean narrative. As these mysterious poetic figures are turned into objects of prose understanding within the pedagogical theme, the resulting

---

[19] *Gedenkausgabe*, vol. 20, *op. cit.* p. 186.

critique of educational authority bears upon the imaginative authority of the preceding narrative.

In so far as the final book of the novel becomes a conscious self-dissolving of the narrative, it takes on an implicit orientation towards both the past and the future rather than consolidating its own present in a mode of conclusion. While inviting the reader to reconsider the preceding narrative as it might now be read from the mentors' point of view, it also prepares for the continuation of Wilhelm's career in what was to prove a radically different kind of book. And within this new consciousness of its own processes, the narrative retrospect also incorporates Wilhelm's aesthetic preoccupations as an integral aspect of its own meaning.

Perhaps the most pregnant of the aphorisms on the Certificate is the last one Wilhelm reads before the Abbé cuts him off, an interruption which is suggestive in itself. Even the Abbé perhaps can't stand to hear these wise sawes repeated cold, and the rest, he says, will abide 'their time'. The readiness is all. This last aphorism, however, which recurs in *WMJ*, states that 'the genuine pupil learns to unravel (or 'to develop', *entwickeln*) from the known what is unknown, and thereby approaches the master.' Like the final book of the novel, this aphorism points both backwards and forwards, from the known to the unknown and *vice versa*. It is ambiguous whether the truth or experience referred to here is actually there in the 'known' form or whether something new has to be discovered. And such words as 'discover' and 'invent' begin to shimmer here, of course, since they rest etymologically on the same ambiguity of the created and the found. However it is interpreted in detail, this aphorism questions whether what is learned can be taught, except obliquely in so far as the posing of the known is the condition for developing the unknown. Teaching, as the exposition of the known, remains necessary although its internal teleology may be illusory. In that respect, the aphorism poses a question not just of understanding but of freedom, a freedom which is not in conflict with authority but is rather encountered within it, and conditional upon it. Such an internal freedom was likewise a central theme of Schiller's *Letters on the Aesthetic Education of Man* written almost contemporaneously with Goethe's work on this novel. Their correspondence is full of fruitful interaction and, whether or not Goethe borrowed from Schiller in this regard, Schiller frequently found in Goethe's intuitive understanding the essential recognitions to which he sought to give discursive articulation.

Schiller saw the value of the aesthetic as lying in the freedom it accords from the polar compulsions of reason and instinct. Rather than seeking to identify these, as in sentimental ideology, or have one dominate the other as in traditional moral thinking, he saw them as both capable of being suspended in, and by, their mutual opposition. In life we are committed to action, even if only at the level of feeling and desire. But all human action, as opposed to purely instinctive reaction, requires a capacity to inhabit one's evaluative commitments with a reflective appreciation of them as such. This inner freedom is a necessary, indeed a defining, feature of the human, and it is most fully known in the aesthetic state of which it is the *proprium*. Schiller values the aesthetic, in other words, as a mode of relation to fundamental beliefs and values which must pervade the moral life at large, but is experienced as such within the aesthetic condition. It was part of Schiller's analytic method, and part of the sentimentalist inheritance, to posit fundamental dualisms to be overcome so that, even in the overcoming, the dualism was still discursively necessary to define the significance. Furthermore, his account of the aesthetic, against the background of sentimental literalism, required emphasis on its distinction from the everyday condition, and to that extent he left himself vulnerable to the later development of a separatist, or aestheticist, understanding of it. Goethe, by contrast, was intuitively holistic and resistant to such dualistic abstractions and, for that very reason, Schiller's terms remain invaluable for understanding him.

Goethe is perhaps one of the first great thinkers of whom it seems appropriate to say that his relation to his own beliefs and values was aesthetic. If there are earlier candidates who might plausibly be described in this way, it was only when the term was developed in the late eighteenth century that it became possible to conceive such a relation to belief. We may think of Shakespeare as having a dramatic relation to truth and value, but that also removes him from the problem. Goethe is much more tangibly the central fact, and implicit material, of his own *oeuvre*. He is personally visible, publicly exposed, in a way that makes his elusiveness in this regard a constant and crucial fact of his writing, and of his being. Of course, to say that his convictions were held in an aesthetic spirit is far from suggesting they were shallowly flexible—indeed, the reverse. For Goethe, the body of experience that makes up a conviction is not susceptible of reduction to principled articulation and its integrity is protected by a constant recognition of this impossibility. As Yeats, another man of strong but elusive convictions, said: 'man can embody truth, but he cannot know it.'[20] Some falsity enters in the very act of translating the dynamic living complex into the fixture of a comprehensible idea and, since words and ideas are the primary means of rehearsing the upshot of experience, Goethe entered into an essentially aesthetic relation to them. His non-coercive way of inhabiting ideas, including even those that express his strongest convictions, is in line with Rousseau's emphasis on experience but

---

[20] W. B. Yeats to Lady Elizabeth Pelham, *The Letters of W. B. Yeats*, ed. Allan Wade (London: Rupert Hart-Davis, 1954) p. 922.

it puts him at the opposite extreme from Rousseau's envisaged exercise of pedagogical authority.

Such a relation to truth, or to the expression of belief, has consequences for the process of humanistic education. Writing of Goethe, Dilthey spoke of the 'teleological character of mental life'.[21] This formulation may recall Kant's approach to a definition of the aesthetic in which he first noted that, although nature has no purpose, we attribute purposiveness to it in order to accommodate it to our understanding.[22] To speak of natural 'laws' is to employ a convenient, if not a necessary, fiction. In that respect, the 'purposiveness without purpose' by which Kant then characterised the aesthetic has a chiasmic opposite in the process of understanding the world. We bring purpose to nature which does not have it, and we suspend instrumental purpose in the concentrated purposiveness of art.

All this offers a fertile analogy with the pedagogical relation. The notion that the still unknown is to be won from the known, in so far as it implies a freedom of purpose that escapes the given, parallels the purposiveness without purpose of the pedagogical relation as a formation of responsible freedom. This is far from being a matter of benign neglect, or just trusting to providence. Like the artist, the teacher must create the concentration of significances, the pressure chamber of meanings, within which the process of understanding is likely to occur. As Schiller put it of Wilhelm: 'In this way, the whole work has a beautiful purposiveness, without the hero having a goal.'[23] For equally in parallel with art, any particular purpose intended to arise from the process is suspended, and it is no less so even if the teacher is in fact motivated by such a didactic intent. As in art, the process is larger than the person who engenders it, and the better it is done the more it escapes ownership. A new entity is formed. Accordingly, at the end of Wilhelm's apprenticeship, Goethe invites us to look back, not just on the internal process of Wilhelm's development, but on the consciously aesthetic modality of its authorial direction as thematised especially in the Abbé's insistence on the providential principle of delay. What for the literalistic Rousseau was a predictive principle resting on certitude, was for Goethe an aesthetically based principle of openness and uncertainty. Even as Wilhelm inhabits a persuasively realist world, the narrative constantly exposes its own teleological drive as a necessary fiction. Goethe, looking back summatively on Wilhelm's education as an intelligible process, recognises its essentially fictional and aesthetic mode of purposiveness.

At the same time, the final book also looks forward in a way that begins to take leave of the whole project of humanistic *Bildung*. As the traditional

---

[21] *Poetry and Experience, op. cit.* p. 185.   [22] *Critique of Judgement, op. cit.* pp. 222–31.
[23] Schiller to Goethe, 8 July 1796. *Gedenkausgabe*, vol. 20, *op. cit.* p. 203.

authority of religion has been opposed to that of medical science, it is to science that Wilhelm's story will increasingly turn. In this respect, the novel does not destroy poetry for prose so much as develop another mode of the poetic. For Goethe lived at perhaps the last moment in the development of modern science in which it could still keep something of its ancient connection with a humanist poetry; after him came the long march to the posthuman. This was, of course, by virtue of an heroic last stand which put him on the losing side of some scientific questions, and his brand of holism was to become a distinctly minority expression, as in the educational practice of Rudolf Steiner. It depended on an assumption of underlying unity by which one discipline could further another and the theme of the open secret linked Goethe's diverse disciplines. In his study of plants, for example, he was engaged by the contemporary discovery, or 'newly opened secrets', of a general principle whereby growth depends on two subordinate principles: the direct upward movement is complemented by a sideways, spiral movement as can be seen on the bark of trees.[24] Only by a balance of these two principles does the plant have the strength to support itself. The fundamental principle in question here required an immense labour of observation and deduction yet is visible on the surface of the phenomenon. And although he does not make the point, the commonality of vocabulary between realms creates a suggestive analogy to personal growth in so far as this requires the lateral movement of error as much as the apparently simple upward movement which education may seek too exclusively to foster. It seems less an analogy than a statement of natural law to say that forced growth is less strong, just as the straight path is too narrow.

Hence, just as art for Goethe was an open secret, so was the natural world as approached through science. Indeed, falling outside human purposiveness, it is even more open to view yet enigmatic to the understanding. Finding a kindred spirit in the Persian poet Hafiz, who was commonly described as 'mystical', he pertinently dismissed this description of him in another poem turning on the open secret:

Offenbar Geheimnis[25]

Sie haben dich, heiliger Hafiz,
Die mystische Zunge genannt

---

[24] 'Spiraltendenz der Vegetation', *Goethes Werke, op. cit.* vol. xiii, pp. 130–48 (131).
[25] Open Secret

They have called you, blessed Hafiz,
The mystical tongue,
And those learned in words
Have not known the worth of the word.

> Und haben, die Wortgelehrten,
> Den Wert des Worts nicht erkannt.
>
> Mystisch heissest du ihnen,
> Weil sie Närrisches bei dir denken
> Und ihren unlautern Wein
> In deinem Namen verschenken.
>
> Du aber bist mystisch rein,
> Weil sie dich nicht verstehn,
> Der du, ohne fromm zu sein, selig bist!
> Das wollen sie dir nicht gestehn.

The supposed mysticism of Hafiz is merely in the eyes of the beholders, whose mystificatory vision might better deserve the term applied, as it is here, in a derisive spirit. Hafiz's blessedness, by contrast, lies not in piously instructing us to see beyond himself and the world, but in what he is, and thereby shows. The poem itself is open in its essentially transparent language of simple statement in which almost the only metaphor is the phrase 'mystische Zunge' (mystical tongue) quoted as a banality of the conventional commentators themselves. Once again, as the language of the poem eschews the conventionally poetic, it points to the different possibilities of the apparently prosaic. Likewise, the strange blend of realism and artifice in *WMA* places the process of Wilhelm's educational formation, and the narrative authority of its telling, under an aesthetic sign, and prepares the way for more radical renunciations, narrative and aesthetic, as well as thematic, in the sequel novel.

> You call them mystical
> Because they think so foolishly of you,
> And pour their profane wine
> In your name.
>
> But you are mystically pure
> Because they do not understand you.
> You who, without being pious, are blessed!
> That they will not understand.
>
> (*Goethes Werke, op. cit.*, vol. ii, p. 24)

4

Pedagogy, Fiction, and the Art of Renunciation: *Wilhelm Meister's Journeymanship, or the Renunciants*

> '... die entsagungsvolle Geschäft des Erziehers...'
> (Wilhelm Dilthey)[1]

Goethe's late novel, *Wilhelm Meisters Wanderjahre* (variously translated as *Wilhelm Meister's Journeymanship* or *Wilhelm Meister's Years of Travel*), is one of the strangest and least readily accessible of works as compared to those of any European novelist of equivalent stature.[2] There are more obscure works, such as *Finnegans Wake*, and more idiosyncratic ones, such as *Tristram Shandy*, but these are deliberately so. No one doubts that they challenge the reader with their pointed and suggestive oddity. The oddness of *WMJ* is of an opposite, apparently anticlimactic, kind which takes to a new level the strangeness within transparency that already characterised *WMA*. The novel is quite transparent in its moment-by-moment narrative, yet is opaque in its overall sense, and difficult at first to see as profoundly meaningful. It can even seem a work of solemn, inward-turned banality as Goethe's creative powers waned; comparable perhaps to the prosaic, religiose didacticism often perceived in Wordsworth's *The Excursion*, a work with some similarity of themes and structure, as compared to the poetic power of *The Prelude*.

The circumstances of its composition and publication have exacerbated the difficulty of its reception. Having long intended a sequel to *WMA*, which he had published over twenty years earlier, Goethe produced a version in 1821 which, owing partly to its critical reception and partly to his own experimental

---

[1] 'The renunciative business of the educator', *Pädagogik: Geschichte und Grundlinien des Systems*, op. cit. p. 171.
[2] I prefer *Journeymanship* as adopted by Eric Blackall since it preserves the connection with Apprenticeship but subsequent quotations are referenced to Waidson's version which preserves Thomas Carlyle's title, *Years of Travel*.

openness, he modified for a final version published in 1829 only a few years before his death. Even then it may be questioned whether it was truly finished and, since the principal narrative in either version is almost buried beneath a variety of interpolated materials, some of which he was known to have already to hand, it could be supposed that he was effectively cobbling together a volume which he could no longer summon the artistic power, or will, to form into a coherent whole. Yet readers attuned to Goethe have always responded to its peculiar demands, and twentieth-century developments especially have provided the context for a more appreciative response. Hermann Broch compared it closely with *Ulysses*, another work whose strangeness lies in its literary mode rather than its worldly reference, the recognisable ordinariness of its Dublin being part of the point.[3] Indeed, if *WMA* internalises the picaresque, and thereby assimilates the previous development of the European novel, *WMJ* already anticipates the modernist break-up of the form. At the same time, as with Sterne, it is a mistake to read it in too much of a modernist spirit and for a sense of its internal artistic logic within Goethe's thought at the time, the English reader may usefully consult Eric Blackall's excellent chapters on this novel.[4] For present purposes, however, it is above all a cardinal moment in the history of *Bildung*. It is the hinge on which the tradition turns from an earlier Enlightenment conception towards the phase of modernity which we still inhabit. The process of *Bildung* is now seen pre-eminently from the viewpoint of the mentor as the centre of gravity has shifted to the special responsibilities and temptations of middle age. Virginia Woolf's compliment to *Middlemarch* for being 'one of the few English novels written for grown-up people' suggests by contrast how *WMJ* is pre-eminently a novel not just for, but peculiarly about, grown-ups.[5] Middle age as a specific phase of life is its theme and its narrative method contrasts accordingly with the story of Wilhelm's youth.

Wilhelm Meister's Journeymanship as Critique of *Wilhelm Meister's Apprenticeship*

The opening narrative premise is that Wilhelm is obliged by the Tower group to spend some years travelling during which he is not to spend more than three nights in one location. This drastically limits the usual possibilities of the novel, such as the continuous dramatisation of relationships developed steadily in time, and almost drives it back to picaresque form. Moreover, the work is peculiarly elusive to summary as it consists largely of a series of sub-narratives

---

[3] Hermann Broch, 'James Joyce und die Gegenwart' (1936) in *Schriften zur Literatur*, 1, *Kritik* (Frankfurt/M: Suhrkamp, 1975) pp. 63–95.
[4] *Goethe and the Novel* (Ithaca and London: Cornell University Press, 1976) pp. 224–69.
[5] See Virginia Woolf, *The Common Reader* (London: Hogarth Press, 1968) p. 213.

from characters, or more commonly from texts, encountered by Wilhelm on his travels. The interest in other life stories that has nurtured his development so far is taken to a point where the relation to the main figure is no longer obvious. They are frequently produced by one or other of the characters as if to insinuate some moral or psychological point that they cannot, or will not, articulate more directly. Yet the stories are thematically linked and Goethe's long-standing method of *Spiegelung*, or mirroring, becomes, in this work, the dominant technique. The stories do more than surround Wilhelm with revelatory images: our sense of his personal development is derived indirectly from this variety of figures, situations, and even of narrative forms.

The interpolated stories are typically domestic in setting with a linking theme of paternal or pedagogical authority. The novel opens with Wilhelm and Felix alone together on a mountain pass and they are frequently referred to throughout the novel not by name but as father and son. Wilhelm has assumed the responsibilities of fatherhood in an unusually abrupt and self-conscious way even though he had already informally fostered the boy. Their first 'action' in the novel is to hear a story of foster fatherhood from a character known only as 'St Joseph the Second'. This is a local carpenter who has met and fallen in love with a woman who was about to give birth to her first child as her husband was killed. 'St Joseph' has married her, assumed the functions of father, built his home on the ruins of an ancient monastery, and modelled his life on an ancestral form of labour which he has inherited from his own father, and which links him strongly to the local community. The novel thus opens with an image of adoptive fatherhood in a richly traditional life form, with overtones of religious piety, but rendered with a note of idyllicism and anachronism that may help explain why it then disappears from the novel for good.

As they travel on, they meet their friend Jarno, now called Montan, who is working alone in the mountains studying rocks. Felix discovers a mysterious locked casket, just before they encounter another group of figures including a wise older woman called Makaria (Greek: Blessed) and a young woman called Hersilie. These live in the highly organised household of Hersilie's uncle who pastes aphorisms from the Koran over the walls of the house. She takes the casket into safe keeping and gives Wilhelm a story to read which she has translated from French. This is the story of the 'Pilgernde Törin' (the Foolish Pilgrim) concerning a beautiful, and evidently well-bred, young woman who has appeared without apparent resources or memory near a country household. Taken in by the family, she proves disruptive as both father and son fall in love with her. Although she seems deliberately to lead them on and humiliate them before her equally sudden departure, she exposes a potential folly in them, especially the father. The situation of a young woman caught between the affections of father and son mirrors the main narrative as Felix becomes attached to Hersilie who in turn seems to feel some attraction for Wilhelm.

As Wilhelm leaves this group, he is given the next interpolated story to read, this time of German provenance, entitled 'Who is the Betrayer?' A young man, Lucidor, is sent by his father to visit a family whose daughter he is expected to marry. His strong sense of duty to his father, enhanced by gratitude for the professional education and prospects the father has provided for him, prevents him from telling his father, or his intended fiancée, that his affections are engaged elsewhere. Although Eric Blackall emphasises the egotistically immature self-involvement of Lucidor, it is worth noting the part played by the older characters.[6] Alone in his bedroom, Lucidor laments his situation aloud unaware that he is audible through a gap in the wall to an older man also staying in the house. The rest of the company, alerted to the situation, keep up a benign facade until his father can be contacted by the other guest, a surrogate father, to release him from the obligation. In a sense several characters have betrayed or deceived but the off-stage father is perhaps the real betrayer even if the power of paternal will emerges most strongly here not in the melodramatic form of unheeding authority but as it is internalised in the rather over-dutiful son.

After this comes the principal interpolated narrative 'The Fifty-Year-Old Man'; a story whose title suggests the novel's centre of gravity. The principal figure is a middle-aged 'Major' whose personal title suggests as much a stage in life as his military rank. When he visits his Baroness sister to further the long-envisaged marriage of his son, Flavio, with her daughter, Hilarie, a marriage that will satisfactorarily combine the family inheritances, he is displeased to be told that Hilarie has fallen in love with someone else; displeased, that is, until he learns that he is the object of her affections. Flattered and moved by the young woman's love he feels, in a significantly counter-natural image, 'the return of his own springtime'.[7] He seeks to rejuvenate his appearance cosmetically, and is subsequently relieved to learn that Flavio has actually fallen in love with a young widow somewhat older than himself. In seeking to resolve the situation, the Major finds himself in a devious relation to his son which prevents him giving the most honest advice. (*WMW*, 182–3; *WMYT*, v, p. 33) When he meets the widow, however, it emerges that Flavio has wooed her partly through his father's poetry, while the father increasingly forms a relationship with her instead of Hilarie. The shifting alignments of the characters perform

---

[6] Eric Blackall, *op. cit.* p. 265.

[7] *Wilhelm Meisters Wanderjahre, Goethes Werke, op. cit.* vol. viii, p. 170; *Wilhelm Meister's Years of Travel*, trans. H. M. Waidson (London: Calder, 1982) vol. 4, p. 24. References are given to the English text although the translations are my own.

a fugal interaction of life phases and functions, while Goethe typically unfolds the personal histories with the same eye that seeks to understand the general processes of nature. This effect is enhanced by the brevity and multiplicity of the stories, and by our consciousness of them as stories with some exemplary import. In contrast to the tragic outcome of his separately published novella *Elective Affinities*, in which the 'scientific' perception of the personal psychology as natural process is made explicit, these four characters eventually recover a proper generational relation, although Hilarie has difficulty in digesting the change. Once again, in this most substantial of the interpolated narratives, the situation echoes that of the principal narrative as Hilarie echoes Hersilie. Furthermore, in this case, these characters from what has seemed a separate sub-narrative, read as if it were a work of fiction, subsequently enter the main narrative. Hilarie and the young widow later travel to Italy and meet Wilhelm by Lake Como where he has gone with an artist friend who wishes to paint the region associated with Mignon, herself a character from what now feels like a different kind of novel. It is here, in an atmosphere of discreet flirtation and in the company of a professional painter, that Wilhelm realises the dilettantism of his own artistic ambitions.

The next major interpolation is in the mode of fantasy as a loquacious barber tells a story of a failed relationship from his youth. This was with a beautiful, wealthy, and mysterious young woman who trusted him to look after a casket he is forbidden to open. She is the princess of a race of tiny beings who need her to intermarry with a human being in order for them not to dwindle out of existence entirely. The casket is the palace where she lives when at her normal size. The barber's unreliability and unfaithfulness, and above all his inability to respect her privacy as symbolised by the casket, prevent him becoming the husband and father that she needs him to be. His second story of 'The Dangerous Wager' is in the farcical mode of the picaresque novel and concerns his insulting an older man by winning a bet that he can pull him by the nose.

The last major interpolation comes from a stranger who joins the Tower Society as they have gathered to discuss their future plans, especially the project of establishing a group in America, and tells them a story from his own youth entitled 'Not too Far'. It begins with a father awaiting with his children the return of his errant wife from a ball. This father rather lacks than imposes authority, and completes the series of interpolated turns on the theme of parental authority. The end of the principal narrative occurs after an episode between Hersilie and Felix. He is by now a young man and expresses his love for her while impetuously breaking the key in the casket she has been protecting. She repulses not so much him as his over-eagerness, and he alarms her by rushing off in a desperate state reminiscent of Werther before his suicide. He falls into the river and nearly drowns but is saved by the now medically trained Wilhelm. He revives to affirm his mature identity as one of the group and is now referred to as brother, rather than son, to Wilhelm.

Although these stories clearly reflect on Wilhelm, or his situation, the effect is rather to gather him into a set of fugal variations on the theme of paternal authority at large. Where maturity is often defined by contrast with the mistakes and follies of youth, this work concentrates on the temptations peculiar to middle-age and the exercise of educational authority. Fatherhood provides a general context of responsibility within which to explore a variety of educational or authoritative relations. None of the characters in the interpolated tales exercises any crudely external will, yet this is precisely what exposes them to more subtle dangers.

Part of the effect of this very different novel lies in its retrospective implication for the reading of *WMA*. Goethe, who was precipitated into publishing the 1821 version by the publication of a sequel by another author, one Friedrich Wilhelm Pustkuchen, was highly aware of Cervantes who was similarly sparked by Alonso Fernández de Avellaneda's spurious sequel into hurrying Part II of *Don Quixote* into print in 1615. Cervantes turned the occasion to brilliant and profound effect by incorporating both the 'false' Quixote, and the false *Quixote*, into the metafictional self-reflections of Part II so that his original novel became Part I of an essentially new work which has only been known since then in its combined form. Goethe's sequel has a more ambiguous and semi-detached relation to its predecessor, growing 'from' it in a double sense. For the continuation of the action, and development of the characters, goes with a radical distancing in meaning and form. Above all, it develops the self-deconstructing potentiality of the last books of *WMA* allowing the reader to appreciate more positively the thematic and narrative turn which was otherwise only hinted at in predominantly negative ways. The danger was of seeing *WMA* as merely losing its momentum rather than regrouping its forces for a radical change in direction. Don Quixote, who is not capable of internal change, is broken by the experiences of Part II, whereas Wilhelm, with his greater pliability, is absorbed in every sense into the new action. And just as the compelling impact of the first five books of *WMA* influenced the nineteenth-century tradition of the *Bildungsroman*, and European fiction at large, so it is the modern, post-Nietzschean fate of *Bildung* which most enables a proper appreciation of this Goethean turn.

Whereas Cervantes' narrative purports to be translated from an Arab historian, Goethe's is collectively produced by the characters themselves and the previous emphasis on the writing down of experience is raised to a new power. The opening premise is that Wilhelm is writing it as a journal sent to Natalie to read as he travels and he gives a significant hint to the reader, as well as to Natalie, in warning her that his account will not be personal, introspective, and emotional but objective and factual. The journal convention, although not rigidly adhered to, creates a sharp contrast with the opening of *WMA* which began with a long, self-involved account of his boyhood enthusiasm for the puppet theatre told in person to a sleepy, hard-working Marianne. Whereas that episode revealed his naive self-enclosure, the act of writing in the later novel is a way of objectifying individual experience, and opening it to collaborative understanding and judgement. It gradually becomes evident that Wilhelm's narrative will form part of an archive, kept by Makaria, and from which the material of the novel has been drawn. Unlike the individual scrolls placed side by side in the Tower library, these materials are to interact in the novel we are reading. Likewise, the narrative of both parts of the novel ends with a series of aphoristic reflections from Makaria's archive which give the generalised form of the aphorism an even greater, and more problematic, prominence than in *WMA*.

As the journal convention dissolves into omniscient narration, the narrative structure marginalises Wilhelm both as a centre of consciousness and as a teleological principle. Since he has already found Natalie, his years of wandering are explicitly released from this traditional narrative telos. In 1851, the novelist Karl Gutzkow was to develop explicitly the notion of a spatialised novel, in which the materials are arranged *nebeneinander*, or spatially, rather than *nacheinander*, temporally, and *WMJ* already seeks such a form reflecting that of the archive on which it is based.[8] The spatialising effect in the novel is also enhanced by the enormous discrepancy between the time accorded to the main narrative and the time required for its action. At the beginning Felix is a small boy: at the end he is a young man. Wilhelm meanwhile forms the decision to become a surgeon and is later assumed to have completed the training. Goethe suggested in *WMA* that the novelistic, as opposed to the dramatic, hero delays the action with reflection, density of inner life, and the slow process of change. On this view, Hamlet was exceptional: a novelistic hero within a dramatic structure, and it is only by virtue of Shakespeare's 'double time' that he is able to mature from the Wittenberg student to the philosophical renunciation of the thirty-year-old in the graveyard.

In that respect, if the parallel between Wilhelm and Hamlet in *WMA* hints at the principle of delay associated with his maturing, in *WMJ* Wilhelm is hardly allowed such a degree of interiority and rather profits from the

---

[8] Karl Gutzkow, postscript to his novel *Die Ritter von Geisle* (1850–1). See also Waltraud Maierhofer, *Wilhelm Meisters Wanderjahre und der Roman des Nebeneinander* (Bielefeld: Aisthesis Verlag, 1990).

book's temporal compressions and elisions. Indeed, the novel recalls once again Cervantes whose interpolated episodes were an indirect way of implying a personal interiority that was not otherwise dramatised. The reader has a powerful impression of knowing Don Quixote and Sancho intimately but neither internal reflection nor authorial omniscience plays a significant part in this.[9] Whereas Cervantes created by oblique means the sense of personal interiority which was to become the central interest of the European novel, Goethe now runs the generic evolution backwards to transcend the personal in Wilhelm. If Wilhelm's personal journal dissolves into a residual convention linking episodes and encounters quite separate from his life, this reflects in a radical, formal way the fact of his maturity. Octavio Paz has noted that the real sign of maturity is a shift in attention from the adolescent's absorption with the self to concentration on an external activity.[10] Significance begins to inhere in the activity, or in the object, itself. The mature self becomes a medium, or tool, while self-knowledge and development may well continue to occur within the activity in a way that could perhaps not be achieved by direct self-inspection or the sheer exercise of moral will. Whereas the Wilhelm of the initiation scene still hardly evinced the maturity that seemed formally to be ascribed to him, the later book treats him structurally as mature, as one who performs a function in a world of which he is not the moral centre.

Wilhelm has joined a group of like-minded, yet highly varied, individuals and personal development has become social and collaborative, arising from constant conversational exchanges as they pool their strengths and watch out for each other's weaknesses. Wilhelm is importantly affected by his conversations with Montan, while he himself acts as mentor to another character, Lenardo, upon whom he imposes renunciant conditions. Having tracked down a bailiff's daughter, the 'Nut Brown Maid', whom Lenardo had to leave in painful circumstances some years before, and for whom he seems now to have a rather excessive concern, Wilhelm ascertains that she is well established and married but tells Lenardo of this only on condition that he refrain from visiting her. Collaboration between equals has a different dynamic and responsibility from the pedagogical relation with an acknowledged pupil although, once this is recognised, it has consequences for the pupil relation too in so far as the pupil is also an independent individual *in potentio*. It can be difficult to distinguish the legitimate exercise of pedagogical authority from personal imposition, a distinction likely to be further blurred by the

---

[9] I discuss this in 'Sancho's Governorship and the "Vanitas" Theme in *Don Quixote Part II*', *MLR* 77/2 (Apr. 1982) pp. 325–38.

[10] Octavio Paz, *The Labyrinth of Solitude*, trans. Lysander Kemp (London: Penguin, 1985) pp. 191–2.

desire to reproduce oneself in the pupil as Hippias sought to do with Agathon.

This distinction becomes more important as the educative goal is no longer justified by the degree of moral and psychological universality still assumed by Rousseau. Rousseau could reasonably suppose that the reproduction of a being essentially similar to himself, or at least to his best ideal of himself, was the appropriate goal. Goethe, by contrast, acknowledges radical difference between individuals, and whole cultures, to the extent of seeing not just their temperaments but their intellectual universes as quasi-natural features essentially incommensurable and not open to change through argument or pedagogy. Anyone lacking a finely attuned awareness of this is in danger of misjudging pedagogical authority. This recognition is a running theme of the series of aphorisms with which the whole novel concludes. For example: 'The latest philosophy of our western neighbours bears witness to the fact that man always returns to what is inborn in him, whatever gestures he may make. And how should this not be so, since it is this innate element that determines his nature and his way of life.' (*WMW*, 464; *WMYT*, vi, 123) Johann Gottfried Herder was a significant mentor to the young Goethe and, according to this distinctly Herderian view, the different thought worlds of individuals and cultures cannot be assessed simply by universal criteria of reason and evidence. They have also an organic character: just as there would be no point in the tiger persuading the leopard to change its spots for stripes. Goethe's irony towards the French Enlightenment here, as towards almost the whole of professional philosophy, rests on an unshakeable sense of his own more subtle and comprehensive mode of thought. And it is appropriate that Goethe's own historical situatedness as a German of a specific moment is inscribed in the narrative viewpoint. By the same token, however, although his aphorism points to a radical scepticism about the effectiveness of intellectual argument, it does not imply falseness or hollowness so much as the need to understand what Nietzsche would call its 'genealogy', its relation to a given life form. And whereas Nietzsche's genealogy would seek to unmask, Goethe's rather indicates the specific necessity of its rootedness. This suggests the limited possibilities of pedagogical formation conducted against the natural grain although there may be a superficial and transitory impression of success.

It is partly to respect this principle that Wilhelm is persuaded by Montan that he should not educate Felix himself but send him to the curious institution known as the Pedagogical Province in which the discovery and nurture of individual talent is a cardinal purpose. A father, however well-meaning, or precisely because of his good intentions, may be the least suitable person to conduct directly the education of his son. In some ways, the Province focuses the character of the novel at large. Wilhelm makes two visits to it: one as he first investigates its suitability and the second after Felix has been there for some time. A supervisor explains to him the institutional principles and practices in an explicitly phased way. His second visit is more revealing as he is in a better position to appreciate what he is being told. (*WMW*, 164–5; *WMYT*, v, 19–20).

The Province institutionalises the principle of 'readiness' which has governed Wilhelm's less formally conducted education, and the same motif pervades the novel more generally. 'St Joseph the Second', for example, only tells his story to Wilhelm because he senses his readiness to appreciate it. (*WMW*, 17; *WMYT*, i, 23) Although the readiness principle was Rousseau's there is a sharp contrast to the seclusion of Emile in that the Pedagogical Province is large enough to be a miniature society and economy in which the boys discover their individual talents by performing the various activities of adult society. The institution seeks a careful balance between social development and individuality, as is especially evident in the matter of uniform dress. Uniform is deliberately rejected as it blocks the child's acquiring that personal balance between social form and individual expression that the institution seeks to foster. The blend of social convention, practicality, fashion, and individual taste expressed in sartorial choice is a conscious aspect of the educative process though one requiring little active direction. Indeed, the institution has learned the power of collective pressure, or fashion, and the greatest danger is of the pupils dressing identically. When this happens, the given style is quietly discouraged.

The pupils conduct their daily lives within a principle of reverence which is not specifically religious or social, and implies no specific locus of ultimate authority. Their three formal gestures, with arms folded on the chest with head upwards; arms behind the back with head bowed; and standing in an upright forward-looking posture, are equivalent to what in other historical establishments might be salutes to a flag or postures of prayer. The gestures express non-sectarian, non-doctrinal reverence for three domains: what is above them, which might include a belief in the divine; what is beneath them in the living earth; and what is on their own plane as the society of other human beings. Reverence for something beyond the self is inculcated from the outset in a supra-personal spirit that is not readily invested in the person of the educator. The Pedagogical Province is a semi-utopian conception in which Goethe explores, with tongue partly in cheek yet with a symbolic earnestness, educational principles and proposals that came in the wake of Rousseau.[11]

---

[11] Blackall gives a useful summary of the secondary literature on the educational theories enshrined in the Province. Blackall, *op. cit.* pp. 317–18.

There is, for example, an ironic allusion to Wilhelm's earlier pursuits in the institution's policy, when a boy shows a talent for theatre, of sending him to exercise it elsewhere. Maybe there is even some authorial self-reference here too. But if it is often hard, as in *Emile*, to draw the line between practical proposals and utopian fancy, this is an indication that the whole episode requires a more symbolic mode of reading. The *Bildungsroman*, with its blend of realism and artifice, explores the relation of principle to practice in a thickly realised yet philosophical spirit and the Pedagogical Province compresses this generic ambivalence into a self-conscious focus. Yet despite its utopian or philosophical heightening, if one faced in the abstract a choice between the Pedagogical Province and the English nineteenth-century public school, and without having the contingent information that the one is a fiction while the other existed historically, a sane observer might find the former not only preferable but more credible. The discouraging of uniform dress, for example, has a practical meaning well understood in the daily practice of the European continent, yet still lost to this day on many British practitioners of education. (*WMW*, 166; *WMYT*, v, 21) The fact that uniform is indeed powerfully symbolic, that it has a psychological impact, and that it rules out inappropriate individualism or clothes snobbery, all the arguments commonly adduced in its favour, are precisely what makes it damaging within a different educational conception.

The mirroring between episodes, such as the thematic use of theatre, can be seen in the way the otherwise unrelated 'Story of the Man of Fifty' includes a parody of the pedagogical process explained immediately before in the Province episodes. The Major, as he becomes his son's rival, slips into the role of pupil and seeks the help of an actor friend in the art of appearing young. As soon as the Major confesses his desire to acquire such cosmetic skills, his friend imposes a rigorous and all-encompassing routine on his 'pupil'. The envisaged stages of initiation will lead to the revelation of the 'higher secrets' of the 'art' which the actor will 'open' to him. (*WMW*, 177–8; *WMYT*, v, 30) As well as the sinister suggestion of black arts, this echoes the graded phases of the boys' education in the Pedagogical Province. Meanwhile, the motives of the educator are put into question. The actor is only too willing to instruct him, remarking: 'Remember, my friend, that man has an intrinsic desire to proselytise; to produce in others, outside himself, the appearance of whatever he prizes; to make them enjoy what he enjoys, and to represent and find himself in them.' (*WMW*, 176–7; *WMYT*, v, 29) There is a hint of the Faust/Mephisto relation as the Major allows himself to be seduced into an ambition, not so much sinful as against the course of nature, while the seducer figure makes many sensible and true observations of a general kind. Once again, although this aphoristic reflection is true and pertinent, it is a ray of light from a dark source and provides no illumination for the Major in his present condition.

As he recovers his moral equilibrium, the Major is relieved to escape the tedious routines required for the appearance of eternal youth. The healthy organism reasserts itself, as it often does in education. Hence the relatively little positive damage done by bad teaching, of which the hidden evil lies rather in the time it wastes. This touches another significant difference from the earlier novel. Being more concerned with pedagogical responsibility than the *de facto* acquisition of experience, *WMJ* is less sympathetic than *WMA* to the principle of fruitful error. In the novel at large what is at stake is not the happy chances of experience, or the individual benefits of error as argued by the Abbé, but the proper conduct of those charged with pedagogical responsibility. In this novel, many would-be mentors, unlike Rousseau's ideal governor, are subject to their own personal proclivities. Hence the 'Story of the Man of Fifty' places its reflections on pedagogy within a story of adult folly while the Province, with its almost hermetic, utopian concentration on the formative process, is embedded in an overall narrative exploring the forces with which its pupils will have to contend in real life. Throughout the switchback experiences of the novel, the pedagogical relation is constantly refracted, reversed, compared, and parodied even as it is earnestly pursued.

Education as Collaborative Fiction

It is evident that the changed conception of educational formation is reflected in a different narrative form. Indeed, the reader may even wonder, as with the Stephen Dedalus of Joyce's *Portrait* and *Ulysses*, whether Wilhelm is strictly speaking the 'same' character or rather two characters from different novels sharing a common body of allusion. There is a fine line between a naturalistic reading that assumes a substantive, complex 'Wilhelm' behind both versions and the retrospective creation of a new character as Wilhelm's opening journal entry significantly modifies our sense of his earlier self. For example, having decided to become a doctor, he writes to Natalie about his boyhood recollection of a country boy who was drowned but might have survived if skilled medical assistance had been available. Wilhelm tells it, very convincingly, as having made a profound impression on him and as underlying his present decision. Yet since this important experience is nowhere hinted at in the narrative of his early life in *WMA*, it indicates how arbitrary the story of a life is likely to be. As the influence of his new companions has guided Wilhelm to develop a useful skill instead of his previous enthusiasm for the theatre, the anecdote is clearly to some unknowable degree an *ex post facto* rationale for his decision. That does not mean that it was not genuinely important, but that its importance can only be retrospectively recognised. Likewise, but for his infatuation with the theatre, and with Marianne, his childhood enthusiasm for the puppet theatre might have remained unrecalled from the background of passive memory. What goes into the narrative of a life is not internally arbitrary, yet it is so by objective criteria outside the subject's life. The archival narrative of *WMJ* plays actively on this borderline where the horizon of the self so closely parallels that of a constructed fiction.

Moreover, *WMJ* constantly introduces written materials which foreground their own textual production, and thereby that of the novel itself. The formal self-consciousness which hovered authorially over the Wilhelm of *WMA* is now absorbed by the major characters as they collectively create the record, and means, of their own development. As part of this, Wilhelm has to write, rather than speak, to Natalie following the peculiar condition of travel imposed on him by his new friends. The subtitle, *or the Renunciants*, has multiple significances in, and for, the novel but renunciation applies very flexibly to persons and circumstances. Indeed, since Wilhelm has chosen to join the Society, this condition, like monastic vows, is both imposed and volitional. Hence, when he makes his decision to become a surgeon, and requires a permanent location for his training, the permission is readily granted. The renunciant conditions, being at once firm and flexible, are like artistic conventions which are freely chosen because they concentrate and enable, yet can themselves be modified by the internal needs of the creativity they help to engender. And this is more than a mere analogy since the renunciant condition imposed on Wilhelm is equally a restriction on the novel itself.

Indeed, the greatest renunciant in the text is no single character but the author, or more strictly, the authorial function as the novel itself embodies the art of renunciation. Wilhelm's renunciant condition of moving on every three nights imposes a formal restriction on the author as when Wilhelm and the artist meet Hilarie and the widow in Italy. Although both men wish to stay and enjoy the company of the women, Wilhelm's restriction imposes itself on the freedom of the narrative. Hence when the women suddenly disappear one morning their attributed motivation reflects, as much as it resolves, a narrative condition. But this relatively mechanical condition suggests more radical renunciations on the part of the author. Goethe seems deliberately to eschew novelistic qualities which he had already shown himself to possess in abundance. His previous writings show him capable of psychological inwardness and penetration in the representation of character; of poetic depth and suggestiveness; and of narrative power and suspense. Yet he largely eschews these, and makes the eschewal itself a significant aspect of the project. Wilhelm is treated authorially in the 'objective' spirit that he was seeking to achieve in his journal. Even more overtly than in *WMA*, characters' names reinforce their functionality. 'St Joseph the Second' voluntarily enacts a form of life he sees as determined (*bestimmte, WMW*, 17) by his parent's choice of his name while the bailiff's daughter who arouses Lenardo's concern is known by different names as she is encountered in different phases of her life. She is in turn Valerine, the Nut Brown Maid, Susanna and die *Gute-Schöne* (the Good and Beautiful). The English word 'renounce' has lost the etymological overtone of utterance still present in 'announce' or 'pronounce' but, in so far as the German term *Entsagung* retains a palpable link with 'saying', it suggests how Goethe exercises the most radical form of renunciation: the power of his own creative utterance.

In this way, even as the novel becomes more pervasively symbolic, it fulfils even more strikingly the withdrawal from poetry already effected towards the end of *WMA* with the 'prosaic' explanation of Mignon and the Harpist. As Wilhelm moves on to the next phase of his life, the sequel seems to be deliberately a novel without 'poetry'. Even the 'apprenticeship' motif, which was essentially a metaphor for Wilhelm's dispersed and unwitting development through the by-paths of error in *WMA*, gives way in *WMJ* to the literal process of medical training. Of course, literally speaking the novel does have poetry, including a great Goethean lyric with which the work ends. Yet even here, as the speaker contemplates Schiller's skull mixed up with other bones in the charnel house, the Hamlet theme is reworked in the less romantic, almost scientific, spirit of the new book. The theme is turned outward to the world with the concluding reflection that, although Schiller has died, the efficacy of his writing will live on. Although this is a traditional argument for the value of poetry, the note of worldly utility has now acquired a special weight within it.

In the same spirit, Goethe takes a knowing artistic risk in giving Lenardo's detailed written account of the working practices in the cottage industry of spinners and weavers. Lenardo is fascinated by this complex communal activity, and wishes to record for the archive a form of life imminently threatened by modernity. Usefulness becomes the criterion on which other values rest. As was to be the case with William Morris, fine art is closely linked to craft and some of the feckless characters from the theatre company, who had been a focus of extraordinary novelistic energy in *WMA*, are encountered again with their personal talents usefully developed. The flirtatious and flighty actress Philine has the skill to assess people's bodies with the eye so as to make perfectly fitting clothes for them without measuring. The art of theatre itself is now seen through a critical, almost Rousseauan, eye. The only other actor in the book is the friend who encourages the Major's artificial rejuvenation, and art generally is considered, if not quite with Rousseau's moral literalism, then by a criterion of realistic, or truthful, representation. The Pedagogical Province gives careful attention to artistic training and one of its guiding principles is expressed in the pupils' song:

> As Nature in its many images
> Reveals only *one* God,
> So through the wide fields of art
> Runs *one* eternal meaning:
> This is the sense of truth
> Which merely adorns itself with beauty.
>
> (*WMW*, 255; *WMYT*, v, 93)

Similarly, Wilhelm takes up surgery, then regarded as among the lowest orders of medical practice, precisely for its hands-on practicality.

It is evident that this novel's renunciations bear specifically on the developmental process of *Bildung*. Thematically, this is most strikingly focused through Montan who forcibly asserts the importance of a specialist knowledge favoured by modern conditions as opposed to the ideal of rounded education through a plurality of subjects.

> ... versatility only makes ready the element in which the one-sided man, who has just now been given sufficient room, can be effective. Yes, the present is the time for specialization; happy is he who understands this and is active in this sense on his own behalf and for others... The best thing is to limit oneself to one craft. For the most limited person it will always remain a craft, for someone better it will be an art, and when the best man does one thing, he does everything, or, to be less paradoxical, in the *one* thing he does expertly he sees the symbol for everything that is done expertly.
>
> (*WMW*, 37; *WMYT*, iv, 38–9)

The novel endorses this view, and the historical analysis on which it is based. The members of the Tower Society reflect on how to live in the new circumstances of modernity and impose, as the universal condition of group membership, the contribution of a specialist skill. Wilhelm becomes a surgeon in response to this requirement.

The specialism theme had an urgent personal significance for Goethe as well as being a major question for his historical epoch. Adam Smith had set forth the economic, and social, advantages of the division of labour, while Schiller in his *Letters on the Aesthetic Education of Man* had regarded the division of functions increasingly required by modern circumstances as a damaging division of the self. The theme of alienation in the conditions of modern labour would be taken up most famously by Marx, but Schiller was more concerned with intellectual specialism. So was Goethe, and his positive appreciation of specialism was precisely within the context of a desired wholeness. Cultural memory still preserves the phrase 'renaissance man' as a potent ideal of personal range within an integral self and if any historical individual since the Renaissance could make a claim to realising this then it is surely Goethe. That makes his turn to specialism particularly significant, if initially surprising, and the important key was the danger of dilettantism he increasingly detected at the heart of the *Bildung* ideal. Dilettantism as the mistaken belief in the possession of artistic talent is an illusion that may be fostered by genuine artistic sensibility. Werther was not just emotionally immature and incidentally a dilettante. Dilettantism is the root of his condition. And as Jarno makes bluntly clear to Wilhelm towards the end of *WMA*, he is the classic amateur actor: identifying with the role rather than creating it with professional detachment. Changes in the meaning of 'dilettante' and 'amateur' indicate in themselves an epochal shift. From honorific terms denoting personal dedication they acquired the derogatory implication of superficial skill in a hobby. For Goethe, the attempt to achieve personal wholeness through a number of activities became a recipe for a multiply self-reinforcing dilettantist illusion while mastery of a single activity disciplines the personality more truly and realistically as a training in thoroughness. It also enforces a sense of the activity rather than the self as the goal. Specialism provides a significant antidote to the danger of absorbing the world into the self.

Moreover, in becoming a surgeon, Wilhelm turns not just to a useful specialism, but to the world of science which has a different relation to the past and to cultural transmission. At that time there was still a close connection, or continuity, between scientific and artistic modes of anatomical knowledge. Artists as well as doctors needed to dissect, and medical knowledge was recorded in artistic images and models. In contrast to 'St Joseph the Second', who built his home and place of work on the site of a religious building, Wilhelm meets a sculptor who no longer has a trade in his specialism of ecclesiastical statues and anticipates the day when he will make complete models of the human body for medical students to use instead of corpses. In the meantime he keeps them hidden as if consciously on the cusp of such an historical cultural turn. Goethe was the last figure of comparable stature whose cosmic vision as an artist was at one with science. His historical world did not as yet impose an absolute diremption on him. Of course, this was at some cost: as has been noted, he fell on the wrong side of some scientific questions but some he got right and, more importantly, his poetic vision was fully informed by a cosmic conception that was not merely 'poetic'. A few decades later, in *Thus Spoke Zarathustra*, Nietzsche would criticise the falsity of the 'poets' even as he expressed himself by deeply poetic means. Similarly, in this novel Goethe does not abandon poetry but seeks a quality of representation consonant with the spirit of science as suggested by his poem to Hafiz quoted above. The poem is a manifesto for Goethe's own poetry and world view. When Wilhelm travels to Italy with the painter his own eyes are opened as he begins to look on nature in the same way as his artist friend, and learns: '... sensitive as he was, to see the world with those eyes in which Nature unfolded the open secret of her beauty.' (*WMW*, 229; *WMYT*, v, 71–2) For Goethe, both art and science are encounters with nature by which the world is properly seen.

Hence *WMJ* seeks to present the world with as little imposed colouring, or 'poetic' heightening, as possible. In *WMA* there was considerable play with motifs from contemporary popular fiction such as the secret society. These motifs were put to serious work even as they enabled Goethe to ironise the whole project. In *WMJ* such play is in an even more throwaway spirit. The mysterious casket found early on by Felix occasions his final, sexually charged, meeting with Hersilie, in which he breaks the key in his impatience, but we never discover any literal contents. It is almost ostentatiously dropped as a mere device that has served its purpose, a concluding emblem of the deliberate anticlimax, the eschewal of, or indifference to, poetic depth in the book as a whole.

In its formal avoidance of wholeness, the novel takes the reader into an open-ended heuristic process. General conditions and attitudes are affirmed, like the gestures of reverence in the Pedagogical Province, and the work is full of local insight and suggestion, but it nonetheless retains an essential reticence and scepticism towards any all-encompassing wisdom; and especially as embodied in its own form. The two parts end with a series of aphorisms and a poem. The final set of aphorisms, explicitly taken 'from Makaria's archive', (*WMW*, 460; *WMYT*, vi, 120) emphasises the source and nature of the whole narrative. The aphorisms enact the repeated attempt at reaching understanding as general truth while jostling and modifying each other so that no one generality encompasses the implication of the work. The necessary impulse to such an all-embracing statement is relativised even as it is exercised, and many of the final aphorisms are implicit reflections on the rationale of the work itself. The opening word of the final sequence is 'secrets': 'The secrets of life's path may, and can, not be revealed . . .' while the theme of the aphorism is repeatedly explored in the text.

The value of aphoristic wisdom and moral maxims had been a matter of debate throughout Goethe's major fiction, as in the conflict between Werther and Albert on the rival merits of individual narrative and general statements of principle. Even more strategic is the emptiness of the maxims which Jarno points out on Wilhelm's Certificate of Apprenticeship. In *WMJ*, when Wilhelm meets the first internal narrator, 'St Joseph the Second', he wishes to hear his story rather than 'generalities' (*WMW*, 15; *WMYT*, iv, 22), but as the book progresses the characters are embroiled in a collective pursuit of understanding for which the aphorism, precisely by its limitations, is both the means and the emblem. If the maxims of the Certificate of Apprenticeship seemed parodically unhelpful as practical guides to conduct, Hersilie attributes a talismanic rather than an instructional value to her uncle's maxims which are displayed all over the house. He has derived the custom from Eastern peoples who display quotations from the Koran 'more in order to honour', she says 'than to understand, them'. (*WMW*, 68; *WMYT*, iv, 64) She also comments on their frequent reversibility of meaning, while the Foolish Pilgrim hides herself, respectably but manipulatively, behind moral maxims. (*WMW* 59; *WMYT*, iv, 56)

Whereas maxims are brief guides to conduct, aphorisms are condensed attempts at understanding. Taken individually, they could be the gist in miniature of a possible novel. But as collected in the collaborative archive, they jostle each other irresolvably and tend even individually to focus the difficulty of immediate action or judgement. Goethe is acutely conscious of the deceptive transposition from experience to idea, especially when the idea is required to be valid in the thought world of another. As Montan observed in one of his first conversations, the very fact of utterance produces its own falsities or miscomprehensions. (*WMW*, 32: *WMYT*, iv, 35) This thought returns as one of the aphorisms in the archive: 'What I truly know, I know only for myself: it is seldom useful to speak it as that usually excites contradiction, deadlock and standstill.' (*WMW*, 476; *WMYT*, vi, 132) Hence, in the teaching relation, 'The genuine pupil learns how to develop the unknown out of the known and so to approach the master.' (*WMW*, 460; *WMYT*, vi, 20) This last aphorism, which occurs in both the Certificate of Apprenticeship and Makaria's archive, is perhaps susceptible of different interpretations in the light of these different contexts. It seems initially to mean that what cannot be taught can be worked out by the pupil, as largely happens with Wilhelm in the first novel. But emphasising the generational experience of historical change to which all parties have to adjust in the second novel, it might suggest how the pupil develops something new out of what the master knows and thereby approaches him not in content but in authority and understanding. Indeed, a young pupil embodies this natural principle of organic development: 'When a man comes together with a woman and a boy is created, so there comes from the known something unknown.' (*WMW*, 461; *WMYT*, vi, 121) As these aphorisms explore what it is to be 'wise' (weis) so they insist on each individual finding his own 'manner' (Weise) of being so. In the aphorism already quoted about French thought, this second meaning perhaps hovers over the concluding words: 'Man always returns to what is inborn in him. And how could it be otherwise as this determines his nature and way of life [*Lebensweise*].'

R. H. Stephenson has closely analysed Goethe's aphorisms as 'wisdom literature' for which an essentially aesthetic relation to truth is the condition.[12] In that respect, Makaria is as much a textual definition as a character in the fiction. After her brief personal appearance she disappears into the texture of the whole. If Natalie, rather than her pious Aunt, the Canoness, was the truly 'beautiful soul' of *WMJ*, Makaria is the culmination of that motif and is manifest more as a moving spirit, and a characteristic form of written utterance, than as a person. The aphorisms represent, that is to say, a striving for impersonality. And yet at the same time, these final aphorisms are often undisguisedly Goethe's own and, as with the reflection on French thought quoted earlier, speak from a specific standpoint. The combination of impersonality and personality is quintessentially Goethean. Blackall emphasises Goethe's conception of the novel, in opposition to the epic, as a *subjective* form.[13] Likewise, Dilthey contrasts Shakespeare's giving himself to the world with Goethe's absorbing the world into himself.[14] His frank use of his own voice at once resists enclosing the work within its own fictive space, and defines its impersonal purview with the signature of his own experience. At the same time, it defines his experience, or the meaning of his experience, as historically representative.

In that respect, the spirit of renunciation represents more than Goethe's own *Altersweisheit*, for it is also, indeed primarily, epochal. Living at a time of extraordinary turbulence and cardinal change, his acute sense of historical loss required a comparable degree of faith in the future. As another aphorism puts it: 'It is rare for someone in old age to become historical to himself, and for his contemporaries to become historical to him, so that he has no one left with whom he either will, or can, engage in controversy.' (*WMW*, 465; *WMYT*, vi, 124) Bakhtin, in his essay on the *Bildungsroman* in European culture, remarked on Goethe's historical sense as a quality of literal vision.[15] Looking at a landscape, he saw in it what it had been and what it might become. Whereas St Joseph the Second, in the rather idyllic opening story, has built a traditional life on the ruins of a monastery, Lenardo records the cottage industry of spinning and weaving as a highly integrated way of life under imminent threat from industrial mechanisation. Goethe sees this epochal change as more fundamental than the political conflicts associated

---

[12] *Goethe's Wisdom Literature: a Study in Aesthetic Transformation* (Bern, Frankfurt/M, and New York: 1983).
[13] Blackall, *op. cit.* p. 275.   [14] *Poetry and Experience*, p. 264.
[15] M. M. Bakhtin, 'The *Bildungsroman* and its Significance in the History of Realism (Towards an Historical Typology of the Novel)', in *Speech Genres and Other Late Essays*, trans. Vera W. McGee, ed. Caryl Emerson and Michael Holquist (Austin: University of Texas Press, 1986), pp. 10–59.

with the French Revolution and, in Bakhtin's formulation, Goethe looks on this ordinary scene with the intense historical interest it would yield for a future generation. So too, the turn to science is as much epochal as personal, seeking to discover the deeper processes of the time as in Montan's argument for specialism. And science, even in the conservative mode of Goethe, looks necessarily to the future.

Where Rousseau envisaged an education in parallel with the argument of *The Social Contract*, Goethe contemplates it within the governing process of history. Just as the individual finds his own form, so history takes its course in a way that it is useless to lament, and damaging to resist. The Tower Society accepts all political views in its members, not just out of tolerance, but reflecting their understanding of ideas as such. If ideas are epiphenomenal in the life of the individual, they are even more so in the process of history. These characters are all caught in a conscious dilemma between the past and the future, their different outlooks being expressed, both practically and symbolically, as the choice between America and Europe. Susanna, the Nut Brown Maid, having married into a weaver family, is almost immediately widowed and then courted by the friend and business partner of her husband. Although she was on the point of emigrating with her husband, her new suitor believes they should make a fresh life at home. Loyalty to her husband's memory makes the choice especially fraught for her and in the end her suitor marries her sister and with the family money modern equipment is bought to secure the future for the whole valley of weavers. (*WMW*, 446–7: *WMYT*, vol. vi, 109) The novel itself seems to endorse neither view exclusively, and the group's debate about whether or not to go to America results in some going and some staying. Individuals follow their own aspirations and talents, while the novel's concern is rather with the quality of the choice, its rationale, and the personal aspirations it embodies. Whatever choice is made, however, historical change involves loss and the spirit of renunciation in a number of these personal choices is crucial to avoiding the various traps of excessive nostalgia, or of mere contempt for the past, or of a disabling fear of the future. An analysis of such damaging psychological dispositions towards history was to be the theme of the second of Nietzsche's *Untimely Meditations*.

Given the collaborative convention of the novel's creation, it is hard to say whether its unfinished nature is an artistic fault or dramatic realism. For it is 'unfinished' not as incomplete so much as unpolished, and permanently open to radical revision. Dramatically, the reader is privileged to read private papers not smoothed and tidied for an exoteric readership and there are several moments where the narrative makes a sudden textual splice. A letter of Lenardo switches abruptly from first to third person in the middle of a paragraph. (*WMW*, 350; *WMYT*, vi, 32) Since these jumps sometimes coincide, as in this case, with revisions of the 1821 text, they may be oversights; yet such a large oversight is difficult to credit while its internal naturalistic explanation is dramatically appropriate. The archive from which the novel is supposedly drawn is precisely an attempt to convert first person experience into general objective understanding, and to transpose the general understanding back into the personal. The problematic interplay of personal and general, of journal and aphorism, is the major preoccupation of the novel, and such jagged textual sutures draw attention precisely to the fault-line which it is the usual business of novelists, especially in the conventions of nineteenth-century realism, to smooth over. Hence, the apparently unfinished novel created from an archive of personal experience exposes dramatically the underlying problematic of the form.

At the same time, however, one hesitates to make too literalistic a case for a dramatic rationale. For we also sense the author using a highly condensed form, impatient of conventional naturalistic amplification, and experimentally open to radical change. In that respect, the novel is like a late Picasso sketch; quick expressive lines doing duty for what could be naturalistically elaborated. In this respect, the novel answers to a category of 'late' work explored by Edward Said in his last years. Said quotes Theodor Adorno on the late work of Beethoven:

The power of subjectivity in the late works of art is the irascible gesture with which it takes leave of the works themselves. It breaks their bounds, not in order to express itself, but in order, expressionless, to cast off the appearance of art. Of the works themselves it leaves only fragments behind, and communicates itself, like a cipher, only through blank spaces from which it has disengaged itself. Touched by death, the hand of the master sets free the masses of material that he used to form; its tears and fissures, witnesses to the finite powerlessness of the I confronted with the Being, are its final work.

As Said paraphrases it:

[the late works of Beethoven] constitute an event in the history of modern culture: a moment when the artist who is fully in command of his medium nevertheless abandons communication with the established social order of which he is a part and achieves a contradictory, alienated relationship with it. His late works are a form of exile from his milieu.[16]

Although Said follows Adorno in attributing these qualities to a spirit of Promethean rebellion which is opposite to the late Goethe's renunciation, the remarks seem eminently germane to Goethe's last novel and thereby suggest something more fundamental in the quality of lateness as such.

[16] *London Review of Books* (5 Aug 2004) p. 3.

In this strange last novel *Bildung* itself is one of the objects of renunciation even as the understanding of this requires a high level of culture. The novel hollows itself out from the inside, while assuming the cultural and historical input of the reader. If its implication has not been widely absorbed, it is above all the later fate of *Bildung* that brings it more clearly into view. For *Bildung* and modernity are in conflict, yet neither is relinquishable. Meanwhile the novel awaits its readers as consciously as the sculptor turned medical model-maker who hid his work until the culture was ready to use it. (*WMJ*, 326; *WMYT*, vi, 14) With its strange texture of lucid opacity, the novel seems to have been written pre-eminently in the spirit of the open secret. Ultimately, it was a book not even for grown-ups, but for the future, which is always both older and younger than the present. And the future, as far as both Goethe and *Bildung* were concerned, was to arrive in an especially significant way with Friedrich Nietzsche.

5

Nietzsche as Educator and the Implosion of *Bildung*

> Posthumous men—like me, for instance—are not so well understood as timely men, but they are *listened to* better. More precisely, we are never understood—and *hence* our authority.[1]
>
> They have learned badly and the best things not at all, they have learned everything too early and too fast...[2]

I noted at the outset that the tradition of negative pedagogy, and of the anxiety of authority, which I am tracing passes through many major thinkers, including those who think primarily in literary and fictional modes. In the mid-nineteenth century a significant such figure, for example, would be Søren Kierkegaard. As a profound religious thinker in an increasingly secular modernity, he found new ways of investigating the traditional religious concern with an order of truth, and an experience of belief, beyond what is rationally demonstrable, or even communicable. Moreover, his early thinking in *The Concept of Irony* (1841) indicates his interest in a literary means, and a philosophical outlook, which link him, on the one hand, to both Plato and late eighteenth-century German thought, notably that of Friedrich Schlegel, and on the other hand to the ironic superstructure of modern writers such as Joyce and Mann. Most significantly, his own mature thought was worked out in texts built around a variety of fictional pseudonyms while at the same time, in contrast to Schiller, he engaged the tension between the ethical and the aesthetic which had become more urgent in his own day. Nonetheless, as a religious thinker, he was ultimately most concerned with the relation to an enigmatic authority rather than with authority's relation to itself. In this respect, he provides significant terms for thinking about Kafka or Beckett, but for the more specific theme of exercising pedagogical authority within

---

[1] *Twilight of the Idols*, trans. R. J. Hollingdale (London: Penguin, 1990) p. 34.
[2] *Thus Spoke Zarathustra*, ed. R. J. Hollingdale (London: Penguin, 1969) p. 223.

the modern fate of *Bildung* it is Nietzsche who offers the most central focus. Moreover, Nietzsche's very positive meditation on Goethe throughout his career, combined with his influence on a variety of modern writers, allows the present story to be told with a detailed thickness of continuing motif.

Goethe provides a significant context for the joint implosion of pedagogical authority and the *Bildung* ideal in Nietzsche, for Nietzsche admired Goethe but was radically critical of the notion of *Bildung* as this was inherited in the mid to late nineteenth century, and especially as institutionalised in Germanophone state education. And Goethe himself, of course, was increasingly institutionalised within this tradition. Whereas Goethe in the Wilhelm Meister novels had radically questioned the project of *Bildung* while overwhelmingly embodying its ideal in himself, Nietzsche separated out these elements which were too much run together in the perception of him. While Goethe's formidably developed talents provided the insight and the motive to detect the danger of dilettantism he saw lurking at the heart of *Bildung*, it remained a highly personal theme for him precisely because of his own artistic aspirations. But the double-bind of an inauthenticity that can only be detected from the inside was carried over in Nietzsche as a more universal historical condition. Nietzsche saw at the secret heart of *Bildung* an unwitting nihilism and with this shift the internal logic becomes almost impossibly strained. How do you express such a critique in a way that can be generally understood; especially when the nature of the 'generality', at the level of both statement and audience, is what is in question?

Nietzsche's Critique of *Bildung*

The critique of *Bildung* is a central concern in Nietzsche's early writings and reaches its self-reflective culmination in *Thus Spoke Zarathustra* which he took to be his cardinal and most ambitious work. *TSZ* is in many respects a black hole at the centre of his thought, as is reflected in its reception history. One of his first works to be known in the Anglophone world in the early years of the twentieth century, and taken most usually as a direct expression of his 'doctrine', it provided at once a colourful and iconic focus for Nietzscheans and a vulnerable example of tediously self-regarding rhodomontade for his critics. Accordingly, in the middle decades of the century many serious students of Nietzsche would advise coming to *TSZ* only when properly familiar with his thought as expressed in more tangible and less aphoristic form. The last decades of the century, however, saw a remarkable resurgence of interest, placing *TSZ* once again at the centre of the *oeuvre*.[3] This accompanied a

---

[3] See, for example, R. Gooding-Williams, *Nietzsche's Dionysian Modernism* (Stanford and Cambridge: Stanford University Press and Cambridge University Press, 1993); Kathleen Higgins,

general shift of attention from the 'content' to the mode of his thought and I wish first to note how TSZ is already embryonic in the early writings for which the predicament of authority is an emergent consciousness seeking formal expression. The most relevant of the early pieces for the pedagogy and *Bildung* themes are his six lectures *On the Future of our Institutions of Cultural Education (Über die Zukunft unserer Bildungsanstalten)* and two of his *Untimely Meditations: The Uses and Disadvantages of History for Life* and *Schopenhauer as Educator.*

Nietzsche believed that the logic of post-religious modernity, the lengthy process which he called 'the death of God', must lead to nihilism. By the death of God he meant not just belief in a personal Deity but the infrastructure of cultural assumptions and practices for which God is the mythic expression. God's death is not the cause of this process but its final realisation. My expression 'lead to', therefore, softens the analysis by implying a speculative condition still to come whereas it is truly a condition already present but unconscious. The fact that this nihilism was self-conscious only in especially thoughtful individuals such as Ivan Karamasov is of little comfort since unconscious nihilism is the greater mischief. Ivan's shocked recognition that 'all is permitted' mitigates the implication of what he perceives while the unwitting nihilist continues to exercise his will-to-power through unexamined habits and opportunist rationalisations. It is possible, for example, to run a great institution, such as a commercial firm, or a nation state, or a university, so that it grows and increases in power, without any real connection to its stated values and purposes. The critique cuts more deeply than the distinction between civilisation and culture which protects the notion of culture by distinguishing it from the external forms of civilisation. The canker is at the heart.

In such a context, culture as a formal acquisition, far from changing this radical condition, may provide the most powerful means of external alibi and internal evasion. Kant had long ago instanced artistic connoisseurs as notoriously trivial, vexatious, and mean-spirited, while Schiller saw that aesthetic education could not substitute for moral character where that was lacking. Yet if for Schiller it was possible for unenlightened spirits to encounter aesthetic objects without undergoing the transformative experience of the aesthetic, the experience at least did no positive harm. In the essay on

---

Nietzsche's Zarathustra (Philadelphia: Temple University Press, 1987); Laurence Lampert, *Nietzsche's Teaching: an Interpretation of Thus Spoke Zarathustra* (New Haven and London: Yale University Press, 1986); Paul Loeb, 'Time, Power and Superhumanity', *Journal of Nietzsche Studies*, 21 (2001) pp. 27–41. Stanley Rosen, *The Mask of Enlightenment: Nietzsche's Zarathustra* (Cambridge: Cambridge University Press, 1995); Gary Shapiro, *Nietzschean Narratives* (Bloomington: Indiana University Press, 1989).

Schopenhauer, Nietzsche gives it a darker inflection, defining as follows the contemporary meaning of *Bildung*: 'To be cultivated means: to hide from oneself how wretched and base one is, how rapacious in going for what one wants, how insatiable in heaping it up, how shameless and selfish in enjoying it.'[4] In contrast, therefore, to the English term 'philistine', derived from Matthew Arnold, denoting a condition outside and hostile to humane culture, Nietzsche coined the expression *Kulturphilister*, or 'culture philistine', (*UM*, 149) to denote a decadent, evil, or banal spirit produced from *within* the circle of cultural knowledge. As the idea of *Bildung* became a conventional aspiration it became hollow, or its potential hollowness became apparent to the diagnostic observer.

Unconscious nihilism is a collective historical condition before it is a personal one, which is why it can remain unconscious. Hence the second *Untimely Meditation*, the essay on history, is an important complement to the Schopenhauer essay in focusing on the general condition. It defines modern educated man as a 'wandering encyclopaedia'. (*UM*, 79, my trans.) He knows, or can know, so much that he can derive no overall wisdom or purpose from this knowledge. The relativistic variety, as well as the sheer quantity, of historical cultural knowledge disables the single-minded purposiveness required for action. The element of *paedia* loses its pedagogical claim once it claims to teach everything to everyone and, in this sad declension of the Enlightenment ideal, the encyclopaedia becomes a *tristrapaedia* indeed.[5] Whereas deeper thinkers might recognise this condition and suffer it consciously, if not thereby avoid it, less demanding minds may find in the acquisition of general cultural knowledge an infinite distraction from such awareness. In opposition to this, Nietzsche rehearses, in the Schopenhauer essay, the same argument for specialism that Goethe had put in *WMJ*, and he poses the sardonic question: '. . . could it perhaps be that that maxim advocating a harmonious development should be applied only to more mediocre natures?'(*UM*, 131) Once the aspiration of leading minds, it has become the very formula for mediocrity, and aspiring mediocrity has its peculiar dangers.

How in these circumstances is an authentic culture to be recognised, or to express its authority? In the lecture series given during his brief tenure of a chair at Basel, Nietzsche comes close to arguing that an institution for humanistic education is a contradiction in terms. The critique is formally attributed, however, to an elderly philosopher encountered in isolation on

---

[4] *Untimely Meditations*, trans. R. J. Hollingdale (Cambridge: Cambridge University Press, 1997) p. 168.

[5] Hugh Kenner has an excellent study of the encyclopaedia theme although he does not include Nietzsche. See *The Stoic Comedians: Flaubert, Joyce, and Beckett* (London: W. H. Allen, 1967).

a hillside with a single companion whose presence makes it possible for his comments to be initially overheard. Authority is in the ear of the listener and the old philosopher speaks only when requested by his young auditors. The embedded fiction has Nietzsche making public what the speaker did not. In this instance, the rather two-dimensional fictional frame does not bracket the truth claims in the complex way that Socrates' report of Diotima's speech on love may be said to do in Plato's *Symposium*. Nonetheless, it suggests a fundamental instinct on Nietzsche's part to dramatise his own unwillingness to speak with direct personal authority on these matters and in that respect it anticipates the complex dramatic method of *TSZ*.

The Schopenhauer essay, which considers the internal contradictions of cultural transmission in more personal terms, is a more complex anticipation of later indirections and fictionalisations. Schopenhauer, whom the essay sets out to praise, becomes as much a Nietzschean *alter ego* as an authority. Just as the account of Wagner in the fourth untimely meditation, *Richard Wagner at Bayreuth*, was to be acknowledged in *Ecce Homo* as partly a self-description, so the analysis of Schopenhauer is highly self-reflexive and his authority increasingly internalised.[6] In setting the cultural historical context, Nietzsche proposes:

... three great images of man which our modern age has set up one after the other and which will no doubt long inspire mortals to a transfiguration of their own lives: they are the man of Rousseau, the man of Goethe and finally the man of Schopenhauer. Of these, the first image possesses the greatest fire and is sure of producing the greatest popular effect; the second is intended only for the few, for contemplative natures in the grand style, and is misunderstood by the crowd. The third demands contemplation only by the most active men; only they can regard it without harm to themselves, for it debilitates the contemplative and frightens away the crowd. (*UM*, 151–2)

In retrospect, Nietzsche's formulation requires an obvious modification. His transformation of Schopenhauer's thought means that, with suitable modification of the description, his own name would now take the third place in this succession, and the essay is an early stage in that process. In recording the impact of Schopenhauer on himself he already starts to translate it into the project and problem of his own writing: 'I hope there are some who understand what I am trying to say with this exhibition of Schopenhauer's destiny...' (*UM*, 176–7). In praising a then unregarded figure, Nietzsche's attention is already directed towards the problem of making himself understood.

Although the three figures are said to represent alternative human images, when Nietzsche's name is substituted for Schopenhauer's it becomes evident

---

[6] *On the Genealogy of Morals and Ecce Homo*, trans. Walter Kaufmann (New York: Random House, 1967) p. 274.

that he has effectively absorbed them all. Despite his always presenting himself as opposed root and branch to Rousseau, he was effectively the Rousseau of a later phase of modernity.[7] Rousseau's work is full of 'anticipations' of Nietzsche just as Nietzsche constantly echoes him. He had to displace Rousseau to reoccupy his space. Hence, while distrusting the mob emotion of *ressentiment* he saw in Rousseau's sentiment, he similarly sought radical renewal through the example of his own integrity as antinomian individual. In the present essay, for instance, a sharp aside on the calumny attracted by the intellectual solitary echoes the same sensitivity over which Rousseau broke with Diderot. (*UM*, 138)[8] But Nietzsche's self-presentation is perforce more indirect, and he learned to combine the overt iconoclasm of Rousseau with the studied elusiveness of Goethe. In emphasising the danger that Schopenhauer's influence might constitute for unsuitable readers, Nietzsche anticipates his own need to speak simultaneously with an exoteric and an esoteric meaning. He was to combine Rousseau's exoteric impact with Goethe's esoteric reserve.

Analytically speaking, therefore, Goethe's critical assimilation of Rousseau provided the fulcrum on which Nietzsche's own chiasmic relation to Rousseau turns. Rousseau's education for responsible freedom in *Emile* required an absolutely controlling authority, a procedure justified by the sentimentalist identification of moral principle and individual feeling. In contrast, Goethe's *WMA*, while ironically adopting the viewpoint of the young hero, allowed its irony to fall on the mentors too. Hence the problems of pedagogic teleology and authoritative guidance, which were optimistically suppressed in *Emile*, were increasingly thematised in that novel and its successor. *Schopenhauer as Educator*, however, fully reverses the order of authority found in *Emile*. Nietzsche presents *himself* as the pupil in search of an educator and his discovery of Schopenhauer proves to be only a step towards inventing, and eventually perhaps becoming, the necessary figure. 'Discovery', 'invention', and 'becoming' were increasingly to overlap in the radical fictiveness of his self-presentation. His elusiveness lies in his being essentially a dramatic character in his own work in a way that Rousseau, in his more literalistic conception, could not be. At the same time, however, the dramatic fiction is not to seem a mere fiction. He had to create an educator out of his own substance to perform the overt function of Rousseau.

In the light of Goethe's positive value as an exemplar in the essay it may be asked why he is not the 'educator' rather than Schopenhauer. One reason is

---

[7] On this relationship see Keith Ansell-Pearson, *Nietzsche contra Rousseau: a Study of Nietzsche's Moral and Political Thought* (Cambridge: Cambridge University Press, 1991).
[8] See ch. 2, n. 17.

that Schopenhauer's epochal relevance significantly dislodges that of Goethe, and of Nietzsche's other life-long intellectual hero, Ralph Waldo Emerson, who provides a culminating quotation for the essay. Both Emerson and Nietzsche taught a psychological holism and self-reliance expressed in their mutual capacity for aphoristic summary. Their common ground was evident in J. B. Burnhill's short-lived, turn-of-the-century Nietzschean journal, *The Eagle and the Serpent* (1898–1903) which placed similar aphorisms by Emerson and Nietzsche in parallel columns.[9] Yet Emerson, like Goethe, looked on modernity from the standpoint of an earlier age in a sense that now requires some elaboration in view particularly of Stanley Cavell's influential advocacy of Emerson as a thinker who deeply influenced Nietzsche.[10] Cavell has noted the multiple influence of Emerson on Nietzsche as part of a sustained campaign to rehabilitate him as a major American thinker despite his not readily satisfying the protocols of later academic philosophy. I sympathise strongly with this endeavour, and the more so as I have urged a comparable recognition of D. H. Lawrence in the context of English and European thought.[11] A common way of formulating the charge against Emerson is that he lacked a sense of evil, a charge that Cavell has persuasively countered. For present purposes, however, it becomes necessary to distinguish between a personal, temperamental or attitudinal optimism and a metaphysical view of the world. Alexander Pope, for example, might be characterised as combining a personal and cultural pessimism with a metaphysical optimism. Emerson's great theme of self-reliance, expressed in apparent lay sermons, has suffered from the fact that he also espoused an ultimately benign view of the universe; and he has, of course, been followed in the twentieth century by an often down-market tradition of American self-help. But the power of his writing is that he did know suffering personally and the positive courage he sought to instil in his readers involved not being blind to evil, but rather turning a blind eye to it, as a calculated and courageous act. It was this deep-lying, instinctive capacity to focus the will for a living purpose which Nietzsche admired in him; a capacity that parallels the willed stance of Nietzschean philosophical 'gaiety' as opposed to the spontaneity of romantic 'joy'. As Nietzsche put it in one of his final works: 'His spirit is always finding reasons for being contented and even grateful; and now and then he verges on the cheerful transcendence of that worthy gentleman who, returning from an

---

[9] *The Eagle and the Serpent*, no. 1 (1898) p. 1.
[10] Most notably in *Conditions Handsome and Unhandsome: the Constitution of Emersonian Perfectionism* (Chicago and London: University of Chicago Press, 1988).
[11] Principally in *D. H. Lawrence: Language and Being* (Cambridge: Cambridge University Press, 1992) and *Literature, Modernism and Myth: Belief and Responsibility in the Twentieth Century* (Cambridge: Cambridge University Press, 1997).

amorous rendezvous *tamquam bene gesta*, said gratefully: "*ut desint vires, tamen est laudanda voluptas.*"' (*TI*, 86)[12] I take it Nietzsche appreciated this quality in Emerson irrespective of a radical difference in their metaphysical world views: a difference that enabled Emerson to be associated with Transcendentalism and the Oversoul while Nietzsche imaged humanity as clever animals on a dying star. Hence, Nietzsche could uphold Emerson's affirmative and, in the most literal sense, en*courag*ing outlook without sharing his underlying *metaphysical* optimism. Indeed, the divergence of underlying world views allowed him a purely assimilative relation to both Emerson and Goethe rather than the agonistic identification that characterised his relation to Schopenhauer who continued to set Nietzsche's agenda throughout his career.

The agonistic relation to Schopenhauer is subtextual in this celebratory essay, but no less significant for that. The essay is virtually silent with respect to Schopenhauer's philosophy mainly because Nietzsche is concerned with the moral quality of the thinker. A further reason, however, is that, while he retained Schopenhauerian premises and concerns throughout his career, he had formulated radical objections to Schopenhauer's arguments several years before writing the essay.[13] For the pedagogical theme, it is significant he should affirm Schopenhauer's educative impact when he had already begun to surpass him. In this respect, I would modify James Conant's view that Emerson was not chosen as the educator because Nietzsche was too close to him, had not outgrown him.[14] While this is true, it was also importantly the case that, for the epochal reasons already outlined, neither Goethe nor Emerson obliged Nietzsche to surpass them in the same way. In this regard, what Nietzsche most gained from Schopenhauer was not an architecture of philosophic thought but a personal image for the future. This is most strikingly focused in his suggestion that, in the absence of educators, the true project of culture must be to produce, by collective endeavour, a future genius. Inverting earlier *Bildung* structure, the educator, now identified as the genius, will be the pupil's creation rather than his guide. By an inverted or anticipatory discipleship, the community of culture is to devote itself to the creation of a higher form:

It seems to be an absurd demand that one man should exist for the sake of another man . . . the question is this: how can your life, the individual life, receive the highest

---

[12] Hollingdale translates: 'that worthy gentleman who, returning from an amorous rendezvous as if things had gone well, said gratefully: "Though the power be lacking, the lust is praiseworthy."'

[13] See *Willing and Nothingness: Schopenhauer as Nietzsche's Educator*, ed. Christopher Janaway (New York: Clarendon Press, 1998).

[14] James Conant, 'Nietzsche's Perfectionism', in *Nietzsche's Postmoralism*, ed. Richard Schacht (Cambridge: Cambridge University Press, 2001) pp. 233–4.

value, the deepest significance?... Certainly only by your living for the good of the rarest and most valuable exemplars, and not for the good of the majority... (*UM*, 162)

The desire to create the higher individual provides both the motive, and the qualification, for entering the 'circle of culture'. (*UM*, 162) As so often in Nietzsche, it is hard to say how far this is to be taken literally or as a regulative metaphor, an iconic focus of value and will. It acts as a noble, disinterested goal which, like the Second Coming, may govern the behaviour and outlook of a like-minded community without immediate historical proof or reward. Unlike the Second Coming, however, it is not a matter of belief but aspiration. The future genius exists as an internal ideal and potentiality in all individuals capable of desiring it, and second-order minds may find a genuine value and dignity in working for such an end. Such proleptic disciples, moreover, escape the danger of epigonism that otherwise shadows discipleship. As Nietzsche was to put it in *Twilight of the Idols*: 'You want to multiply yourself by ten, by a hundred? you are seeking followers?—Seek *noughts.*' (*TI*, 34)

The idea of devoting one's own life to the production of a future genius has been the subject of much debate, or rather perhaps of a sustained misreading of it as elitist, a reading which has been decisively answered by Stanley Cavell and his colleague James Conant, the latter in an authoritatively detailed article.[15] Both show that Nietzsche's conception is not exclusivist except in so far as it requires the reader to accept the personal challenge that genius constitutes. They also indicate the substantial borrowing from Emerson whose introductory essay to *Representative Men*, for example, 'On the Uses of Great Men', repeatedly emphasises that greatness, or 'genius', is not to be interpreted as indicating something different in kind from the ordinary but is challenging, and enabling, precisely as an achievement from within our own kind. But such a misreading of Nietzsche has perhaps grown up partly because he sharpens the challenge and the paradox of this idea. Whereas in Emerson great men exist and naturally have such an impact in their world, Nietzsche makes the project more lonely, utopian, and against the grain. According to his three modern images, Goethean man, in contrast to the populism of Rousseau, is already a model only for the few, and is almost necessarily misunderstood by the unsuitable reader. He even runs the constant internal risk that 'he may degenerate to a philistine'. (*UM*, 152) Schopenhauer was positively dangerous to the wrong reader. In this context, it is unlikely that the future educator will be able to use the limpidly public, sermonic expression of Emerson.

---

[15] Cavell, *Conditions Handsome op. cit.* esp. pp. 53–6 cites 'The American Scholar' and the Divinity School Address. Conant, *op. cit.* pp. 181–257.

The anxiety of reductive influence gives rise to Nietzsche's mordant warning against what has since become the familiar, almost structural, condition of the modern humanistic academy:

> He who nowadays knows how to open up a new field within which even the weakest heads can labour with some degree of success becomes famous in a very short time: so great is the crowd that at once presses in. Every one of these loyal and grateful people is at the same time a misfortune for the master; to be sure, since they all imitate him and his defects then seem disproportionately great and exaggerated because they appear in such tiny individuals, while it is the opposite with his virtues, which are proportionately diminished when the same individuals display them. (*UM*, 171–2)

A mere perusal of book titles from many academic publishers confirms the continuing melancholy truth of this comment. By this analysis, the more 'successful' the educator, the more real damage he or she is likely to do. By contrast, even as Nietzsche questions the ideal of *Bildung*, his future educator continues the function of the mentor within the self-deconstructing tradition of the *Bildungsroman* understood not as a postmodern *mise en abyme* but as resistance to banalisation. Marc Redfield has described the *Bildungsroman* as a 'phantom formation' to indicate the retrospective creation of the genre, but his image also reflects its mode of survival through a radical self-deconstruction at the heart of its major texts.[16] Conversely, even as the *Bildung* process acknowledged its own problematic and inconclusive nature, the genre continued to be haunted by the formative pressure of a pedagogic teleology, the goal of achieved wholeness. The upshot of this double truth is that the teleological idea, or ideal, is *necessary* to *Bildung* but should not be *equated* with it. In that respect, Nietzsche does not so much end the tradition as turn its whole cloth inside out to reveal the other side of its pattern. He initiates a modern phase of the tradition, as in *The Magic Mountain* (1924), in which the internal instability of the *Bildungsroman* will be privileged over its optimistic teleology of purpose. Likewise, Nietzsche's notion of the future genius, whose creation guides the present, weirdly extends the phantom status of the mentor in the tradition. This hypothetical genius of the future, strangely transhistorical yet emergent from history, is a further embryonic intimation of Zarathustra which in this case also opens the question whether Nietzsche *is* Zarathustra or only one of those who works towards him. Before proceeding to *Thus Spoke Zarathustra*, however, it is relevant to note some of the paradoxes of felt historicity which are explored in the companion essay, *On the Uses and Disadvantages of History for Life*.

---

[16] Marc Redfield, *Phantom Formations: Aesthetic Ideology and the Bildungsroman* (Ithaca and London: Cornell University Press, 1996).

Bildung in History

The History essay is as much about *Bildung* as history: it historicises *Bildung* and experiences history as *Bildung*. Indeed, for Nietzsche, the contemporary crisis of *Bildung* lay in its being doubly overwhelmed by history. It had become unsustainable through an over-development of historical consciousness which was in itself a new historical experience. The condition of 'wandering encyclopaedia' was a product of Enlightenment culture institutionalised and democratised in the nineteenth century and, as he contemplates the history theme through the medium of *Bildung*, he is significantly immersed in the condition he describes. R. J. Hollingdale echoes other biographers and commentators in noting the peculiarly intense interrelation between life and thought in Nietzsche and the special penetration of the history essay lies in the inward experience of his personal existence as a microcosm of the historical condition.[17] The condition was not so much a generality perceived *outside* himself as constitutive *of* the self. The Schopenhauer essay emphasised the dissolution of the substantive *ego*: ' . . . if the hare has seven skins, man can slough off seventy times seven and still not be able to say: "this is really you, this is no longer the outer shell." ' (*UM*, 129) Likewise, the 'wandering encyclopaedia' image has its proper force only if the category of personal identity is already deconstructed. It is not the culture possessed that matters, but the culture one is.

The mutual porousness of self and history in Nietzsche is cardinal and, experiencing history in the way he did, Nietzsche once again enacted a chiasmic reversal of the eighteenth-century origins of *Bildung*. *Bildung* arose from the attempt to apply within the personal sphere models of development drawn from the massive collective processes of cultural history, and pre-history, as these came to consciousness in Enlightenment thought. An ideal of humanity as such rather than the formation of the individual was the driving motive and intellectual focus. As *Emile* attempted to preserve the naturalness of the pupil against the intrinsically corrupting effects of socialisation, its intellectual hinterland necessarily included Rousseau's reflections elsewhere on the origins of community and culture at large. In retrospect, however, his speculations about human evolution were anthropologically naive, and particularly in his assumption that the individual *precedes* community rather than being its *product*. In that respect, Rousseau's regenerative genius depended on what the Nietzsche of the history essay might theoretically have approved: a relative absence of historical sense and his conviction that you could start afresh from here. By contrast, a major shift in subsequent philosophical

---

[17] *Thus Spoke Zarathustra, op. cit.* p. 11.

anthropology, stemming most notably from the historical sense of the German Enlightenment, was the recognition that the category of the individual had itself to be created out of a long collective evolution: the process Thomas Mann was to call '... the birth of the ego out of the mythical collective'.[18]

Hence, when Herder and Lessing wrote their treatises on the 'education of mankind' they were concerned in the first instance not with individual pedagogic formation but with the collective evolution of human culture which it also served.[19] The pedagogical formation of the individual drew on this collective momentum. On such a model, the self is ideally a growing point of humanity as a whole, and contains the whole of humanity within itself, although the modern conception of the individual as irreducible and autonomous difference was developing from the same complex of thought. Rousseau, as the author of a first major modern autobiography, equivocated over whether the interest of his own case lay in his specialness or his representativeness, and it was incompatible with his literalism to negotiate the fine line between imperial ego and self-abnegating impersonality. Goethe, however, as the major inheritor of this Enlightenment vision, constantly overrode, and creatively obfuscated, this distinction. The narrative of *WMJ* encompasses undisguisedly personal aphoristic and poetic reflections just as the autobiographical impulse is everywhere assimilated to the impersonality of an epochal consciousness. In the subsequent development of the *Bildungsroman*, however, the growth of the individual became the central focus and goal in a way that Goethe had resisted. His irony *vis-à-vis* Wilhelm's ambitions in *WMA* is partly an irony against the category of the self-directing individual as such, and in *WMJ* the characters place themselves consciously within the historical process. But in the major nineteenth-century successors, such as Gottfried Keller's *Der Grüne Heinrich* (1854–5) and Adalbert Stifter's *Nachsommer* (1857), the purview narrows despite the cultural ambitions of the heroes, ambition which in Stifter's case especially entails a reverence for the past. Culture is increasingly privatised and becomes more susceptible to the Nietzschean critique of secret self-interest.

In Nietzsche himself the personal motive of *Bildung* is once again merged inextricably with a collective history but within a changed awareness of both the individual and the historical process. The new historical condition of the 'wandering encyclopaedia' implies a grotesque reversal of the Enlightenment ideal: instead of the individual being the growing point of humanity, it is merely

---

[18] See 'Joseph und seine Brüder: ein Vortrag', *Gesammelte Werke* (Frankfurt: Fischer, 1960) vol. xi, p. 665.

[19] J. G. Herder, see *Auch eine Philosophie der Geschichte zur Bildung der Menschheit* (1774), *Ideen zur Philosophie der Geschichte der Menschheit* (1784–91), and G. E. Lessing, *Die Erziehung der Menschengeschlechts* (1780).

the receptacle and, on Nietzsche's reading, increasingly the waste-basket, of history. This latter image comes from Borges' 'Funes the Memorius', whose unfortunate hero lives out Nietzsche's thought experiment, in the history essay, of the paralysing, insomniac condition of one who has no capacity to forget:

Imagine the extremest possible example of a man who did not possess the power of forgetting at all. . . . Like a true pupil of Heraclitus he would in the end hardly dare to raise his finger . . . A man who wanted to feel historically through and through would be like one forcibly deprived of sleep, or an animal that had to live only by rumination and ever repeated rumination . . . *There is a degree of sleeplessness, of rumination, of the historical sense, which is harmful and ultimately fatal to the living thing, whether this living thing be a man or a people or a culture.* (*UM*, 62)[20]

Bildung is once again dissolved back into historical process but within a paralysing, rather than a progressive, model of the historical condition. In this context, Nietzsche's idea of working towards the production of the future genius is a recovery of Enlightenment affirmation but now only conceivable as an audacious image challenging the common value of individual self-cultivation. It transposes the collective into the individual purpose in such a way as to deny the unearned assumption that the individual as such is the highest value. Only the great individual instantiates this value although, of course, Nietzsche saw this as a positive challenge for all individuals. The Schopenhauer essay opens by reflecting on the arbitrariness of individual existence in history and goes on to argue the importance for each individual of creating a personal significance: 'the fact of our existing at all in this here-and-now must be the strongest incentive for us to live according to our own laws and standards.' (*UM*, 128) His problem will be to realise, or even to articulate, this demanding conception of the individual.

Nietzsche's sense of the arbitrariness of personal historical existence is an important complementary aspect of his own felt historicity. He constantly 'presents' himself as a philosophical time-lord living in the present only as a visitor from afar. The tension between the felt historicity of the self and its historical arbitrariness lends psychological force to the otherwise abstract categories through which he seeks to overcome the wandering encyclopaedia condition. Effective historical existence requires an intuitive admixture of what he called the 'unhistorical' and the 'superhistorical' spirits. Combining the focused instinct of the animal with the detachment of the religious sage, enables a capacity for the decisive deed with an inner remove from the scene of action. The crucial point is the intuitive combination. Neither the

---

[20] J-L. Borges, *Labyrinths*, ed. Donald A. Yates and James E. Irby (London: Penguin, 1970) pp. 87–95.

unhistorical nor the superhistorical standpoints are desirable, or even possible, by themselves. Nietzsche's notion of the superhistorical as a viewpoint, not removed from historical reality but suffusing it, is a crucial anticipation of literary modernism. It provides the metaphysical and psychological rationale for the spatialising, and mythicising, of the temporal in modernist narrative. The mythical viewpoint of *Ulysses*, for example, is not incompatible with an intense interest in Irish political history.[21] So too, the elaborated definition of the superhistorical in the history essay helps to clarify a relation of time to understanding which is likewise emergent in the Schopenhauer essay.

In some respects Nietzsche's encounter with Schopenhauer is quite traditional as he records the initial impact within his then condition:

It was in this condition of need, distress and desire that I came to know Schopenhauer.

I am one of those readers who when they have read one page of him know for certain that they will go on to read all the pages and will pay heed to every word he ever said. (*UM*, 133)

This could be an episode of intellectual discovery from a *Bildungsroman*. Yet Nietzsche's account overall records more than the *coup de foudre* effect of the first reading. It catches as an instant, as it were visionary, recognition something crucial about Schopenhauer's thought *per se*: it is itself the expression of a world view which is either taken in as a whole or not at all.

We cannot determine at all closely how early in his life Schopenhauer must have perceived this picture of life in all its details and as he sought to reproduce it in all his subsequent writings; we can demonstrate that he saw this tremendous vision as a young man, and can well believe he had already seen it as a child. (*UM*, 182)

Schopenhauer's is a superhistorical vision to be superhistorically grasped, which suggests a more fundamental reason for Nietzsche's apparent lack of interest in it as a logically argued system. In his own century, Schopenhauer influenced artists rather than academic philosophers and he is in some degree himself a prophetic artist rather than a philosopher as conventionally conceived. His mode of thought exemplifies the exception in Nature that Nietzsche saw as characteristic of genius: it constitutes a 'leap' in cultural evolution (*UM*, 159) and a similar leap is required to follow it. By the same token, Schopenhauer's vision lurks as a permanent trans-temporal possibility available at any moment of sufficient insight or courage. Like the Proustian recognition, it can only be encountered *in* time yet may occur at *any* time.

---

[21] After the mid-century dominance of an 'aestheticist' view of Joyce, the last two decades of the twentieth century saw a stream of publications on his interest in history and politics. See for example: James Fairhall, *Ulysses and the Question of History* (Cambridge: Cambridge University Press, 1993), Robert Spoo, *James Joyce and the Language of History* (Oxford: Oxford University Press, 1994), Emer Nolan, *James Joyce and Nationalism* (London: Routledge, 1995).

Nietzsche is especially sensitive to this because his writings too, although they may be read and reread, will frequently only open themselves, if at all, to a flood of recognition rather than through the methodical process of argument. That was the importance of aphorism. Experience speaks to experience, or else not at all, although it is by the same token fatally open to illusory understanding.

Likewise, achieving the right balance of the historical, unhistorical, and superhistorical spirits requires an instinct that could hardly be taught, or perhaps even learned. Once again, Goethe provided the significant example. Without using the term, Dilthey saw Goethe as having a naturally superhistorical attitude.[22] Whereas Schiller, he thought, had a stronger sense of history in progressive terms, Goethe saw the past universalistically through the trans-historical demands of his own personality, and of his art. Indeed, their different relation to the political was the basis of Goethe's initial reserve towards Schiller. Yet this is not to deny Goethe's acute historical sense for they are two sides of the same coin. Indeed, Goethe's sense of history exemplifies Nietzsche's insistence that the superhistorical is only valuable as an informing consciousness within history although it may appear to contemporaries as mere detachment. Nicholas Boyle's biography of Goethe continually brings out this aspect of his relation to his time. Nietzsche understood very well this value in Goethe but, as philosopher rather than poet, he had to find a discursive means of expressing such a double relation to history, and for an audience not likely to understand its spirit. The emergent complex of an historical/superhistorical vision, along with its resultant rhetorical impasse, further prepares for the figure of Zarathustra.

Nietzsche as Educator/Zarathustra as Prophet

Nietzsche's writing continues to affect countless readers with something like the impact he records Schopenhauer having on him, and he seems more timely a hundred years after his death. But if his self-description as 'untimely' means not just being *against* the time but being *incomprehensible* to it, how did his thought survive to address the future? In these early essays he frequently appeals to posterity but as his career developed he was to embed a readerly futurity more cunningly and constitutively in the writing itself. In so far as the word 'prophet' is appropriate to Nietzsche its double meaning is especially to the point. The prophet was originally one who gave unwelcome truths to his contemporaries, truths that they may find unbelievable or incomprehensible. It has acquired the secondary meaning of foretelling the future by supernatural

---

[22] Wilhelm Dilthey, *Poetry and Experience, op. cit.* pp. 275–82.

means. Nietzsche is a prophet in the primary sense and yet he secretly foretells the future through texts which await it.

His predicament *vis-à-vis* his contemporaries is figured in his image in *The Gay Science* of the madman who comes into the market place in the 'bright morning hours' with a lantern to announce the death of God.[23] His madness is as much perceived as substantive, and in so far as he *is* mad it is not for what he says but for the mistake that he himself recognises when he smashes his lantern saying 'I have come too early'. Like light still arriving from a dead star, the event has already occurred but remains unconscious. The lantern in daylight is an image of the open secret. At once genuinely and ironically, he struggles to illuminate from a limited, personal source what is, in the strict sense, blindingly obvious. Nietzsche's own rhetorical equivalent of the lantern in daylight was to develop forms of expression very different from either Emerson's secular sermons or Goethe's Olympian self-enclosure: he incorporated Rousseau's fire into a cunningly delayed relation to history. If the madman is another anticipation of Zarathustra, *TSZ* is Nietzsche's most intensively self-reflective representation of the limits of his own authority and, in its dramatic structure, it enacts a detailed chiasmic reversal of the representation of authority in *Emile*.

TSZ contrasts most crucially with *Emile* in being a conscious fiction although the fact that Zarathustra expresses genuinely Nietzschean doctrine served for a long time to obscure the significance of this. Until quite recently, Zarathustra has been taken rather as a spokesman for Nietzsche in a self-inflationary mode of pseudo-biblical prophecy. That reading had seemed justified because the fictive gap is not a doctrinal one but that is precisely the point, that it is a mode of self-recognition, and a self-recognition not so much in a personal, or introspective, as a structural sense. The personal sincerity/authenticity of Nietzsche or Zarathustra is not the point so much as the objective impact on the listeners, the condition of authority as such. Goethe's increasingly sceptical focus on the mentor culminates in *TSZ* as the mentor becomes the central figure. Rousseau's near absolute confidence in pedagogical authority is replaced by Nietzsche's near absolute scepticism. Authority, which was part of the unconscious of Rousseau, and was disguised by unmarked fiction, is now thrown into relief by Nietzsche's use of a consciously fictive *alter ego*. In the course of the narrative, the very title of the work begins to shimmer. Initially the apparent formula of unquestioned authority echoing 'this is the word of the Lord', it takes on the minimal implication: 'that is what he *said*.'

The customary text of *TSZ* consists of four parts of which the fourth has an ambiguous status. Nietzsche added it later and circulated it only to a limited

[23] *The Gay Science*, trans. Walter Kaufmann (New York: Random House, 1974) p. 181.

circle of friends. He also considered adding possible further parts. Without entering the resultant debates about the text, it is enough to note that both aspects, its possible inconclusiveness and its ambiguous circle of readership, are entirely germane to the internal drama of the work itself which is centred on Zarathustra's unresolved search for a comprehending audience. In the Prologue that opens Part I, Zarathustra descends from his mountain cave to the town of the Motley Cow where his public teaching is interrupted by a rope-dancer who attempts to cross the town square. The rope-dancer is followed by a buffoon who, in jumping over him on the rope, causes him to fall to his death. Zarathustra carries away the body for burial, and it becomes increasingly clear that the rope-dancer is a figure of Zarathustra himself. Less immediately obvious is his parallel with the buffoon as well. For even as Zarathustra sets out to teach demonstratively his doctrine of traversing the difficult rope stretched between man and superman, so he also jumps over the pedagogical difficulty this presents for an audience who are not ready. He attempts to jump over himself. The quasi-allegorical method here, of rope-dancer and buffoon, is at once pre-modern and postmodern, and it avoids any personal pathos through a strange mixture of earnestness and farce. Strategically, it avoids any introspective access to Zarathustra and embodies his predicament in external and structural terms. Although Zarathustra subsequently communes with himself, as when he talks to his 'heart', this emphasis governs the narrative throughout.

The subsequent sections of the narrative re-enact the initial difficulty with increasing intensity as Zarathustra seeks progressively more limited and choice audiences only to find their incomprehension the more intrinsic and ineradicable. At the end of the Prologue, he decides to speak in future not to the public but to 'companions'. At this stage he is teaching the doctrine of the superman, or the special individual, which any of them might conceivably become. Accordingly, at the end of Part I, like one of Goethe's mentor figures in *WMA*, he deliberately withdraws to his mountain cave in order to free his disciples, now that the seed of the doctrine has been sown, to become truly independent as he has taught them. The possibly empty circularity of teaching independence, however, lurks, unnoticed in the teaching itself: 'Believe me, my brothers!' he repeats (*ASZ*, 30; *TSZ*, 59), yet a little later he criticises the former teachers of religion who 'want to be believed in'. (*ASZ*, 32; *TSZ*, 61)[24] This latter formulation, it may be noted, emphasises the authority of the teacher rather than that of the doctrine. All discipleship contains this crucial ambiguity.

---

[24] *Also Sprach Zarathustra*, ed. Giorgio Colli and Mazzino Montinari (Stuttgart: Reclam, 1994); *Thus Spake Zarathustra, op. cit.* All subsequent references are to these editions.

At the opening of Part II he has been waiting like a sower for the seed to grow but, with his 'longing for those whom he loved', his wisdom has increased till it 'caused him pain by its abundance'. (*ASZ*, 83; *TSZ*, 107) As the sower image modulates into that of imminent male discharge, it may suggest a sexual motivation of pedagogy going back to the Socratic model, or that it is a parallel need as absolute as generation. Zarathustra's solitude is partly proud and chosen but it is mainly an enforced and painful isolation such as Nietzsche had noted of Schopenhauer and Goethe in the Schopenhauer essay. Also lurking in the opening imagery, therefore, is the onanistic possibility that the seed has been, and will be, cast fruitlessly upon the ground. The self-enclosure is in the pedagogical circle as well as in the emotional isolation, and the means by which he seeks to teach the general overcoming of the contemporary condition is similarly problematic. 'Willing liberates: that is the true doctrine of will and freedom—' (*ASZ*, 88; *TSZ*, 111), he declares, but the will itself proves to be caught in circular paradoxes. In so far as *TSZ* is the story of Zarathustra's learning as well as his teaching, it is centrally focused on the problem of the will.

Early in Part I, he had proposed three fundamental 'metamorphoses' of being which underlie formal philosophical world views: the camel, the lion, and the child. The 'camel' is the spirit which endures, and carries willingly the burden of duty. The lion throws off the burden, exerts his will defiantly, and corresponds in effect to the iconoclasm of Zarathustra. But the will in this mode is too purely reactive, it is exerted *against*. Hence the third image is of the 'child', the 'self-propelling wheel'. (*ASZ*, 26; *TSZ*, 55) Zarathustra seeks but never achieves this final metamorphosis. Zarathustra recognises the fundamental reality of the will in all creatures: 'Where I found a living creature, there I found will to power.' (*ASZ*, 118; *TSZ*, 137) But the will, as an organic need, does not for conscious beings have the simple goals of purely animal life. Hence the mistaken 'will to truth' of the philosophers (*ASZ*, 105; *TSZ*, 126) and, even more importantly, the will to revenge (*ASZ*, 102; *TSZ*, 123) which often conceals itself within the will to truth. Hence too the importance of the two figures not mentioned by name, Rousseau and Schopenhauer, whose images help to bring the problem of the will to its most intense, and therefore ultimately productive, focus.

The spirit of Rousseau, whose image of man was said to possess 'the greatest fire', (*UM*, 151) is imaged more demeaningly now as the 'firedog'. (*ASZ*, 136; *TSZ*, 153) The spirit of *ressentiment*, the desire to take revenge on the past, is the great modern temptation that Nietzsche always laid at the door of Rousseau, and Zarathustra himself has little difficulty in holding it at bay. A more subtle temptation immediately follows, however, as he hears a Soothsayer whose words 'went to Zarathustra's heart and transformed him'. (*ASZ*, 139;

TSZ, 156) Overcome by the 'melancholy' of the Schopenhauerian image of life, he falls into a sleep in which he has the most terrifying of his dream visions. In a high wind, a black coffin is hurled at him which breaks and vomits 'forth a thousand peals of laugher... a thousand masks of children, angels, owls, fools, and child-sized buttterflies...'(*ASZ*, 141; *TSZ*, 157) When he recounts the dream, a disciple gives it the positive and flattering interpretation that Zarathustra is the wind which will banish these nightmare images. This response, however, far from heartening him, is the point at which his own mission falters. He 'gazed long into the face of the disciple who had interpreted the dream, and shook his head'. (*ASZ*, 142; *TSZ*, 159) No dialogue seems possible here: just an ambiguously shocked recognition on Zarathustra's part. In keeping with the externality of Zarathustra's dramatisation, his response may be shock at the traducing of the teaching, or a deeper shock of recognition concerning the true meaning of the teaching itself. Either way, it is after this exchange that he formulates more precisely the paradox of the will which, in overcoming *ressentiment*, will need to perform the impossible feat of willing backwards: 'The will cannot will backwards... that is the will's most lonely affliction'. (*ASZ*, 145; *TSZ*, 161)

As Zarathustra returns to his cave at the end of Part II his mood is in sharp contrast to that of his previous withdrawal. He now retires reluctantly into an afflicted solitude. The solitude is deeper because far from trusting the independent development of his disciples, he now knows the depth of their incomprehension. The solitude, moreover, is more than spatial, it is increasingly temporal. For as the various dream visions, and other hints, suggest, he is increasingly living not so much in a different time as with a different sense of the meaning of time. This is suggested in the opening of Part III: 'The time has passed when accidents could befall me; and what *could* still come to me that was not already my own?' (*ASZ*, 157; *TSZ*, 173)[25] The rhetorical question suggests precisely an internalising, a making his own, of temporal chance and destiny. Zarathustra comes to realise that the contradiction of willing backwards has a solution in the willing of the eternal recurrence but this is as difficult to accept as it is to understand. Meanwhile he has another horrifying vision, this time of a young shepherd being choked by a black snake in his mouth. Unable to pull it free, Zarathustra involuntarily tells him to bite its head off. He asks: '*Who* is the man into whose throat all that is heaviest and blackest will thus crawl?' (*ASZ*, 165; *TSZ*, 180) The man proves to be an image of Zarathustra himself for whom, as for Nietzsche, the notion of the eternal return initially presented itself as horrifying. Zarathustra

---

[25] Paul Loeb, *op. cit.*, has discussed the verbal and narrative paradoxes of time in *TSZ* as evidence of Zarathustra's intuition, or memory, of transcending time.

has to learn to accept it. The snake, an image of chthonic life, like Zarathustra's serpent, and an image of eternity, prevents the man from speaking though he may express his will in biting it.

The degree to which Zarathustra manages to accept it remains uncertain. In the section 'The Convalescent' the doctrine of the eternal return is directly affirmed but it comes from Zarathustra's animals, the eagle and the serpent. And Zarathustra's response is far from affirmative. 'When the animals had spoken these words they fell silent and expected that Zarathustra would say something to them: but Zarathustra did not hear that they were silent. On the contrary, he lay still with closed eyes like a sleeper, although he was not asleep: for he was conversing with his soul.' (*ASZ*, 232; *TSZ*, 238) As with the earlier response of the disciple, the effect is to drive Zarathustra further into reflective solitude. In this case, however, it is clearer that what is at stake is not some error in what they have said. Rather the reverse: they state very clearly the doctrine but in doing so they perhaps bring home to him the gap between the abstract statement and the possibility of living it which they confidently, or encouragingly, attribute to him. The situation might be contrasted with Socrates' quoting of Diotima in giving 'his' definition of love in the *Symposium*. Recognising the limits of his own purely dialectical mode of thought, he reports what she said, and affirms his belief in her. Zarathustra, by contrast, appears to disown the statement even though it expresses the inner logic of his teaching as that has been developed throughout the narrative. Hence even the ending of Part III, which affirms the eternal recurrence in dithyrambic verse, sees it as depending on his successful mating with life, and it is open to the possibility that the very nature of his insight will have cut him off further from general comprehension. So far he has learned from his pedagogical failures but precisely as he approaches the core of his doctrine, he places himself outside the pedagogical relationship. Part IV substantiates this as he engages with a variety of representative 'higher men', including once again an image of Schopenhauer, who have seen through the old orders, and should therefore be sympathetic to his new doctrine, but who once again can only traduce it. Indeed, his ultimate temptation in Part IV is the Schopenhauerian virtue of compassion which is cognate with that of the teacher.

It is evident, then, that the dramatic structure of *TSZ* enacts Zarathustra's deepening pedagogical failure. But such a summary obscures the fact that the bulk of the narrative in Parts I to III is nonetheless taken up with Zarathustra's aphoristic expression of Nietzschean doctrine. In that respect it is easy to see why it has so often been read doctrinally. Reading the work dramatically rather than doctrinally, however, does not negate such a reading: it rather shows the narrative strategy to have an important double function. It both gives that doctrine the exoteric expression which remains a primary function of the work, and enacts dramatically the way Zarathustra is constantly seduced into expository self-confidence. Over and over again, it is only at the end of an extended exposition that his failure to make himself truly understood is suddenly brought home. At the same time, as he is repeatedly driven into self-reflective isolation, pedagogical failure teaches him not just about the failures of pedagogy, but about the very doctrine he wishes to expound. For what is at stake in the doctrine has now shifted from understanding to will, from the supposedly inter-personal to the irreducibly personal. The shift from knowledge or understanding to will is of cardinal importance. It has been the source of much miscomprehension in Nietzsche commentary, and is the fulcrum of Nietzsche's chiasmic reversal of Rousseau.

What Zarathustra teaches is not strictly the 'eternal recurrence' but *willing* the eternal recurrence. Much ink has been spilt on the plausibility of the idea of the eternal recurrence but, in so far as its use in *TSZ* is concerned, this often obscures the point by missing the order of significance which it claims. The point can be clarified by contrast with the orders of knowledge and belief which are being challenged. Nietzsche objected to the Socratic/Platonic privileging of the order of knowledge, and the inauguration of this as the primary concern for subsequent philosophy. Knowledge, for him, always serves, albeit unconsciously, the interests of the will to power. He typically questions, therefore, not the knowledge itself but the value and motivation of its pursuit. It followed from the Platonic commitment to knowledge that it was superior to belief: even true belief is inferior to knowledge. Christianity, however, lends a new significance to belief. Its central statement is a *Credo* and there is a moral value in belief which would be undermined by knowledge. If God could be known as the objects of science can be known then there would be no virtue in believing in him. Christian tradition has encompassed, or veered between, on the one hand the desire to have faith find support in knowledge and reason, and on the other hand the need to emphasise its difference as in the formula: *Credo quia absurdum*. The latter is crucial and such an emphasis on belief is a step closer to Nietzsche's recognition of myth as the underlying reality of culture although in *TSZ* belief is treated, not as mythic health, but as a form of self-deception, including the disciples' belief in Zarathustra himself. The eternal recurrence, then, is not primarily an object of either knowledge or belief since it signifies precisely a shift from both these orders to that of the will.

The eternal recurrence, therefore, is not argued in *TSZ* as a cosmological truth, and Nietzsche left his reflections on that possibility unpublished. Nor is it even presented as a belief that he seeks to make plausible. On the contrary, it is presented as a stupendous thought, in which the willing of its truth is a highest test of character. Just as faith has its moral value in standing in opposition to knowledge and reason, so this expression of will takes its significance from its opposition to both knowledge and plausible belief. Reconciling it to these would lose the force of the affirmation. The shift to the order of will also explains Nietzsche's otherwise puzzling account of his visionary moment on 1 August 1881 in which, he says, the idea of the eternal recurrence first came to him.[26] It would be puzzling because he had already used this idea in one of his earliest works, the essay on history. He suggested in that essay a thought experiment by which to test anyone's capacity truly to live in the present rather than in nostalgia and regret for the past or hopeful anticipation of the future. (*UM*, 65) Such a rare person would be able to answer affirmatively the question of whether they could bear to live over and over again exactly the same life. In the history essay, however, the question remains abstract and hypothetical, and is directed to no one in particular. When the same image is used again in *The Gay Science* in a passage which directly anticipates *TSZ*, it has a deeper aura of horror as it is whispered to the reader by a secret demon and implies the horrifying prospect imaged later by the black snake in the shepherd's mouth.[27] The *idea* had long been in Nietzsche's mind but this sequence of its uses denotes an increasing internalisation of it as a focus of the will. Only in *TSZ* do we get close to the internal process of its being willed. But that is also to recognise something crucial about the will itself.

The shift to the order of will rather than knowledge seems arbitrary, and to many readers repellent or dangerous. That is why it is important to recognise that it is not so arbitrary as it may at first appear, or a matter of choice. For the deeper process underlying the shift is the recognition that, just as the mutual overlapping of knowledge and belief makes their discrimination elusive, so will is not a separable order either. On the contrary, it is the unconscious of knowledge and even more so of belief. The reason belief is treated with scant respect through much of *TSZ* is that it is so patently an unacknowledged function of the will, or the function of a weak will. As Cicero once said, men will readily believe what they wish to be true. Once again, will is a traditionally acknowledged aspect of belief, crucial to its moral distinction from knowledge, but usually in a way that disguises its subtending *of* the belief. Augustine's *Confessions*, for example, are a distant forebear of *TSZ* in being the dramatic narrative of a successful teacher who increasingly questions in the process what it is that he has to teach. The inner story of his conversion separates out the moment of his intellectual conviction from that of his surrender to it.[28]

---

[26] *Ecce Homo*, *op. cit.* p. 295.
[27] *The Gay Science*, *op. cit.* p. 273.
[28] Augustine, *The Confessions*, Bk, 8, *op. cit.* pp. 133–54.

The greatest suspense lies between the two. Yet even as his will comes into line with his conviction he also treats it as secondary: the will is experienced within a theological framework which to that extent obfuscates the function of the will as such. For the theological conviction after all is itself, and even more crucially, a matter of will. Nietzsche reverses the traditional order of will and belief to recognise the will as primordial. It operates not just in the moments of conscious decision, but in the unconscious universe of value that subtends the decision.

For Nietzsche, the underlying reality of the will to power governs belief wherever fundamental conceptions of life are concerned and it is important to recognise the practical force of this. The will to power is not the vulgar desire for domination which was often foisted on him in his early reception and which he himself diagnosed as a symptom of weakness. It is closer to the ancient Greek ideal of flourishing but with a modern naturalistic edge countering the moral idealisms which modernity has also inherited. Nor is it offered in the first instance as a moral, or even an amoral, ideal. It is not something to aspire to: just an unillusioned recognition of the way things are. Its immediate value lies in the shedding of illusion. By contrast, discussions of belief by many, such as religious believers, who would consider themselves opposed to Nietzsche often vindicate his analysis by enacting it. Arguments for a given belief will frequently turn not on its plausibility but on its preferability as a form of life which is precisely Nietzsche's argument for the cultural significance of myth. Likewise, objections to the notion of the will to power as the fundamental motive in living organisms including the human are often phrased as distaste for the moral implications, or supposed moral implications, of what is in itself proposed as a neutral truth. Of course, one may object to the specific uses to which Nietzsche puts the idea but that is strictly a different matter. It is rare that objections to the notion itself are not governed by preference, which is to say in effect by a contrary will to power.

The will to power, then, is for Nietzsche the supreme open secret. It is no longer the open secret of Nature, as in Goethe's usage, but now, more elusively, of life understood in a qualitative rather than a simply biological sense. The shift in term is crucial. Life is known intuitively within the self yet always through the medium of interpretation and as resistant to objective articulation. Whereas Goethe could rest in, and on, Nature, Nietzsche recognises that life has to be sustained as, and by, will. Hence the elusiveness of his invocation of science. In *TSZ* he affirms the will to eternal recurrence in implicit opposition to scientific knowledge. Yet in unpublished notebooks he declares that eternal recurrence, at least as the extreme form of nihilism, is 'the *most scientific* of all hypotheses'. And that the 'energy of knowledge and of strength *compels* such a belief'. (Nietzsche's emphases)[29] His language in saying so, however, is not that of science as usually understood so much as will to power. In his own 'gay science' he sought a science of life in a fundamentally qualitative sense for which the will was a crucial factor. The open secret of the will, therefore, has a multi-layered obscurity. Will is not only hidden within knowledge and belief: these obscure the deeper quality of life by which that will is itself subtended. Not surprisingly, all this can be expressed in prophetic pedagogy only in the mode of the open secret.

Hence the willing of the eternal recurrence in Part III grows from a double-layered analysis of the will. The suffusive, deconstructive recognition of will as the unconscious of all belief enables a more positive process of thought leading to Zarathustra's specific affirmation. In Part II, Zarathustra puzzles over the riddle of how to will backwards. It is hard to escape the condition of *ressentiment* associated above all with Rousseau, a condition in which history and the personal past have already robbed us of a free and full existence. If one could retrospectively will the past as a matter of choice, as one can assume a debt not personally incurred, then the hostile power of the past would be overcome although the proposal formulated in that way rather suggests a raising of *ressentiment* to an even higher intensity just as the Christian redemption from sin intensifies the significance of sin. But backward willing is the riddle, or *Rätsel*, for which Zarathustra's enigmatic counsel of the eternal recurrence offers the solution in Part III. The predicament seems initially to require a 'redemption', or *Erlösung*, but here the common English versions miss one of the verbal resonances which permeate the text. Whereas the English 'redemption' etymologically suggests the payment of a debt, and therefore some element introduced from the outside, the word *Erlösung* is cognate with solving, dissolving, and release. The 'redemption', *Erlösung*, depends upon a *Lösung*, solution, of the riddle. This redemption will be achieved from within the secular terms of the riddle itself. Hence, whereas willing backwards still has the overtones of *ressentiment*, the eternal recurrence is an image of the absolute value of the present. It incorporates the superhistorical not as detachment from the present but as a maximal concentration within it. By the same token, however, even as Zarathustra/Nietzsche lucidly acknowledges the role of the will, he puts himself outside of what can be interpersonally argued. His idea can be truly known and judged, if at all, only by a personality of equal life-quality, or will to power.

Nietzsche's analysis of the will reverses the model of authority in Rousseau. With his belief in the identity of nature and reason Rousseau elides the

---

[29] Friedrich Nietzsche, *Writings from the Late Notebooks*, ed. Rüdiger Bittner, trans. Kate Sturge (Cambridge: Cambridge University Press, 2003) p. 118.

problem of will. If protected from corruption, Emile will 'naturally' will what is reasonable. But the iron hand is always within the velvet glove, just as Rousseau's forebear, the genuinely child-centred Locke, will have to thrash a boy for just one sin: obstinacy. The will must be either elided or suppressed. And if Nietzsche could be said likewise to merge reason with nature, it is not by the upward assimilation of nature to reason but by the downward assimilation of reason to the purposes of the will. And in this respect Goethe once again represents a mid point. A central theme and structural principle of *WMA* is the ambiguity between narrative destiny and the free will of the hero. In the novels these principles are ultimately as happily combined for Wilhelm as they are for Emile, but in Wilhelm's case it is partly by virtue, as in *Tom Jones*, of his destiny being overtly fictional. At the end, Wilhelm retrospectively wills the providence of Goethe's fiction, as he has done unconsciously throughout. Goethe's way of resolving the antinomy of destiny and free will in fiction, while using the same medium to keep the two principles in overt tension, reflects an attitude expressed in his own life and which Nietzsche affirmed in one of his last works, *Twilight of the Idols*. In what is perhaps his nearest instantiation of the Overman, Nietzsche describes Goethe's *amor fati*, his complete willing of his own destiny: 'A spirit thus *emancipated* stands in the midst of the universe with a joyous and trusting fatalism, in the faith that only what is separate and individual may be rejected, that in the totality everything is redeemed and affirmed . . . ' (*TI*, 114) Where Rousseau elides the will on which he nonetheless depends, Zarathustra's will cancels the *ressentiment* Rousseau otherwise bequeathed to posterity.

The reverse symmetry of the relation to Rousseau is also evident in their uses of the child. Nietzsche is principally concerned with philosophical systems not as intellectual structures but as expressions of temperament and life-quality. Hence his allegorical method by which he distinguishes in Part I between the spirits of the camel, the lion, and the child. The child's naivety, in the Schillerian sense of unreflective wholeness, would overcome the lion's need to assert its will but this state, the 'self-propelling wheel', is not achieved. At the end, to be sure, Zarathustra awaits his 'children', but we hardly know even then, were they to appear, whether they would not still be his children only in the sense of being his intellectual offspring, simply more disciples. Earlier reference to children suggests this hopeful but still lesser possibility:

> Once the creator sought companions and children of *his* hope: and behold, it turned out that he could not find them, except he first create them himself.
> Thus am I in the midst of my work, going to my children and turning from them: for the sake of his children must Zarathustra perfect himself.   (*ASZ*, 166; *TSZ*, 181)

These children seem not quite the 'child' who, as the 'self-propelling wheel', figuratively anticipates the enigma of the eternal recurrence. Hence, whereas Rousseau starts with an empirical child, or rather the idea of an empirical child, which may be recognised on closer inspection as a philosophical fiction, Nietzsche starts with a sage seeking the condition of the child which he himself recognises only too well to be a philosophical fiction. The child he wishes to produce through his love for eternity is, in the first instance, himself. This child is not the object of authority, but at once its goal and its source. In a complex way, of course, this might be said too of Rousseau's child who is equally utopian but unwittingly so. As always, Nietzsche's chiasmic reversal of Rousseau is as much a sublation as a denial.

All these features help to create the curious double action of *TSZ*. The emphasis on the will spells out why the central doctrine cannot be rationally enforced while the text expresses his doctrine within the dramatised recognition of its contemporary incomprehension. In this way, as a number of recent commentators have realised, Nietzsche created a text which could bide its time.[30] The future is preserved in this, as in other aphoristic works, as a more constitutive version of the open secret: not verbally hidden, but secret until understood. And in the event, his writing for futurity balanced the opposite dangers of comprehension and incomprehension with remarkable success. His texts have stayed alive in provoking and engaging successive generations while resisting interpretative closure. There is something more here than the openness of all great thinkers to competing interpretations: he seemed to realise this potentiality in advance as a rhetorical principle. In effect, he raised to a higher power the elusiveness of earlier mentor figures of the *Bildungsroman* who similarly sought to avoid premature understanding.

Yet the immediate effect, of course, is exactly the opposite: where Goethe drew an overt veil of mystery *around* himself, Nietzsche seems constantly to draw directly *upon* himself, even to expose himself, as his own primary material. In Nietzsche's case, as much as in Rousseau's, the author's personality is a primary exhibit but more obliquely so. For what Nietzsche reveals is rather the elusiveness of the self, and especially his own. Precisely in his apparent self-reference, his rhetoric is as 'dark and veiled' as the ego itself. (*UM*, 129) And by the same token, what he exemplifies is highly elusive when we seek to give it concrete instantiation beyond the rhetorical contexts of its definition. All readers are required in a significant measure to create their own Nietzsches. The meaning of the 'overman', for example, is defined clearly enough in its rhetorical contexts but retains a teasing indeterminacy at the

---

[30] Of the many critics who take up this theme Stanley Rosen treats it most directly in, *The Mask of Enlightenment* (Cambridge: Cambridge University Press, 1995).

level of any imagined instantiation. It takes on practical meaning only from the image the reader places within it, or the quality of life attributed to it. It is pre-eminently an idea defined by the personality which inhabits it. That points to more intrinsic, not just 'rhetorical', reasons why his works have kept their openness to the future and remained so problematic. The vicious circularity of ideas and experience enforces the critical question of in what sense Nietzsche instantiates, and thereby underwrites experientially, the meaning of his own works.

Nietzsche as Personal Exemplar

If Nietzsche found the educative value of Schopenhauer to lie not so much in his ideas as in the 'honesty' of his thought, this is because Nietzsche, more than almost any other major thinker, questions what is meant by 'thought' or 'ideas' when abstracted from their living contexts. The interestedness with which ideas are held, particularly if they are fundamental ideas, gives a built-in falsification to the necessary act of trans-personal, or trans-historical, abstraction through which we define them *as* ideas. The typical difficulty here lies not in our being unaware of this so much as in assuming too readily a particular relation between ideas and life. Opposing parties in argument, for example, tend to infer the personality type, or the moral conduct, they believe to be entailed by a given set of ideas rather than espousing Ezra Pound's opposite principle that the value of an idea depends on the nature of the person who holds it. If Nietzsche himself has notably suffered from this tendency, it is partly because there is in him a peculiarly close, and therefore elusive, interdependence of personality and thought. The originality and difficulty of Nietzsche's thought lay in its active instantiation of this philosophical holism, in seeing ideas always epiphenomenally as functions of the will to power, itself defined through the quality of life it affirms. The 'death of God' was the death of an idea in this sense: it would take generations to discover what the demise of the idea would mean as a change in life form. And the old idea would not really be dead until that new form had superseded it. Hence Nietzsche conducted philosophical thinking against its traditional ideal of objectivity, and sought to expose, with 'genealogical' insight, the function of ideas as psychological motives. This is familiar enough in relation to the ideas of others, but to pursue a positive philosophical project of one's own in this spirit is peculiarly demanding. Philosophical thought conceived in this way is not a licence to embrace the subjective, but rather assumes a burden of impersonality as that term might be understood in relation to major artistic creation. That is why the temperamental arbitrariness of Schopenhauer's philosophy, which would be a stumbling block to many, was for Nietzsche precisely the sign of its authenticity as a personal vision raised to an impersonal power. The truth value of Schopenhauer's thought lay in the first instance not in its objective persuasiveness as an intellectual system but in his heroic embracing of his personal fate as the bearer of this vision.

By the same token, the future impact of ideas is not merely difficult to guess, it may be illusory in principle. An 'idea' assimilated by a later generation enters a different body of experience and is no longer the same idea. Nietzsche was to remark elsewhere, for example, on the ennobling effect of liberational ideals before the liberation occurs, and their different significance afterwards.[31] Likewise, when iconoclasm becomes received wisdom, it retains its abstract 'meaning' while changing its significance. And in so far as new thought tends to be assimilated only to the extent that it ceases to be threatening, that a life form now exists to contain it, then it is possible to go from the iconoclastic to the banal without the intervening stage of being understood. Nietzsche himself did not entirely escape this fate and if he has survived persistent reduction and banalisation this is partly owing to the built-in resistance of his writing as seen in TSZ. But that in turn leads to the other horn of the prophetic dilemma. How does Nietzsche, if he understands his own thought, already embody it personally and experientially?

I have commented on the non-introspective, allegorical method of Zarathustra's presentation. Within a short fiction spanning many years, we are invited to infer an inner life with long periods of private reflection to which we have no further access. Yet in so far as he is a fiction, of course, Zarathustra, like any fictional being, has no such inner being. He exists only in rhetoric: his own and that of the text. To be sure, in realist fiction we are accustomed to accepting the dramatic illusion, or convention, of a permanent inner life in characters such as Elizabeth Bennet or Anna Karenina. The pathos and significance of their stories depend on this. But Zarathustra as allegorical and philosophical fiction is hardly endowed with such a realist psychological hinterground and, precisely in that respect, he provides a further reflection on Nietzsche himself. For if we say that Zarathustra is a fictional possibility of Nietzsche, that does not tidy up the relation so much as open it up to more vertiginous regress. The figure we call Nietzsche, in accordance with everything that figure says about identity, is a highly constructed and largely textual being, a creation, in some imponderable measure, of his own will. Hence Zarathustra's dramatised selfhood is a telling emblem of something not sufficiently noticed about Nietzsche himself: what Daniel Conway calls 'the

---

[31] 'Liberal institutions immediately cease to be liberal as soon as they are attained', *TI, op. cit.* p. 103.

self-referential blind spot that vitiates his critical enterprise'.[32] For he seems to exist almost exclusively as an exemplary figure created by his own rhetoric. I have stressed the rhetorical control, the psychological penetration, and the historical absorbency, from which Nietzsche derives his authority. Yet these qualities are compatible with, and may even entail, a corresponding blind spot with regard to a more ordinary mode of self-awareness. Peter Stern, and others, have remarked that Nietzsche, as thinker, was almost blank in the 'realm of association', the everyday need for political and social interaction.[33] There is a less noticed, internal corollary of this in his relation to his self. While he was certainly not a man who 'evaded his genius' (*UM*, 128), the mortal sin of the Nietzschean ethic, that may have meant evading, or of being unable to see, something else. His insight into the general condition of his time derives from his existing to himself as conceptualised in the intellectual inheritance outlined in this study, as if having even to himself a purely exemplary existence defined by the problematics of *Bildung*. And even here he cannot escape the general truth he applied in *Beyond Good and Evil* to all philosophers: that they create world views out of their personal biographies. In that regard, his very strength in making himself a world-historical exemplar fosters a blind spot at a more common level of self-knowledge.

In one sense this is both well-recognised and inconsequential. When Nietzsche describes himself in *The Gay Science* as one of the 'premature births', the phrase is as poignant as it is pregnant.[34] Along with his extraordinary prescience goes the image of one but half made up and sent into the world before his time, not in the sinister sense of Shakespeare's Richard III, but as one radically vulnerable and unwhole. Most modern commentators, including many highly sympathetic to Nietzsche, would accept that, whatever the power of his diagnoses, he himself never embodied the overcoming, or the integral being, that was variously envisaged in such notions as the 'overman' or a 'dancing Socrates'. Although his iconoclasm was undeniably affirmative in spirit, it is hard the believe that he was able personally to internalise, in Joyce's words, 'the wisdom he has written or the laws he has revealed'.[35] This in itself implies no adverse judgement. As the preceding discussion has emphasised, herein lies the enduring strength of his writing. Unlike Rousseau, Nietzsche did not identify his exemplary value with his biographical personality, and nor is he therefore essentially vulnerable to attack on that ground. At the same

---

[32] Daniel Conway, in *Why Nietzsche Still?* ed. Alan D. Schrift (Berkeley and Los Angeles: University of California Press, 2000) p. 33.

[33] Peter Stern, *Nietzsche*, Fontana Classics (Glasgow: Collins, 1978) p. 146.

[34] *The Gay Science, op. cit.* p. 279.

[35] James Joyce, *Ulysses*, ed. Hans Walter Gabler *et al.* (London: Bodley Head, 1986) p. 162, ll. 7–8.

time, the very impersonality of his self-reference, while brilliantly serving his rhetorical purposes, suggests a possible blank at the heart of his own experience of the self. Whereas we usually think of impersonality as hard to achieve, it is as if Nietzsche lived overwhelmingly on that plane rather than a personal one. What is the Nietzschean self behind the rhetorical persona? It may be a vertiginous hollow, a volcanic inferno, or an averagely sick animal for all we can directly know from the published *oeuvre* in which he figures so strongly

The question of Nietzsche's self-knowledge is frequently met with reference to his self-presentation in *Ecce Homo* and to Freud's memorable remark that he had 'a more penetrating knowledge of himself than any other man who ever lived, or was ever likely to live'.[36] He may have done, but the question is whether we can know this of him, and what exactly it means. The two familiar references rather reinforce and clarify the point I am making. His self-reference in *Ecce Homo*, apart from any other questions about the nature and purpose of that work, is in the spirit of what has been seen in other works. Even as he apparently steps forward to address the reader personally, we sense only the more strongly the dramatic control of his continuing performance. He speaks of himself variously as the litmus of the historical condition, or as the genius, but always in the impersonal context of his functions. Freud's remark is even more telling in this regard and helps to define more closely the nature of Nietzsche's exemplarity. Ernest Jones notes that Freud kept a wary distance from Nietzsche who had only too evidently anticipated some of his own major insights. His hyperbolic compliment just quoted, made after attending a reading of Nietzsche in October 1908, is both pre-emptive and assimilative, as Jones's own comment implicitly suggests: 'From the first explorer of the unconscious this is a handsome compliment.' The compliment attributes to Nietzsche a power of recognition for which the Freudian terms are an implicit condition. Nietzsche, it suggests, has looked into himself, and like Freud as explorer of the unconscious, he has discovered the pre-civilised domain of primordial instinct. What Freud implicitly praises in Nietzsche is not personal self-knowledge so much as the recognition of a universal discovery for which Freud is the Columbus. The remark suggests, therefore, that he could look through himself to another level of exemplarity in the manner I have been suggesting throughout the present chapter. In this respect, Nietzsche recovered what Hegel saw as the ancient Greek meaning of 'know thyself', referring not to the individual personality but to the human as such.[37]

---

[36] Ernest Jones, *Sigmund Freud: Life and Work*, vol. 2, *Years of Maturity 1901–1919* (London: Hogarth Press, 1967) p. 385.
[37] Georg Wilhelm Friedrich Hegel, *The Philosophy of History* (New York: Dover, 1956) p. 220.

At the same time, the conjunction of Freud and Nietzsche usefully highlights the difference between their respective notions of the unconscious in a way that also bears on this study. It is a difference whereby Freud's model might be seen as a mystification of Nietzsche's. Freud's tragic conception of civilisation as founded on instinctual repression and sublimation is challenged by Nietzsche's sense of tragedy as Dionysian affirmation. And Freud's tendency to reify the unconscious as the realm of the inaccessible is different from uses of the term that might be derived from Nietzsche's less systematically theorised account of the psyche. Throughout this study the word 'unconscious' has been used in a Nietzschean sense of the 'open secret'; not so much inaccessible as unnoticed. It is more in keeping with the spirit of late twentieth-century deconstruction for which Nietzsche is a philosophical, and Joyce a literary, patron. Joyce's genius was for turning depth into surface in the spirit precisely of Nietzsche's view of the ancient Greeks as being superficial out of profundity.[38] Deconstruction exposes the unconscious of texts not by means of depth analysis, such as by invoking the secret structures of myth, repression etc., but through the internal logic of their own textuality. Likewise, the denial of the substantive subject which accompanies most forms of deconstructive analysis is one of its problematic aspects, both theoretically in terms of agency and *ad hominem* in its frequent manifestation of personal *ego* in the writing. I am suggesting this question is already present, both positively and negatively, in Nietzsche. His capacity to question the substantive *ego* is closely allied to his capacity, noted by Hollingdale and others, to experience his personal existence impersonally as a function of the historical culture. Nietzsche seems really to have lived a deconstructive *ego*.

I emphasise this aspect because it helps to explain why his greatest force lies in his diagnostic and critical insight rather than in the affirmation by which it is theoretically informed. The authenticity of the affirmation is not in question. His diagnostic rhetoric has a hyperbolic energy and control, a focused power of wit, which make it in itself an effective form of affirmation. His writing, even in the act of rejection, constitutes an essential assertion of life. In that respect, his remark on Schopenhauer bears, once again, more truly upon himself: 'there is a kind of denying and destroying that is a discharge of that mighty longing for sanctification and salvation.' (*UM*, 153) But what is at stake is something else: the possibility of testing instantiation, the turning of speculative rhetoric into concrete possibility. By living so fully *in* the rhetoric, the affirmation lives it too completely *as* rhetoric. We cannot inspect more directly what quality of life underwrites the overcoming of dark diagnosis with

---

[38] The remark is in *Nietzsche contra Wagner*. See *The Portable Nietzsche*, ed. and trans. Walter Kaufmann (London: Chatto and Windus, 1971) p. 683.

optimistic affirmation. To that extent he cannot entirely escape the condition he recognises in contemporary philosophical forms of vitalism. He observes that, in contrast to the ancient Greeks whose vitality was evident even as they condemned human life, 'it is precisely the more modern philosophers who are among the mightiest promoters of life'. (*UM*, 145) Hence, for all his deconstructive self-awareness, or precisely because of it, it was not within his power to instantiate heuristically his own intuitions. We have too little to get hold of and test, as Keats put it, 'on the pulses'.[39] In that sense, *Zarathustra*, as reverse *Bildungsroman* and conscious fiction, is importantly not a novel at all.

But if Nietzsche could give little concrete guidance in the affirmative art of living, several of the modernist generation in literature were to offer such testing specificities within the conditions, and the metaphysic, which he had defined. It is worth noting here that the term *Bildungsroman* was given its present currency only as late as 1904 by Wilhelm Dilthey. In the nineteenth century the term was used by several critics but remained a nonce term.[40] That may reflect the fact that the ideal of all-round *Bildung* was a newly active concern of the later period for which the institutionalised, classic status of Goethe was being enlisted. A nonce tradition of fiction influenced by Goethe became reified into a programmatic genre concerned with the achievement of personal wholeness through cultural acquisition. Anglophone modernism had a parallel anxiety over a widely presumed loss of personal and cultural wholeness as focused, for example, in the currency of the phrase 'dissociation of sensibility', a conception which was also derived from, or fathered on, an earlier period of literary history. W. B. Yeats, Thomas Mann, and James Joyce variously took up aspects of the Nietzschean problematic but in important respects they were all too close to Nietzsche's own mode of rhetoric and thought to test it in the most crucial ways. In this regard, the modern thinker for whom his legacy was most significantly, because contrastively, embodied, and for whom the complex interrelations of pedagogy and wholeness remained central, was the philosophically alert poet, novelist, and cultural prophet, D. H. Lawrence.

[39] Letter to Reynolds, 3 May 1818. *The Letters of John Keats*, ed. Maurice Buxton Forman, 2nd edn. (Oxford: Oxford University Press, 1935) p. 142.
[40] See on this James Hardin, ed., *op. cit.* Several contributors cover this theme but especially Hartmut Steinecke, pp. 89–92.

Part II

6

'The Passion of Instruction': D. H. Lawrence and Wholeness versus *Bildung*

'Thought is man in his wholeness, wholly attending'[1]

Of all European novelists, it was Thomas Mann who showed the most substantial and self-evident impact of Nietzsche and, not surprisingly, the tradition of the *Bildungsroman* comes close to imploding in his hands. In *The Magic Mountain* (1924) the vein of pedagogical scepticism that runs through the genre from the outset becomes, as it were, the dominant note.[2] But if Mann provided an especially appropriate literary medium for Nietzsche's thought it was partly because, by Anglo-Saxon models and assumptions, he was not so much a novelist as an orchestrator of philosophical and cultural themes.[3] Part of the difficulty of Nietzsche's thought lies in determining at what level of rhetorical or speculative bracketing particular arguments or statements are to be taken. Mann's extraordinary skill was to create the internal framings and obliquities by which passionately held convictions can resonate with both a dangerous power and an eerie emptiness. He creates literary equivalents of Nietzsche's perspectival heurism and hyperbole. In such fictions, he was able to enact an internal resistance to the Nietzschean legacy, an internal agon that notably culminated in *Doctor Faustus* (1947). But in significant respects,

---

[1] 'Thought', *The Complete Poems of D. H. Lawrence*, ed. Vivian de Sola Pinto and Warren Roberts (New York: Viking, 1964) vol. ii, p. 673.

[2] As a further twist of the pedagogical theme, in Mann's last major novel, *Doctor Faustus*, the uncanny schoolboy precocity of Adrian Leverkuhn makes him, in Serenus Zeitblom's words, the bad pupil who is top of the class. *Doctor Faustus*, trans. H. T. Lowe-Porter (London: Penguin, 1968) p. 47.

[3] He may have been acknowledging something like this in the following comment: '... when I hear myself being called "the foremost novelist of the age" I want to hide my head. Nonsense! I am no such thing; Joseph Conrad was, as people ought to know. I could never have written *Nostromo*, nor the magnificent *Lord Jim*; and if he could not have written *The Magic Mountain* or *Doctor Faustus*, the account balances out very much in his favor.' Letter to Irita van Doren, 28 Aug. 1951, *The Letters of Thomas Mann*, sel. and trans. by Richard and Clara Winston (London: Penguin, 1975) p. 445.

his special suitability for the mediation of Nietzschean thought meant that he could not achieve the distance required for a sufficiently radical critique. His very lucidity creates a blind spot whereby Nietzschean notions of the Dionysian 'other' to civilisation, or the asociality of the artist, act very often as unexamined premises in Mann's fiction. As fictional premises, they are overtly hypothetical in a fundamental sense, and yet their hypothetical nature cannot be truly examined as such within a fiction that is dependent on them. The brilliance of *Doctor Faustus*, for example, lies partly in the way the terms of the historical allegory invested in the modern German composer, Adrian Leverkuhn, are built up within the narrative, as for example through the lectures of Wendell Kretschmar. The allegory, that is to say, does not rest crudely on the ground either of history, or of an *a priori* theory, but creates itself as a consciously speculative lens through which to view that history. By the same token, however, the work is vulnerable when a reader, such as Michael Beddow, questions in more literal terms the historical justification of the allegory.[4] For, indeed, the work has in some measure to invite such questioning even as it evades it.

In this respect, D. H. Lawrence is the significant parallel to Thomas Mann. Stated in the abstract, the themes and diagnoses of these two writers are remarkably similar although their literary universes were poles apart, as each of them recognised.[5] Seeing the parallel between them, therefore, is to recognise them as lines which could never meet. As Karl Kerenyi anticipated, from its first conception, Mann's *Joseph and his Brothers* (1933–43), as the modern narration of a generational saga following a Biblical model, lends itself to close comparison with Lawrence's *The Rainbow* (1915). But for present purposes the significant parallel is between *The Magic Mountain* and *Women in Love* (1920).[6] Both were diagnostic studies of modern European culture conceived before the war of 1914–18. Each was rewritten after the war with the wartime experience thematically assimilated. In Lawrence's case publication of an earlier version in 1916 was impossible after the banning of *The Rainbow*, while Mann delayed completion of his novel until he had sufficiently digested

---

[4] Michael Beddow, *Thomas Mann's Doctor Faustus* (Cambridge: Cambridge University Press, 1994).

[5] See Lawrence's review of *Death in Venice* in *Phoenix: the Posthumous Papers of D. H. Lawrence*, ed. Edward D. McDonald (London: Heinemann, 1961) pp. 308–13, and *Mythology and Humanism: The Correspondence of Thomas Mann and Karl Kerenyi*, trans. Alexander Gelley (Ithaca NY: Cornell University Press, 1975) p. 77.

[6] For a sustained comparison of Mann with *Women in Love* see T. E. Apter, *Thomas Mann: The Devil's Advocate* (London: 1978). Apter makes shrewd points though with perhaps insufficient attention to the difference in literary and philosophical worlds. See also Michael Bell, 'D. H. Lawrence and Thomas Mann: *Unbewuste Brüderschaft*', *Études Lawrenciennes*, 10 (1994) 187–97.

the experience of the war.[7] Both employ a symbolic geography of the psyche: Mann's ranging with cultural horizontality from American to Russian while Lawrence's depth psychology runs vertically from Nordic to African. Both books concern intellectuals, and subject the processes of intellection and argument to radical scepticism. For both of them, a setting in alpine snows figures a deathly condition of the culture as each diagnoses the ambiguity of living and deathly tendencies in love, in sickness, and in art. Both use a modernist spatialisation of narrative for the analysis of a modern condition which threatens to place a terminus on the temporal processes of both history and *Bildung* although both works are ultimately affirmative and unclosed.

And yet despite these similarities, comparison seems almost perverse given the difference in imaginative universes and philosophical or psychological premises. Part of the difference is that Mann's orchestration of ambivalences is usually at a high level of abstraction while his decorously controlled irony takes the reader into its privileged viewpoint. For example, the horror that Castorp sees in the 'Snow' episode, of witches tearing apart and consuming a child, is essentially literary and symbolic. Generations of readers have, therefore, been intellectually stirred and emotionally moved by the book, but not perhaps viscerally disturbed. Lawrence, by contrast, creates no such veil of art or overt ironic distance. In a book replete with bitter argument and psychological, as well as physical, violence the writing is as raw as the feeling. And it is this quality that most divides the readership. I take it all readers find Lawrence difficult to read at times, but for different reasons. Some, like Thomas Mann writing to Kerenyi, will be unable to stomach his 'hectic sensuality', while others will see something at stake in his mode of writing for which a writer like Mann has no equivalent. Thomas Mann is ultimately too decorous to be a fully adequate vehicle of Nietzschean thought: in Mann, Nietzsche's challenging harshness is softened while his heuristic mobility is reified into system. Lawrence, by contrast, while having the essential artistic control, philosophical intelligence, and psychological insight, has the visceral directness, self-exposure, and readerly discomfort that Nietzsche's thought properly entails.

If Lawrence engaged the parts of Nietzsche that Thomas Mann did not reach, this reflects a significant shift with respect to all the principal authors still to be discussed. Modern critics have emphasised that the *Bildungsroman* performs its most important pedagogical function *on* the reader rather than *in* the hero. But this is, of course, to speak primarily of the implied reader created by the narrative self-consciousness of the genre. With Nietzsche, the emphasis shifts rather to a challenge felt by the actual reader and enacted in

---

[7] See *Tagebücher* (Frankfurt/M: Fischer, 1979) pp. 200–1.

the partisanship of literal responses. Of course, Lawrence, like F. R. Leavis and J. M. Coetzee, has an implied reader, but the consciousness that the real reader is likely not to endorse the Lawrencean values or diagnoses becomes increasingly strong in his major fiction until it virtually dissolves the dramatic form of the novel itself.[8] In that respect, Thomas Mann kept faith with the ironic artistry of the *Bildungsroman* while Lawrence is the significantly testing inheritor of the Nietzschean problematic.

Lawrence was a teacher before becoming a writer with a distinctly prophetic orientation. His central concern was with a quality of being, variously described as wholeness, singleness, and spontaneity, which was difficult to articulate with its proper experiential force, and especially against the grain of the culture. Despite his articulacy, therefore, he constantly experienced the futility of both pedagogy and prophecy on matters of fundamental value. Since then the culture has moved notionally in 'his' direction in becoming more 'liberated', which is largely an incomprehending banalisation, while his positive vision of wholeness remains largely unknown. He is a writer for whom the reception is almost as significant as the work itself and the open secret theme reaches a new level with the phenomenon of educated incomprehension. In his fine introduction to Lawrence's letters, Aldous Huxley remarked that he had known personally many of the leading figures of his time but whereas others seemed more talented in various ways than himself, Lawrence struck him uniquely as being different in kind rather than degree.[9] To his credit, although he was himself an intellectual through and through, Huxley could recognise, and honour, Lawrence's otherness in precisely that regard. Lawrence always offers this challenge to academically educated readers who need to take seriously, rather than with the intended irony, T. S. Eliot's comment that Lawrence was 'incapable of what is ordinarily called thinking'.[10] Many are now educated confidently to look down on Lawrence as a thinker, and in a sense that is right. For no more than with Nietzsche would it be appropriate to look *up* to him in a spirit of discipleship. But any looking down should be a matter of questioning the ground on which one stands, and the wholeness with which one thinks. Of course, this is not to say that Lawrence himself consistently enjoyed wholeness of being either in his art or in his personal life. On the contrary, it is only as an achievement against the odds, and with the experience of being deeply unwhole, that it acquires its significance. The value lies in the criterion and the struggle; the insight these generated; and the works of representative sanity by which these are vindicated. Since few of us are simply

[8] I trace this complex process in *D. H. Lawrence: Language and Being* (Cambridge: Cambridge University Press, 1992).
[9] *The Letters of D. H. Lawrence*, ed. Aldous Huxley (London: Heinemann, 1932) p. xxx.
[10] *After Strange Gods* (London: Faber, 1934) p. 48. The book was of course withdrawn by Eliot.

whole, he is overwhelmingly concerned with diagnosing the spirit of different kinds of failure which often means distinguishing the potentially creative from the merely decadent or stultifying.

At the end of the 1914–18 war, while still revising *Women in Love*, he wrote a number of articles which were not published but were rewritten two years later as a long essay on the 'Education of the People'. This was just after the Fisher Education Act of 1918 which was intended to put the national education system on a new footing, and to extend the education of non-academic children.[11] In the essay, he sought to define the integral singleness of being for which education should aim: 'The Japanese know that one flower is lovelier than many flowers. Alone, one flower lives and has its own integral wonder. Massed with other flowers, it has a being-in-common, and this being-in-common is always inferior to the single aloneness of one creature.'[12] The essay remained unpublished in his lifetime and its often hyperbolic tone and substance suggest an awareness that, despite its underlying seriousness in arguing an education for wholeness, its recommendations were unlikely to be adopted in the national educational system. And if it was difficult for Lawrence to translate his vision of life into a literary or pedagogical practice, it remains peculiarly difficult to 'teach' him. The danger is of turning him into something teachable, and no doubt the school or seminar room only too often transposes the quick of Lawrencean life into pedagogical banality. But the proposition can also be reversed: the pedagogical context throws Lawrencean quickness into relief. The pedagogy theme within his work focuses the difficulty of defining such quickness of being, or of giving it a generalisable value beyond the manifold individual instantiations in his *oeuvre*, yet the 'struggle into verbal consciousness',[13] which provides the essential action of *Women in Love*, is necessary and unavoidable. In engaging these questions, Lawrence takes forward the expressive predicaments seen in Goethe and Nietzsche.

The Passion of Instruction

As Lawrence resigned from his teaching career and sought to establish himself as a full-time writer, he also started the thinking that would lead to his major novels: *The Rainbow* and *Women in Love*. One central character, Ursula

---

[11] H. A. Fisher, a historian, was the President of the wartime Board of Education. The promotors of the act sought to establish a truly national system of school education and extend the leaving age for all pupils till eighteen. The 1944 Education Act sought the same extension, also without success.

[12] *Reflections on the Death of a Porcupine and Other Essays*, ed. Michael Herbert (Cambridge: Cambridge University Press, 1988) p.139.

[13] *Women in Love*, ed. David Farmer, Lindeth Vasey, and John Worthen (Cambridge: Cambridge University Press, 1987) p. 486.

Brangwen, is a school-teacher and Rupert Birkin, with whom she forms a life relationship, is a school inspector. *WL* is generally acknowledged to be the most important and summative of Lawrence's novels, and as I have indicated elsewhere it is also the fulcrum on which his novelistic *oeuvre* turns.[14] Its internal fulcrum is Birkin's abortive struggle for pedagogical authority. In that respect, he is Lawrence's Zarathustra.

The two novels, initially conceived as one, became very different in kind. *R*, concerned with the Brangwens' family and social history echoes nineteenth-century historical form and has the future-oriented image of the rainbow as its defining symbol. *WL*, concerned with the modern generation, is a spatialised narrative structuring the psyche as a geographical polarity of Nordic and African. This strikingly parallels Goethe's shift from the teleological movement of *WMA* to the archival and symbolic spatialising of *WMJ*. Likewise, after Joyce's *A Portrait of the Artist as a Young Man*, the story of Stephen Dedalus' would-be teleological *Bildung* gives way to the paradigmatic instance of modernist superhistorical spatialising in *Ulysses*. On Stephen's return to Dublin, however, as an apparent stalling of his previous onward quest, he finds himself in the ironic position of teaching history to schoolboys, and it is fitting that the two 'Lawrencean' characters, Birkin and Ursula, have their first substantive conversation in a chapter entitled 'Class-room'. As in Yeats' 'Among School Children', which I believe to be his greatest poem, the elementary classroom is the fitting location for a wounded affirmation of wholeness arising from an emotional action of mingled repression and recognition. Misplaced idealism is already at work in the cultural initiation of the young.

As Michael Ragussis has analysed in detail, *WL* is the novel in which Lawrence first developed his heuristic method of exploring a theme through key terms which constantly shift in meaning.[15] The word 'individual', for example, represents both the isolated ego of modernity and the integral wholeness that Lawrence sought to foster. Such words are not fixed by a defined 'idea' but constantly shift according to context. Even as he developed this exploratory orientation towards the future, however, he found himself fighting on two fronts. For this is also the work in which he began to struggle radically with the question of his own authority. As he entered his full power and thematic range as a novelist, so he became fully conscious of the difficulty in communicating his world view at all, and specifically in the form of the novel. In *WL*, these difficulties are contained within the frame of the novel by

[14] See *D. H. Lawrence: Language and Being* op. cit., the chapter on *WL* and *passim*.
[15] Michael Ragussis, *The Subterfuge of Art: Language and the Romantic Tradition* (Baltimore: Johns Hopkins University Press, 1978).

their becoming a thematic focus in their own right as the 'Class-room' episode already indicates.

Ursula's life as a teacher in WL seems strikingly different from her initiation in R. In the earlier novel she suffered from the obligation to exercise an institutional authority for which the common manifestations were largely false and vulgar. Nonetheless she developed the necessary second skin and, whatever the brute social reality of elementary school teaching in the period, or at any time, good teachers will create their own worlds within it. She appears now to be relatively content and successful, and in genuine rapport with her pupils. The afternoon has darkened and, as she has not broken the mood by switching on the lights, the pupils' heads are illuminated by the red-gold light of the sun. As the window lets in the outside world of nature, the door effectively shuts out social and institutional intrusion while Ursula is 'absorbed in the passion of instruction'. (WL, 35) This phrase seems highly positive and suggests her professional maturity in making the emotional investment she had initially made too naively. She had at first imagined herself in a loving, highly personal, relation to her pupils, and admired by her colleagues. But genuine passion in Lawrence is always impersonalising and she has now developed a truly pedagogical relation focused through the subject. Teachers may legitimately take satisfaction in the love of their pupils, but only as an outcome, not as the motive. Accordingly, while absorbed in the passion of instruction, Ursula no longer places herself on the level of the pupils, and part of her is held in reserve.

At the same time, the *word* 'passion' in Lawrence frequently, even predominantly, has overtones of falsity as, for example, in his critique of John Galsworthy, and Ursula is not entirely free of such an implication.[16] Likewise, there can be a measure of emotional alibi in professional reserve, as occurs with Dr Fergusson in the 'The Horse-Dealer's Daughter'.[17] The underlying reason for Ursula's reserve is suggested in the sentence: 'The day had gone by like so many more, in an activity that was like a trance.' (WL, 35) Throughout the early part of the novel Ursula lives in a trance. She performs her daily round as if cut off from any deeper connection with herself or with others. This elusively separate quality maddens her father and attracts Birkin in the episode of the abortive proposal. (WL, 258–61) It attracts him because her instinctive reserve with respect to her deeper self is not a sign of repression but of keeping herself *in* reserve. It suggests a potential equivalent in her of his own desire for singleness in relationship, a desire he tries to express as a mutual non-possessiveness in the image of 'star' equilibrium. Yet they fall into mutual

---

[16] *Study of Thomas Hardy and Other Essays*, ed. Bruce Steele (Cambridge: Cambridge University Press, 1985) pp. 209–20.
[17] I have discussed this story at length in *Literature, Modernism and Myth* (Cambridge: Cambridge University Press, 1997) pp. 97–111.

misunderstanding because, while she is naturally single but seeks relationship, he has experienced relationship only as engulfing his singleness. Although she enjoys intuitively the singleness he consciously seeks, it has not been an issue for her because she has never been challenged to a true commitment. In her former relationship with Anton Skrebensky, her assertion of singleness was destructive for him without being properly educative for her.[18] Hence her state of 'trance' is ambivalent. While reflecting a genuine absorption in her activity, it also signals a deeper lack of fulfilment in her life and her state of half-consciousness is in keeping with the unnoticed darkening of the room. Lawrence's fiction typically concerns a twilight zone of half-awareness. Birkin, however, is the principal dramatic agent of the novel's 'struggle into verbal consciousness' and when he comes into the room he interrupts the atmosphere by switching on the lights. The episode then proceeds to a characteristic double process: it overtly thematises the nature of knowledge in a bitter and unresolved argument while subtextually dramatising the same question in a more positive countermovement.

As the pupils learn about catkins, Birkin insists on attention to the object, or what he calls the 'fact', rather than the 'subjective impression'. (WL, 36) They should draw a brief visual notation of the essential form with no purpose of self-expression. In seeking to remove the sentimentalism which obscures perception and knowledge Birkin, in his insistence on fact, almost plays the Gradgrind figure from Dickens' *Hard Times*. When Hermione Roddice arrives, however, she questions the value of forcing the pupils into consciousness at all.

Readers generally recognise that Hermione gives a reductive version of Birkin/Lawrence's own convictions, and is indeed the 'Lawrence' of popular reputation. Birkin experiences the nightmare and nemesis of all teaching as she parrots his own view. It is worth pausing, however, on the exact nature of what is wrong with what she says: ' "Hadn't they better be anything than grow up crippled, crippled in their souls, crippled in their feelings—so thrown back—so turned back on themselves—incapable—" Hermione clenched her fist like one in a trance— "of any spontaneous action, always deliberate, always burdened with choice, never carried away." ' (WL, 40) Her critique is clearly self-reflexive: it is she who is most crippled and unable to be 'carried away' which she imagines as the alternative. But while critics are broadly right to see her incomprehending relation to Birkin/Lawrence's meaning, it is not clear how far this can be deduced, as is often supposed, simply from her form of words. For Lawrence gives due emphasis elsewhere to the point she is making.

---

[18] Cf. *The Rainbow*, ed. Mark Kinkead-Weekes (Cambridge: Cambridge University Press, 1989) pp. 443–5.

Moreover, he is frequently hyperbolic, and open to self-parody, as occurs in the episode of 'Gudrun in the Pompadour'. (*WL*, 382–5) He could express himself pretty much in Hermione's words, and in his essay on the 'Education of the People' he gives equally intense expression to a similar thought: 'the human being craves for change in his automatism. Sometimes it seems to him horrible that he must, in a fixed routine, get up in the morning and put his clothes on, day in, day out. He can't bear his automatism. He is beside himself in his self-consciousness.'[19] Birkin's attack on Hermione, therefore, has to be essentially *ad feminam* in a way that almost *requires* authorial intervention. There is a constant narrative emphasis on her peculiar manner: her 'convulsed movement', her 'sing-song' voice, and the 'queer rumbling in her throat'. (*WL*, 40) The reference to her bodily gesture is intruded even into her speech. Lawrence has no choice but to put his thumb in the scale in his presentation of her, for the problem is not that she cannot understand, but that *she* cannot understand. The same general idea or form of words has a radically different significance not so much *for* her, as *in* her. By Ezra Pound's principle that the value of the idea inheres in the quality of the personality which inhabits it, when she argues for wholeness, she is not in error, so much as 'wholly' wrong. In this respect, she typifies a certain fatedness in the novel's characterisation generally.

In response, Birkin is soon caught in his own 'passion of instruction' as he tries to explain the falsity of experience known only 'in the head'. Neither of the women understand him although, objectively speaking, he makes his point as clearly as could be imagined. Hermione parallels Ursula by being in her own kind of 'trance', and does not wish, or could not afford, to understand. But the point is obscure to Ursula too because what he says has no experiential significance for her as he expresses it. He has the idea but cannot experience the singleness, while she possesses the intuitive singleness without the idea of it. Hence the depth of his 'exasperation' as he speaks while 'hating his own metaphors'. (*WL*, 40) He feels intensely the revulsion expressed by Nietzsche in *Twilight of the Idols*: 'Our true experiences are not at all garrulous.... Whatever we have words for we have got beyond. In all talk there is a grain of contempt. Language, it seems, was invented only for what is average, medium, communicable. With language the speaker immediately vulgarises himself.' (*TI*, 94) Birkin's predicament also recalls Goethe's aphorism: 'What I really know, I know only for myself. A spoken word is rarely useful; it mostly excites contradiction, deadlock and standstill.' (*WMYT*, 132) But Birkin would not emulate Goethe's Olympian detachment, and there is a further, self-directed edge in his exasperation. Even as he attacks Hermione's purely mental sensuality, his anger, as in the Nietzsche passage, hints at a measure of

---

[19] *RDP, op. cit.* p. 131.

self-recognition: her condition is only a more extreme and unknowing version of his own. Hence, when he tells her that her 'loathsome little skull... ought to be cracked like a nut' (*WL*, 40) he unwittingly anticipates the service she will shortly perform for him with a lump of lapis lazuli. (*WL*, 105) When she strikes him, he implicitly accepts her rough justice, as the blow to the head of the Lawrencean spokesman expresses the author's own self-exasperation.

While the characters argue apparently fruitlessly about the nature of knowledge, the narrative explores the same term subtextually. In bringing the light of consciousness so abruptly into the scene, Birkin does not create understanding, but his passion breaks Ursula out of her trance. She thinks of 'solving her problems, in the light of his words' (*WL*, 43) until, at the end, she switches off the lights and, after a moment of absorption, 'began to cry, bitterly, bitterly weeping: but whether for misery or joy she never knew'. (*WL*, 45) The moment of potential emotional growth explicitly eludes her knowledge. A modern equivalent is needed for her grandfather, Tom Brangwen's, relation to his wife, Lydia: 'He did not know her any better, any more fully, now that he knew her altogether.' (*R*, 91) In *R*, the narrative commentary at this moment separates out in Tom and Lydia these modes of knowing which they could not articulate. Ursula and Birkin, by contrast, are driven to articulate their own feelings and the episode shows them making the first steps towards another kind of knowing which they themselves do not yet know.

The focus has shifted from the formal academic knowledge required by the school children to emotional understanding in the principal characters. Lawrence recognised these were different orders but he would put them on a continuum whereby they inform each other. He describes elsewhere the special processes of the 'emotional mind' when arriving at a decision or negotiating a crisis:

Now the emotional mind... is not logical. It is a psychological fact, that when we are thinking emotionally or passionately, thinking and feeling at the same time, we do not think rationally: and therefore, and therefore, and therefore. Instead, the mind makes curious swoops and circles. It touches the point of pain or interest, then sweeps away again in a cycle, coils round and approaches again the point of pain or interest. There is a curious spiral rhythm, and the mind approaches again and again the point of concern, repeats itself, goes back, destroys the time-sequence entirely, so that time ceases to exist as the mind stoops to the quarry, then leaves it without striking, soars, hovers, turns, swoops, stoops again, still does not strike, yet is nearer, nearer, reels away again, wheels off into the air, even forgets, quite forgets, yet again turns, bends, circles slowly, swoops and stoops again, until at last there is the closing-in, and the clutch of a decision or a resolve.[20]

[20] *Phoenix, op. cit.* pp. 249–50.

Lawrence defines this as the special behaviour of the '*emotional* mind' but equally of the 'emotional *mind*'. When his language hovers on oxymoron, due weight must be given to both sides. He did not separate off the 'emotional' but saw it is an integral and implicit aspect of all thinking. This is easy and uncontroversial to say, perhaps easier now than in Lawrence's time, but it remains no less difficult to realise. His fiction typically dramatises the momentary process of understanding in the twilight region in which it is never fixed. Vital truth of the kind in question here is not a proposition to be reached and retained so much as a constant momentary adjustment to the inner and outer worlds. Its coherence is to be judged by a vertical criterion of wholeness rather than a horizontal consistency. At its best, however, Lawrence's discursive prose also achieves this with its constant working through of underlying emotional themes. His notion of a 'poetry of the present' may stand for a more general mental outlook: whatever is consciously formulated as knowledge is constantly open to being superseded, which is why he is not to be read doctrinally. It is not just that he constantly revises, explores, and changes his mind. Even where a particular attitude or conception has not apparently changed, it is no longer the recognition pertaining to the individual moment: 'My yea! of today is oddly different from my yea! of yesterday.' (*STH*, 196) Both Goethe and Nietzsche understood this very well in their own ways and there is, once again, a curious functional equivalence to Goethe through chiasmic opposition. Lawrence's relation to his own beliefs was hardly to be described as aesthetic and yet the heurism of fiction played a vital role in the internal process of his understanding. His literary criticism provides a particularly useful example of a discursive mode combining exploratory thought and feeling.

In his reading, Lawrence could study wholeness in others. Just as Birkin aspires to wholeness, and acknowledges that a certain process of dissolution may have to be undergone on the way to achieving this, so Lawrence read individual works and entire literary traditions in this light. He came to see the modern Russians, for example, with their remarkable explorations of dissolution and disintegration, as effectively caught in a psychological impasse. Their very self-consciousness had effectively blocked other possibilities of renewal or self-perception. Hence his approval of V. V. Rozanov, who 'when he is not Russianizing, is the first Russian really to see it, and to recover, if unstably, the old human wholeness'. (*Phoenix*, 370) By contrast, the apparently familiar works of the American tradition, still often classified at that time as adventure books, children's stories, or religious and moral allegories, had for him a subtextual life which was partly repressed, but also released, by the conscious moral alibis of the authors. American idealism, including the idealism of money-making, is a loss of wholeness, and the consciously asserted freedom of Americans is 'a rattling of chains'.²¹ Despite their rhetoric of freedom, the early settlers 'hated the flowing ease of humour in the old Europe'. (*SCAL*, 17) Yet half-consciously, beneath the moral rhetoric, the shock and expansion to the soul in the American adventure created new psychic possibilities.

Studies in Classic American Literature, also known by Lawrence's intended title of *The Symbolic Meaning*, remains one of the most original and significant treatments of the national literature. Lawrence explores the twilight zone of consciousness in the writing of the classic American authors, and enacts his opening injunction: 'Never trust the artist. Trust the tale.' (*SCAL*, 14) This maxim is his one abiding legacy as a critic although it has since been reinvented in different terms, and thereby sometimes traduced. Roland Barthes' notion of 'The Death of the Author', in its eagerness to demystify the Gallic institution of authorship, loses something vital.²² For Lawrence, the text reveals the wholeness or otherwise of the psyche in which it was created. On this model, the wholeness of the critic is on test too in entering into the agonistic struggle of the author. Lawrence's critical procedure is to read testingly alongside the author's imagined process of creation. Intending the essays to be delivered as lectures in America, he adopted an informal, highly personalised manner which initially seems an irritating affectation but is actually functional. It constantly focuses the arena of responsibility in the author while never allowing authorship to be reified or mystified. His ostentatious avoidance of a professional academic register also has a more general implication. There is much at stake for a criterion of wholeness in his use of the most common terms for complex thought, and this applies pre-eminently to the word 'wholeness' itself.

The word 'whole' is of such common usage and general meaning that it can be little more than a place-holder for the significance Lawrence requires it to bear. He is obliged, therefore, to be quite concrete in instantiating it. He steals no parasitical ride on terms of art, and gives the word a precise force only through its contexts. In that regard, its usage is at one with its meaning. By the same token, such everyday vocabulary is peculiarly vulnerable when detached from its context. It carries no implicit warning of being a term of art. This has been highly significant for his reception. His informal discourse has obscured the distinctiveness of Lawrencean wholeness. Only if you recognise it as a serious conception does it reveal itself as something quite new. This may seem at first a surprising claim. Lawrence's wholeness has plenty of antecedents

---

[21] *Studies in Classic American Literature*, ed. Ezra Greenspan, Lindeth Vasey, and John Worthen (Cambridge: Cambridge University Press, 2003) p. 17.

[22] Reprinted in David Lodge, ed., *Modern Criticism and Theory* (London and New York: Longman, 1988) pp. 167–72.

particularly within traditional religious thought, in romantic literature and criticism, and in modern psychological theory. Yet on closer inspection, the very wealth of general models points to an opposite recognition: that there is no one really very like Lawrence in this essential respect. His aphoristic statement that 'thought is the whole man, wholly attending' might, for example, have come from Emerson, but it would then be of a piece, in its generality, with Emerson's essentially public rhetoric. In Lawrence, by contrast, the summative remark takes its force from the variety of ways in which it is dramatically instantiated. As a self-standing generalisation, it is as empty as the maxims on Wilhelm Meister's Certificate of Apprenticeship. What is distinctive in Lawrence resists recognition and dissemination as 'thought' because it is so closely, and properly, tied to its occasions. As 'thought' it is fatally vulnerable to banality.

Comparison with Emerson brings home the epochal reasons for Lawrence's distinctiveness. 'Wholeness' was a modernist preoccupation in a new and urgent way and Lawrence, following Nietzsche, acknowledged most radically, and positively, that wholeness must be achieved in a spirit of metaphysical independence from moral, religious or social orders. Of course, he took these dimensions of human existence seriously, but he understood and judged them by his own criterion of wholeness. These other orders rather depend on it. Schiller's contrast of the 'naive' and the 'sentimental' is a related Enlightenment conception, and the modernist generation variously reflected on failure of wholeness as, for example, in the notion of a 'dissociation of sensibility'. In so far as the Schillerian and modernist notions assume a long-term, collective historical process they hardly admit of being overcome. The modern subject is constituted in these terms which, Schiller thought, only the genius of Goethe could transcend. At the same time, however, in so far as the modern, post-Nietzschean, generation saw that metaphysical orders of value had collapsed, it was possible for responsibility and value to reside in a newly independent way within the integrity of the self. It became possible, and necessary, to think wholeness as such rather than as the overcoming of a given dichotomy. In this respect, the epochal context was both a predicament and an opportunity for which Lawrence's rejection of the 'old stable ego' as defined within a 'moral conception' was cardinal.[23] Post-Rousseauan concern with wholeness, authenticity or sincerity still remained for a long time within the conceptual structure of eighteenth-century sentiment. It was a matter of living up to an extra-personal conception assumed to be prior in value. In Lawrence, by contrast, the impersonal was fully internalised and it was he who most fully

---

[23] Letter to Edward Garnett, 5 June 1914. *The Letters of D. H. Lawrence*, vol. 2, ed. George J. Zytaruk and James T. Boulton (Cambridge: Cambridge University Press, 1981) p. 183.

recognised this as an affirmative possibility: that the wholeness of the self was a pure living purpose not dependent on other orders of value or belief. His radical grasp of this possibility helped to make him incomprehensible to other modernists who were in many respects fighting conservative rearguard actions within their various iconoclasms. But Ezra Pound, who after a brief friendship came to dislike Lawrence personally, always recognised that Lawrence had understood the treatment of modern subjects before he had.[24] That is a high compliment in Pound's book and it was perhaps truer, or more philosophically radical, than Pound realised.

The point can be reinforced by reference to Jeff Wallace's study *D. H. Lawrence, Science and the Posthuman*.[25] Wallace explores in some detail the reading in nineteenth-century thought about science that influenced the dissolution of the 'old stable ego' in Lawrence and he indicates how Lawrence thereby anticipates the 'posthuman' as it has been variously discussed by Gilles Deleuze and Katherine Hayles. Given the diminished reputation of Lawrence in the Anglophone academy, the book is timely in its substance yet polemically distracted by its context. Informed readers of Lawrence, while welcoming the documentation of this moment in literary and intellectual history, will not find the thrust of Wallace's argument new or controversial but he is writing for those who think this author is hopelessly outdated. For this reason, he wishes to explode the supposedly naive humanism of Leavis on which an older reception of Lawrence was based. The problem here, however, is that Lawrence continued to value, and to develop, human wholeness and singleness *within* the recognitions that have come to be called posthuman. In his letter to Garnett rejecting the 'old stable ego' he also refused Marinetti's separation of the human and the non-human. Once this second-order, reconstructed sense of the human has been realised, therefore, it remains the significant emphasis in his work and in that sense Leavis's claim for Lawrence's moral exemplarity was entirely appropriate even though Lawrence's Nietzschean posthumanism is the underlying condition. The desire to present an up-to-date Lawrence can sometimes obscure the fact that we already have one, and may introduce an over-compensatory distortion, as happens I would say with Amit Chaudhuri's 'postmodern' Lawrence.[26]

In sum, Lawrence's 'singleness' is one of the most direct and substantive answers to Nietzsche's call for an affirmative conception of the ego in modernity; a call that emerges from the dissolution of the ego and of the

---

[24] Letter to Harriet Monroe, Mar. 1913. *The Letters of Ezra Pound 1907–1941* (New York: Harcourt, Brace and World, 1950) p. 17.

[25] (London: Palgrave, 2005).

[26] *D. H. Lawrence and Difference: Postcoloniality and the Poetry of the Present* (Oxford: Oxford University Press, 2003).

traditional model of all-round *Bildung*. But if it is not widely recognised that Lawrence fits the space left by Nietzsche's critique of *Bildung*, it is because he so radically changes the terms, and the line of significance becomes clearer when he is linked to the internal deconstruction of these terms in Nietzsche and Goethe.

Lawrence and Nietzsche

Nietzsche's critique of *Bildung* in the early writings led to several controversial and sketchy resolutions in his later *oeuvre*. His personal example is no adequate guide, and his central notion of the 'Overman' provides only the specifications for a position which remains to be filled: the talented individual who answers to specifications often proves to be very different from the abstract personality that might be constructed from them in advance. While Nietzsche's conceptual universe has continued to govern much of his posterity, the truest development of his inheritance might be one that radically alters its terms. One who transcended the felt sense of impasse or paradox in the notion, for example, of the 'dancing Socrates', might not seem to be answering the specifications at all. I believe that Lawrence represents precisely this mixture of similarity and difference in relation to Nietzsche. His general, if ambivalent, responsiveness to Nietzsche is well known.[27] Lawrence clearly assimilated Nietzsche substantially although in a critical spirit far short of discipleship. Whereas the relation is often understood either through Nietzsche's philosophical, or Lawrence's novelistic, terms, I want to focus on their interaction by which Lawrence emerges as a fulfilment of the Nietzschean conception by being its significant anti-type. Here it is necessary to expand what has been said of his literary criticism to encompass his relation to high culture at large.

Sons and Lovers and *The Rainbow* are sometimes referred to, in the more generalised Anglophone usage, as *Bildungsromane*. But Lawrence, like Nietzsche, runs significantly counter to the values of *Bildung* and if R is his major *Bildungsroman* then WL is his significant questioning of *Bildung*; just as the process of *Bildung* in Goethe's WMA is subjected to radical critique in WMJ. In Lawrence's case it is a matter of how the possession of culture is recognised or defined. Lawrence was a highly cultivated man. He had an excellent knowledge of European art and of French, German, Italian, and Spanish literatures at first hand as shown in his translations, reviews, and introductions. His pioneering study of American literature remains a classic

---

[27] For a book-length study see Colin Milton, *Lawrence and Nietzsche* (Aberdeen: University of Aberdeen Press, 1987).

on its theme, and if his intensive reading of Russian was not linguistically at first hand, he was close to those for whom it was.[28] And yet no one, including himself or his admirers, would usually think to describe him in such way. It would seem to miss the point. Overtly cultivated friends, such as Ford Madox Hueffer (Ford) and Aldous Huxley, were impressed by his range of reading and knowledge, but the value lies in his way of ingesting and deploying it.[29] Moreover, from a distance, or for observers with more conventional criteria, he was clearly not recognised as having a cultivated mind. His strength, his absurdities, and his partial incomprehensibility lay in his being so *sui generis*; living 'according to (his) own laws and standards' as Nietzsche recommended in the Schopenhauer essay. (*UM*, 128) It is not always easy to distinguish this from the naive and self-willed commitment to the 'inner voice' which T. S. Eliot spoke of with scorn.[30]

Lawrence and Nietzsche have undergone opposite critical destinies in the latter decades of the twentieth century. Lawrence's reputation, at least in the academy, has declined as the evident absurdities and extremities which are part of his heurism have been read in an assumed spirit of doctrinal dogmatism. In contrast, Nietzsche's comparable moments are now seen as rhetorically controlled and bracketed. The reasons for this difference lie partly in their self-presentation. Once one attends to it, it is evident that Nietzsche is always in rhetorical command of his persona, whereas it is essential for Lawrence to make himself genuinely vulnerable. He could make a fool of himself in pursuing a larger theme and was not unduly concerned to protect a self-image. Accordingly, even allowing for the *ad hominem* naivety of much early Lawrence criticism, a genuine difference is reflected in the way his biography can legitimately be adduced in interpreting him, whereas Nietzsche's thought is rarely to be *explained* in such terms. All this points to the cardinal difference that Lawrence provides a concrete instantiation, a testing 'on the pulses', which Nietzsche does not attempt. It is easy to say, as Lawrence said of himself, that he is an emotional and spiritual explorer. The bland formula satisfies all parties. But imaginative exploration will have no real force if it is felt to be *only* 'imaginary'. It requires the capacity to be wholly committed within the momentary process. Just as Nietzsche's thought experiments keep the reader on the back foot of

---

[28] He knew Constance Garnett, who translated Dostoevsky, and his friend, Middleton Murry, wrote a book on him.

[29] Hueffer said that 'he moved amongst the high things of culture with tranquil assurance' and Huxley that he 'had a large store of knowledge, he did not like to say so, but *he did*. He was very well read.' John Worthen, *D. H. Lawrence: The Early Years: 1885–1912* (Cambridge: Cambridge University Press, 1992) pp. 121–2, 560.

[30] *Selected Essays* (London: Faber, 1961) pp. 26–8.

uncertainty as to how literally they are to be taken, so Lawrence, but even more so, pushes uncomfortable speculations with an apparently unreserved literalism. Genuine emotional exploration will almost of necessity be rough-edged, literalistic, assertive, unguarded, and, above all, whole-hearted in its moment by moment commitment. Only gradually, do we realise the longer-term underlying freedom or insouciance, the capacity to see round, and walk free of, his apparent obsessions. When he praised insouciance, the capacity 'to sit like a dandelion on its own stem', it was in reaction against the ideas of others, but more importantly he could exercise this quality in relation to his own.[31]

While *WL* is Lawrence's first major work to acknowledge the impact of Nietzsche, and to develop the Lawrencean mode of exploratory imaginative testing, it evinces some epochal confusion as well as an authentic transformation of Nietzsche's thought. Gerald Crich, the industrialist with militaristic overtones, is the figure explicitly associated with Nietzsche rather than Rupert Birkin who is the figure with truly Nietzschean insight. Hence Birkin criticises the *Wille zur Macht* that he sees in Gerald and opposes to it a *volonté de pouvoir* glossed as a capacity to act rather than to exert power: 'It is a volonté de pouvoir, if you like, a will to ability, taking pouvoir as a verb.' (*WL*, 150) But it is Birkin's critique of the overt assertion of power as a symptom of insecurity which is truly Nietzschean, echoing Nietzsche's own critique of Bismarckian Germany. Lawrence has inverted the Nietzschean meaning by associating Gerald with the will to power because he is really responding to the common perception of Nietzsche at this time. The Great War of 1914–18 saw a widespread demonising of Nietzsche as the supposed expression of German power lust.[32] Yet if Lawrence is in some sense reinventing the true Nietzschean meaning, Birkin's phrasing nonetheless gives the idea a genuinely different inflection.

If the Nietzschean 'Overman', who embodies the will-to-power, remains an ambitious and ambiguous figure, this is because he is at least partly a rhetorical device designed to highlight the radical nature of the problem he is notionally being adduced to overcome. By contrast, Lawrence's concern with singleness, spontaneity, and wholeness proposes something much more ordinary which puts the Nietzschean thought to work. It is a testing domestication of Nietzsche, as Birkin's shift from noun to verb emphasises, in making it a mode of action. Birkin's early argument with Gerald Crich about 'spontaneity', arising in response to the inconsequential event of the bride and groom's behaviour at a

---

[31] *Phoenix II: Uncollected, Unpublished and Other Prose Works by D. H. Lawrence*, ed. Warren Roberts and Harry T. Moore (London: Heinemann, 1968) p. 533.

[32] The tendency of the period even at academic rather than journalistic levels is suggested in the title of George Santayana's *Egotism in German Philosophy* (1916).

society wedding, proposes an everyday Nietzscheanism as the effective agenda of the novel:

> '... I think it was perfectly good form in Laura to bolt from Lupton to the church door. It was almost a masterpiece in good form. It's the hardest thing in the world to act spontaneously on one's impulses—and it's the only really gentlemanly thing to do—provided you are fit to do it.'
>
> . . . .
>
> 'Then I'm afraid I can't come up to your expectations here, at any rate—You think people should do just as they like?'
> 'I think they always do. But I should like them to like the purely individual thing in themselves, which makes them act in singleness. And they only like to do the collective thing.'
> 'And I,' said Gerald grimly, 'shouldn't like to be in a world of people who acted individually and spontaneously, as you call it.—We should have everybody cutting everybody else's throat in five minutes.'
> 'That means *you* would like to be cutting everybody else's throat,' said Birkin.
>
> . . . .
>
> 'It's a nasty view of things, Gerald,' said Birkin, 'and no wonder you are afraid of yourself and your own unhappiness.' (*WL*, 32–3)

In *The Gay Science*, which was echoed in 'Le gai savaire', Lawrence's intended title of his 'Study of Thomas Hardy', Nietzsche expresses the same insight:

> I find those people disagreeable in whom every natural inclination immediately becomes a sickness, something that disfigures them or is downright infamous: it is *they* that have seduced us to hold that man's inclinations and instincts are evil. *They* are the cause of our great injustice against our nature, against all nature. There are enough people who *might well* entrust themselves to their instincts with grace and without care; but they do not, from fear of this imagined 'evil character' of nature. That is why we find so little nobility among men; for it will always be the mark of nobility that one feels no fear of oneself... (*GS*, 236)

In making the general psychological point, Birkin likewise diagnoses an unacknowleged fear of the self and limits the exercise of spontaneity to those special cases who have a natural nobility evidently independent of social rank. The novel sets out to enact the practical implications of this claim.

Unlike Nietzsche, Birkin seeks singleness of being within relationship, especially the sexual relationship, and hence his other major idea of 'star-equilibrium'. In *The Gay Science* Nietzsche uses the image of 'star friendship' as a positive model of estranged male relations. (*GS*, 225–6) For him, enemies had an important positive function in providing a necessary challenge and the star is an image of isolation. For Birkin/Lawrence, by contrast, the separation of the stars is an image of singleness *within* a close and continuing relationship. It privileges the gravitational connection rather than the pure separation of Nietzsche. And its being a permanent sexual bond, rather than Nietzsche's male relationship, is crucial. If Nietzsche was relatively blank on the 'sphere of association', then sexuality was the most striking instance of this. When he compared unfavourably the modern love-match to the impersonal institution of marriage, he evinced the same unproblematised transposition of the personal into the impersonal that characterises his rhetorical use of himself in his aphoristic formulations.[33] By contrast, Lawrence seeks to achieve the full weight of the impersonal *within* the personal, an emotional, intrinsic equivalent of traditional marriage, and this remains perhaps the most difficult issue in his thought at large.

Indeed, the whole relation to the feminine is a crucial difference between Lawrence and Nietzsche. Although Nietzsche's comments on women are often directed at the cultural construction of the feminine, he undoubtedly evinces a radical misogynistic apartness. By contrast, Lawrence's notorious and tedious assertions of masculinity are clearly reactive and compensatory. Above all, they are belied by the female identification that runs throughout his work. In their first extended conversation alone, Birkin's star image provokes one of his sharpest disagreements with Ursula. Understanding it as a model of satellitic female dependence, she gave a lead to the hostile feminist criticism which has been largely responsible for Lawrence's occlusion in the Anglophone academy of the late twentieth century. What is most significantly at stake here, however, is the clash between Lawrence's heurism and the self-conviction of late twentieth-century ideological critique. After critics of the 1950s, notably F. R. Leavis, had sought to sift out what mattered in Lawrence, and given him a cultural authority he never had in his lifetime, this authority was merged in the 1960s with his reputation as an antinomian sexual prophet, to create, over Leavis's protests, the 'Lawrence' of popular posterity.[34] Kate Millet's *Sexual Politics* (1971) attacked this 'Lawrence' in shocking ignorance of Lawrence or of his serious critical history, and the reception of the book confirmed a more general cultural amnesia. It set a course for future ideologically driven readings. Lawrence meanwhile has continued to have intelligently sympathetic women readers and one of the finest and most timely studies of him in the period is Carol Siegel's *Lawrence Among the Women* (1991). Siegel places Lawrence in a tradition of women writers: the Victorians, such as George Eliot and the Brontës, from whom he learned; his contemporaries, some of them professional writers, with whom he

---

[33] *TI*, 105.
[34] Leavis deplored the serious literary and moral claims made for *Lady Chatterley's Lover* during the 1962 trial against Penguin Books. See *Nor Shall my Sword* (London: Chatto and Windus, 1972) p. 31.

collaborated; and subsequent women writers for whom he was an important influence or point of reference.

But Lawrence's female identification has an importance beyond sexual politics. The argument between Birkin and Ursula is conducted in a gendered language, and is one of the moments in which he is most intensely disgusted with his own articulacy. One may suspect Hélène Cixous' claims for a female mode of language as being internally incoherent, polemically driven, and undemonstrable, but Deborah Tannen's sociolinguistic observations confirm general experience.[35] She distinguishes the relational character of 'female' speech from the factual and objective nature of 'male' speech. This difference can be seen throughout Lawrence's *oeuvre*, as when Mrs Gascoyne, in the play *The Daughter-in-law*, scornfully dismisses her son for quoting his wife: 'Tha'rt a fool, our Luther. If ter ta'es a woman at 'er word, well, tha deserves what ter gets.'[36] These differences are not, of course, tied simply to biological sex and the significant point about Lawrence is that 'female' speech as so defined is his normal mode, as is evident in the dramatic process of *The Daughter-in-law* itself. Wholeness to the emotional moment rather than consistency over a period is the essential condition of his creative heurism. One might say, therefore, that if you take Lawrence at his word, you deserve what you get although that is what academic ideological reading, irrespective of sexual difference, has largely continued to do. In truth, while Lawrence has been consciously excluded for his reactionary masculinism, he has been more significantly unheard as a woman.

Of course, Lawrence's creative heurism was very different from the ordinary processes of emotional argument. It required above all an artistic impersonality. But the common root is nonetheless vital, and artistic impersonality echoes at a different level the 'impersonal' look that Lydia Brangwen gives her husband after childbirth. (R, 77) Lawrence's awareness of the dissolved ego as a positive mode of connectedness to both human and non-human otherness transposes the Nietzschean problematic of the self into a multitude of positive, practical, concrete investigations of human wholeness throughout his *oeuvre*. Lawrence's female identification is crucial here and it significantly distinguishes him not just from Nietzsche but from Goethe who remained for Nietzsche the great exemplar of the Overman as achieved wholeness. Lawrence's sympathies reach back more sympathetically, past Goethe, to Rousseau.

[35] 'The Laugh of the Medusa', in *New French Feminisms*, ed. Elaine Marks and Isabelle de Courtivron (London: Harvester, 1980); Deborah Tanner, *You Just Don't Understand: Women and Men in Conversation* (London: Virago, 1991).
[36] *The Plays*, ed. Hans-Wilhelm Schwarze and John Worthen (Cambridge: Cambridge University Press, 1999) p. 345.

Lawrence versus Goethe

Despite Lawrence's positive interest in German culture, and his appreciation of its lyric tradition in which Goethe is a pre-eminent instance, he shared a typical English distaste for the consciously self-cultivated *Geheimrat*. In *Mr Noon*, a novel begun before and completed after the Great War, the hero, Gilbert Noon, another ex-school-teacher, speaks for the author when he regrets Goethe's 'setting up the stunt of German Godlikeness and superhumanness'.[37] Lawrence's informal phrasing catches a compressed historical insight in seeing the link between Goethe, Nietzsche, and contemporary Germany. In *WL* Gudrun and Loerke play at historical/cultural charades invoking the world of Goethe's Weimar along with other Enlightenment figures. Their mockery, as what would now be characterised as a postmodern indulgence in their own deracination, is quite different from Lawrence's, yet he incorporates it into his own. For he also saw the Weimar self-consciousness, however worthy in itself and in its day, as part of the long history of inner evacuation of meaning in modern culture. Gudrun and Loerke are ultimately descendants of the same tradition and, in their postmodern play with cultural forms and histories, a once noble ideal of cultivation is bitten by its own tail. 'It was a sentimental delight to reconstruct the world of Goethe at Weimar, or of Schiller and poverty and faithful love, or to see again Jean-Jacques in his quakings, or Voltaire at Ferney, or Frederick the Great reading his own poetry.' (*WL*, 453) Their 'sentimental' delight has the eighteenth-century implication of self-conscious, rather than merely mawkish, enjoyment of feeling and two points emerge from this moment: a general and a more specific one. The first is that, through Gudrun and Loerke in the post-war German context, Lawrence catches the numbed equivalent of what Nietzsche's critique of culture had already declared. It is not that these high points of humane culture have lost their intrinsic value but that sensitive individuals can no longer respond to them as before. And for later readers the fact that German artists and writers were to face a more devastating version of this condition after the next war lends it a further historical pathos. The more specific point, however, is that Goethe's youthful novel, *The Sorrows of the Young Werther*, was an early phase in the internal critique of sensibility by which it was to evolve, through many transformations, into Lawrence's sophisticated

---

[37] *Mr Noon*, ed. Lindeth Vasey (Cambridge: Cambridge University Press, 1984) p. 184. See also his much later letter to Aldous Huxley deploring in *WMA* 'the perversity of intellectualised sex' and 'the utter incapacity for any *development* of contact with any other human being' 27 Mar. 1928. *The Letters of D. H. Lawrence*, vol. 6, ed. James T. Boulton, Margaret Boulton, and Gerald Lacy (Cambridge: Cambridge University Press, 1991) p. 342.

concern for emotional integrity and human wholeness.[38] Lawrence, therefore, was more sympathetic than Nietzsche to the underlying spirit of Rousseau even as he distanced himself from the 'quakings' of Rousseau's idealism. He may have had Rousseau in mind elsewhere when, contesting a naive modern commitment to the idea of equality, he nonetheless says: 'no idea which has passionately swayed mankind can be altogether wrong.' (*RDP*, 100) Hence, the arguments between Birkin and Gerald rehearse with an opposite force those between Werther and his friend, Albert; or Wilhelm and Jarno over the Certificate of Apprenticeship. But it is now the spirit of Rousseau which gets the better of the argument as Birkin's argument for 'spontaneity' is a more sophisticated version of a case that Werther would have found sympathetic.

Indeed, the discussion is initiated through a classically Goethean disagreement over the aphorism. Whereas both Werther and Wilhelm found generalisations irritating in a way that reflects their own immaturity, that position is reversed in Lawrence. Gerald declares:

'If you're doing a thing, do it properly, and if you're not going to do it properly, leave it alone.'
'Very nice aphorism,' said Birkin.
'Don't you agree?' asked Gerald.
'Quite,' said Birkin, 'Only it bores me rather, when you become aphoristic.'
'Damn you, Rupert, you want all the aphorisms your own way,' said Gerald.
'No, I want them out of the way, and you're always shoving them in to it.'

(*WL*, 32)

Moral generalisation typically reflects a commitment to a socially based conception to which the eighteenth-century man of feeling, such as Werther, was opposed. But whereas Werther counterposed what he saw unproblematically as acting on the feelings, this has now become Birkin/Lawrence's much more demanding notion of 'spontaneity'. Yet although Birkin holds his own in argument more successfully than Werther, he cannot enforce his viewpoint against conventional wisdom. In this episode, Gerald has just remarked on Birkin's own expressive vulnerability: 'Is that an aphorism or a cliché?' (*WL*, 32) The real irony hovering over Birkin, as in his argument with Hermione, is not his personal inadequacy, or that he cannot make his point, but that even when it is well articulated it is not understood. Or the words are understood without the substantive meaning. Goethe, of course, is neither Werther nor Albert and he effectively combines their rival modes in his own increasingly flexible and relativistic use of aphorism until, in *WMJ*, it has virtually reversed

---

[38] I trace this development in *Sentimentalism, Ethics and the Culture of Feeling, op. cit.*

its implication. As in several examples already discussed, his aphorisms frequently reflect on their own hollowness. In that respect, although approaching from the opposite direction, he arrives at a similar awareness to Lawrence: what Nietzsche refers to as his 'noble pliability'. (*UM*, 155) Lawrence parallels Goethe in a different key: his moment-by-moment wholeness of being is the chiasmic opposite of Goethe's cultivated completeness. Both are difficult to enforce as criteria, however, and that is why, as with Nietzsche, a peculiar burden rests on their own implicit exemplarity.

In both Goethe and Lawrence there is an inescapable element of self-reference as the internal standard of a highly integrated personality is an implicit premise of the *oeuvre*. This was the missing factor in the unresolvable polarity of Werther and Albert, as it is still for Gerald too. In the spontaneity argument, although Birkin detects Gerald's own murderousness as the basis of his fear of being murdered, he nonetheless goes a long way to conceding Gerald's general point with his proviso that 'you're fit to do it' and his comment that 'it is the only gentlemanly thing to do'. How widespread is the capacity for such spontaneity likely to be? Will it be as rare as the Nietzschean Overman? Both Goethe and Lawrence invoke a notion of aristocracy to define their ideal personality type. Goethe spoke quite literally in a social world where he had daily intercourse with aristocrats exercising an accepted and responsible authority even if their continuing function and value had become an urgent question in his time. He reflected this epochal pressure by transposing the aristocrat into a model of the artist as one able to cultivate his own individual development as an end in itself in contradistinction to the bourgeois whose priority must be economic productivity. Goethe's own ennoblement reflected both aspects: it was necessary for his official position in the Weimar court, and it acknowledged the personal and artistic achievement which ultimately underwrote that position. Lawrence adopts a more metaphorical and internalised notion of aristocracy to express the quality of proper singleness. In the intentional scheme of *Lady Chatterley's Lover*, Oliver Mellors, rather than Clifford Chatterley, is the more truly aristocratic.

Birkin's notion of 'singleness' is a pre-ethical mode of being which governs, rather than denies, the ethical and is in this respect an equivalent of Nietzsche's genealogical attempt to recover nobility beneath the ethical, to recover *virtu* beneath virtue. Yet the argument of *The Genealogy of Morals* remains at a high level of generality and it is not merely philistine to ask what exactly we are to make of it in practice, if indeed it has any practical bearing. As usual, Nietzsche gives little guidance at that level, and what he gives at various moments in his *oeuvre* can be worrying. Whereas Lawrence sought a constructive working equivalent within the modern psyche, Nietzsche's historical diagnosis led him to speak favourably of examples of renaissance brutality. Nietzsche is dangerous to the mediocre reader in the same way that he defined Schopenhauer as being. He expresses necessary truths or radical speculations which are resistant to democratisation and there is much in his thought that would be mischievous if put naively into action. In some measure this applies to Lawrence, and perhaps even to Goethe, too. In all three, the image of nobility, which always tends to sound weakly assertive and self-referential, points to an underlying problem of treating individual genius as representative.

For Lawrence, there was no contradiction in seeking singleness for all. All human beings are equal before the law, while in their talents and qualities of being they are neither equal nor unequal, they are incomparable. But the capacity to experience and affirm such singleness is not common and it shows up especially in the context of universal state education. Lawrence should be a major source of insight into education. His creative work is powered by a prophetic motive, and many of his friends and acquaintances testified to his educative impact in daily life. He clearly loved showing and explaining things in a way which, one can surmise, would have underwritten his successful experience as a school-teacher. Yet it may be that in drawing upon the example of his own singleness he has everything and nothing to teach us about teaching.

Lawrence and Education

Lawrence's essay on 'The Education of the People' reflects the difficulty of generalising from genius and the fact that it remained unpublished in his lifetime is as much emblematic as adventitious. It recalls the spirit of Rousseau in many ways. It begins with the formative moments of early childhood, objects to children being 'swaddled in fixed beliefs' (*RDP*, 114), and adopts the principle of minimal and delayed instruction: 'First rule, leave him alone. Second rule, leave him alone. Third rule, leave him alone.' (*RDP*, 121) Authority would be more frankly exercised as authority, as the inescapable function of adult responsibility, and this is still based on the underlying principle of not prematurely reasoning with the child. Lawrence favours a tough, unsentimental regime which harks back through Rousseau to Sparta.

The essay shares with Plato's *Republic*, Rousseau's *Emile*, and Goethe's Pedagogical Province a pervasive ambiguity between practical recommendations, general principles, and utopian aspirations. All communicate a sense of literal, even urgent, practicality while hinting at a philosophical concern for which the practical measures are essentially a metaphor. In Lawrence's case, this is pointed up by a pervasive hyperbole designed to draw attention to the radical shift in cultural assumptions which is the underlying point. The essay begins with a tellingly realistic diagnosis of the condition of the elementary teacher in state education, but as he proceeds to his positive recommendations his proposals are often fancifully hyperbolic. With evident reference to his own experience of mother love, he recommends:

> ... babies should invariably be taken away from their modern mothers and given, not to yearning and maternal old maids, but to rather stupid fat women who can't be bothered with them. There should be a league for the prevention of maternal love, as there is a society for the prevention of cruelty to animals.   (*RDP*, 121)

The hyperbole enforces a general psychological point against the grain of the culture. One might say that it is immoderately expressed but what would the moderate form of this insight be? It can only be expressed as a rhetorical extremity. Like his predecessors, Lawrence radically challenges his existing sociocultural world. Plato would educate for a society of philosopher kings; Rousseau for a society of free and responsible citizens; Goethe for a world that embraces modernity intelligently by preserving traditional values and ideals; while Lawrence imagines a world in which whole and single individuals are educated in a universal state system.

In all these works the tension between nature and authority is reflected in the theme of necessary deception. Plato made his selection of pupils for different life functions on the basis of what he frankly called the Great Lie, or Myth. Rousseau sought to overcome the contradiction of *exercising* the unmediated authority of *nature* by a series of running deceptions and manipulations, although he too is quite frank with the reader, or the intending tutor, about the need for this. In Goethe, there is no deception so much as a freely acknowledged artifice although the supervisors in the Province preserve a measure of secrecy about their methods. In Lawrence, however, an endemic social lie has become unsustainable: national education in his day was ideally for the development of the individual but for the great majority it was a purely functional preparation for the world of work. Hence the pupils are aware of the constitutive dishonesty while the educational establishment is in denial. 'It is no wonder the young workmen sneer at all idealism, all idealists, and at everything higher than wages and short hours. They are having their own back on the lie, and on the liars, that educated them in school.' (*RDP*, 93) Lawrence would meet this condition with a genuine education for wholeness. He emphasises the damage done by a consciousness aroused, not just prematurely, but falsely. What is not done in a spirit of true wholeness is actively damaging—pretty much the point that Hermione Roddice wished to make. Whatever the practical merit of his proposals, his diagnosis has a prescient relevance to the brutalised debasement of popular culture in Britain in the later twentieth century.

While wholeness is potentially universal, only a minority would be capable of 'the struggle into verbal consciousness' and Lawrence, like Plato, would select for academic education on intrinsic ability, not social and economic background. In this respect, he belongs, in British terms, to a pre-1960s world, the era when a socialist government could establish a selective school system and the academic minority would become the professionals of the new generation. At the same time, Lawrence would not subscribe to the values of conventional social hierarchy and follows Rousseau and Goethe in stressing the importance for all children of learning a physical trade or handcraft. Rousseau, educating a single, economically advantaged individual, wished to inculcate a spirit of genuine personal independence; as in his own practice of music copying. The socially privileged Emile would thereby rise to the true dignity of being a man. In the self-selecting intake of Goethe's Pedagogical Province, it was part of the rounded education and a means of discovering individual talent. The boys were guided to specialise as their individual abilities emerged. Lawrence has a different emphasis as he seeks to educate for wholeness in a complete population and the learning of physical skills is crucial to this.

> The point about any handwork is that it should not be mind work. Supposing we are learning to solder a kettle. The theory is told in a dozen words. But it is not a question of applying a theory. It is a question of *knowing*, by direct physical contact, your kettle-substance, your kettle curves, your solder, your soldering iron, your fire, your resin, and all the fusing, slipping interaction of all these. (*RDP*, 154)

Although the bulk of the people are not to be forced into intellectual awareness, handicraft is for everyone because it represents the centre of gravity of the whole. Handicraft is a means of personal wholeness before it is an economic specialism. Once again, this points to a widely acknowledged lack in late twentieth-century Britain: the absence of training for, and appreciation of, practical skills, although the fact continues to be lamented without a concerted will to change the underlying cultural attitudes.

Guidance in the life direction of children is envisaged with an authority greater even than that of Goethe's supervisors and Plato's guardians: '... vital understanding belongs to the masters of life. And all the professionals in our new world are not mere technical experts: they are life directors.' (*RDP*, 108) The authority assumed here bears less on a realistic practice for education in the given social culture and rather reflects Lawrence's calling as novelist, psychologist, and social prophet. For although all these works attempt to generalise from genius, his essay, in its hyperbolic frankness, reveals most sharply the intrinsic difficulty of this. In Plato's *Republic* the discourse of order in the individual psyche and of the state are effectively identical so that little tension emerges between them. Microcosm and macrocosm are made up of the same elements. In *Emile*, the *de facto* conflict between the individual and the general case can be felt despite the optimistic rhetoric but the tension remains largely subtextual. In Goethe, in so far as the unique individuality of the hero is the governing premise and goal, Goethe's own genius both underwrites and overwhelms the narrative. Lawrence, however, is even more problematic in this regard. His best fiction is underwritten by a philosophical vision, and *vice versa*, but wherever this vision begins to become separably prophetic within the creative context, it is in danger of overwhelming the integrity of the work. Likewise, the practical requirements of a teaching regime for the generality of young children force a similar tension into the open.

The enduring truth in the essay is that human wholeness has no privileged cultural locus and Lawrence's most telling image of it is an everyday physical activity performed with a concentrated attention to being that few would find in the supposedly 'higher' cultural experiences.

> The actual doing things is in itself a joy. If I wash the dishes I learn a quick, light touch of china and earthenware, the feel of it, the weight and roll and poise of it, the peculiar hotness, the quickness and slowness of its surface. I am at the middle of an infinite complexity of motions and adjustments and quick, apprehensive contacts. Nimble faculties hover and play along my nerves, the primal consciousness is alert in me. Apart from all the moral or practical satisfaction derived from a thing well done, I have the *mindless* motor activity and reaction in primal consciousness, which is a pure satisfaction. If I am well and satisfied as a human being, a large part of my life must pass in mindless motion, quick, busy activity in which I am neither bought nor sold, but acting alone and free from the centre of my own active isolation. Not self-consciously, however. Not watching my own reactions. If I wash dishes, I wash them to get them clean. Nothing else.
>
> Every man must learn to be proud and single and alone, and after that, he will be worth knowing. (*RDP*, 151)

Washing dishes was not for him a lower kind of activity and he is known to have performed many of the domestic chores in contrast to Frieda von Richthofen's 'aristocratic' indifference. For him, the 'higher' cultural activities were no more or less organically connected with the capacity for fully experiencing one's being-in-the-world.

Indeed, his description of washing-up echoes his reflections on the 'writing' of a novel. He thinks of the physical act: his hand having its own kind of 'cleverness' as it 'slips gaily along', and 'jumps like a grasshopper to dot an i . . .'. (*STH*, 193). Likewise, his typical images for the 'morality' of the novel, such as putting 'the thumb in the scale', conceive the criterion of anti-Cartesian and literary wholeness through a physical action of the hand. In the same essay he states his criterion of wholeness in relation to art:

> I very much like all these bits of me to be set trembling with life and the wisdom of life. But I do ask that the whole of me shall tremble in its wholeness, some time or other.
>
> And this, of course, must happen to me, living.
>
> But as far as it can happen from a communication, it can only happen when a whole novel communicates itself to me. The Bible—but *all* the Bible—and Homer, and Shakespeare: these are the supreme old novels. . . . Which means that in their wholeness they affect the whole man alive, which is the man himself, beyond any part of him . . .
>
> Me, man alive, I am a curious assembly of incongruous parts. My yea! of today is oddly different from my yea! of yesterday. My tears of tomorrow will have nothing to do with my tears of a year ago. . . .
>
> In all this change, I maintain a certain integrity. But woe betide me if I try to put my finger on it. . . .   (*STH*, 196–7)

Although the 'I' that speaks here is philosophically representative it is also highly personal as the meaning is underwritten by Lawrence's especially acute sense of lived being in the world. The reason he survives the notorious unevenness of his written *oeuvre* is that his genius was primarily for life and being, flame-like values which are intrinsically fluctuating.

He evidently believed that such wholeness of being could be more widely experienced if *it*, instead of intellectual attainment conceived in isolation, was the goal of education. It is a compelling and affirmative vision on which we should never turn our backs, yet we may at the same time wonder to what extent it was a projection of his own genius. Many people read Lawrence without learning from him; and of those who respond to his quickness, how many have actually been taught, or guided to do so? Or does one rather have to have the inkling already in order to understand? The relation between Lawrence and education is a highly-charged, mutually illuminating, tension bringing home with special force the utopian condition which is at once the predicament, and the motive, of all worthwhile humanistic education, while his own example remains permanently elusive: at once familiar, transparent and inaccessible.

7

The Importance of being Frank: Criticism, Collaboration, Pedagogy in F. R. Leavis

When the literary critic F. R. Leavis (1895–1978) is read alongside the creative artists considered so far, his teaching of literature in the mid-twentieth century brings the same complex of themes to a further focus historically and analytically. His practical pedagogy of imaginative literature intensifies the impasse exemplified in the preceding fictions of pedagogy because Leavis's criticism, as well as representing a distinctive view of literature in relation to human life and history, was directed primarily to a pedagogical purpose. This must be borne in mind, for example, in relation to his exclusionary judgements, as in the opening section of *The Great Tradition*. Given the limited amount that can be read with any thoroughness in an undergraduate degree, he considered that bold pedagogical choices have to be made although both he, and his major collaborator, Q. D. Leavis, assumed a responsible teacher could make these only on the basis of wide personal reading.

The urgency of his pedagogical mission, and his insistence on its immediate application to the social and institutional culture of the day, made his criticism controversial for its manner as well as its substance and his personal engagement has often made him seem a merely idiosyncratic case. Despite his immense impact on the reading and teaching of English literature in British universities and secondary schools in the middle decades of the twentieth century, therefore, by the latter part of the century he had become known largely through the reductive image of a naively dogmatic and reactionary moralist guarding a narrow literary 'canon'. When properly understood, however, he is highly representative precisely where he most pushes against the limits of the teachable and, once again, fiction as an ontological category is at the heart of the question. Initially engaged by poetry, Leavis increasingly concerned himself with the 'poetic' creativity of the novel although his emphasis on a genre, and authors, popularly associated with a straightforward moral realism tended to confirm his reputation as a simple moralist. To question this simplistic response to him, which is partly engendered by his deceptive transparency, it is necessary to unpack a number of his implicit premises.

Later academic practice has largely replaced his conception with radically different ones, and often with a view to privileging different histories although, as I have shown elsewhere, there has also been a recurrent practice of dismissing his supposedly naive conception in order to reinvent it in a weaker form.[1] This latter phenomenon points to the closeness of the representative and the incommunicable at the heart of his critical practice and I revisit him as one of those apparently marginal instances who reveal the premises and problems which are hidden in mainstream practice. He formed his conception of criticism by reflecting on what for him were the self-evident properties of language, and the difficulty of conveying the self-evident, the pedagogy of the open secret, was the increasingly conscious predicament at the heart of his *oeuvre*.

His emphasis on the importance of critical assessment requires in itself some contextual appreciation. He was of the generation that pioneered the study of English, the vernacular literature, as an independent discipline. Although it had been taught as a university subject through much of the nineteenth century, in the teens of the twentieth century, especially under the influence of modern writers, it became newly conscious of its problematic, and potentially ambitious, status. It had previously been modelled on the study of the classical languages with an admixture of Germanic philology. In so far as the classical literatures were closed, and traditionally represented a collective source of humane wisdom, their value as an object of knowledge and appreciation appeared both fixed and self-evident. It was therefore possible to exercise taste and judgement within the historically defined field of the classical literatures without being required on every occasion to justify the constitution of the field *per se*. But the generation of Eliot, Joyce, and Pound brought home how illusory it was to study English literature, even of the relatively distant past, in that way. They showed not just the importance of contemporary writing, but that the contemporary involves a constant revaluation of the past. Hence, although vernacular literary study requires philological knowledge and 'aesthetic' appreciation, the field cannot be constituted wholly in those terms. In that sense, criticism precedes scholarship. At the same time, however, as long as given cultural habits and social consensus are in place, it is possible to proceed on a day-to-day basis as if the field were a 'natural' given. Leavis was the figure who brought the modernist revolution most strongly into the academy by throwing the historical field into question. For him, judgements

---

[1] See 'What Price Collaboration? The Case of F. R. Leavis' in *Critical Ethics*, ed. Dominic Rainsford and Tim Woods (London: Macmillan, 1999) pp. 23–39.

about individual authors and works were not just *within* the field, but always and necessarily *about* it. In each instance, the whole enterprise of studying the vernacular literature was at stake. His criticism consciously lived out the radical responsibility of the critical discipline as such and, in so far as the problems commonly ascribed to him as an individual case were actually universal ones, he represented a repressed unconscious of the literary academy. Or he was like Socrates and Wittgenstein in seeing problems underlying common uses of words including most notably the word 'literary' whose elusive significance is the primary subject of this chapter.

By an ironic logic, later commentators seeking to question and reconfigure the teaching syllabus have perceived him as responsible for imposing a 'canon' rather than as the significant forebear who saw that the received tradition is always necessarily in question. Indeed, the now clichéd metaphor of the 'canon', which Leavis would not have adopted, is itself a tendentious vulgarism expressing, or repressing, this very confusion. But the misapprehension goes beyond the choice of authors and texts to reflect the constitution of the field, not just in content, but in kind. Later questioning of a traditional reading list has been primarily political as texts are foregrounded on ideological, or politically representative, grounds. Persuasive arguments can be made in these terms, of course, but they are radically different from Leavis's terms. Meanwhile 'new historical' commentary characteristically uses 'literary' texts for historically illustrative purposes in a way that makes it unnecessary for them to be discussed as literature. They can be discussed in the same terms by historians. Leavis, although not unaware of political implications in the construction of syllabi, was concerned for the literary field as a distinctive domain. Where literature is in question, moral, political or historical significance comes *through* the special mode of the literary. For him, every critical judgement sustained the significance of the literary field, not just qualitatively, but generically.

The later elision of literature as a significant category is sometimes proclaimed consciously, but is often implicit and by default.[2] Just as the term 'poetry' can mean both a generic formal use of language, by which we merely know where to shelve it in the library, and a judgement of significance, so the more general term 'literature' has both a descriptive and an evaluative use. Much confusion arises from not distinguishing these, and thinking through their order of priority. Rather than recognising a body of material as literature, some of which is outstandingly good, Leavis used the term primarily in its

---

[2] For example, excerpts from Terry Eagleton's *Literary Theory and Introduction* (Oxford: Blackwell, 1983) are presented in an anthology for students *Literature in the Modern World*, ed. Dennis Walder (New York: Oxford University Press, 1990) pp. 21–5. Eagleton's brisk populism attacks the straw man of literature as an 'objective, descriptive category', effectively to elide the category of literary art.

qualitative sense and only on that basis as subtending the field. The recurrent objection that he accorded too much value to the 'literary' arises from missing the ambitious significance he attributed to it. Conversely, it is hard to see how anyone, personal modesty notwithstanding, could justify studying and teaching literature at public expense without a comparably ambitious conception. Where self-cultivation had dwindled to a superior form of hobby, Leavis wished to give it a fully public value. One can, of course, object that his ambition in a modern democratic context was as utopian as Plato's philosopher king in an earlier era but even such a pragmatic objection needs first to assess the full weight of the case.

Cultural amnesia with respect to Leavis extends to once broadly held conceptions of language, creativity, and historical understanding which he assumed. Whereas the modern university study of English was established in the teens and twenties of the century within a view of the nature of language that was widely accepted in a largely passive and implicit way, the latter half of the century saw the spread of opposed conceptions which were highly self-conscious and theorised. The earlier view was less explicitly theorised since, apart from not being significantly threatened within the discipline, it prized the unconscious dimension of language as the source of creativity. Hence it neither lent itself to, nor saw the value of, more theoretical articulation. Later conceptions, however, most notably those associated with the term 'deconstruction', typically sought to expose the unconscious of language in the spirit of what Paul Ricoeur has called 'the hermeneutics of suspicion'.[3] The relative lack of Anglophone theorisation of the earlier conception has helped to make it invisible to a later generation while many intrinsic features of language came to be widely understood only through the later, deconstructive lens. The outcome is a widespread, genuine innocence by the late twentieth century that such a rival conception existed. It is necessary, therefore, to set out this positive conception before considering the difficulties to which it gave rise. The argument of the preceding chapters helps to illuminate both aspects.

Language, Creativity, History

Leavis seems to have formed his understanding of language, creativity, and history directly from his contemplation of creative literature and the reflections of several great writers. In so far as he wished to express this in general terms, he found in his early career virtually no philosophically articulated model

---

[3] Ricoeur uses this phrase in *The Rule of Metaphor*, trans. Robert Czerny *et al.* (London: Routledge and Kegan Paul, 1978) p. 285, and gives it a fuller historical explanation in *Freud and Philosophy: an Essay in Interpretation*, trans. Denis Savage (New Haven and London: Yale University Press, 1970) pp. 32–6.

in the Anglophone world and, in a famous exchange with René Wellek, he disputed the value of providing a philosophically principled account of his critical practice.[4] Likewise, he frequently disparaged the contribution of philosophy to the understanding of language. In so far as this has been taken for an hostility to philosophy *per se*, two points need to be made. One is that he wished criticism and philosophy to be clearly *distinguished*, and the other is that he found the Anglophone academic philosophy of his day singularly unhelpful to his concerns precisely because he had a philosophically significant conception of language. In that regard, his close parallels in German thought help to clarify his implicit conception while sharpening the distinction between properly philosophical reflection and Leavis's critical concerns. The principal German parallel, combining the themes of language, literature, creativity, and history, is the *Lebensphilosophie* of Wilhelm Dilthey (1833–1911) while a more purely philosophical parallel can be found in late essays on poetry, language, and thought by Martin Heidegger (1889–1976). When Leavis eventually found Anglophone philosophers on whom he could draw, one was the then rare, British Heideggerean, Marjorie Grene.

Dilthey and Leavis reached a common set of recognitions from opposite directions. Dilthey, meditating on the special problems of understanding the historical past, and the interpretation of texts, privileged the concentrated, inward evidence of art and especially literature as the art of language. Conversely, Leavis meditating on the nature and authority of great literary art, valued it as the most inward and complex understanding of history. They shared a view of literature as, not just reflecting history, but embodying it. As H-G. Gadamer puts it: 'historical understanding proves to be a kind of literary criticism writ large.'[5] Dilthey's life work was centred on producing an adequate conception of historiographical practice. Post-Enlightenment culture had developed an immense historical knowledge and a powerful capacity for historical understanding but, for Dilthey, the understanding of history itself was still at a pre-critical stage and required an equivalent of Kant's foundational critiques in the realms of knowledge, ethics, and art. Failing that, a constantly seductive model was that of natural science which Dilthey, like Nietzsche and others, saw as inappropriate to history. His *Introduction to the Human Sciences* (1863) sought to place the humanities in general on a proper disciplinary footing distinct from the natural sciences. Leavis similarly insisted on the *discipline* of English as having a strictness comparable to, but different from, the scientific. It may be significant that Dilthey never completed his projected critique of

---

[4] 'Literary Criticism and Philosophy', in *The Common Pursuit* (London: Chatto and Windus, 1952) pp. 211–22.
[5] Hans-Georg Gadamer, *Truth and Method, op. cit.* p. 339.

historical reason for, apart from personal and circumstantial factors, he had a radical resistance to systematic and generalised thought. It is as if the general formulation is necessarily inadequate to the experience and, perhaps for this very reason, he had a formidable sense of historical significance as inhering within the experience of the past. 'Experience' in this context means not external events so much as the inward digestion by human consciousness, most notably in great works of literature. Leavis had a similarly radical scepticism about historical generalisation with a comparable insistence on reading literature as historically evidential. Literary texts are most evidential, that is to say, not by what they refer to, but by what they are.

Dilthey conceived great art as treating human concerns with such impersonality as to constitute a permanently available form of historical understanding beyond the means of scientific or theoretical enquiry. In great art life discloses itself and, although a trained skill is required to obtain it, such understanding is in principle objective and certain:

... in the struggle of practical interests every expression can be deceptive and its interpretation changed with the change in our situation. But, in great works, because some content of the mind separates itself from its creator, the poet, artist, or writer, we enter a sphere in which deception ends. No truly great work of art can, according to the conditions which hold good and are to be developed later, wish to give the illusion of a mental content foreign to its author; indeed it does not want to say anything about its author. Truthful in itself it stands—fixed, visible, permanent: and, because of this, a skilled and certain understanding of it is possible. Thus there arises in the confines between science and action a circle in which life discloses itself at a depth inaccessible to observation, reflection and theory. (*Gesammelte Schriften*, vii, 206–7)

In his later years, when Leavis sought to express his own conception in more theoretical terms, notably in *The Living Principle: 'English' as a Discipline of Thought* (1975), he gave a highly Diltheyan account of the relation of literary art to history:

All writers of major creative works are driven by the need to achieve a fuller and more penetrating consciousness of that to which we belong, or of the 'Something other than itself' on which the 'physical world ultimately depends'... The English language in the full sense is alive, or becomes for the creative writer alive, with hints, apprehensions and intuitions. They go back to earlier cultural phases. The writer is alive in his own time, and the character of his response, the selective individual nature of his creative receptivity, will be determined by his sense—intensely individual—of the modern human condition...

He needs all the resources of the language his growing command of his theme can make spontaneous—can recruit towards the achieving of an organic wholeness: his theme itself is (being inescapably a prompting) an effort to develop, in realizing and presenting it, living continuity....

> ... The 'living principle' itself is an apprehended totality of what, as registered in the language, has been won or established in immemorial human living. I say, 'an apprehended totality', for, in the nature of things, there can be no one total upshot: for every major writer it is different—there are many potentialities and no statistically determinable values. We call a writer major when we judge that his wisdom, more deeply and robustly rooted, represents a more securely poised resultant, one more fully comprehensive and humanly better centred—considerations bearing crucially on future growth—than any ordinarily brilliant person could offer us.[6]

The formulations are characteristically different. Dilthey assumes the existence of great art, speaks of it as acting under its own laws and, when he rises to general statement, it is with a note of grandly idealised assertion and certitude. By contrast, Leavis focuses on both the creation and the recognition of such art as an ongoing, difficult process for the individuals concerned. His own prose, as so often, seems to enact the struggle of which he speaks. Nonetheless, the crucial point in common is the model of history as constituted by, and known through, the creative activity of language.

Such an historical understanding is the centre of gravity of Leavis's criticism. His judgements of relative quality or importance are not by some independently 'aesthetic' criterion, or expressions of personal moral 'taste', but as concentrations of historical significance with a continuing bearing for the present. That is the intended force of 'great' in *The Great Tradition* and it gives the more fundamental reason for his pedagogical 'exclusions'. Like Dilthey, and subsequently Heidegger, he invoked a criterion of historical significance which few writers in any generation would be likely to satisfy, and the common charge of excessively narrow taste must be seen in this light.

His Diltheyan emphasis on creative 'impersonality' echoed that of modern authors such as Eliot, Joyce, and Lawrence. Almost all the modernist generation emphasised the need to separate, if not the work, then the significance of the work, from the personality of the writer. But they meant different things by this. For Leavis, there was more at stake than the internal dynamic of the artwork considered in isolation: a Flaubertian disappearance of the author. As for Dilthey, an artist is adjudged to be 'major' not just through personal expressiveness, but as the medium by which new emotions, intuitions, and forms of being 'for the race, as it were' come into existence. Seeing this quality, for example, in Blake made him, for Leavis, a great artist whatever the crankiness that pervades so much of his *oeuvre*. Indeed, Blake's doctrinal content throws his true value into relief:

---

[6] *The Living Principle: English as a Discipline of Thought* (London: Chatto and Windus, 1975) pp. 68–9.

I don't myself believe that Blake had any comprehensive guiding wisdom to offer, but it was his genius to be capable of a complete disinterestedness, and therefore of a complete sincerity. He had a rare integrity, and a rare sense of responsibility as a focus of life. His experience was *his* because only in the individual focus can there be experience, but his concern to perceive and understand was undeflected by egotism, or by any impulse to protect an image of himself.[7]

Impersonality is not a technique to be applied, so much as personality at full stretch. A work becomes impersonal in this ambitious sense by a higher sincerity in its author in discovering his or her own deepest intuitions in dialogue not just with the subject-matter but with the promptings of language itself. Leavis saw this quality, for example, in the opening of Eliot's 'East Coker' and always used the word 'sincerity' in this sense, not as a merely personal attribute of the biographical artist but as a judgement of achieved impersonality in the work.

This view of history not as external events reflected in language, but as made within and by language, is highly consequential for what it means to understand the past. Dilthey placed special weight on the word *Verstehen* (to understand) since part of the difference between history and the natural sciences is that we can understand human beings inwardly, even if they are of a different historical culture, although we cannot explain them. In contrast, science allows us to explain the world but not to understand it in the sense that we understand our fellow beings. Where science gives certitude and predictability, history gives a depth of empathic understanding within protocols of interpretation. Dilthey, in line with earlier German tradition, distinguishes and limits the claims of science without demonising it. These disciplines are complementary modes within the common creation of a human world, a recognition for which Goethe's life and work stand as the abiding instance. English culture, on the other hand, has tended to produce an assumed opposition between disciplines, an opposition exacerbated by the educational tendency throughout the nineteenth and twentieth centuries to specialise in one or other area from an early age. Accordingly, Leavis was often perceived by British observers as espousing the 'literary' in an oppositional spirit although his respect for science was always evident. His discussion of *Little Dorrit* emphasises the creative urge of Daniel Doyce, the scientific inventor, in parallel with that of the author while the phrase in the above quotation, 'something other than itself... on which the physical world ultimately depends', is taken from R. G. Collingwood's *The Idea of Nature*. And in Leavis's best known discussion of this question, *Two Cultures? The Significance of C. P. Snow* (1962), his original lecture was published with the essay of a science student, Michael Yudkin,

---

[7] *Lectures in America*, with Q. D. Leavis (London: Chatto and Windus, 1969) p. 77.

reinforcing the case from a scientific point of view. Yet in the British public sphere of the day, Charles Snow was widely accepted as making a case for closing the educational gap and Leavis as resisting it. In fact, Leavis was seeking to show that Snow assumed the gap, and in a way that revealed his ignorance of what creative literature, and therefore any culture, was. *The Living Principle* was to spell out more fully the conception of culture, which can only be a common culture, on which 'literary' creation depends.

Dilthey's model of understanding gave special importance to what he called *Erlebnis*, or 'lived experience', a close parallel for the Jamesian criterion of 'felt life' which underwrites Leavis's criticism.[8] The German words *Erfahrung* and *Erlebnis* are both translatable as 'experience' but whereas the former is connected etymologically to travelling the latter is connected to living. One can travel without internalising the experience it offers, while a stay-at-home may live more intensely. Leavis, who lived in Cambridge virtually all his life, was sceptical about claims to cultural *Erfahrung* but had a formidable intensity of lived experience. 'Experience' in this sense is manifestly elusive to both articulation and judgement. While Dilthey theorised the resistance of experience to theorising, Leavis expressed his meditation on history in the intuitive complex of his praxis, as a creative writer might do, and he avoided any tendency to translate, or interpret, the literary work into terms other than its own. He rather sought to sink into the experience of the work, but to put it in that way throws an ambiguity into relief. For this experience can be neither that merely of the verbal text nor the personal and historical experience of the writer: it is the transient and elusive relation between them in the act of creation. Hence Leavis's reading was typically an intense participation, not so much in the fictional world of the work, as in the author's creative process in producing it; as if the work were being freshly created each time, with each re-reading, in the reader/critic's imagination: 'It is a creative process . . . ' a more deliberate following through of that process of creation in response to the poet's words.[9] Similarly, although Dilthey was more concerned with the philosophical problems of interpretation than the act of criticism, he was equally insistent on the inwardness and immediacy of relation to the text. He saw textual understanding as a difficult form of 'divination', and borrowed from Schleiermacher the notion of a reading which 'apprehends an author through the same creative act—albeit conceived

---

[8] The phrase is from James's Preface to *The Portrait of a Lady* and Leavis quotes it to enforce his critique of the later James: *The Great Tradition, George Eliot, Henry James, Joseph Conrad* (London: Chatto and Windus, 1948) p. 168.

[9] *English Literature in Our Time and the University* (London: Chatto and Windus, 1969) p. 48.

as receptivity—that generated the work in the first place'.[10] Properly to appreciate a work of genius requires a measure of what he called 'congeniality'. Such an empathic reliving of the original creativity (what Dilthey called *Nacherlebung*) was necessary to re-animate the historical process of the author. Dilthey's *Nacherlebung* catches the intensely inward participation of Leavisian reading. By the same token, in Leavis's case, such a re-animating of the openness of the past, implicitly recovering the possibility of its *not* having been created, provides a suggestive insight into historical potentiality in the present.

All this suggests a peculiar difficulty in locating the authority of the critical discourse. Ideally, this is not a function of the critic but of the text, or of the author whom the critic invokes. Hannah Arendt speaks suggestively of a shift in the modern scientific era from the 'why' to the 'how', from metaphysical questions of ultimate purpose to observation of process.[11] Although Leavis is obviously concerned with ultimate questions, Arendt's distinction is quite apt to his agnostic focus on the creative process of the writer. The critic's capacity for an impersonal submission to the process implied by the text is the equivalent of the scientist's objectivity although it is achieved as a high level of emotional intuition and skill rather than by technical protocols. This may explain why Leavis seemed to have more ready sympathy for scientists than for most 'literary' critics. At the same time, in so far as great literary art is the royal road to historical self-understanding, its elusiveness to protocols of scientific certitude is a necessary consequence. There is no alternative to personal judgement, which will always be more than 'aesthetic' or 'literary'.

Hence both Dilthey and Leavis emphasised the individual as the inescapable locus of both significant artistic achievement and responsible criticism. As Leavis put it, with reference to Blake: 'only in the individual can there be experience.' Likewise, summarising the development of historical consciousness in and after the Enlightenment, Dilthey put much of the Leavisian view in a nutshell:

And in Germany the point was finally reached where the conception of society according to the natural system passed into a true historical consciousness. Herder found in the disposition of the individual that which changes and constitutes historical progress. The medium through which this progress was studied in Germany was art, especially poetry. (*Introduction to the Human Sciences*, 215)

The act of creation in language mediates between the self and history, and the emphasis on the individual within the collective process led both Dilthey and

---

[10] *Selected Works*, vol. iv, *Hermeneutics and the Study of History*, ed. Rudolf A. Makkreel and Frithjof Rodi (Princeton NJ: Princeton University Press, 1996) pp. 130, 158.
[11] *The Human Condition, op. cit.* pp. 295–6, 307.

Leavis to dwell on the multi-layered implications of the word 'to mean'. Dilthey observes: 'There is a relation, strange as it is important, between purpose and meaning, which we have already noticed in the life of the individual, and which asserts itself in history.' (*Meaning in History*, 163) Meaning must be personally intended yet can only arise from a potentiality already present in the language. Our meanings do not belong simply to ourselves and entail responsibility to the whole. As Leavis put it:

> The focal words for me at present are 'mean' and 'meaning'. The ease with which one shifts from one force of the word 'mean' to another is significant. The protest, 'Oh, but that isn't what I meant by the word', might very well have issued as, 'But that isn't what I meant to mean'. . . . It seems to me that some presence of the force of 'intend' is necessary to the meaning of 'means'.
>
> . . . Thought about language should entail the full and firm recognition that words 'mean' because individual human beings have meant the meaning, and that there is no meaning unless individual human beings can meet in it, the completing of the element of 'intend' being represented by the responding someone's certitude that the last condition obtains. (*LP*, 37–8)

The deconstructive recognition that language 'speaks through' us is incorporated here to enforce responsibility. Linguistic meaning is underwritten by a purposiveness which can only be manifest through individuals and yet is inseparable from the general potential of meaning in the language at large. The point, Leavis suggests, is at once self-evident and yet, for that very reason, overlooked. By the end of the twentieth century, it came to be overlooked in a different way: the dissolution of the self in the constitution of meaning became a banality and in doing so it often lost, or reversed, its original force. Despite corrective emphases in Derrida, for example, the individual is now widely perceived as an illusory subjectivity rather than a focus of responsibility.[12]

The emphasis on criticism as responsibility contrasts with Dilthey's successor, Martin Heidegger, whose philosophical power became notoriously uncoupled from civic responsibility.[13] His major philosophical claim was that Western man had suffered, since the time of Socrates at least, a progressive and disastrous forgetfulness of Being. In this respect, he developed a long-standing view of the ancient Greeks as enjoying an un-alienated relation to themselves and the world. With the growth of Socratic ideals of knowledge,

---

[12] See, for example, 'Eating Well: On the Calculation of the Subject, an Interview with Jacques Derrida', in *Who Comes After the Subject*, ed. Eduardo Cadova, Peter Conner, and Jean-Luc Nancy (London, Routledge, 1991).

[13] Recent Anglophone debate about Heidegger's politics was largely sparked by Victor Farias, *Heidegger and Nazism*, trans. Paul Burrell (Philadelphia: Temple University Press, 1989). For a good summary discussion see Miguel de Beistegui, *Heidegger and the Political* (London and New York: Routledge, 1998).

however, the world had become a congeries of external entities susceptible to explanation and technical manipulation in which the mystery of its sheer Being was obscured. In this condition, personal being, and even language, became infected with inauthenticity. Leavis had an equivalent grand narrative. Long after the phrase, though not perhaps the underlying idea, fell out of fashion, he maintained T. S. Eliot's notion of a 'dissociation of sensibility' to argue a more recent historical process of alienation within the self, a coming apart of thought and feeling, occurring particularly with the rise of modern instrumental reason in the seventeenth century.[14] This was his equivalent of Heideggerean 'inauthenticity', just as what he called the 'technologico-Benthamite' culture echoed Heidegger's notion of the merely instrumental, the *Gestell*.[15]

I have explored elsewhere the parallels and differences between Heidegger and Leavis.[16] Here a couple of points require emphasis: that for Heidegger great art is philosophically significant, and that his difficulties of expression are even more overt. The expressive difficulties may indeed be taken as the way into the substantive questions.

Heidegger's account of Being is not fully susceptible to argument. Indeed, *ex hypothesi* the conventional processes of argument are likely to remove us even further from recognition of it. As Heidegger says, it is the hardest thing in the world truly to see what is before our eyes.[17] As might be inferred from the title of his lecture course, *What is Called Thinking*, Heidegger was as incapable as Lawrence of 'what is ordinarily called thinking'.[18] Late essays, such as 'The Way to Language' or 'The Thing', evade the ordinary processes of argument to enact a gradual unfolding of recognitions through meditating on the historically layered meanings of words.[19] In most circumstances argument by etymology would be a classic error yet it is appropriate in his case. For etymology reveals not the supposedly 'true' meaning of the modern word, but that another meaning has been lost. Forgetfulness of Being is reflected in linguistic change. So, for example, he traces the word 'thing' back to an original

---

[14] *Nor Shall My Sword* (London: Chatto and Windus, 1972) p. 124.
[15] 'The Question Concerning Technology', in *The Question Concerning Technology and Other Essays*, trans. William Lovitt (New York: Harper and Row, 1977) pp. 3–35.
[16] *F. R. Leavis* (London: Routledge, 1988) pp. 35–54.
[17] 'The task of properly seeing what we have had in front of us all along may appear to be very simple, yet this kind of seeing and grasping is actually very difficult.' *Gesamtausgabe*, vol. 29/30, *Die Grundbegriffe der Metaphysik* (*The Fundamental Concepts of Metaphysics*), ed. Friedrich Wilhelm von Hermann (Frankfurt/M: Vittorio Klostermann, 1983) p. 91.
[18] *What is Called Thinking*, trans. J. Glenn Gray and F. Wieck (New York: Harper and Row, 1968).
[19] See *On the Way to Language*, trans Albert Hofstadter (New York: Harper and Row, 1971) pp. 111–36; *Poetry, Language, Thought*, trans. Alfred Hofstadter (New York, Harper and Row, 1971) pp. 165–86.

Germanic use as 'matter of concern' rather than its modern implication of an external, inanimate object. The mode of argument is itself closer to poetry than philosophy and may achieve its essentially meditative purpose even where the etymological claim is fanciful. Heidegger's properly philosophical language is notoriously obscure although extraordinarily precise in its own way. It likewise requires a measure of willingness from the reader to go along with it. Judged by many to be the major philosophical mind of the twentieth century, he causes even sympathetic readers constantly to ask themselves whether his thought is truly profound or merely banal. This is quite appropriate for, as Heidegger indicates in his *Parmenides* lectures, Being is the ultimate open secret and in constant danger of being lost between the self-evident and the incommunicable.[20]

Despite the radical questions that hang over him, Heidegger is the culmination of a classic tradition of European thought and the intellectual problems he poses have a significant parallel in Leavis. Heidegger sought to go a stratum deeper than Nietzsche's end of metaphysics. If value, as Nietzsche insisted, is prior to the Socratic question of knowledge, since we seek to know what we will to know, then the question of Being, Heidegger argued, is prior to value. For Leavis, as for Nietzsche and Lawrence, the fundamental term is 'life', which is perhaps even more discursively vulnerable than 'Being'. 'Life' here does not imply a metaphysical vitalism in which life is a causal entity or force.[21] It is an assessment of phenomenal quality rather than a noumenal claim. Taken in this sense, it underwrites Leavis's criticism although he resists the philosophical focus Heidegger sought with respect to Being. Heidegger focused Being by its distinction from the myriad empirical beings, whereas life as an internally discriminable scale of value, rather than a mere biological fact, is only manifest in specific living beings. Heidegger may indeed be more profound yet the shift to the term 'life' in Nietzsche signals a more immediate foreground of concerns that Heidegger's thought slights in ways that his own life notoriously illustrated. Leavis shares the Nietzschean problematic and in a late essay entitled 'Life is a Necessary Word', he confronts the joint necessity and vacuity of the word.[22] It is necessary yet can only be a frame of reference, a place-holder term, within which specific manifestations of living quality must be judged. By confronting the primordial basis of judgement in this exposed way, Leavis is not importing something that could be left out of the critical

---

[20] *Gesamtausgabe*, vol. 54, *Parmenides*, ed. Manfred S. Frings (Frankfurt/M: Vittorio Klostermann, 1982) p. 93.

[21] Nietzsche was characteristically scathing on modern life-force philosophies: 'it is precisely the more modern philosophers who are among the mightiest promoters of life . . . ' *UM, op. cit.* p. 145.

[22] ' "Life" *is* a Necessary Word', *NSMS, op. cit.* pp. 11–37.

act but, like Nietzsche, is making explicit the evaluative decisions which are otherwise being made subliminally and habitually. Quality of life is his open secret; and hence in his case too the constant proximity of profoundly realised judgement and the threat of banality.

For Heidegger also the royal road to remembrance of Being is through the non-discursive route of art and, as with Dilthey and Leavis, only great art is in question. The art object, experienced in the mode of purposiveness without purpose, eludes instrumentality and thereby allows Being to be manifest. He argues with telling reference to poetry and art but for an essentially philosophical purpose which does not depend on specific critical discrimination.[23] Likewise, forgetfulness of Being is essentially a philosophical myth which can survive a measure of cultural historical vulnerability, the word 'myth' here meaning, not falsehood, but a world view. By contrast, Leavis's 'dissociation of sensibility' lies between such a philosophical myth and a detailed historical case. It partakes of philosophical myth in its order of significance, and if it had been referred to as the aftermath of the Cartesian split, or as a form of alienation, it might well have been less readily dismissed; yet the chosen phrase indicates how it depends crucially on the reading of literary texts in specific cultural moments. Hence, whereas Heidegger adduced poets such as Hölderlin and Rilke as philosophically illustrative, Leavis's use of poetry was historically evidential. Leavis's philosophical and historical claim is, therefore, inextricable from specific acts of criticism. This doubleness indicates why Leavis was at once deeply committed to the significance of the artistic imagination and yet hostile to the term 'aesthetic'. For apart from objecting to the residual aestheticism of the early twentieth century, and to loosely obscurantist belle-lettrist usage, his avoidance of the term 'aesthetic' importantly complements, and defines, his commitment to the 'literary'.

Leavis's great difficulty was to communicate a radically philosophical recognition for which criticism, as participation in the creative act, was the necessary medium. Readers tended to respond to the critical foreground of the judgement without seeing the underlying philosophical claim other than as naive moralism or vitalism. His judgements were taken to be judgements about the world through a literary occasion rather than as judgements of a specifically imaginative achievement. His belief in the *creative* rather than *reflective* relation of poetic art to life entails that the object is always in the first instance essentially imaginative. It is hard to keep this distinct in the mind because, of course, there is also in imaginative literature a level of referential

---

[23] This is a brief summary. For an excellent examination of the internal changes in Heidegger's thinking on art see Julian Young, *Heidegger's Philosophy of Art* (Cambridge: Cambridge University Press, 2001).

reflection that it shares with general usage. But what makes it poetry, for Leavis, is its heuristic openness to what is not, or is not yet. At the same time, even if this confusion is avoided, poetic language cannot be merely imaginary in any sense that cuts it off from extra-aesthetic usage. As Leavis would say, while you must discuss literature as literature 'and not as another thing', there are no 'purely literary values'.[24]

Suzanne Langer's account of 'poeisis' in *Feeling and Form* gets close to the point:

> The word 'life' is used in two distinct senses, ignoring the many esoteric or special senses it may have besides: the biological sense, in which life is the characteristic functioning of organisms, and is opposed to 'death'; and the social sense, in which 'life' is *what happens*, what the organism (or, if you will, the soul) encounters and has to contend with. In the first sense, all art has the character of life, because every work must have organic character, and it usually makes sense to speak of its 'fundamental rhythm'. But 'life' in the second sense belongs peculiarly to poetic art, namely, as its primary illusion. The semblance of experienced events, the illusion of life, is established with the opening line; the reader is confronted at once with a virtual order of experiences . . . [25]

In distinguishing the different senses of 'life', Langer recognises their mutual implication. The two meanings are in some sense present both within art and outside it. In particular, the virtuality of poetic 'life' reflects a virtuality already implied whenever human life, as Leavis would call it, is in question. What poets do is, after all, only a superior version of what we all do all the time. At the same time, as her Schillerian use of 'semblance' indicates, Langer finds it necessary to insist on the virtuality of life in poetry because its encompassing character constantly obscures this aesthetic premise even where the literary form or artifice is quite overt. Similarly, the virtuality of 'life' in poetry is the condition of Leavis's reading although his emphasis falls on critical discrimination. For critical purposes the aesthetic premise is not immediately relevant because the aesthetic is a mode of relation to value, not a value in itself. One must be careful, therefore, not to confuse Leavis's specific objections to uses of the *term* 'aesthetic' with an objection to the aesthetic *as such*. In his review of the Twickenham edition of Pope, for example, he comments that a critic would do well to avoid the word 'aesthetic'.[26] In view of his larger conception of language and creativity, the inference to draw here is a double one: in the philosophical consideration

---

[24] *Anna Karenina and Other Essays* (London: Chatto and Windus, 1967) p. 195. See also *The Common Pursuit* (London: Chatto and Windus, 1952) pp. 183, 280.
[25] *Feeling and Form* (London: Routledge and Kegan Paul, 1953) p. 214.
[26] *The Common Pursuit, op. cit.* p. 89; *NSMS, op. cit.* p. 97.

of art as such the concept of the aesthetic is of the essence, but where any specific critical judgement is in question invoking of the aesthetic is almost always a confusion. Leavis's critical concern, which required specific emphasis on quality, obscured for many readers the ontological discrimination, the virtuality, which is the condition of poetic 'life'. In Nietzsche, likewise, the 'vitalist' emphasis of *Twilight of the Idols* does not deny the aesthetic model of *The Birth of Tragedy*. They are mutually necessary: *Twilight* is primarily a cultural critique while *Birth* is centrally concerned with a metaphysical and cultural definition of the aesthetic.

Leavis, then, was in accord with Schiller and Nietzsche in seeing the aesthetic imagination not as separate from, but as vital to, the conduct of life although in his time it had acquired the separatist overtones of aestheti*cism*. In *Twilight*, Nietzsche was to speak dismissively of the morally idealistic Schiller as the 'moral trumpeter of Säckingen', yet he praised him in *The Birth of Tragedy* for his aesthetic penetration.[27] Schiller had dismissed naturalistic interpretations of the dramatic chorus as moral commentary, or the voice of the community, to affirm its function in *separating* the stage action from ordinary life. Nietzsche quotes Schiller's wonderfully suggestive description of the dramatic chorus as a 'living wall'.[28] Although Nietzsche follows Schiller in emphasising the separation, they were both sensitive to the subtext of the phrase which catches the doubleness of the aesthetic, or the literary. Even though the chorus is a wall that separates, it is formed of the living and mediates the staged significance it has made possible back into the world of life. It surrounds the action with a circle of concentrated concern within the midst of life. For Schiller, the moral is the unconscious condition of the aesthetic, just as the aesthetic is the condition of the moral.

The parallel with Schiller and Nietzsche suggests why Leavis constitutes a radical change within the Arnoldian tradition with which he is commonly identified. Whereas Matthew Arnold had a conception of high culture as intrinsically ennobling, Leavis's conception was practically the opposite. Although the seeming transparency of his reading may suggest an effectiveness emanating directly from the text, it is the demonstrative act of responsive reading which is crucial. As Schiller had recognised, great literature cannot convey wisdom and insight where these qualities are absent in the reader, it can only enhance and educate them where they exist. Hence the significant locus of the problem, as for Nietzsche, was now in the notion of culture itself as the medium of reception. Whereas Arnold contrasted culture and philistinism, Leavis saw in British academic and literary culture the equivalent of Nietzsche's *Bildungsphilister*, the culture philistine. For him, the academic

[27] *The Twilight of the Idols*, op. cit p. 78.   [28] *The Birth of Tragedy*, op. cit. p. 58.

and higher journalistic worlds were standing examples of the inefficacy of sheer acquaintance with 'the best that has been thought and said' in producing the properly whole and human individual. In so far as the case for a publicly funded literary academy tends conventionally to rest upon an implicit, inertial Arnoldianism, Leavis was once again exposing its unconscious.

In sum, the historicist *Lebensphilosophie* of Dilthey combined with the phenonemological philosophy of Being in Heidegger articulate the considered view of language, poetic creativity, and historical significance that underwrites Leavis's criticism. At the same time, comparison with Nietzsche suggests both the internal strains and the external difficulties of authoritative articulation which this conception presented, especially within the context of the institutionalised academy. Like Nietzsche, he found himself at the limits of the communicable.

Pedagogy versus Collaboration

I have emphasised how Leavis's conception privileges the impersonal within the personal, and the representative within the individual but, of course, the same logic applies equally in the opposite direction: the representative is only enacted through the individual and, as the etymology of the word arbitrary indicates, one person's act of grave public judgement is another's personal whim. As Dilthey observes: 'The capacity to make a profound judgement about a great poet... is akin to creative ability.'[29] There remains a question, therefore, as to how well in practice Leavis enacted in his criticism the impersonality he valued in the great creative artists. The pedagogical relation throws this into relief because, like Nietzsche, he exercised a compelling authority on sympathetic recipients who were often self-identified as disciples. At the same time, he declared an 'aversion from the word "teach"' and preferred to dissolve it into the 'collaborative' and the 'creative':

If one's concern is essentially with literature one doesn't think of oneself as 'teaching'. One thinks of oneself as engaged with one's students in the business of criticism—which, of its nature, is collaborative. The student, on his part, ought to be able to think of himself as belonging to a collaborative community formed by the English School as a whole, undergraduates, graduate students and permanencies, and the more, let me add parenthetically, he can feel that it transcends departmental frontiers the better, the community being a model or paradigm of the ideal—for it doesn't now exist—educated public that (ideally) makes possible at any time a performance of the function of criticism. The collaboration is essentially a creative one. (*NSMS*, 109)

[29] *Poetry and Experience, op. cit.* p. 131.

By honouring this ideal in decades of practice, Leavis also revealed its internal strains. In principle, he sought collaboration. Any critical judgement invites the response 'Yes, but . . . ' to be followed by 'qualifications, corrections, shifts of emphasis, additions, refinements'. (*ELTU*, 47) Yet his very phrasing here indicates in advance the limited scope of these counter-terms. The envisaged dialogue is little more than a tuning-up of the original judgement. To see, for example, in the comic and self-conscious tradition of Fielding, Sterne, and Joyce the possibility of major status or interest comparable to, albeit very different in kind from, Austen, George Eliot, and James, would be in itself an effective disqualification from participating in the Leavisian dialogue on the English novel. Collaboration is strongly governed by the self-fulfilling exclusivity of the pedagogical circle and to stay within it is to be a virtual disciple for, once such fundamental judgements have been articulated, it is difficult to endorse them, even with authentic and independent exercise of understanding, without the semblance of epigonism.

Leavis's best criticism was so authoritative because of its seeming transparency. He submits himself to the literary work, in the first instance, as a pupil, seeking to re-enact its creative process. In the participatory act of *Nacherlebung* he seeks the maximum inwardness with the work, and therefore seems to place the reader in the same relation to it, with no more than hortatory and ostensive gestures of focused attention. Hence the curious mixture of density and transparency in his critical prose as it struggles with the logic of the open secret. Its Jamesian syntactical complexity constantly eludes premature comprehension while holding the self-evident in view. This is why, even at its best, his commentary can flicker in the reader's perception between the definitive and the vacuous. For the same reason, however, although his criticism at its best has an incomparable conviction and gravitas, it leaves even then little space for internal dissent. The *de facto* authority obfuscates the difference between fundamental disagreement from a standpoint of equality, and failure to understand, whether through immaturity and lack of experience or through some defect of personality. This difficulty was especially acute in so far as 'maturity' was itself a key criterion in Leavisian judgements.

Once again, the significance of his case lies not in being unusual in principle but in bringing these universal tensions to the surface. Life judgements reveal the personality of the judge as much as the nature of the object and Leavis lived out the logic of his position by exposing himself to judgement, or by making explicit the self-exposure of others. The definitive instance of the latter was his critique of Charles Snow's Rede lecture in which Snow, as mentioned earlier, had deplored the perceived gap between the 'two cultures' of the arts and the sciences. Snow's authority to comment on 'literary' culture was implicitly underwritten by his own pretensions as a novelist while, for Leavis, the quality of the novels, as well as the style of Snow's commentary, indicated the emptiness of his notion of culture. An *ad hominem* critique was therefore of the essence.

In his later years, Leavis sought to give a principled account of his practice while feeling even more acutely the pressure of his isolation within the culture at large. In accordance with his ostensive procedure, he argued through critical discussion of two authors who had come to be exemplary for him. *The Living Principle*, which gives central weight to an extended critique of T. S. Eliot's *Four Quartets*, complements the exemplary value of *Thought, Words and Creativity: Art and Thought in Lawrence* (1976). Leavis's assessment of a writer's 'major' status involves more than historical representativeness. The author must constitute a desirable growing point in the culture. James Joyce, for example, was the example for Leavis of a bad representativeness: one who increasingly embodied, even exploited, the spirit of the time without seeking to overcome it. (*LP*, 284) Underlying the critical/historical judgement, in other words, is a life judgement as to the fundamental tendency of the author. This double focus is especially significant for his differing responses to Eliot and Lawrence. Both writers have manifest points of vulnerability, Lawrence the more strikingly so for most readers. Indeed, Leavis immediately acknowledged the force of Eliot's early criticism and poetry while it took him some years to develop his appreciation of Lawrence. This latter point is worth remembering since the late twentieth-century academy has often rediscovered the obvious vulnerabilities of Lawrence without recognising that the high value Leavis's generation came to place on him was not in ignorance of these, but despite them.

To many observers, however, Leavis seemed to adopt an increasingly uncritical identification with Lawrence and an irrepressible hostility to Eliot. There were tactical reasons for this emphasis in the enormous authority acquired by Eliot in the academy and the relatively late appreciation of Lawrence, itself largely the result of Leavis's own efforts. But there were also more intrinsic reasons. Although Leavis continued to see Eliot as the supremely important poet of his generation, and *Four Quartets* exemplified a major heuristic imagination at work, he found crucial weaknesses in him, as for example in parts of the *Four Quartets*: moments of archness, of self-protection, of flinching from life, which interfered with the impersonality that enabled his true creativity. Eliot's failings mattered because they touched the essential. By contrast, Lawrence's extremities and absurdities did not damage what was essential in his creativity. In fact they were an aspect of his heuristic openness: his emotional truth and moral sanity were intrinsically connected to his falsities and follies through his ability to detect and discard them. Above all, as with Blake, Lawrence's heurism, even when absurd or extreme, was not hampered or distorted by a concern for self-image.

I believe that Leavis's overall judgement locally distorts his reading of Eliot's *Four Quartets* just as he seriously underestimates the significance of Joyce. The point, however, is not to argue these judgements yet again, but to indicate the authentic predicament they illuminate. As with Charles Snow, they are inescapably *ad hominem* and, since the fundamental values at stake are *ex hypothesi* not open to other forms of grounding, it was dangerous for him even to negotiate them. Any compromise risks the whole. As Milan Kundera has pointed out, the word 'collaboration' has been rendered deeply ambivalent in the course of twentieth-century history.[30] Is it possible to collaborate in the positive and necessary sense without the contamination of betrayal? In that respect, every morally aware individual, especially if working in an institution, finds a place on a spectrum of moral possibilities in which there is no ideally clean location. Many local goods can only be served through compromise. Leavis is one who refused compromise and gained thereby a powerful but narrowly based authority. If his purity of conviction did not become a mere conviction of purity, it drew the collaborative circle to a tightness very different from either Goethe's Olympian elusiveness or Lawrence's underlying insouciance. Moreover, the representative value of the individual rightly acknowledged in the case of a great artist may create a disproportionate burden of significance for lesser individuals who can plausibly be seen as cultural portents. The 'portentous' Snow had made himself a target and Leavis's critique of Eliot, for all its trenchancy of *ad hominem* judgement is personally decorous, but the investment of such meaning in individuals is in danger of depersonalising rather than impersonalising.

In this respect, he seemed not to internalise the qualities he valued, with real insight and eloquence, in Blake and Lawrence. His few paragraphs comparing Eliot's essay on *Hamlet* to Lawrence's account of an Italian village production of the play are masterly. (*ELTU*, 154–5) Yet Lawrence's literary criticism is quite unlike Leavis's. Although much of it is radically diagnostic, and it is always highly personal, it has a humour that is not personally destructive so much as a way of establishing, not just a sense of proportion, but of essential difference. His great theme as poet and novelist, after all, was otherness, including that of other human beings, both as individuals and as types. In his literary reading he likewise sought to define his relation to the author as 'other', and could in a measure appreciate the existence of a radically different mode of being, as for example in reviewing Ernest Hemingway.[31] Lawrence is

---

[30] Milan Kundera, *The Art of the Novel*, trans. Linda Asher (London: Faber, 1988) p. 125.
[31] See his review of 'In Our Time', *Phoenix, op. cit.* pp. 365–6.

perhaps the supreme example of critical reading as *Nacherlebung*. He typically follows the creative process closely from the inside except that, in his case, it is to quarrel and compete where necessary with the original author. Hence his penetrative reading of American literature. Yet in Lawrence the novelistic sympathy which exposes, also in a measure accepts and sustains. This is explicit, for example, in his conclusion on Melville:

> Melville was, at the core, a mystic and an idealist.
> Perhaps, so am I.
> And he stuck to his ideal guns.
> I abandon mine.
>
> (*SCAL*, 136)

In his best criticism, Leavis had a remarkable capacity for impersonality, for placing himself at the disposal of the material. Yet as with Nietzsche, this seemed to be at the cost of a more ordinary personal dimension. He seemed not to have the easy wholeness of the Lawrence and Blake who matter, and in whose dismissive comments, however radical and heartfelt, there is already a restorative balance at work, and where the personality of the other does not seem to be felt as an ultimate threat. By contrast, with whatever mixture of intrinsic or circumstantial reasons, Leavis broke relationships even with his closest collaborators. If one reads the accounts not of his enemies, but of his friends, it is hard to escape the thought that the ambiguity of the collaborative-cum-pedagogical circle had an intrinsically paranoid potentiality.[32] In this he remains exemplary, a permanent instance of the limits of a given conception of humanistic criticism and pedagogy when its inner logic is lived consistently.

The compelling analogy is with Rousseau. Leavis stands before the text, as Rousseau stood before nature, claiming an authority beyond himself yet instantiated necessarily within himself in a way that cannot brook compromise. At the same time, both were possessed of powerful visions which transcend the criticisms to which they were inevitably vulnerable. The analogy is worth pursuing for its epochal value in relation to the pedagogical theme of the open secret for, although Leavis was not a literalist like Rousseau, and had a view of literary meaning predicated precisely on the power of the imagination, he nonetheless saw the relation to language in an essentially comparable light. His own intense responsiveness to language figured a crucial truth about the condition of the human world and in that respect Leavisian immediacy and integrity, although fundamentally different in principle, echo Rousseau at another level. So too, Rousseau's metaphysical horror of acting in the *Letter*

---

[32] *The Cambridge Quarterly*, F. R. Leavis Special Issue, 25/4 (1996).

to d'Alembert was predicated on his literalistic assumptions; yet Leavis, in his very different thought world, and for all his acceptance of the imagination, shares something of Rousseau's horror.

A hint of this can be seen in his comments on the histrionic self-presentation of the Irishmen, Joyce and Yeats.[33] He saw them as given to posing, as presenting a self-image, in a way that conflicted with the impersonality of creative art. But there is something more intrinsic at work. His own way of reading, of *Nacherlebung*, was *internally* dramatic. His commentaries on poetry and fiction stress a dramatic 'action' within the language such as to justify his notion of poetic language as 'enactive'.[34] In so far as reading was for him an internal dramatic performance seeking to recover immediate communion with the creative expression, even the speech of a dramatic character is most importantly part of the overall authorial utterance. This is the truly dramatic focus in his reading of Shakespeare. *Scrutiny* helped to pioneer the modern concentration on language in contrast to the emphasis on character typified by A. C. Bradley. This was fruitful in its day, yet it thereby neglected in some measure the aspect of theatre as such and there was some point to John Newton's later suggestion that the journal had significantly 'failed' with Shakespeare in comparison with Bradley's sense of dramatic character in action, a suggestion that caused another rift between Leavis and a collaborator.[35] Leavis's suspicion of the theatrical arose from the need not to be centre stage, but to be the stage itself. This is not egoism or solipsism, so much as the demand for complete immersion in the language of the text.

Rousseau's *Letter to d'Alembert* touches sublimity in its mixture of the compelling and the absurd, and especially so in his extended defence of Alceste, the central character of Molière's *Misanthrope* (1666). The well-known ambivalence of Alceste, especially for modern audiences, is that he is indeed a figure of moral integrity and intelligence but in Molière's radically social conception, these very qualities are problematic, even risible, when they are allowed to become socially isolating or disruptive. Rousseau, however, identified with Alceste as an honest and intelligent man refusing to compromise with the world around him. There is a poignant comedy in Rousseau's defence of a literary character who prefigures his own literal descent into paranoic isolation. And just as Rousseau laid the foundations for world-historical change which would extend, through many transformations, to Leavis, so the shadow of Alceste reaches him too. For both of them, any compromise is catastrophic, and the realm of literary criticism, not worth such

---

[33] See *Lectures in America, op. cit.* pp. 75–6.

[34] I discuss this conception in *F. R. Leavis, op. cit.* pp. 41–4.

[35] Newton largely excepts Leavis from his critique. J. M. Newton, '*Scrutiny*'s Failure with Shakespeare', *The Cambridge Quarterly*, 1/2 (Spring 1966) pp. 144–77.

an absolute stand in the eyes of more worldly bystanders, is the significant arena. The values for which they stand are, though profoundly representative, vulnerably invested in their isolated integrity.

If Rousseau's sympathy with Alceste reflects an epochal shift, so his parallel with Leavis is historically chiasmic in so far as Leavis marks the end of the era of Rousseau. The category of the modern individual, for which Rousseau represented in many ways the birth pangs, was itself dissolving over Leavis's lifetime, into the now familiar, later modern, versions of socially constructed subjectivity. Once again, conceptions of language are at the heart of the question. If Rousseau used a language of social reason identified with nature, Leavis respected language as pregnant with a collective history. Joyce rejected such umbilical connections except as objects of critical play.[36] Where Lawrence's genius saw the depth in apparent surface, Joyce's genius was for turning apparent depth into surface. These two conceptions are incommensurable, and ultimately unreconcilable, although each for that very reason needs the awareness of the other to escape its own possible impoverishment. It seems that Leavis's conception of language, and the corresponding relation of the individual to the communal, no longer compels. It may indeed be that a variety of developments, such as the global use of English for technical and commercial purposes, and the increase of computer translation, will completely change the human relation to language so as to render impossible an older conception of poetry. Such a development, like the death of God, would be another event of catastrophic proportions that may pass unnoticed.

Meanwhile, the tension between the individual and the representative in Rousseau is re-enacted chiasmically in Leavis. Instead of the individual providing the focus of responsibility *within* the collective, the individual has come to be seen rather as an illusion *of* the collective. What most divides the latter part of the twentieth century from major writers of the modernist generation is their commitment to a single culture in which discriminations of life quality made by individuals of unusual wisdom and insight should have a representative force. Of course, this was slipping away at the time as they constantly complained, but the complaints themselves indicate the implicit norm. This was the authority assumed to be necessary by Eliot, Pound, and Yeats. By contrast, the multicultural world of the late twentieth century no longer subscribes even notionally to such an ideal. There is an analogy, and partial cause, in the mid-twentieth-century shift of political commitment from class analysis to identity politics. The morally authoritative model of racial exclusion has left a ready-made structure of feeling whereby members of any

---

[36] *Ulysses*, ed. Walter Gabler *et al.* (New York: Vintage, 1986) p. 32.

self-identified group, from middle-class women to public smokers, can present themselves, whatever their individual position of advantage, as oppressed. The point here is not to deny the reality of relative oppression or disadvantage but to indicate how the absence of a commonly accepted vantage-point is linked to the seductions of morally solipsistic *ressentiment*. This is turn undermines the authority of the genuinely outstanding writer as being ultimately no more than an interested voice. The moral authority of fiction in a post-colonial, multicultural world is the concern of the next chapter.

8

The Novelist, the Lecturer, and the Limits of Persuasion: J. M. Coetzee and Elizabeth Costello on the Lives of Animals and Men

Excuse me for talking in this way. I am trying to be frank.[1]

The white South African born novelist and academic, J. M. Coetzee, is in my view one of the most important writers of fiction at the turn of the twenty-first century. In pursuing discomforting recognitions, he has intensified, and made even more self-conscious, the predicament of moral and literary authority. As novelist, academic teacher, and citizen, living through one of the most painful cultural conditions of the epoch, officialised racism, Coetzee has exercised the power, and examined the claims, of the literary imagination with a peculiar and multi-layered intensity but also with a deceptive transparency. For where Leavis's insistence on the human values at stake in a literary work made him seem to the casual eye a moral literalist, Coetzee has increasingly emphasised the mediation of fiction, or of the 'aesthetic' as it might be understood by Schiller, and yet he has been similarly subjected to literalistic reading. While such responses may be taken as testifying to the authentic power of felt reality and moral passion in the work, they nonetheless distort its meaning.

Coetzee has long been discomforting to read but increasingly the index of his authenticity has come to be the resistance he arouses, if not the repression he reveals, in many of his readers. If his novel *Disgrace* (1999), for example, was meant actively to elicit such a response it certainly succeeded. Some readers reacted with literalistic political objections compounded, I would surmise, by distaste for its central character, the disgraced university lecturer, David

---

[1] David Lurie in J. M. Coetzee, *Disgrace* (London: Secker and Warburg, 1999) p. 166.

Lurie.[2] For although few readers would admit to simply identifying character and author, or to forgetting that it is a work of imaginative literature, it is not clear that the implications of these distinctions are fully understood. The response to Coetzee, and his evident awareness of such a response within the text, raises with unusual urgency the nature of the 'literary' in relation to the 'real'. Without collapsing author into character, one could take as a significant clue Lurie's remark: 'Excuse me for talking in this way. I am trying to be frank.' For it would seem that Coetzee's own frankness is exercised in the mode of the open secret, constantly made available through, and yet significantly bracketed as, literature. In Coetzee, the literary as such proves over and again to be the radically discomforting, and yet indispensable, category for a certain kind of truth telling. In that respect, his case suggests that T. S. Eliot's famous line got it slightly wrong. It is not, unfortunately, the case that 'humankind cannot stand very much reality'.[3] As another Eliot, the novelist, insisted, we can stand it only too well because we are so 'well-wadded with stupidity'.[4] What many of us cannot stand is truth, which is the distinction at stake in the question of reality and fiction in Coetzee. For Coetzee, although he also writes as an academic essayist, does his most significant thinking not just in, but through the mode of, fiction.

Disgrace has a characteristic blend of directness and obliquity. The narrative of Lurie's rather louche affair with one of his students, his self-destructive refusal to make the required apology before a university tribunal, and the violent rape of his daughter by three marauding black youths, is discomfortingly direct with virtually no distance from Lurie's own viewpoint. Yet as Derek Attridge notes, if the aspect of disgrace not just in him but in the whole situation is only too evident, it is ultimately there to hint at its opposite, the possibility of something that might tentatively be called grace.[5] Lurie's lack of self-righteousness, or even moral pragmatism, as focused by his response to the tribunal, allows him, or perhaps the reader through him, to glimpse such a possibility. In this regard, he is like some Lawrencean characters, such as Aaron Sisson, whose behaviour is a perverse, but somehow necessary, rejection of ordinary social and ethical expectations. The perverseness focuses attention on something at stake beyond the immediate ethical and instrumental considerations within which it nonetheless arises. At the end, following his loss of

---

[2] For a record and discussion of responses to *Disgrace* see Derek Attridge and Peter D. McDonald, eds., *Interventions*, 4/3 (2002). Coetzee subsequently changed his domicile from South Africa to Australia.

[3] *Complete Poems and Plays of T. S. Eliot* (New York: Harcourt Brace, 1930) p. 118.

[4] George Eliot, *Middlemarch*, bk. 2, ch. 20, ed. David Carroll (Oxford: Clarendon Press, 1986) p. 189.

[5] Derek Attridge, 'Age of Bronze, State of Grace: *Disgrace*', in *J. M. Coetzee and the Ethics of Reading* (Chicago and London: University of Chicago Press, 2004) pp. 162–91.

employment, Lurie assists in the humane killing of stray dogs. His creaturely relation with these non-human animals becomes a clue to a different relation to the other, and to himself. In this respect, the novel is thematically related to *The Lives of Animals*, a generic hybrid which explores the writerly stance underlying the fiction.[6]

Invited to participate in the annual series of Tanner lectures at Princeton University in 1998, Coetzee read out the story of an elderly fictional novelist, Elizabeth Costello, who, when invited to lecture at a US university, causes embarrassment by speaking on the theme of eating and farming animals to which she is passionately opposed. Four subsequent lecturers responded to Coetzee/Costello's theme from a variety of disciplinary standpoints. All the lectures were then published in a single volume which is the text on which the present discussion is principally based. The choice of this text now requires some explanation, however, as the Elizabeth Costello figure has since been developed in remarkable ways. First, since its original publication, the lecture/story has been reprinted with only minor changes, but without the other contributors' responses, in a volume comprising a sequence of other fictions, some of them already published, based on the figure of Elizabeth Costello.[7] This later volume, entitled *Elizabeth Costello* (2003), is in effect a new novel in so far as a number of once separate stories now take the implicit form of a continuous narrative. I believe that the resulting work, even as it generates new interests of its own, nonetheless, in so far as it establishes Costello as a more conventionally fictional character, significantly flattens the immediate effect of the original lecture. By privileging her continuity as a character, it blunts the discomforting edge of her irruption into a real historical occasion as embodied, in the original publication, by the responses of the other contributors. Indeed, there was a bemused, but condescending, note in some of its reviews which suggests that the later volume has enclosed itself in a purer fictionality whose formal self-consciousness comes too close to an emptily postmodern game.[8] At the same time, however, *Elizabeth Costello* develops another important aspect of Coetzee's later work: a radical scepticism about the authority of the literary imagination *per se*. In its new context, the bleakness of her predicament in *Lives* is retrospectively imbued with Coetzee's, and increasingly her own, doubt concerning the Leavisian conviction on which her life's work has been based. In 2005, the novel *Slow Man* explored an even more audacious possibility in placing Costello apparently within one of her own fictional texts. Once again, however, she is in a fictional space that effectively

[6] J. M. Coetzee, Marjorie Garber, Peter Singer, Wendy Doninger, and Barbara Smuts, *The Lives of Animals* (Princeton University Press, 1999).
[7] *Elizabeth Costello* (London: Secker and Warburg, 2003).
[8] See, for example, Oliver Herford, 'Tears for Dead Fish', *TLS* 5 Sept. (2003) pp. 5–6.

pre-empts the literal intervention of the Tanner lecture on which I wish to focus.

Costello's Lecture

The moral discomfort caused by Costello's lecture is focused by its rhetorical centre-piece: an analogy between the industrialised slaughter of animals and the mass killing of Jews in the Shoah. There is also a specifically disciplinary discomfort in that, while she draws on poets as her authorities, and is dismissive of discursive or instrumental reason, her son John, who works in the same university, is married to an unemployed philosophy Ph.D. John's wife, Norma, dislikes Costello as much for her modes of argument as for the absoluteness of her convictions. Coetzee's *oeuvre* includes many works which, whatever their internal self-questioning, are clearly definable as either fiction or discursive essay. But here, with a mixture of formal ingenuity and apparently casual opportunism, Coetzee has devised a work which genuinely answers to each category and thereby succeeds in radically destabilising both. In *Lives* the questions of response and of fictionality are overtly thematised yet still with the deceptive transparency that characterises the meta-fictional self-questioning in almost all of his fiction. So deceptive indeed that even this work, which raises these questions so frontally, has been read at a first order level, as largely occurs with the four respondents whose contributions are included in the original volume.[9] Only Marjorie Garber, at the end of her lecture, hints at the literary self-reflection achieved by Coetzee's narrative frame. Of course, such a response is not simply wrong. In so far as the fictional novelist Elizabeth Costello has put into the public domain a passionately held conviction about the relations of human beings with animals, the work is a telling contribution to a significant debate and the last two respondents take it straightforwardly in that spirit. Nonetheless, as a fiction it has a significance beyond the apparent topic of Costello's lecture, and transforms the truth claims of her argument. The work examines with bleak lucidity the relation of the morally convinced speaker both to her audience and to her self.

It is necessary, therefore, to appreciate some of the governing structures of the fiction in which the lecture is embedded, although this may at first

---

[9] Garber raises the question of literary truth but does not explore it. Singer is disturbed by what he sees as Coetzee's self-protective indirection and, by attempting to respond in narrative form, he indicates how widely he has missed the point. Doninger and Smuts contribute interestingly to the substantive question of the human relation to animals without distinguishing Costello from Coetzee. The British Channel 4 TV dramatisation likewise placed it in a series of programmes about animals.

seem to be enquiring too curiously into an obvious device. One can readily see why a notoriously reticent male author, often thought to be rather affectless, should construct a fiction in which views close to his own are expressed by a woman of forthright conviction and passionate intensity. As he has said in an interview: 'When a real passion of feeling is let loose in discursive prose, you feel you are reading the utterances of a madman.... The novel, on the other hand, allows the writer to *stage* his passion.'[10] No doubt Costello is a defensive or liberating device for the writer: a way of getting certain things said for which passionate intensity is of the essence, and which Coetzee does not feel able to say in his own voice. But that leaves the propositional statement essentially the same within its fictional frame, and leaves it open to the objection apparently felt by the first respondent, the philosopher Peter Singer, that Coetzee wishes evasively to eat his cake and have it. There is something more at stake, something already hinted at in the reference to 'passionate intensity', in so far as in Yeats's case the best alternative, or at least the alternative of the 'best', was silence.[11] Coetzee shares Yeats's unease yet cannot be silent: he faces an abyss which Yeats's rhetoric often passed by. Coetzee's relation to Costello is rather suggested by his remark on another Elizabeth, the female central consciousness in *Age of Iron*: 'There is no ethical imperative that I claim access to. Elizabeth is the one who believes in *should*, who believes in *believes in*. As for me, the book is written, it will be published, nothing can stop it. The deed is done, what power was available to me is exercised.' (*DP* 250) *Lives* is a closely structured examination of why Coetzee himself, at least as author, cannot readily believe in 'believes in'.

Costello, it seems, is more than a defensive displacement comparable to Rousseau's attribution of his own views to the Savoyard Vicar in *Emile*. Coetzee has fictionalised not so much himself as his function, and his relation to Costello should not be thought of as ironic if that implies substantive divergence from her convictions. For difference of views would distract from the more radical question: Coetzee places *en abyme* conviction as such, what it means to have one, how it can be communicated, and such questioning of conviction is the more telling if it is his own. At the same time, by placing Costello's argument *en abyme* Coetzee reverses, or greatly expands, the more obvious thematic focus of the work. Within the narrative, the Jewish poet, Abraham Stern, is offended by Costello's use of the Shoah as an analogy for her case about animals; and Ian Hacking, in a sympathetic and penetrating

---

[10] J. M. Coetzee, *Doubling the Point: Essays and Interviews*, ed. David Attwell (Cambridge, Mass. and London: Harvard University Press, 1992) pp. 60–1.

[11] W. B. Yeats, 'The Second Coming', *Collected Poems* (London: Macmillan, 1950) p. 211.

review, confessed to sharing Stern's unease.[12] But Hacking too was reading it here simply as a real lecture, as if he were on the same narrative, plane as Stern. In Coetzee's fictional narrative, by contrast, the central theme is as much the Shoah itself with the animal theme as an analytic device for unsettling conventional ways of thinking about it. The animal theme is a Trojan horse designed to deconstruct the authority of conviction, and to test the power of persuasion, in relation to all fundamental, and morally urgent, life issues such as the Shoah, or Apartheid.

While dramatising Costello's conviction, Coetzee's narrative neither endorses nor dissents from her views. And it is significantly neutral on her interpretations of other authors since; in drawing other writers into the powerful vortex of her lecture she radically traduces almost all of them and, if she were to be seen as a straightforward mouthpiece for Coetzee, then his readings would be questionable and disingenuous. For the innocent reader is nowhere tipped off that some of the authors most heavily criticised by Costello express precisely the views she goes on to articulate against them. She unwittingly plagiarises the very writers she excoriates. But as Costello's readings they are entirely in character. She misreads her authors because she leaps over their terms and discourse. Her antipathy to their way of thinking apparently blinds her to what they are saying. This places her, if not Coetzee, in an ambiguous relation to these sources; just as Coetzee elsewhere leaves it an open question whether D. H. Lawrence, a critic very like Costello, has misread Swift or has offered 'a reading of genius'. (*DP*, 309) Like Lawrence or Leavis, Costello tends to override the distancing ironies within a work and go directly for the existential premises of its creation, premises which are not separable from an *ad hominem* judgement of its creator.

The questions of existential judgement and communicability raised by Costello's lecture are dramatically thematised in the surrounding narrative. These questions have both an outward bearing on the speaker's relation to her audience and, through that, an inward bearing on her relation to herself. She asks after our knowledge of the 'other' and how we can communicate what we think we know. The animal theme focuses these themes within a specific history of philosophical debate and cultural change. Dominant assumptions respecting human continuity with, or distinction from, animals shifted over the course of the twentieth century. Traditional definitions of the human were based on such unique capacities as reason, language, and tool-making. Not only have these once-confident boundaries become increasingly blurred but the general emphasis has also shifted: we are now less concerned for our distinction from animals and more for our commonality with them,

---

[12] Ian Hacking, 'Our Fellow Animals', *NYRB*, 47/11 (29 June 2000) 20–6.

including above all the capacity to feel pain. Costello feels this commonality with an immediate intensity overriding the slow shift in culture and the minute processes of argumentation in several disciplines. Her intuitive and apodictic leap, which makes her relation to other thinkers so hostile, is not just an objection to their discourse, we may infer, but to their making the matter open to question at all. If it is a matter of 'rational' debate the pass is already sold. Or as she puts it: 'something in me resists, foreseeing in that step the concession of the entire battle.' (*Lives*, 25) At the same time, her espousal of poetry against philosophical and scientific reason rather confuses the issue since her philosopher, scientist, and poets are actually close to each other and provide parallel vindications of her own argument. It is worth tracing some of the delicacies she overrides in these authors since the narrative as a whole is a literary, if not poetic, development of their combined insights and thereby sharpens the point of her disagreement.

She invokes Blake, Lawrence, and Ted Hughes to affirm the integrity of all animals' lives, and to challenge Thomas Nagel's philosophical exposure of the anthropomorphic fallacy in his essay 'What is it like to be a bat?'[13] Actually, as Hacking points out in his review, Nagel is not her opponent here but her ally. Arguing against materialist reductions of consciousness, he makes her point in advance. The phenomenon of consciousness in living beings is irreducible and, in denying that we can know what it is *like* to be a bat, Nagel assumes, and indeed emphasises, that the creature has *some* mode of phenomenological subjectivity. From her point of view, this Thomas's doubt is benign, for if we cannot know the internal being of animals we cannot know that our everyday intuitions of emotional continuity with them are mistaken. His anti-anthropomorphic scepticism gives an absolute protection to the otherness of the non-human creature; a point made by the respondent Wendy Doninger as if *contra* Nagel. (*Lives*, 103) Costello also misses the point in her use of the poets. Citing Blake and Lawrence as predecessors, she concentrates on Ted Hughes. In truth, by opting for Hughes she simplifies her own case and appears to fall for a common misreading of Lawrence's animal poems. She supposes him to be claiming internal understanding of animal modes of being as if he were naively anthropomorphic in the way Nagel has analysed. But the *pons asinorum* in reading his animal poems is the recognition that he does not naively assume he knows what it is like to be a fish, tortoise or humming bird. On the contrary, these poems typically depend on an anthropomorphism which is bracketed, or as Derrida might say, 'under erasure'. The being of these creatures is unknowable and the poems typically

---

[13] Thomas Nagel, *Mortal Questions* (Cambridge: Cambridge University Press, 1970) pp. 165–80.

show the concentrated exercise of sympathetic imagination which is required to confront experientially, rather than to recognise theoretically, their radical otherness.

And such an intuition of otherness is the condition of a creaturely connection such as Lurie perhaps finds at the end of *Disgrace*. For in a simple formula there can be no otherness without relation, and no relation without otherness. For Lawrence, therefore, the anthropomorphic, or one might simply say the human, imagination is the necessary condition for a more complex recognition. The other life form is in some unknowable measure both continuous with and different from the human, and what is ultimately at stake for him is an extension of *human* being rather than a claim to full internal knowledge, or imaginative possession, of the other life form in *itself*. Indeed, if the other form could be so known, it would no longer lend itself to this imaginative extension of human awareness. At the same time, otherness is the necessary condition of relationship. Hence, the naive sense of encountering another mode of being which many readers take from Lawrence's animal poetry is not wrong, but he achieves his acts of sympathetic attention precisely through the awareness of radical otherness. In comparison, Hughes's poems on animals, however remarkable, are more open to the charge of naive anthropomorphism precisely because of their tendency to melodramatic, all-too-human, insistence on the inhuman; a point Costello goes on to acknowledge in commenting on the ultimately ideal, or 'Platonic', significance of Hughes's 'Jaguar'. (*Lives*, 53–4) Lawrence, then, anticipates Costello's affirmation of continuity with the animal precisely by accommodating the epistemological condition which she overrides and which Nagel articulates discursively.

Reflecting on his reluctance to kill a porcupine which had become a pest on his Taos farm, he pondered the double relation of human to animal, our difference and continuity, and found a discursively irresolvable conflict over killing it. On the one hand, there is a hierarchy of life by which one order of being dominates or devours another. On the other hand, all individual creatures have an incommensurable vitality, a fullness of being in the 'fourth dimension' (*RDP*, 358–63) which is an absolute value. As he puts it: '. . . one truth does not displace another. Even apparently contradictory truths do not displace one another. Logic is far too coarse to make the subtle distinctions life demands.' (*RDP*, 357) Costello privileges Lawrence's second truth at the expense of the first.

To do so, she first seeks to nail Nagel through a virtuoso parallel between two texts of respectively scientific and literary provenance: Wolfgang Köhler's *The Mentality of Apes* and Franz Kafka's 'Report for an Academy' both dating from 1917. I say 'virtuoso' because, as with her analogy of industrial farming and the Shoah, what seems philosophically arbitrary or rambling is poetically precise in its imaginative connections. She recounts how Köhler, whose title might for us recall Lévy-Bruhl's *Primitive Mentality* (1922),[14] sought to measure experimentally the intelligence of an ape called Sultan by accustoming him to being fed by a keeper who then places his food in progressively more difficult locations. Costello imagines a different thought process for 'Sultan' in which, instead of puzzling out how to reach the bananas, he wonders why the keeper has suddenly withdrawn the kindly relationship. By a doubled and reversed anthropomorphising, she imagines the ape having to work out what the human being is thinking, or feeling. Objectively speaking, although she does not conceive it in this way, Costello too exercises a bracketed anthropomorphising here. She can have no idea what the ape actually experienced, or if such a formulation is even meaningful. She needs simply to challenge Köhler's version. The further significance of the captivity theme, however, is that Costello, just like Nagel and Lawrence, sees the comparability between human and animal life as lying in their fullness of their own being. Our modes of being may be incomprehensibly different but the fact and the fullness of it is a point of sympathy and connection: 'To be a living bat is to be full of being; being fully a bat is like being fully human.' (*Lives*, 45) The authentically Lawrencean ring of this affirmation makes one wonder if Costello, or Coetzee, is more aware of Lawrence than either wishes to let on.

The deeper connection with Lawrence, however, is that he sees no localised, special problem of otherness with respect to animals: all relations are radically other and his interest in the more overt instances, racial, sexual or animal, is precisely to reveal the occluded otherness of all human beings which habit, including habits of language and consciousness, disguises as knowledge. The real problem of otherness is our failure to experience it in the human beings closest to us. Moreover, Lawrence's case also reminds us, as did Adam Smith, that sympathy is not necessarily positive.[15] In the human realm particularly, we not only have relative degrees of mutual comprehension, but comprehension may also focus significant discontinuity. Sympathy under a negative sign is a primary motif for Lawrence, as it evidently is for Costello too in the delivery of her lecture. In this respect, her identification with the animal has a further import for her relation to her audience.

---

[14] Lucien Lévy-Bruhl, trans. L. A. Clare (London and New York: Allen and Unwin, 1923). It is also known as *How Natives Think*.

[15] Adam Smith modified Francis Hutcheson's and David Hume's notions of 'sympathy' as emotional *identification* to a more judgemental view of the impartial spectator as *understanding* subjective states whether approving or disapproving. Hence his phrase 'sympathetic resentment'. Adam Smith, *The Theory of Moral Sentiments*, ed. D. D. Raphael and A. I. MacFie (Oxford: Oxford University Press, 1979) p. 78.

Costello and the Audience

Costello's reading of Köhler differs from that of most of his readers, including her first questioner who refers to his 'benign psychological experiments'. (*Lives*, 36) Far from simply isolating Sultan in the way she suggests, Köhler visits an established group of chimpanzees and ends his study with a long appendix on their sociality which begins: 'It is hardly an exaggeration to say that a chimpanzee kept in solitude is not a real chimpanzee at all.'[16] In fact, she acknowledges this aspect of Köhler, but believes that Köhler himself, as a scientist rather than a poet, cannot properly acknowledge it, does not know its significance. For her, the very fact of captivity at all provides a sufficient basis for her parallel with Kafka's Red Peter, an ape who has been captured from Africa and attained a limited freedom by assuming human characteristics. Red Peter has developed the traditional capacity of the ape for imitation to the point where he has acquired speech and can lecture to an academic audience although his motive was not to become *human* but to escape captivity as an *ape*. Within the multiple suggestiveness of Kafka's fable, Red Peter overcomes the otherness of species although he denies that he now has access to his earlier ape-being any more than his human audience have to theirs. His ambiguity of species has a double value for Costello. It helps her anthropomorphising of Sultan against Köhler's putative dehumanising of him while at the same time he provides a model of her own alienation. Even as she insists on his continuity with the human, he figures forth her discomfort in delivering her lecture to an audience of what she feels to be radically alien beings. Her alienness does not derive essentially from being a writer, and a writer can represent a general condition. But as a famous writer she is especially exposed: she is called upon to articulate, and as it were perform, her personal convictions in public. And it is the fate of some writers, such as Kafka, Lawrence, Costello, and Coetzee, to be radically at variance with their culture.

The point can be enforced by extending the network of Costello's possible intertexts to include one she does not cite: Max Scheler's *The Nature of Sympathy* first published in 1913. In the revised edition of 1922 Scheler, while admiring Köhler's book, disputes his claim that the apes truly experience mutual sympathy, seeing it rather as an emotional infection tied to the present moment. He also quotes approvingly Bertrand Russell's *Principles of Social Reconstruction* (1916) and thereby touches on a *locus classicus* of intra-human otherness. For Russell's book was the outcome on his side of a joint proposal for social renewal which he had briefly undertaken with D. H. Lawrence at

---

[16] Wolfgang Köhler, *The Mentality of Apes*, trans. Ella Winter (London and Boston: Routledge and Kegan Paul, 1917, 1925, rev. 1927) p. 282.

the beginning of the 1914-18 war. Despite their joint opposition to the war, Lawrence soon realised his fundamental difference from Russell and wrote to him proposing that they become 'strangers'.[17] Russell's statements of social principle, as quoted by Scheler, would be for most people, perhaps even including Lawrence, well-meaning enough in their generality. Indeed some of the last sentences of *Reflections on the Death of a Porcupine* are close to Russell in phrasing as well as analysis.[18] But just as Hermione Roddice traduced Birkin's Lawrencean meaning within the same form of words, so Russell's abstraction was symptomatic for Lawrence of what he came to see as a fundamental incapacity for true fellow-feeling. Russell, in his view, had developed elaborate mental substitutes for sympathetic connection. If Lawrence was the modern author with the most radical appreciation of the incommensurability of world views, or perhaps one should say 'world feelings', then he had a chiasmic counterpart in the philosopher Wittgenstein for whom mutual understanding depended on a shared 'form of life'. Although Wittgenstein had received even more sustained and generous patronage from Russell than Lawrence did, he likewise felt obliged to make a formal break with him.[19] Both Lawrence and Wittgenstein shared language with Russell but inhabited it in different ways which the formal commonality threw into relief. Wittgenstein later remarked: 'It is what human beings *say* that is true or false; and they agree in the *language* they use. That is not agreement in opinions but in form of life.'[20] But their mutual relation to Russell invites the opposite formula: human beings may agree in their opinions but disagree, if not in the language they use, then in their use of language. In other words, the same formal system of linguistic signs, particularly when operating at a high level of generality, may mask radical differences in forms of life. In such circumstances, the difference may be evident to one party and not the other. And by the same logic, it may be incommunicable in any terms that do not traduce it. Seen in this light, we may infer that Costello has quite intelligibly blanked out Köhler's emphasis on simian sympathies, or Nagel's on fullness of being, because they have for her the same abstract hollowness as Lawrence saw in the social concern of Russell.

[17] 14 Sept. 1915. *The Letters of D. H. Lawrence*, vol. 2, ed. George Zytaruk and James T. Boulton (Cambridge: Cambridge University Press, 1981) p. 392.
[18] Compare Lawrence's 'We are losing vitality, owing to money and money standards...' (*RDP*, 363) to Russell's 'I wish to show how the worship of money is both an effect and a cause of diminishing vitality, and how our institutions might be changed so as to make the worship of money grow less and the general vitality grow more.' Max Scheler, *The Nature of Sympathy*, trans. Peter Heath (London: Routledge and Kegan Paul, 1950) p. 108 n.
[19] For some relevant comments on this fundamental difference see Ray Monk, *Ludwig Wittgenstein: the Duty of Genius* (London: Vintage, 1990) p. 53.
[20] Ludwig Wittgenstein, *Philosophical Investigations*, trans. G. E. M. Anscombe (Cambridge: Cambridge University Press, 1992) p. 88e.

Hence where human relations are concerned, Costello is far from being given to that form of clubbism which Leavis called 'flank-rubbing'. Like him, she not only suffers an embattled isolation, she deliberately exacerbates it in order to face the challenge, or to bring it fully into view. Just as her remarks on animals reflect her own estrangement from her surrounding human culture, so she pursues the confinement theme into a deliberately discomforting realm: 'Fullness of being is a state hard to sustain in confinement. Confinement to prison is the form of punishment that the west favours and does its best to impose on the rest of the world through the means of condemning other forms of punishment (beating, torture, mutilation, execution) as cruel and unnatural.' (*Lives*, 46) This comment on liberal views of punishment is likely to disturb some readers. Is she, or Coetzee, arguing for the acceptance of these other punishments, or simply making a more general diagnostic observation in the spirit of Nietzschean thought experiment? I take it the true point for Coetzee at least is not a first order commentary on penal practice but pushing at the boundaries of the acceptable to test fundamental commonalities of value which are hard to bring fully to consciousness, and which are not open to purely discursive justification. The Jewish poet, Abraham Stern, affronted by what he takes to be Costello's moral equation of animal farming with the Shoah, declines 'breaking bread' (*Lives*, 82) with her, just as she does with the writer, Michael Leahy. (*Lives*, 66) Partly novel and partly philosophical dialogue, Coetzee's text follows both Fielding's *Tom Jones* and Plato's *Symposium* in drawing on the image of the shared meal but only to insist on the corollary of exclusion. Knowledge of the other, whether porcupine or human, may entail rejection.

In the latter part of his career, Lawrence felt, like the elderly Costello, a radical sense of estrangement from the norms of his culture and there is a close analogy to her embedded lecture in the opening of his Mexican novel, *The Plumed Serpent* (1926). His earlier version, now published as *Quetzalcoatl*, is a more moderate treatment of the theme but it is as if he wished precisely to subject it, and the reader, to a testing extremity.[21] The final version is generally, and I think rightly, regarded as a failure, with much solemn absurdity, and multiple offensiveness, interspersed with uniquely brilliant passages. The present interest, however, lies in the immediate challenge he makes to the reader through the heroine, Kate Leslie. Where Costello is suspicious of bullfight ritual (*Lives*, 52), Lawrence begins with a bullfight at which the disembowelling of a horse arouses Kate Leslie's absolute disgust. As the bull's horn works slowly up and down in the horse's rear it suggests, as another variation of bracketed anthropomorphism, an obscene parody of

---

[21] *Quetzalcoatl*, ed. Louis Martz (New York: New Directions, 1995).

human rather than equine sexuality. She is even more horrified by the crowd's enjoyment of the spectacle, and her male companions' failure to share her response. Her attitude to Mexico will change, but Lawrence is not ironising her reaction. Indeed, by using her emotional viewpoint, and stressing her moral isolation, he throws an implicit metafictional challenge to the reader: a problem of evaluative commonality. If you do not respond to the event as Kate Leslie does, you cannot significantly enter the evaluative world of the fiction, although you can read the words and may have the illusion of doing so. Like her male companions, you may see and yet not see the same event.[22] Lawrence's Leslie and Coetzee's Costello are figures of authorial moral isolation, an effect reinforced by their both being gendered female in strongly masculinist cultures.

Costello's daughter-in-law is the character most outraged by the novelist's flouting of social and academic norms and her name, Norma, is a word-play prepared early in the text (*Lives*, 60). Her son, John, seeks to comfort his wife on the eve of his mother's departure with the thought that 'In a few hours she'll be gone, then we can return to normal.' (*Lives*, 119) But as the elderly Elizabeth is driven to the airport by John, she proves to be the one crying in the wilderness; a wilderness, in her case, of no monkeys. She confesses tearfully that the comparison of farm animals with Shoah victims is not rhetorical for her, nor even a matter of strongly held conviction. She is in the grip of an emotional response which radically destabilises both her own identity and her sense of social normality:

'. . . I no longer know where I am. I seem to move around perfectly easily among people, to have perfectly normal relations with them. Is it possible, I ask myself, that all of them are participants in a crime of stupefying proportions? Am I fantasizing it all? I must be mad! Yet every day I see the evidences. The very people I suspect produce the evidence, exhibit it, offer it to me. Corpses. Fragments of corpses that they have bought for money.' (*Lives*, 20–1)

Costello's confession of her minority conviction has a universal structure. She is the emblem of any humane citizen living within an evil social culture but is seen within Coetzee's narrative frame with an analytic *Verfremdung*. Her predicament is moral, political, and philosophical. With what discourse or criteria do you mount a case against the implicit norms of your own culture? If the animal theme provides a completely naturalistic example within our cultural epoch of what we can see to be a more general problem, it also has more specific resonances for the theme of conviction.

---

[22] I discuss this episode of *The Plumed Serpent* in *D. H. Lawrence: Language and Being* (Cambridge: Cambridge University Press, 1992) pp. 187–98.

Faced with the need to kill the porcupine Lawrence was caught between the incommensurable recognitions of living hierarchy as opposed to the equal fullness of being in living creatures. There is no Kantian universal imperative to guide him, and his essay records his characteristic process of thinking, or feeling, his way to action. Through Costello, Coetzee problematises even more sharply the nature of existential decisions which cannot be decided as a matter of reason. She replies to her first questioner: ' "If principles are what you want to take away from this talk, I would have to respond, open your heart and listen to what your heart says." ' (*Lives*, 52–3) Her problem is that her conviction must not just be understood by others as a possible 'position', it must be felt apodictically as a living truth to which there is no alternative. Indeed, the word 'position', after being used casually in the body of the narrative (*Lives*, 25, 48, 60), is put under pressure at the end. As John drives his mother to the airport we recall how he met her with little physical warmth or touch. He now apologises for his wife's hostility by saying 'I don't think she is in a position to sympathise.' (*Lives*, 68) In a context now charged with resonances of philosophical discussion, sympathy, and physicality, the word 'position' lends itself to multiple implication. While John means merely that Norma is overrun with domestic obligations and resentful at her lack of an academic career, his phrase also suggests her adoption of an intellectual posture which excludes the act of sympathy. On that reading her position ceases to be simply circumstantial as internal resistance connives with external conditions. If thought is 'man in his wholeness wholly attending', then philosophy can be a way of avoiding thought, and that leads to the second focus of the fiction: the relation to the self.

Costello and the Self

If Costello's situation as lecturer focuses her isolation, her difficulty in enforcing her own conviction on others, it has an equally forceful inward reference with regard to her self-assurance. Her reply that you must 'listen to what your heart says' echoes the words of Rousseau's Savoyard Vicar but Coetzee does not subscribe to the transparency of the Rousseauvian self.[23] On the contrary, as she confesses, when Costello's anguished intensity in espousing a currently minority viewpoint is seen, through the eyes of others, as deeply eccentric, almost mad, those same eyes make her feel this too. The intensity of her belief, and of her belief in 'believes in', ultimately rebounds to threaten her belief in herself. After all, despite her belief in the unlimited power of the

---

[23] '... Je ne voulais pas philosopher avec vous, mais vous aider à connaitre votre coeur.' *Emile*, 377.

sympathetic imagination, she is confessedly unable to exercise it in favour of the carnivorous majority. In this respect, her conviction is something she rather suffers than espouses and the nature of her conviction is to be placed under increasing pressure in *Elizabeth Costello*.

It is extremely difficult to live outside of cultural norms although the variety of norms available to most of us may disguise this fact. It is possible, for example, to gravitate from a provincial racist culture to a larger world in which such attitudes are abhorrent. But this, however desirable, is a change of norms. Such an individual can feel morally endorsed even while politically exposed. The issue there is more typically one of moral courage *within* a normative conviction. But Costello's response to the farming of animals puts the word 'normal' under a more radical kind of epochal strain. Over the course of the twentieth century, public anti-semitic discourse has become unacceptable but we still eat animals. The imbalance between these questions makes them not, as Abraham Stern thought, a cheap analogy but an analytic device. Coetzee uses a contemporaneous but asymmetrical cultural change to focus the question of how far any convictions are functions of norms.

Joseph Conrad memorably focused what we might call the *Lord Jim* problem: that we can never know for sure our own capacity for moral endurance under pressure. But the revelation which destroys Jim, disturbs Marlow, and provokes Captain Brierly to suicide, depends on their all clearly acknowledging the moral requirements for being 'one of us'.[24] Costello, however, embodies a different level of the question: who is 'one of us' in the first place? The psychologist, Ruth Orkin, uses the phrase for the relation of men and apes (*Lives*, 39) but it has most importantly an intra-human bearing. By the end of the twentieth century we know from several famous psychological experiments that individuals who in the abstract sincerely repudiate cruel or inhumane behaviour will, in the majority of cases, adopt it if they are placed even in a consciously artificial micro-culture in which it is endorsed as normal towards designated subgroups.[25] Modern history, of course, has conducted equivalent experiments with notorious success on whole populations. The degree to which the self is constructed from implicit norms, which may themselves shift and change, is in principle unknowable. By allowing Costello to use the Shoah to express her anguish about animals, Coetzee is using the animal theme to illuminate not just the psychology of the Shoah, or of Apartheid, but of the historical

---

[24] 'One of us' is Conrad's motif phrase in *Lord Jim* signifying a professional and moral community.
[25] On, for example, the Stanford experiment see: P. G. Zimbardo, C. Maslach, and G. Haney, 'Reflections on the Stanford Prison Experiment: Genesis, Transformations, Consequences', in T. Blass, ed., *Obedience to Authority: Current Perspectives on the Milgram Paradigm* (Maharah NJ: Erlbaum, 2000) pp. 193–237.

judgements made about them. How many of those who sincerely subscribe to the anti-racist culture of the late twentieth century would have done so at the beginning of it? How many are exercising truly independent moral responsibility, and how many are animated precisely by the mass emotions of their own day? This is not a question of sincerity, which is broadly knowable, but of authenticity, which is more elusive. Coetzee's narrative of minority and majority convictions does not destabilise moral norms as such, but our internal relation to them, and our consequent capacity to judge others. Never mind the bat, or the chimp, what is it like to be a racist? Not what *would* it be like for *me* to be one, but what *is* it like for the *other*, including the other that I might have been? And if we cannot say, how securely can we judge? Or more subtly and crucially, what is it like to be a non-racist? On the available evidence, how many of us are actually in a position to know for sure that even we are one of us?

The predicament focused by Coetzee's narrative is that citizens of modernity, particularly when inhabiting political orders of some approximative democracy, have urgent obligations to exercise moral authority, but have little secure right to claim, or to enforce, it. As moral individuals and citizens, most of us can, and do, live with this, but a writer whose texts are of their nature public moral interventions can hardly avoid the implicit claim to authority inscribed in them. And where the political stakes are both urgent and painful the predicament is the more intense. Coetzee's fiction constantly negotiates this question as an implicit and integral aspect of the narrative and it would seem that, invited to give a public lecture, he has found a way of inscribing the same double awareness into its internal logic. Even to the extent perhaps of making the predicament itself the primary subject. Costello's simple and passionate conviction is genuinely admirable and therefore only the more seductive. In this respect, she is less like the author, for whom she partly deputises, and more like some of his most hostile readers. We might all wish to live in a simpler world, and we need the motivating focus of simple convictions, but Coetzee is bleakly aware of the noumenal core of the moral self.

The generic overlay of academic lecture, narrative fiction, and philosophical dialogue allows this internal tension to be embodied as different ways of inhabiting language. Although Costello appeals to poetry, her own language is not conventionally 'poetic', and Coetzee's is even less so. His characteristic mode is a minimalist prose giving an immediate impression of transparency but with a luminously enigmatic aura. In *Lives* the bare tautness of the language brings to the surface those dead metaphors which are the most likely locus of unexamined norms. The habitual premises of a culture are the hardest to scrutinise in being at once pervasive and banal, which may be why Costello, while espousing poetic against philosophical thought, remarks: 'Like most writers, I have a literal cast of mind.' (*Lives*, 42). Her very literalism is Coetzee's means for a resonant rhyming of ideas and psychological formations. In reversing and literalising the analogy of the Jews being killed like cattle, Costello allows Coetzee to illuminate not just the state of mind in which the Shoah could occur but the difficulty of internalising this well-known history as moral self-knowledge.

In contrast to Rousseau's merging of educational treatise, novel, and philosophy, Coetzee's tight structure of lecture/story/philosophical dialogue provides an analytic counterpart to *Disgrace* in which Coetzee's tautly minimalist technique pressures the most common terms to reveal unnoticed meanings. It may be because I am one of the apparently few who find the word 'holocaust' distasteful as a reference to the attempted extermination of the European Jews, that I also find the conclusion of *Disgrace* has its full force. Lurie's final statement about the dog he has been preserving from incineration: 'I am giving him up' (*Disgrace*, 220) resists analytic articulation. Obliquely invoking the Shoah, it speaks from the abyss of the self, combining both betrayal and abnegation within a transcendent, but not quite religious, implication of sacrifice. He does not say, and perhaps cannot know, whether he is acting selfishly or generously at the level of motivation, but he is willing to do the right thing by a fellow creature, the essential nature of the recognition being focused precisely by the objective triviality of the occasion. Costello has something similar in mind when she speaks not of moral conviction but of saving her 'soul'. (*Lives*, 43) Whereas Schiller could give a human account of what he meant by 'grace', in Coetzee's world the word denotes a noumenal value glimpsed at best through negative reflections and faint echoes of religious meaning. So for example, we might take the university president's anticipation of 'tomorrow's offering' (*Lives*, 45) as a hint that Costello is not merely preparing to speak *for* the animals but is about to put herself in their place, effectively sacrificing herself as a respected social identity.

Meanwhile, beneath Costello's distress at the end of *Lives*, we may sense something of Coetzee's own scepticism about the value of the literary, which is to say the moral, imagination in which she still believes so intensely. In *Elizabeth Costello*, which has 'lessons' rather than chapters, the two 'Lives' episodes are followed by 'The Humanities in Africa' and 'The Problem of Evil'. In the first, Costello's sister, a missionary nun, questions the impact of classical culture in the context of African history. In the second, Costello finds herself questioning the novelist Paul Webb's painfully detailed account of the slow executions of Hitler's would-be assassins. Just as in *The Master of Petersburg* (1994) Coetzee questioned the dark sources of the literary imagination, so here he questions its effects on both writer and reader. The force of evil may be greater than the imagination can uncorruptedly contain. By the end of the work Costello is forced into what we infer to be Coetzee's own position: even when her salvation depends upon it, she can, as a writer, no longer believe in 'believes in'.

In *Lives*, following her earlier remarks on academic education as a 'narrow, self-regenerating intellectual tradition whose forte is reasoning' (*Lives*, 35), there is an aetiological reflection on her own predicament in her remark on Sultan: 'only the experimenter's single-minded regimentation forces him to concentrate on it.' (*Lives*, 30) 'Concentration' is another term of focal ambivalence. While modern history has lent it a dark inflection, educational institutions are inescapably sites of induced concentration. Concentration is necessary to thought, including the mode of thought known as artistic creation which is notably exemplified in Coetzee's own taut narratives. The mode of concentration is all and Coetzee is suspicious of ideological confinements including, perhaps especially, those with unimpeachable motives. Taut in avoiding the merely taught, his lecture/story/dialogue positions, not just Costello, but writer and reader too within a tight structure of generic enclosures with no evident exit from its moral concentration. And yet, even here, as with all the previous writers discussed, the author's predicament provides the pressure chamber in which a charge of recognition passes to the reader, and that has to remain the final emphasis for the pedagogical theme.

Conclusion

The preceding chapters have traced an *ad hoc* tradition of pedagogical scepticism in which writers with some urgent wisdom to impart have felt the limited likelihood, even sometimes the impossibility, of doing so. The authors discussed in the first part seem principally to have exercised an ironic literary command of this truth while with those discussed after the Nietzschean turn it becomes a more literal predicament. And yet the testimony of many readers indicates that all these writers have been remarkably successful in conveying their different visions or bodies of experience; especially so if judged by intensity of impact rather than breadth of acceptance. They were all great teachers and their negative pedagogy is far from equating with pedagogical negativism.

This might be taken to mean that their pedagogical anxiety was unnecessary, or was merely a rhetorical subterfuge. But the evidence of these texts points over and over again to a more significant and intrinsic relation: the scepticism is a crucial internal dynamic by which the work defines its demands, or rather the demands of its subject, upon the reader. And that in turn begins to explain why a recurrent feature of this internal dynamic is a recourse to fiction. Fiction, that is to say, is not just a sympathetic vehicle for the pedagogical content as a body of accumulated experience, but by its ontological transposition it gives an important regulative definition, both pre-emptive and creative, to the exercise of pedagogical authority. Despite the institutional reality of authority in the teaching relation in many everyday contexts, indeed precisely because of this, there is an important focus for reflection here on its intrinsically creative and hypothetical character. Above all, its oblique and subjunctive nature seems to be of the essence.

This latter aspect has become more important because of the dual process that has been seen in the preceding texts: along with the specifically pedagogical scepticism there has been a deepening scepticism about the value of *Bildung* as such. With varying degrees of sophistication, a variety of ideological critiques over the late twentieth century have convergently encouraged the belief that high culture is effectively, if often unconsciously, a means of maintaining social dominance. Pierre Bourdieu is among the most distinguished thinkers to have encouraged such a view of culture as a form of social capital.[1] In respect of the authors discussed in the preceding chapters, it has been evident at least since Nietzsche that high culture has such a social meaning, and that for given individuals it may have no further meaning. But only in the late twentieth century has there grown up the widespread tendency to regard it, or at least to speak of it, as *merely* that. The authors discussed in this study, by contrast, have maintained the double recognition: that the traditional high points of human culture, however open to revaluation, are supremely important even although, being helpless to enforce this value where it is not acknowledged, they are always vulnerable to positive abuse. The pedagogical danger of the later, one-sided conception is that culturally deprived students will be less likely to be introduced to the major achievements from which a sense of the value of literature and art as such is usually derived. To that extent it is a major *trahison des clercs* as well as perhaps providing a further example of the principle of unteachability.

In practice, of course, it may be that relatively few of those who polemically adopt this ideological view really live it as a belief, or will maintain it in its strong form if challenged. It is only too possible to trade on the power of great literature even while denying it in the abstract and, in that respect, the often agonised dual consciousness of the authors considered here has its mirror image in a pervasive academic double-think. And this may be thought of not simply as a moral failing but in a spirit of intellectual diagnosis. Experience may be traduced by the habitual modes of thinking: we may get away with going wrong in the head because we do not live what we think we think. In that respect, modern ideological critique, at its lower and more disseminated levels, is an equivalent of the eighteenth-century moral literalism against which Kant and Schiller developed their conception of the aesthetic. Their aesthetic conception was truer to the actual experience of the more demanding literature of sentiment in the period, and it is a version of this conception which is now constantly occluded by ritually attacking the straw man of aestheticism, or the ideological connivance of the aesthetic. A positive appreciation of the aesthetic is therefore significant for both aspects of my double theme. It crucially underwrites the understanding of *Bildung* itself and it bears upon the spirit in which that might be taught. It will be appropriate, therefore, to close with some reflection on the possibly practical implications for a humanistic pedagogy of what has been said in the preceding chapters.

[1] As, for example, in the following summary of Bourdieu's thought in a magisterial anthology of modern critical thought: 'Bourdieu challenges Kant's claim that our judgements about art are disinterested, arguing instead that cultivated sensibilities both derive from and produce a "cultural capital" that is tied to economic and social advantages.' *The Norton Anthology of Theory and Criticism*, ed. Vincent B. Leitch *et al.* (New York: Norton, 2001) p. 1806.

Conclusion 237

What has emerged from the preceding exposition is, unfortunately, an open secret, in both senses. Good teachers have always known it while, by the logic of the open secret, every generation has to discover it anew. And in each generation there are those for whom it remains closed. More specifically and practically, the desire to increase numbers in higher education over the last few decades has meant in Britain, and in varying degrees elsewhere, a dilution, at least numerically, of the pedagogical relationship. This has been accompanied by compensatory initiatives for making teaching itself more effective. It is difficult to assess such widespread and multifarious developments justly, and dualistic polemical positions are always seductive. But one can at least say that effectiveness is in the eye of the beholder and in some of the more directive conceptions of pedagogy the circuitous process of the 'Socratic' method, by turns exhilarating and infuriating, does not fare well. A new professional cadre has emerged in tertiary education to organise training sessions for tutors in which good pedagogical practice is to be disseminated, and judged, irrespective, it is reassuringly affirmed, of any knowledge of the subject matter, or even of the discipline concerned. Attendance at such a session produced for the present writer the reward of at least one memorable *trouvaille*. One of the 'bullet-point' advertising recommendations for an MA course was that it involved 'No Wasted Learning'. This phrase might indeed have been latinised and taken as the motto of a great educational institution, as who would say 'there is no wasted learning', although that, alas, was not the implication with which the phrase was used.

In a world where the effective is thought of as the instrumentally 'efficient', two questionable models continue to flank the conception of humanistic teaching that would emerge from the preceding discussion. The instructional model is perennial, and enough has now been said to indicate its limitations beyond the realms of fact and technique which are its proper object. At the same time, every error tends to generate its counter-error and in this case the opposite, more modern, model is the encouragement of independent discussion between students, the success of which is judged by a more or less explicit criterion of animated participation. In its simple form, this model is an exact equivalent of the open-ended, or postmodern, relativity that is often recommended at more exalted levels for the reading of texts. Of course, where group teaching is concerned, engaged discussion is of the essence but, as contemplation of the preceding authors may help to indicate, the criteria of its usefulness are highly elusive. This is partly because any notion of success or failure in humanistic teaching is itself profoundly ambiguous, and the absence of a specific instructional goal does not imply that the field is simply to be left open. Some highly purposive concentration is required if only as the occasion of a significant reaction. This latter possibility is indeed indicated archetypally by the succession of thinkers I have invoked. Goethe, like many of his generation, assimilated Rousseau profoundly but his internal struggle, almost literally a life and death struggle, to transform him is already evident in his early novel, *The Sorrows of the Young Werther*. At a more emblematic level, Goethe was asked to advise on the education of the infant Schopenhauer, and later encouraged his early publication; yet Schopenhauer represents the radical reversal of Goethe's benign conception of nature. Nietzsche in turn honoured Schopenhauer as his educator at a time when he had significantly outgrown Schopenhauer's thought. Once again, this latter point is not a concessive limitation of influence but its essence for it is only by the concentration of power within the pedagogical circle that the energy and significance for its true transformation are created. And Schopenhauer, of course, continued to provide the premises and agenda for Nietzsche's thought even as he reversed its implication. Hence the ambiguity of Goethe's aphorism: 'The genuine pupil learns how to unravel what is unknown from what is known, and approaches close to the master.' The pupil closest to the master may be the one who strikes out most independently and approaches him not in identity of content but in equality of understanding. As I remarked at the outset, on the basis of this principle all humanistic educators may inscribe over their desks, in a positive not cynical spirit, the reflection that education does so much less damage than it might because students, especially the best ones, can always be relied upon to do something quite different with it. But the problem for the educator is to invest this negative truth with a positive and practical realisation, and it is in that respect that the preceding texts show the notion of the aesthetic to provide a crucial model.

Schiller believed that the capacity to adopt an aesthetic relation, a mental stance of non-instrumental reflection, towards one's own values is fundamental to human freedom and responsibility. For him, 'aesthetic education' did not just mean education in matters specifically artistic, although these would be well within the spirit of his argument. It is rather that having the capacity for such an aesthetic attitude at the heart of consciousness at all times constitutes the educative effect. All human beings exercise such a capacity intuitively to some degree, but they possess their humanity most fully when it is raised to the purity, intensity, and self-consciousness which are the *proprium* of art. And his conception, by focusing the purity of non-instrumental reflection within the artistic context, helps to avoid the inappropriately free-floating effect of aesthetic detachment in the moral and social spheres. It opposes aestheticism. This was the double emphasis that he believed was required, for example, both in the immediate aftermath of the French Revolution and *vis-à-vis* the longer-term philosophical movement of moral sentimentalism.

Conclusion 239

The present argument draws a further conclusion for our own time from Schiller's thought by emphasising that educational authority should itself be exercised in an aesthetic spirit. The skill is to incorporate both sides of the Kantian formula of 'purposiveness without purpose'. There must be an intensely concentrated purpose in the experiential structure the teacher creates around the pupil although the pupil should not be a direct object of the teacher's formative will. Rousseau gave an enduring *image* of this in his recommendation that the governor must renounce personal authority and pretend to be merely an older friend, no more than another character, as it were, within the pupil's story. But within Rousseau's conception this was too much of a pretence, while the governor effectively enacted the pedagogical will elaborated by the author. By contrast, Goethe constantly explored the intrinsic perplexity of the pedagogue in his mentor characters. Even while as author he created the benign providence of the hero's experience, the book acknowledges both the fictiveness of Wilhelm's good fortune and the limitations of pedagogical influence. In Goethe, pedagogical scepticism is the counterpart of a positive trust; a trust which, although undoubtedly reflecting an authentic world view, is itself given a frankly fictional expression through and through. In Goethe, as in Nietzsche, a radical scepticism is something that the strong spirit is able to afford rather than something to be suffered. This curious mixture of near absolute scepticism and near absolute trust underwrites the Schillerian aesthetic spirit of Goethe's pedagogical fiction. Just as Schiller speaks of the aesthetic state as simultaneously complete fullness and complete emptiness, Goethe's novels combine plenitude and vacuity.[2] A similar duality should be the goal of pedagogy.

In so far as this provides a generally significant model, it reflects the most ancient Western tradition of pedagogy. Indeed, I hope it will have been no wasted effort if the upshot of the preceding argument is ultimately to have taken the reader round another familiar circle, an historical one this time, making the eternal return to the Platonic *Dialogues*. For the figure of Socrates can be understood in different ways which the preceding chapters may help to illuminate. Jacques Rancière, in his important and engaging meditation on the pedagogical thought of Joseph Jacotot, gives a highly critical account of Socrates. Unable to work in France after the 1815 Restoration, Jacotot secured a post at the University of Louvain despite his inability to speak Dutch and his students' inability to speak French. Having available a bilingual edition of Fénélon's *Télémaque*, he asked his students to learn French from it with no instructional intervention. Remarkably, the students, being powerfully motivated to learn, produced essays in French and thereby led

---

[2] *Aesthetic Letters*, op. cit. pp. 145–7.

Jacotot to recognise the supererogatory nature of pedagogy at all times. The story constitutes a brilliant and iconic *aperçu* which should stand over the desk of all educational practitioners and theorists. In developing this thought, Jacotot and Rancière stress the inequality which the pedagogical relation does not just assume but fosters. All pedagogy brutalises, and Socrates for both of them is not an exception but the extreme example.

That is why the Socratic method, apparently so close to the universal teaching, actually represents the most redoubtable form of its brutalisation. The Socratic method of interrogation, while claiming to lead the pupil to his own understanding, is in fact that of a dressage master: 'He commands all the movements, the marches and counter-marches... By one detour after another the pupil's mind arrives at a goal it had never thought of at the outset. Astonished to reach it, he turns, sees his guide, and astonishment gives way to admiration; an admiration which brutalises. The pupil feels how, left simply to himself, he would not have followed this route.[3]

There is an important point here: the Socratic method, especially when disseminated as a *method*, is indeed open to a secret exercise of control akin to that seen in Rousseau. And Rancière, with his radical objection to inequality, endorses Jacotot's condemnation with a hyperbolic earnestness that recalls Lawrence on similar topics. In contrast to this, the implication of the previous chapters is that some form of pedagogical authority is not only a practical and *de facto* necessity, it is a positive benefit and obligation, and yet it must also accommodate a radical scepticism about its own function. The trick is to include the openness of discovery with the creative pressure that Jacotot's Dutch students supplied with their desire to learn. Rancière, again like Lawrence, argues that there is an expressive need in all individuals, a need whose heterogeneity cannot be readily hierarchised. Indeed, 'the artist needs equality as the instructor needs inequality.' (*Maître ignorant*, 120) But art also involves the other aspect I wish to emphasise here: a concentration such as is most readily seen, and appreciated, in works of art is likewise a condition for the dynamic of learning. So too, this is the more fruitful way to understand the internal pressure generated within the Platonic *Dialogues*.

Although a body of doctrine is traditionally attributed to Plato, his Socrates, the commonly acknowledged archetype of humanistic teaching, typically expounds no doctrine of his own. Moreover, Socrates exists for later readers almost entirely in the ambiguously historical and philosophical, but perhaps above all, the literary medium of the *Dialogues*. At the same time, we sense in Socrates' elusiveness as thinker and pedagogue, as real and performed self, a controlling consciousness matching Plato's from within. In Socrates's typical

---

[3] *Le maître ignorant, cinq leçons sur l'émancipation intellectuelle* (Paris: Fayard, 1987) p. 101.

relation to the ephebe figure, such as Phaedrus, he encircles his interlocutor intellectually while allowing the young man's progressive puzzlement to remain the dynamic centre of the fiction. The pupil is at the centre of a circle whose circumference is everywhere and nowhere. It moves like an horizon, sometimes revealing new vistas. In that respect, the circle is creative and protective as well as pressurising. But yes, it is pressurising; it constantly drives the young man, or the opponent back into himself as happens with later *Bildungsromane*. But because this is done so directly by the mentor it throws the paradox of freedom and discipleship into sharp relief. Socrates is the admired teacher because he challenges and disturbs; which is why he remains a teacher of the few. What those few might ultimately do with the experience remains in many cases unknown although the *Dialogues* themselves are an act of homage which in their artistry also take possession of Socrates. For once again, as with the *Bildungsroman*, the educative beneficiary is ultimately less the Socratic interlocutor than the Platonic reader: the meaning lies a little beyond and above the action that is narrated. If the Platonic dialogue is the enduring image of humanistic teaching it is partly because it employs the concentrated purposiveness of the aesthetic with no instrumentally defined purpose. It is generally recognised that great literary art usually acquires its significant authority by its avoidance of the merely didactic, and with all the same temptations of didacticism, self-display, and facile authority, good teaching is the legitimate sibling of great art. Constant acknowledgement of this kinship is a prophylactic against the perennial abuses of pedagogy.

Bibliography

Ansell-Pearson, Keith, *Nietzsche contra Rousseau: a Study of Nietzsche's Moral and Political Thought* (Cambridge: Cambridge University Press, 1991)
Apter, T. E., *Thomas Mann: The Devil's Advocate* (London: Macmillan, 1978)
Arendt, Hannah, *The Human Condition* (Chicago and London: University of Chicago Press, 1958)
Aristotle, *The Politics*, trans. T. A. Sinclair, rev. Trevor J. Saunders (London: Penguin, 1992)
Attridge, Derek, *J. M. Coetzee and the Ethics of Reading* (Chicago and London: University of Chicago Press, 2004) pp. 162–9
―――― and Peter McDonald, eds., *Interventions*, 4/3 (2002)
Augustine, *Confessions*, trans. Henry Chadwick (Oxford: Oxford University Press, 1992)
Bahktin, M. M., *Speech Genres and Other Late Essays*, trans. Vera W. McGee, ed. Caryl Emerson and Michael Holquist (Austin: University of Texas Press, 1986)
Beddow, Michael, *Thomas Mann's Doctor Faustus* (Cambridge: Cambridge University Press, 1994)
Bell, Michael, *D. H. Lawrence: Language and Being* (Cambridge: Cambridge University Press, 1992)
―――― *F. R. Leavis* (London: Routledge, 1988)
―――― *Literature, Modernism and Myth: Belief and Responsibility in the Twentieth Century* (Cambridge: Cambridge University Press, 1997)
―――― 'Narration as Action: Bekenntnisse einer schöne Seele and Angela Carter's *Nights and the Circus*', *German Life and Letters*, 45/1 (Jan. 1992) pp. 16–32
―――― 'Sancho's Governorship and the "Vanitas" Theme in *Don Quixote Part II*', MLR 77/2 (Apr., 1982) pp. 325–38
―――― *The Sentiment of Reality: Truth of Feeling in the European Novel* (London: Unwin, 1983)
―――― *Sentimentalism, Ethics and the Culture of Feeling* (London: Palgrave, 2000)
―――― 'Sterne in the Twentieth Century', *Laurence Sterne in Modernism and Postmodernism*, ed. David Peirce and Peter de Voogd (Amsterdam and Atlanta Ga.: Rodopi, 1996) pp. 39–54
―――― 'Unbewusste Brüderschaft: D. H. Lawrence and Thomas Mann', *Études Lawrenciennes*, 10 (1994) pp. 187–197
―――― 'What Price Collaboration? The Case of F. R. Leavis,' in *Critical Ethics*, ed. Dominic Rainsford and Tim Woods (London: Macmillan, 1999) pp. 23–39

Blackall, Eric, *Goethe and the Novel* (Ithaca and London: Cornell University Press, 1976)
Blass, T., ed., *Obedience to Authority: Current Perspectives on the Milgram Paradigm* (Maharah NJ: Erlbaum, 2000)
Blanckenburg, Friedrich von, *Versuch über den Roman*, facsimile edition of 1774, ed. Eberhard Lämmert (Stultgart: Metzler, 1965)
Bloch, Jean, *Rousseauism and Education in Eighteenth-Century France* (Oxford: Voltaire Foundation, 1995)
Bloom, Harold, *The Anxiety of Influence: a Theory of Poetry* (New York: Oxford University Press, 1973)
Booth, Frank, *Robert Raikes of Gloucester* (Redhill: National Christian Education Council, 1980)
Borges, Jorge-Luis, *Labyrinths*, trans. Donald A. Yates and James E. Irby (London: Penguin, 1970)
Boswell, James, *Life of Johnson* (New York and London: Oxford University Press, 1960)
Boyle, Nicholas, *Goethe: the Poet and the Age* (Oxford: Clarendon Press, 1991)
_____ ed., *Goethe and the English-speaking World* (Rochester NY: Camden House, 2001)
Broch, Hermann, *Schriften zur Literatur*, I, *Kritik* (Frankfurt/M: Suhrkamp, 1975)
Buddecke, Wolfram, *C. M. Wielands Entwicklungsbegriff und die Geschichte des Agathon* (Göttingen: Vandenhoeck and Ruprecht, 1966)
Cassirer, Ernst, *Rousseau, Kant, Goethe* (New York: Harper, 1963)
Cavell, Stanley, *Conditions Handsome and Unhandsome: the Constitution of Emersonian Perfectionism* (Chicago and London: University of Chicago Press, 1988)
Chaudhuri, Amit, *D. H. Lawrence and Difference: Postcoloniality and the Poetry of the Present* (Oxford: Oxford University Press, 2003)
Cixous, Hélène, 'The Laugh of the Medusa', in *New French Feminisms*, ed. Elaine Mark and Isabelle de Courtivron (London: Harvester, 1980)
Clark, Robert T., *Herder: His Life and Thought* (University of California Press, 1969)
Coetzee, J. M., *Disgrace* (London: Secker and Warburg, 1999)
_____ *Doubling the Point: Essays and Interviews*, ed. David Attwell (Cambridge, Mass. and London: Harvard University Press, 1992)
_____ *Elizabeth Costello* (London: Secker and Warburg, 2003)
_____, Marjorie Garber, Peter Singer, Wendy Doninger, and Barbara Smuts, *The Lives of Animals* (Princeton: Princeton University Press, 1999)
Conant, James, 'Nietzsche's Perfectionism', in *Nietzsche's Postmoralism*, ed. Richard Schacht (Cambridge: Cambridge University Press, 2001) pp. 181–257
Derrida, Jacques, *Of Grammatology*, trans. Gayatri Chakravorty Spivak (Baltimore and London: Johns Hopkins University Press, 1976)
_____ *Who Comes after the Subject?* ed. Eduardo Cadova, Peter Conner, and Jean-Luc Nancy (London and New York: Routledge, 1991)
Dilthey, Wilhelm, *Pädagogik: Geschichte und Grundlinien des Systems* in *Gesammmelte Schriften* (Stuttgart and Gottingen: Vandenhoeck and Ruprecht, 1986)
_____ *Poetry and Experience*, ed. Rudolf A. Makkreel and Frithjof Rodi (Princeton NJ: Princeton University Press, 1955)

____ *Selected Works*, vol. iv, *Hermeneutics and the Study of History*, ed. Rudolf A. Makkreel and Frithjof Rodi (Princeton NJ: Princeton University Press, 1996)

Edgeworth, Maria and Richard, *Essays on Practical Education*, 3rd edn. (London: J. Johnson, 1811)

Eliot, George, *Middlemarch*, ed. David Carroll (Oxford: Clarendon Press, 1986)

____ *Selected Critical Writings*, ed. Rosemary Ashton (Oxford and New York: Oxford University Press, 1992)

Eliot, T. S., *After Strange Gods* (London: Faber, 1932)

____ *Complete Poems and Plays of T. S. Eliot* (New York: Harcourt Brace, 1930)

____ *On Poetry and Poets* (New York: Farrar, Straus and Giroux, 1966)

____ *Selected Essays* (London: Faber, 1961)

Fairhall, James, *Ulysses and the Question of History* (Cambridge: Cambridge University Press, 1993)

Farias, Victor, *Heidegger and Nazism*, trans. Paul Burrell (Philadelphia: Temple University Press, 1989)

Fodor, Jerry, 'Is it a Bird? Problems with Old and New Approaches to the Theory of Concepts', *TLS* 17 Jan. (2003) pp. 3–4.

Fraiman, Susan, *Unbecoming Women: British Women Writers and the Novel of Development* (New York: Columbia University Press, 1993)

Gadamer, H-G., *Truth and Method*, trans. revised by Joel Weinsheimer and Donald G. Marshall (London: Sheed and Ward, 1989)

____ *Conversations with Eckermann*, trans. David Luke and Robert Pick (London: Oswald Wolff, 1996)

Goethe, Johann Wolfgang von, *Goethes Werke*, 14 vols. (Hamburgischer Ausgabe), ed. Erich Trunz (Munich: Beck, rev. edn. 1981): *Die Leiden des Jungen Werthers*, vol. vi; 'Empirrhema', vol. i; 'Offenbar Geheinnis', vol. ii; 'Spiraltendenz der Vegetation', vol. xiii; *Wilhelm Meisters Lehrjahre*, vol. vii; *Wilhelm Meisters Wanderjahre*, vol. viii

____ *Wilhelm Meister's Apprenticeship*, trans. H. M. Waidson (London: Calder, 1977)

____ *Wilhelm Meister's Years of Travel*, trans. H. M. Waidson (London: Calder, 1982).

Gooding-Williams, Robert, *Nietzsche's Dionysian Modernism* (Stanford and Cambridge: Stanford University Press and Cambridge University Press, 1993)

Green, Gayle, *Changing the Story: Feminist Fiction and the Tradition* (Bloomington and Indianapolis: Indiana University Press, 1991)

Greenspan, Ezra, Lindeth Vaisey, and John Worthen, *Studies in Classic American Literature* (Cambridge: Cambridge University Press, 2003).

Gutzkow, Karl, *Die Ritter von Geisle* (1850/1)

Haas, Rosemary, *Die Turmgesellschaft in Wilhelm Meisters Lehrjahre: zur Geschichte des Geheimbandromans und der Romantheorie im 18 Jahrhundert* (Bern and Frankfurt/M: Herbert Lang Peter Lang, 1975)

Hacking, Ian, 'Our Fellow Animals', *NYRB*, 47/11 (29 June 2000) pp. 165–80.

Hardin, James, ed., *Reflection and Action: Essays on the Bildungsroman* (Columbia SC: University of South Carolina Press, 1991)

Hegel, Georg Wilhelm Friedrich, *The Philosophy of History* (New York: Dover, 1956)

Heidegger, Martin, *Gesamtausgabe*, vol. 54, *Parmenides*, ed. Manfred S. Frings (Frankfurt/M: Vittorio Klostermann, 1982); and vol. 29/30, *Die Grundbegriffe der Metaphysik*, ed. Friedrich Wilhelm von Hermann (1983)
―― *Poetry, Language, Thought*, trans. Alfred Hofstadter (New York, Harper and Row, 1971)
―― *The Question Concerning Technology and Other Essays*, trans. William Lovitt (New York; Harper and Row, 1997)
―― *What is Called Thinking*, trans. J. Glenn Gray and F. Wieck (New York: Harper and Row, 1968)
Herder, J. G., *Auch eine Philosophie der Geschichte zur Bildung der Menschheit*, ed. Hans Dieter Irmscher (Stuttgart: Reclam, 1990)
―― *Ideen zur Philosophie der Geschichte der Menschheit*, ed. Martin Bollacher (Frankfurt/M: Deutsche Klassiker Verlag, 1989)
Herford, Oliver, 'Tears for Dead Fish', *TLS* 5 Sept. (2003) pp. 5–6
Higgins, Kathleen, *Nietzsche's Zarathustra* (Philadelphia: Temple University Press, 1987)
Janaway, Christopher, ed., *Willing and Nothingness: Schopenhauer as Nietzsche's Educator* (New York: Clarendon Press, 1998)
Jimack, Peter, *La Genèse et la redaction de l'Émile de Jean-Jacques Rousseau. Études sur l'histoire de l'ouvrage jusqu'à sa parution. Studies in Voltaire and the Eighteenth Century*, vol. xiii (Geneva: Institut et Musée Voltaire, 1960)
Jones, Ernest, *Sigmund Freud: Life and Work* (London: Hogarth Press, 1967)
Joyce, James, *A Portrait of the Artist as a Young Man*, ed. Chester G. Anderson and Richard Ellman (New York: Viking, 1965)
―― *Ulysses*, ed. Hans Walter Gabler *et al.* (London: Bodley Head, 1986) p. 162, ll. 7–8
Kant, Immanuel, *Critique of Judgement*, trans. J. H. Bernard (New York: Hafner, 1972)
―― *Critique of Practical Reason*, trans. Lewis White Beck (New York: Macmillan, 1993)
Keats, John, *The Letters of John Keats*, ed. Maurice Buxton Forman, 2nd edn. (Oxford: Oxford University Press, 1935)
Kenner, Hugh, *The Stoic Comedians: Flaubert, Joyce, and Beckett* (London: W. H. Allen, 1967)
Köhler, Wolfgang, *The Mentality of Apes*, trans. Ella Winter (London and Boston: Routledge and Kegan Paul, 1917, 1925, rev. edn., 1927)
Kundera, Milan, *The Art of the Novel*, trans. Linda Asher (London: Faber, 1988)
La Fare, *Le Gouverneur, ou essai sur l'éducation* (London and Paris 1768)
Lampert, Laurence, *Nietzsche's Teaching: an Interpretation of Thus Spoke Zarathustra* (New Haven and London Yale University Press, 1986)
Langer, Suzanne, *Feeling and Form* (London: Routledge and Kegan Paul, 1953)
―― *The Complete Poems of D. H. Lawrence*, ed. Vivian de Sola Pinto and Warren Roberts (New York: Viking, 1964)
―― *The Letters of D. H. Lawrence*, ed. Aldous Huxley (London: Heinemann, 1932)
―― *The Letters of D. H. Lawrence*, vol. 2, ed. George J. Zytaruk and James T. Boulton (Cambridge: Cambridge University Press, 1981)

—— *The Letters of D. H. Lawrence*, vol. 6, ed. James T. Boulton, Margaret Boulton, and Gerald Lacy (Cambridge: Cambridge University Press, 1991)

Lawrence, D. H., *Mr Noon*, ed. Lindeth Vasey (Cambridge: Cambridge University Press, 1997)

—— *Phoenix: the Posthumous Papers of D. H. Lawrence*, ed. Edward D. McDonald (London: Heinemann, 1961)

—— *Phoenix II: Uncollected, Unpublished and Other Prose Works by D. H. Lawrence*, ed. Warren Roberts and Harry T. Moore (London: Heinemann, 1968)

—— *The Plays*, ed. Hans-Wilhelm Schwarze and John Worthen (Cambridge: Cambridge University Press, 1999)

—— *Quetzalcoatl*, ed. Louis Martz (New York: New Directions, 1995)

—— *The Rainbow*, ed. Mark Kinkead-Weekes (Cambridge: Cambridge University Press, 1989)

—— *Reflections on the Death of a Porcupine and Other Essays*, ed. Michael Herbert (Cambridge: Cambridge University Press, 1988)

—— *Studies in Classic American Literature*, ed. Ezra Greenspan, Lindeth Vasey, and John Worthen (Cambridge: Cambridge University Press, 2003)

—— *Study of Thomas Hardy and Other Essays*, ed. Bruce Steele (Cambridge: Cambridge University Press, 1985)

—— *Women in Love*, ed. David Farmer, Lindeth Vasey, and John Worthen (Cambridge: Cambridge University Press, 1987)

Leavis, F. R., *Anna Karenina and Other Essays* (London: Chatto and Windus, 1967)

—— *Dickens the Novelist*, with Q. D. Leavis (London: Penguin, 1980)

—— *English Literature in Our Time and the University* (London: Chatto and Windus, 1969)

—— *Nor Shall my Sword* (London: Chatto and Windus, 1972)

—— *The Common Pursuit* (London: Chatto and Windus, 1952)

—— *Lectures in America*, with Q. D. Leavis (London: Chatto and Windus, 1969)

—— *The Living Principle: English as a Discipline of Thought* (London: Chatto and Windus, 1975)

Lessing, Gotthold Ephraim, *Die Erziehung der Menschengeschlecht*, ed. Helmut Göbel (Munich: Karl Hauser, 1979)

—— *Hamburgische Dramaturgie*, ed. Klaus L. Berghahn (Stuttgart: Reclam, 1981)

Lévy-Bruhl, Lucien, *Primitive Mentality*, trans. L. A. Clare (London and New York: Allen and Unwin, 1923)

Lillyman, William J., ed., *Goethe's Narrative Fictions: the Irvine Goethe Symposium* (Berlin and New York: de Gruyter, 1983)

Locke, John, *Some Thoughts Concerning Education*, ed. John W. and Jean S. Yolton (Oxford: Clarendon Press, 1989)

Lodge, David, ed., *Modern Criticism and Theory* (London and New York: Longman, 1988)

Loeb, Paul, 'Time, Power and Superhumanity', *Journal of Nietzsche Studies*, 21 (2001) pp. 27–41.

Lukačs, Georg, *Studies in European Realism* (New York: Grosset and Dunlap, 1964)

Lyotard, J-P., *La Condition Postmoderne* (Paris: Minuit, 1979)
McCarthy, John A., *Christoph Martin Wieland* (Boston: Twayne, 1979)
Maierhofer, Waltraud, *Wilhelm Meisters Wanderjahre und der Roman des Nebeneinander* (Bielefeld: Aisthesis Verlag, 1990)
Mann, Thomas, *Doctor Faustus*, trans. H. T. Lowe-Porter (London: Penguin, 1968)
—— 'Joseph und Seiner Brüder: ein Vortrag', *Gesammelte Werke* (Frankfurt/M: Fischer, 1960) vol. xi
—— *Mythology and Humanism: the Correspondence of Thomas Mann and Karl Kerenyi*, trans. Alexander Gelley, (Ithaca NY: Cornell University Press, 1975)
—— *Tagebücher* (Frankfurt/M: Fischer, 1979)
—— *The Letters of Thomas Mann*, sel. and trans. Richard and Clara Winston (London: Penguin, 1975)
Michelsen, Peter, *Laurence Sterne und des deutschen Roman des achtzehnten Jahrhunderts* (Göttingen: Vandenhoeck und Ruprecht, 1962)
Millett, Kate, *Sexual Politics* (London: Sphere Books, 1971)
Milton, Colin, *Lawrence and Nietzsche* (Aberdeen: University of Aberdeen Press, 1987)
Minden, Michael, *The German Bildungsroman: Incest and Inheritance* (Cambridge: Cambridge University Press, 1997)
Monk, Ray, *Ludwig Wittgenstein: the Duty of Genius* (London: Vintage, 1990)
Nagel, Thomas, *Mortal Questions* (Cambridge: Cambridge University Press, 1970)
Newton, John, ''*Scrutiny*'s Failure with Shakespeare', *The Cambridge Quarterly*, 1/2 (Spring, 1966), pp. 144–77
Nietzsche, Friedrich, *On the Genealogy of Morals and Ecce Homo*, trans. Walter Kaufmann (New York: Random House, 1967)
—— *The Gay Science*, trans. Walter Kaufmann (New York: Random House, 1974)
—— *Thus Spoke Zarathustra*, trans. R. J. Hollingdale (London: Penguin, 1969)
—— *Twilight of the Idols*, trans. R. J. Hollingdale (London: Penguin, 1990)
—— *Also Sprach Zarathustra*, ed. Giorgio Colli and Mazzino Montinari (Stuttgart: Reclam, 1994)
—— *Untimely Meditations*, trans. R. J. Hollingdale (Cambridge: Cambridge University Press, 1997)
—— *Writings from the Late Notebooks*, ed. Rüdiger Bittner, trans. Kate Sturge (Cambridge: Cambridge University Press, 2003)
Nolan, Emer, *James Joyce and Nationalism* (London: Routledge, 1995)
Ong, Walter, *Orality and Literacy: the Technologising of the Word* (London and New York: Methuen, 1982)
Pax, Octavio, *The Labyrinth of Solitude*, trans. Lysander Kemp (London: Penguin, 1985)
Peters, Gary, *Irony and Singularity: Aesthetic Education from Kant to Levinas* (Aldershot: Ashgate, 2005)
Pierce, David and Peter de Voogd, eds., *Laurence Sterne in Modernism and Postmodernism* (Amsterdam and Atlanta Ga.: Rodopi, 1966)
Plato, *The Dialogues of Plato*, trans. B. Jowett (Oxford: Clarendon Press, 1953)
Pound, Ezra, *The Letters of Ezra Pound 1907–1941* (New York: Harcourt Brace and World, 1950)

―― *The Spirit of Romance* (London: Peter Owen, 1952)
Ragussis, Michael, *The Subterfuge of Art: Language and the Romantic Tradition* (Baltimore: Johns Hopkins University Press, 1978)
Rancière, Jacques, *Le maître ignorant: cinq leçons sur l'émancipation intellectuelle* (Paris: Fayard, 1987)
Redfield, Marc, *Phantom Formations: Aesthetic Ideology and the Bildungsroman* (Ithaca and London: Cornell University Press, 1996)
Richardson, Samuel, *Selected Letters of Samuel Richardson*, ed. John Carroll (Oxford: Oxford University Press, 1964)
Ricoeur, Paul, *Freud and Philosophy: an Essay in Interpretation*, trans. Denis Savage (New Haven and London: Yale University Press, 1970)
―― *The Rule of Metaphor*, trans. Robert Czerny et al., (London: Routledge and Kegan Paul, 1978)
Rosen, Stanley, *The Mask of Enlightenment: Nietzsche's Zarathustra* (Cambridge: Cambridge University Press, 1995)
Rousseau, Jean Jacques, *The Confessions*, trans. J. M. Cohen (London: Penguin, 1953)
―― *Emile, or On Education*, trans. Allan Bloom (London: Penguin, 1991)
―― *Émile, ou de l'education*, ed. Michel Launay (Paris: Garnier-Flammarion, 1966)
―― *Julie, ou la nouvelle Héloïse* (Paris: Garnier, 1960)
―― *Lettre à d'Alembert* (Paris: Gallimard, 1995)
―― *Oeuvres complètes*, Bibliothèque de la pléiade, ed. Bernard Gagnebin and Marcel Raymond (Paris: Gallimard, 1959–)
Scheler, Max, *The Nature of Sympathy*, trans. Peter Heath (London: Routledge and Kegan Paul, 1954)
Schelling, Joseph von, *The Philosophy of Art*, trans. Douglas W. Stott (Minneapolis: University of Minnesota Press, 1989)
Schiller, Friedrich, *On the Aesthetic Education of Man in a Series of Letters*, trans. Elizabeth M. Wilkinson and L. A. Willoughby (Oxford: Clarendon Press, 1967)
―― *On the Naïve and Sentimental in Literature*, trans. Helen Watanabe O'Kelly (Manchester: Carcanet, 1981)
Schlegel, Dorothy B., *Shaftesbury and the French Deists* (Chapel Hill NC: University of North Carolina Press, 1956)
Schrift, Alan D., ed., *Why Nietzsche Still?* (University of California Press, 2000)
Shapiro, Gary, *Nietzschean Narratives* (Bloomington: Indiana University Press, 1989)
Siegel, Carol, *Lawrence Among the Women: Wavering Boundaries in Women's Literary Traditions* (Charlottesville Va.: University of Virginia Press, 1991)
Smith, Adam, *The Theory of Moral Sentiments*, ed. D. D. Raphael and A. I. MacFie (Oxford: Oxford University Press, 1979)
Spoo, Robert, *James Joyce and the Language of History* (Oxford: Oxford University Press, 1994)
Staël, Germaine de, *Lettres sur les ouvrages et le caractère de J-J. Rousseau* (1788)
Starobinski, Jean, *Jean-Jacques Rousseau: Transparency and Obstruction*, trans. Arthur Goldhammer (Chicago and London: Chicago University Press, 1988)
Steiner, George, *The Lessons of the Masters* (Cambridge, Mass. and London: Harvard University Press, 2003)

Stephenson, R. H. *Goethe's Wisdom Literature, a Study in Aesthetic Transformation* (Bern: Lang, 1983)

Stern, Peter, *Nietzsche* (Glasgow: Collins, 1978)

Sterne, Laurence, *The Life and Opinions of Tristram Shandy*, ed. James A. Work (New York: Odyssey Press, 1940)

Stifter, Adalbert, *Der Nachsommer*, in *Gesammelte Werke*, ed. Konrad Steffen, vol. 7 (Basel and Stuttgart: Birkhauser, 1965)

Swales, Martin, *The German Bildungsroman from Wieland to Hesse* (Princeton: Princeton University Press, 1978)

Swift, Jonathon, *Gulliver's Travels*, ed. Peter Dixon and John Chalker (London: Penguin, 1985)

Tanner, Deborah, *You Just Don't Understand: Men and Women in Conversation* (London: Virago, 1991)

Walder, Dennis, ed., *Literature in the Modern World* (New York: Oxford University Press, 1990)

Wallace, Jeff, *D. H. Lawrence, Science and the Posthuman* (London: Palgrave, 2005)

Wieland, Christoph Martin, *Geschichte des Agathon*, ed. Fritz Martini (Stuttgart: Reclam, 1979)

―― *The History of Agathon*, 4 vols. (London: Cadell, 1773)

Wittgenstein, Ludwig, *Tractatus Logico-Philosophicus*, trans. D. F. Pears and B. F. McGuiness (London: Routledge and Kegan Paul, 1963)

―― *Philosophical Investigations*, trans. G. E. M. Anscombe (Cambridge: Cambridge University Press, 1992)

Wollstonecraft, Mary, *A Vindication of the Rights of Woman* (1792)

Worthen, John, *D. H. Lawrence: The Early Years, 1885–1912* (Cambridge: Cambridge University Press, 1992)

Woolf, Virginia, *The Common Reader* (London: Hogarth Press, 1963)

Yeats, W. B., *Collected Poems* (London: Macmillan, 1950)

―― *The Letters of W. B. Yeats*, ed. Allan Wade (London: Rupert Hart-Davis, 1954)

Index

Addison, Joseph 24
Adorno, Theodor 128
aesthetic 10, 13, 25, 36–7, 47, 58–9, 68, 72, 75, 83–4, 100, 103–5, 107, 132, 143 n., 175, 194, 199, 202, 206–8, 217, 236, 238–41
Aquinas, Thomas 6
Arendt, Hannah 63, 85, 202
Aristotle 6, 17–18, 63, 85
Arnold, Matthew 133, 208
Attridge, Derek 218
Augustine 7, 151–2
Austen, Jane 157, 210
Avellaneda, Alonso Fernández de 113

Bakhtin, Mikhail 126–7
Barthes, Roland 176
Bauer, Wilfried 98
Beckett, Samuel 12, 40, 130
Beddow, Michael 166
Beethoven, Ludwig van 128
Bible 3, 145
Bildungsroman 5–8, 10–12, 26–7, 32, 35, 47, 67, 69, 82–3, 85–6, 113, 126, 139, 141, 155, 161, 165, 167–8, 179, 241
Blackall, Eric 109, 111, 126
Blake, William 199–200, 202, 212–13, 223
Blankenburg, Friedrich von 66
Bloom, Harold 4
Bordieu, Pierre 6, 235–6
Borges, Jorge-Luis 29, 50, 60, 142
Boswell, James 7
Boyle, Nicholas 93, 144
Bradley, Andrew C. 214
Broch, Hermann 109
Brontës 183
Buddecke, Wolfram 67
Burnhill, John 136

Calderon de la Barca, Pedro 46
Cassirer, Ernst 48
Cavell, Stanley 136, 138
Cervantes, Miguel Saavedra de 6, 29, 46, 66, 85, 89, 113, 115
Chaudhuri, Amit 178
Christ, Jesus 49–50

Cicero 151
Cixous, Hélène 184
Coetzee, J. M. 11–13, 168, 217–14
  Disgrace 217–19, 224, 233
  Elizabeth Costello 219, 231, 233
  Lives of Animals 219–34
  Master of Petersburg 233
Collingwood, R. G. 200
Conant, James 137–8
Conrad, Joseph 231
Conway, Daniel 157–8

Dante Aligheri 87–8
Defoe, Daniel 9, 38–9
Deleuze, Gilles 178
Derrida, Jacques 23, 30–1, 223
Dickens, Charles 172, 200
Diderot, Denis 8, 26, 135
Dilthey, Wilhelm 6, 8, 105, 108, 126, 144, 161, 197–203, 206, 209
Doninger, Wendy 223
Dostoevsky, Fyodor 132
Dupont, Pierre-Samuel 43

Eagleton, Terry 195
Edel, Leon 35
Edgeworth, Maria and Richard 43–4, 50
Eliot, George 88, 95, 109, 183, 210, 218
Eliot, T. S. 87, 168, 194, 199–200, 204, 218
Emerson, Ralph Waldo 136–8, 145, 177

Farias, Victor 203
Fénelon, François de Salignac de la Mothe 34, 239
Fielding, Henry 6–7, 9, 65, 68–9, 154, 210, 228
Flaubert, Gustave 94, 199
Fraiman, Susan 32
Frederick the Great 185
Ford, Ford Madox 180
Freud, Sigmund 159–60

Gadamer, Hans-Georg 6–7, 197
Galsworthy, John 171
Garber, Marjorie 220

Garnett, Edward 178
Gide, André 87
Goethe, Johann Wolfgang von 4, 10–11, 13, 27, 35, 47, 51, 65, 87–129, 131, 134–8, 145, 152, 155, 161, 169, 173, 177, 184–91, 200, 212, 238–9
  Elective Affinities 112
  Poetry and Truth 93
  Werther 7, 25–6, 50, 73, 95–7, 112, 123–4, 185–7, 238
  WMA 11, 60, 86–108, 141, 154, 170, 177, 179, 186–9
  WMJ 11, 108–29, 133, 141, 170, 179, 188
Gosse, Edmund 55
Gottsched, Johann Christoph 66
Green, Gayle 32
Grene, Marjorie 197
Gutzkow, Karl 114

Haas, Rosemary 97
Hacking, Ian 221–2
Hafiz 106–7, 123
Hamman, J. G. 22
Hayles, Katherine 178
Hegel, G. W. F. 8. 159
Heidegger, Martin 70, 197, 199, 203–6, 209
Hemingway, Ernest 212
Heraclitus 142
Herder, J. G. 5, 48, 67, 93, 116, 141, 202
Hölderlin 206
Hollingdale, R. J. 140, 160
Homer 88
Hueffer, Ford Madox, *see* Ford
Hughes, Ted 223–4
Humboldt, Wilhelm von 5
Huxley, Aldous 168, 180

Jacotot, Joseph 239–40
James, Henry 35, 88, 201, 210
James, William 35
Jimack, Peter 36
Johnson, Samuel 6–8, 10, 19, 37
Jones, Ernest 159
Joyce, James 108, 160–1, 194, 199, 210, 214, 215
  Portrait 94, 119, 170
  Ulysses 97, 109, 119, 143, 158, 170

Kafka, Franz 12, 130, 224–6
Kant, Immanuel 6–7, 24, 47, 71–2, 83, 88, 105, 132, 197, 230, 236, 239

Karl August, Duke of Saxe-Weimar 81
Keats, John 161
Keller, Gottfried 141
Kenner, Hugh 133
Kerenyi, Karl 166
Kierkegaard, Søren 130
Köhler, Wolfgang 224–5
Kundera, Milan 212

Laclos, Choderlos de 7, 42, 71
La Fare, de 43
La Fontaine, Jean de 38
Langer, Suzanne 207
Lawrence D. H. 6–7, 11, 13, 23, 25, 30, 70, 94, 136, 161, 165–92, 199, 211–13, 215, 218, 222–30, 240
  The Daughter-in law 184
  'Education of the People' 169, 188–92
  'Horse-Dealer's Daughter' 171
  Lady Chatterley's Lover 187
  Mr Noon 185
  The Plumed Serpent 228–9
  Quetzalcoatl 228
  Sons and Lovers 179
  Studies in Classic American Literature 176, 213
  Rainbow 166, 169–70, 172, 174, 179, 184
  Reflections on the Death of a Porcupine 227
  Women in Love 166–74, 181–2, 185–8
Leavis, F. R. 11, 13, 168, 183, 193–216, 217, 219, 222, 228
Leavis, Q. D. 193
Lessing, G. E. 66, 141
Lévy-Bruhl, Lucien 225
literalism 10, 38–40, 42–4, 46–7, 51, 62, 65–6, 68, 95, 104, 135, 213–14, 217, 236
Locke, John 18, 29–30, 46, 50, 55–6, 58–60, 154
Lukaćs, Georg 8

Malborough, John Churchill, 1st Duke of 53, 63
Mann, Thomas 11, 65, 73, 94, 139, 141, 161, 165–7
Marinetti, Filippo Tommaso 178
Marx, Karl 63, 122
Melville, Hermann 213
Michelet, Jules 32
Michelsen, Peter 84
Mill, J. S. 55

Index

Millett, Kate 183
Molière 24, 214
Montesquieu, Charles-Louis de Secondat 67
More, Hannah 3
Morris, William 121
Mozart, Wolfgang Amadeus, *Don Giovanni* 76

Nagel, Thomas 223–5, 227
Newton, John 214
Nietzsche, Friedrich 1, 4, 10–11, 13, 23, 70, 88, 113, 116, 129, 130–92, 205, 209, 213, 228, 236, 238
  Beyond Good and Evil 158
  Birth of Tragedy 208
  Ecce Homo 134, 151, 159
  Gay Science 145, 151, 158, 182
  Genealogy of Morals 187
  On the Future of Our Institutions of Cultural Education 132–3
  Richard Wagner in Bayreuth 134
  Schopenhauer as Educator 132, 133–40, 142–3, 156–8, 161, 180, 187
  Thus Spoke Zarathustra 11, 123, 131–2, 139, 144–61
  Twilight of the Idols 137, 138, 154, 157, 173, 183, 208
  Uses and Disadvantages of History 127, 132–3, 139–40, 151, 197

Ong, Walter 31
open secret 1, 4, 82–3, 84–5, 89, 98, 106–7, 124, 129, 145, 152–3, 155, 160, 168, 194, 210, 218, 237
Ovid 75

Paine, Thomas, *The Rights of Man* 3
Paz, Octavio 115
pedagogical circle 1, 3, 19, 27, 29, 73, 82, 147, 210
Peters, Gary 6
Picasso, Pablo 128
Plato 6, 66–72, 74, 79–80, 134, 150, 224, 228, 239–41
  Republic 5, 49, 78–9, 85, 188–9, 196
  see also Socrates
Pope, Alexander 136, 207
Pound, Ezra 75, 173, 178, 194, 215
Proust, Marcel 61, 88, 143
Pustkuchen, Friedrich Wilhelm 113

Rabelais, François 56
Ragussis, Michael 170
Raikes, Robert 3
Rancière, Jacques 6, 239–40
Redfield, Marc 139
Richardson, Samuel 7, 9–10, 42, 53, 71
Ricoeur, Paul 196
Rilke, Rainer Maria 206
Rousseau, Jean-Jacques 13–14, 17–51, 56–7, 60, 67, 73, 75, 83, 93–4, 104–5, 116, 134–5, 138, 145, 147, 150, 153–4, 184, 238, 240
  Confessions 18, 20, 26, 33, 37, 96, 141
  Emile 3, 10–11, 17–53, 55, 58, 60, 62, 67–8, 69, 71–2, 74, 77, 79, 81–2, 84, 91–2, 96, 98–100, 118–19, 140, 145, 154–5, 188–9, 191, 221, 230
  Julie 7, 20, 23, 33, 35, 37–8, 41, 74
  Letter to d'Alembert 36, 40, 213–15
  Social Contract 48, 127
  The Solitaries 41, 51
Rozanov, V. V. 175
Russell, Bertrand 226–7

Sade, Marquis de 71
Said, Edward 128
Saussure, Ferdinand de 30–1
sentimentalism 9–10, 19, 22–4, 41, 56, 62, 64, 66, 95, 104, 135, 238
Scheler, Max 226–7
Schelling, F. W. 89, 101
Schiller, Friedrich 5, 36, 47, 71, 91, 98, 100, 121, 130, 144, 154, 177, 185, 233, 236, 238–41
  Aesthetic Education of Man 13–14, 58–9, 68, 83–5, 103–4, 122, 132, 207–8, 217
Schleiermacher, F. D. E. 201
Schopenhauer, Arthur 148, 238
  see also Nietzsche
Senancour, Etienne Pivert de 96
Shaftesbury, Anthony Ashley Cooper, 3rd Earl of 24–5
Shakespeare, William 46, 88, 104, 126, 158
  Hamlet 90, 93, 114, 121, 212
Siegel, Carol 183
Singer, Peter 221
Smith, Adam 122
Snow, C. P. 200–1, 210, 212
Socrates 1, 4–5, 49–50, 72, 134, 147, 149, 150, 195, 203, 237, 239–41

Stael, Germane de 33
Starobinski, Jean 18–19, 22
Steiner, George 12
Steiner, Rudolf 106
Stephenson, R. H. 87, 126
Stern, Peter 158
Sterne, Laurence 8–9, 10, 51–64, 65, 108–9, 210,
Stifter, Adalbert 2, 83, 141
Swales, Martin 85
Swift, Jonathan 6, 45–6, 222

Tannen, Deborah 184
Tolstoy 157

utopianism 43, 51, 84–5, 117–19, 138, 192, 196

Voltaire 6, 19, 67, 185

Wallace, Jeff 178
Wellek, René 197
Wieland, Christoph Martin 10, 51, **65–86**, 89, 116
Winkelmann, J. J. 78
Wittgenstein, Ludwig 101, 195, 227
Wollstonecraft, Mary 33
Wordsworth, William 32, 108
Woolf, Virginia 109

Xenophon 54, 63, 65, 74, 81, 85

Yeats, W. B. 104, 161, 170, 214–15, 221
Yudkin, Michael 200